# THE SOUL OF BUSINESS ONLINE [9 IN 1]

All the Knowledge and Investment Strategies to Unlock
Your First 6-Figure Dividend

*David Lazarus*

The information herein is offered for informational purposes solely and is universal as so. The presentation of the information is without contract or any type of guarantee assurance.

The trademarks that are used are without any consent and the publication of the trademark is without permission or backing by the trademark owner. All trademarks and brands within this book are for clarifying purposes only and are owned by the owners themselves, not affiliated with this document.

# Table of Contents

## SWING TRADING FOR BEGINNERS

## SWING TRADING ADVANCED COURSE

## DAY TRADING FOR BEGINNERS

## STOCK MARKET INVESTING FOR BEGINNERS

## STOCK MARKET INVESTING - ADVANCED COURSE -

## DEDUCTING | THE RIGHT WAY

## BOOKKEEPING AND QUICKBOOKS MADE EASY

# SWING TRADING FOR BEGINNERS

*David Lazarus*

# Table of Contents

# Introduction

Approaching swing trading from the angle of guesswork is a recipe for financial woes! Unfortunately, many people approach swing trading from this line of thinking. They jump in with little or no knowledge, lose their investments and go crying.

There are others who do not know the difference between the various types of trades available on the stock market, so they confuse one for the other, applying right methods or techniques to the wrong trade.

Still, there are those who are really impatient to learn the ropes, and they end up using half-baked knowledge to cause themselves financial shipwreck. They half-heartedly study some few tips and run amok with their new found knowledge that would magically transform them into self-made millionaire traders. Sadly, most of these types of imaginary self-made millionaires soon learn the hard way that becoming successful trading online demands the same level of commitment and dedication required to become successful at anything in life – online or offline.

Throughout this book, I have used terms that you may not be familiar to you. Kindly turn to the last chapter of this book to familiarize yourself with the list of terminologies commonly used in swing trading and their meanings. You derive two benefits from doing this. Firstly, it is easy to get lost and frustrated trying to keep up with the trading lingo. Understanding their meanings will give you a clearer insight into what you are learning. Secondly, it minimizes your chances of gambling – you understand exactly what to do and what not to do. So before you jump into guessing what chart patterns are or reading indicators that you are not properly equipped to interpret, kindly get used to these terminologies.

Some of the terminologies are not used in this book because they are not necessarily related to swing trading. However, I have deliberately expanded the list to cover stock trading in general so as to help you broaden your horizon.

# Chapter 1: Basics about Swing Trading

## Swing Trading Without a Guide

Here's what many novices do when they attempt to trade on the stock market. First, they lack the patience to learn anything aside from how to click on the "call" and "put" option or the "buy" and "sell" option. Then they invest some capital (probably $500) in stock and begin to trade. The next day, they find that they have lost almost everything, so they run to their favorite web browser and type in "how to trade stock online" and click the search button. They talk to a few friends (and probably family too) and invest some more capital (maybe $1,000 because they are more confident this time). But they soon discover that trading is not like gambling and they simply quit.

A lot of people attempt trading and fail because they do not have proper guidance. They lack the necessary knowledge to succeed at trading. They do not have the patience to learn how to trade. And they do not have a strategy – a definite plan. What they rely on is pure guesswork. And for some who have both the knowledge and a good plan, they lack the discipline to stick to their plans. They are too emotionally attached to trade outcomes that they cannot follow through with their plans. Their strategies are good on paper, but when it comes to implementation, they just can't stay true to their strategies.

They are those who are hell-bent on finding the best technical indicator so that they can throw every single dollar into it. It is like a magic formula that will churn out millions. They believe all they need to do is find the infallible indicator, follow it, and make a killing. Rinse and repeat! But they too soon discover that the best technical indicator on its own is a fast lane to financial trauma.

As a beginner who is attempting to trade, your best guide is not the crowd. Following what others are doing may affect your account in ways that are not too pleasant for you. Learning the fundamentals of a company is okay, but that may not contribute anything meaningful to your swing trading decisions. Burying yourself diligently in studying a company's profit/earnings ratio, profit margins, book value, etc., to determine if they are the perfect company for you, and then throwing your all of your money into the company may prove fatal.

My aim is to get you to sidestep pit holes so that you do not take a nosedive and plunge into misery. The risk involved in trading is very high as it is; do not add your ignorance or impatience to it. Take the time to study the strategies outlined in this guide before attempting your first trade.

## Swing Trading: What It Is

Swing trading is a method of trading stocks or securities with the aim of making quick profits from powerful short-term price movements of the market. Usually, swing trading involves holding a stock for a period between 2 to 5 days (or even a few weeks).

A swing trader (obviously, that's someone who does swing trading), doesn't concern him or herself so much about every single detail of a company or about their products or services. As a matter of fact, a swing trader may not even bother to know what the name of a company is before trading its stock. In other words, if you are a swing trader or planning on becoming one, your focus is not so much on the company. You do not make your trading decisions based on the types of products they sell or who they are. Your choice to trade a company's stock as a swing trader is purely based on demand and supply. Period!

Swing trading does not need you to spend the whole day in front of a computer watching, studying, monitoring charts, trades, and price movements, etc. It gives you enough room to do other things, which is why many swing traders have a day job and treat swing trading as a part-time venture.

Basically, your job as a swing trader is to study indicators to determine what the dominant trend of a stock is. When you are sure of this trend the next step is to be on the lookout for a brief retrace and subsequent return of the dominant trend after which you should enter the trade. This is why swing trading works so well. You are simply trading along the direction of a confirmed trend.

When you are choosing a stock to trade, ask yourself the following questions: is there cash flow in this stock? Right now, is cash coming into this stock or is cash going out? In what way can I minimize risk while trading this stock and maximizing profit as quickly as possible? Your success as a swing trader hinges largely on how well you are able to figure out answers to these pertinent questions. But since this is a swing trading guidebook for beginners, I shall help you to figure out the best answers to these questions so that you will avoid the likely traps along the trading path.

But before you start trading, consider the following.

**Before You Trade...**

What type of swing trader do you want to be? Take enough time to think about this. What is your main motive? Do you want an additional source of income, or are you looking for a primary source of income? How many hours in a day are you ready to devout to swing trading? Will you be watching the market all day? (By the way, watching the market all day doesn't guarantee that you will be more successful).

Opening a trading or brokerage account is all good and well, but before you do that, you need to ascertain what this new trading venture is to you. What level of commitment are you looking to give to swing trading?

*Part-Time Income*

A lot of swing traders fall into this category, and it is for a good reason. First of all, generating income from swing trading on a part-time basis is a way of removing unnecessary pressure from the swing trader. You are sure that your income stream is not limited to only swing trading. It makes you less emotionally invested in trade outcomes. You have a day job that guarantees income even if you slip-up in your swing trading. Typically, swing traders who generate income from swing trading on a part-time basis are more clearheaded when they analyze strategies after the close of work and then implement these strategies the next trading day.

It is not necessary for them to monitor the market all day because they can utilize the stop loss order to minimize losses. It is a good ambition to be a full-time swing trader, but it is better if you start first as a part-time swing trader so that you can watch your progress over a long period of time without the added pressure of thinking about making money for sustenance. With enough practice, you can gradually switch into full-time swing trading.

As a beginner venturing into swing trading, I would recommend that you start your trading experience with paper trading. This is trading without real money. However, do not let whatever successes you have with paper trading get into your head and make you commence real money trading with a large portion of your capital. It is best always to start small when using real money.

## Full-Time Income

As a beginner, it is very risky to quit your job and plunge headlong into swing trading when you have not spent enough time gathering experience in trading. And what I mean by enough time is at least several months of swing trading to learn the ropes and see a major shift in self-discipline that results in good trade returns.

You must be well prepared to handle pressure, working long hours per day to monitor and study trades noting their performances before the market hours, during trading, and after the closing bell.

Full-time swing trading can be very stressful. You will be under constant pressure to generate a steady cash flow since this is your primary source of income. And we all know what happens to a person who is under pressure to produce financial gains when he or she is losing trades. They tend to trade more! Unless you have disciplined yourself to be calm even in the face of apparent failure, you will be tempted to abandon your well-thought-out plans and strategies, and follow your emotions and disregard everything you have learned. The sudden realization that they have nothing else to fall back on is likely to push them into haphazard trading. A swing trader (especially one who is a full-time swing trader) must be emotionally detached from the outcome of trades. Listening to your emotion is practically the same as gambling.

The best way to handle pressure in the face of apparent failure is to retreat for a while and take a closer look at why you are failing. Going back to the strategy and determining what went wrong may bring about more insights. Trading more when faced with failure doesn't guarantee success. If anything, it is a sure way to more failure.

While quitting your job and swing trading from home (in your pajamas) is an appealing idea for some, before you do that make sure you have real successes based on proven strategies and not some mere fluke or lucky winning streak.

*Your Techniques*

The methods you employ in your swing trading depend on whether you choose to be a full-time swing trader entering and exiting trades at day time or part-time swing trader entering trades after the close of market.

If you are a full-time swing trader, you have the choice of using the intraday price action to properly time your trade entry and exit. On the other hand, if you are a part-time swing trader, you will normally enter a trade order after the markets are closed and then use the stop-loss order to exit trades when you are losing money.

Whatever the case (full-time or part-time), you need to learn how to analyze the market for you to trade successfully. You need to learn how to read patterns on a stock chart (technical analysis). Additionally, you have the option of also learning about the company whose stocks you are trading. Their sales, earnings, plus other fundamentals (fundamental analysis) will help you make informed decisions.

However, this option is only important if you intend to invest in the company for the long haul. If your interest in a company is just a quick, short trade of its stock, you need not bother yourself so much about the fundamentals of the company. So that you know; it is cumbersome and very demanding to learn all about a company's fundamental. For beginners, I strongly suggest you use that time and energy to first master how to swing trade properly before you bother yourself with fundamental analysis.

## Choosing What to Trade

So, you want to be a swing trader? Great! What are you trading? What are you buying and selling on the market? You need to put up a plan and on that plan (which is your business plan), you have to state exactly what you will be trading.

Here are a few securities you can choose from:

*Stocks*: almost everyone (traders or not) are familiar with stocks. Basically, stocks are public equities. The ease of trading this type of security has made a lot of swing traders concentrate on trading only stocks. In the United State, most stocks trade on a daily basis; however, other countries may not trade stocks that frequently. The diversity of stocks makes this choice a more popular one.

*Commodities*: silver, crude oil, gold, etc. are all commodities that are attractive in the futures market. Although a swing trader can make good earnings from short-term price swings of commodities, they come with some level of risks that is completely different from equity trading.

*Forex market*: this is also known as the currency market or foreign exchange market. With a daily turnover placed at an average of $3.21 trillion, this is by far the largest market the world over! If you intend to trade forex as a swing trader, be sure to confirm that your intended currency pair is listed in the forex market. A few of them are USD,

British pound sterling, Euro, AUD (Australian Dollar), Japanese yen, etc. Also note that not every broker offers forex trading, which means you need to verify from your chosen broker before including this in your plan.

*Options*: this refers to the type of contract where someone buys an investment that gives them the option (not necessarily an obligation) to purchase an underlying asset at some specified price before an expiration date. Do note, however, that options are not a recommended trading vehicle for swing traders. It is very risky to trade options as a swing trader as they are not very liquid.

### Choosing Your Market

The stocks or securities you chose to trade will, to a very large extent, determine what market you will be able to trade them. You can choose from many different markets. Here's is a few of the big names.

- New York Stock Exchange (NYSE)
- Tokyo Stock Exchange (TSE/TYO)
- Euronext (EUXTF)
- National Association of Securities Dealers Automated Quotations (NASDAQ)
- Hong Kong Stock Exchange (HKEX)
- American Stock Exchange (AMEX)
- Shenzhen Stock Exchange (SZSE)
- London Stock Exchange (LSE)

- Shanghai Stock Exchange (SSE)

Before you choose a market, do take some time to research what stocks or securities trade on that market. If you want to trade commodities such as gold, coal, crude oil, ethanol, soybean, corn, silver, etc., you should keep in mind as I have mentioned earlier that trading these commodities are a different ball game entirely and the risks are higher than swing trading stocks.

## Different Types of Trading

Generally, there is day trading, swing trading, and buy-and-hold investing. The investment time frame, market approach, and source of data for these trading are completely different. It is important to know the differences in these types of trading so that you do not waste your time and effort chasing what is not relevant to you as a swing trader.

### Day Trading

Holding any position overnight is not an option for a day trader since there is a high chance of losing a large chunk of their investment because of the gap that is created in the price of the stock or security if left overnight. Day trading involves close observation of movements in price on a continuous basis to enable the day trader to determine when to enter or exit a trade. Usually, their trade duration lasts from few minutes to a couple of hours, but generally not overnight or beyond the close of trade for the day.

This set of traders pay more taxes and commissions than the swing trader because movement in prices in a day is due largely to demand and supply of shares in short-term and the holding period is much shorter compared to the swing trader.

The fundamentals of a company are not so much of great concern for the day trader as the psychology of a major buyer or seller in the stock market. They understand that short-term movements in price can be greatly influenced by a major investor, so day traders do all they can to pay close attention to the chatter in the stock market to determine if the noise is dying down or becoming louder.

### Buy-and-Hold Investing

Short-term price swings are not the concerns of buy-and-hold investors. They are focused on studying the market for longer periods of time to determine what stocks and securities will perform well over in the long run.

These categories of investors do not invest to generate current income or cash flow. They are concerned with building or growing their wealth over a long period of time. Unlike swing trading which focuses on generating quick cash flow, buy-and-hold focuses on long-term investing. They are like the vultures of the stock market – the vulture being a patient bird will wait a long time for its idea to prove true and then move in on its prey!

Buy-and-hold investors are relatively passive compared to swing traders. They put less amount of time and effort into trading than the swing trader does. Also, these types of investors find it difficult to profit from shorting or going on the short position as compared to the swinger trader whose aim is to make profits both from the long positions and the short positions.

**In this Chapter...**

You have learned the following:

- Swing trading is basically guess work if you do not have a guide. You are effectively throwing away your hard earned money if you attempt to trade stocks without proper guidance.
- Swing trading is short-term trading. It seeks to make profits from quick but powerful price movements.
- Typically, a swing trader does not stay long in one position. Usually, they hold a position for a couple of days to a few weeks.
- A swing trader's primary concern is with demand and supply, not a company's fundamentals.

- Before you trade a stock, determine if there is an active interest in the stock. Is money coming in or going out of this stock in this very moment?

Before you begin trading, determine whether you want to be a part-time or full-time swing trader. Also give due consideration to what types of stock you will trade, where to trade them, and which techniques you will employ for your swing trading.

# Chapter 2: Beginner's Guide

Let us begin by learning the simple, elementary yet essential fundamentals of swing trading. Beginners who skip this elementary knowledge are setting themselves up for failure. So pay close attention to this part of your learning.

Basically, there is a predictable pattern in the movement of stocks. And the good news is that this pattern can be learned and mastered. When I say "predictable pattern," I do not mean that you will be 100 percent accurate at all times. If that were the case, then there is no risk to swing trading or all types of stock trading in general. What I mean by "predictable pattern" is this: stock traders generally have a way of trading stocks that follow a similar pattern. Knowing this pattern is a vital key to your success in trading stocks or securities.

This is where technical analysis comes to play. You see, everything you need to know about a stock is on the stock's chart. However, you need to know how to read the messages on the stock chart by using technical analysis. So what exactly is technical analysis? Well, just in case you have not deduced it from what I have been saying so far, it is the art and science of reading, understanding, and unraveling the messages on a stock chart. In other words, the technical analysis gives you the tool with which to read the subtle messages hidden in plain sight on the stock chart.

The stock market is basically made up of people and institutions buying and selling stocks. They have fears, hopes, and doubts as they trade. Will the price of this stock drop after I purchase it? What if it falls and becomes a liability for me? Will I profit from buying into a company's shares? Perhaps I should hold on a bit for the price of this stock to go up before I sell and make a better profit. Or do I sell now before the market come crashing?

These are all emotions that determine what happens on the stock market. And the interesting part is that they are all expressed on a stock chart. So, when you can successfully use technical analysis to read in between the lines and decode what the heartbeat of the market is, you will be handsomely rewarded. On the other hand, if you do not know how to read the market and you blindly throw money around in the hope of making some profits, you will be punished for your ignorance. Unfortunately for many traders, this is the path they choose. Technical analysis only becomes an option after they have been severely punished by the market.

We are, however, going to avoid those costly mistakes that will cost us money by first of all learning how to read the stock chart using technical tools. Do not bother so much about memorizing definitions and names of tools. Rather, give your undivided attention to how they work and how to use them. And by all means, do not feel intimidated by the term "technical analysis." It is simpler than it sounds. However, I must add that simple does not necessarily translate to easy. So you do need to give it the level of seriousness that it deserves.

The tools for analyzing stock charts which we shall be discussing in this guide will help you to uncover the prevailing or dominant trend of a stock, and then to trade along those trends. If you use the tools well, you should be able to stay on track with a trend for as long as it is ongoing and then jump out when you begin to see signs that the trend is about to change.

In this guide, you will be introduced to tools such as volume, support, resistance, trends, trend lines, etc. These are the most elementary yet essential tools you will need for technical analysis. The more tools you use for your swing trading, the better the results. I strongly advise that you should never base your trading decisions on one tool alone; I mean, what then will be the purpose of having a lot of tools to help you discover a trend if only one is sufficient?

The thing is, when it comes to swing trading (and in fact, stock trading in general), you need several tools to give you the same message as a confirmation that your analysis is accurate (at least to a large extent) so that you can make informed and balanced decisions.

All of the above notwithstanding, it is necessary to mention here that technical analysis is not a hundred percent spot-on. Like I mentioned earlier, what would be the risk in swing trading if there is a full-proof way of trading? None, right?

Nevertheless, these tools have a way of increasing your odds at making better trading decisions.

Now, without further ado, let us truly begin.

## Ups and Downs

The two price patterns that are important to us at this beginner level are the upward trend (uptrend) and the downward trend (downtrend). As a complete beginner to swing trading, it will be in your best interest to avoid trading when market prices show a sideways movement. That sideways price movement is usually referred to as trading ranges or a choppy market. We shall talk briefly on that later.

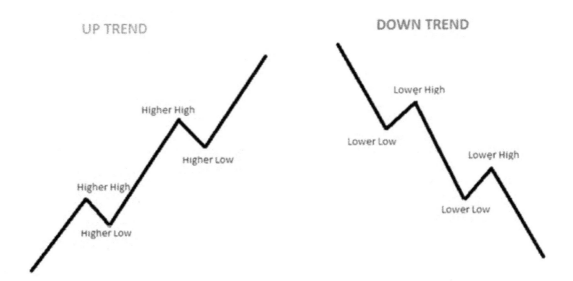

*Image source: https://www.niftytradingacademy.com/wp-content/uploads/2016/01/Display-1-Chart-showing-Up-and-Down-Trends.png*

## Uptrend

When the prices of stocks start to go higher than previous high prices (higher highs) and when they fall, they tend to be higher than previous low positions (higher lows), we say the price of the stock is in an uptrend.

The chart below perfectly illustrates this. It shows the price movement of a stock in an uptrend which retractor pullback (moves downward) briefly before returning upwards again. As we go along in this guide, I will show you why you should buy during a pullback when you are trading a stock that has a dominant uptrend.

## Downtrend

On the flip side of the uptrend is, of course, the downtrend. When the highest price movement of a stock starts to fall lower than previous high prices (lower highs) and when the prices take a nosedive lower than the previous low prices (lower lows), we can safely say that the stock is in a downtrend.

Here is another chart that explains the concept of downtrend better (they say a picture is worth more than a thousand words!). This chart below shows the price movement of a stock in a downtrend which takes a quick retrace or pulls up (moves upward) before continuing its downwards movement again. As we go along, I shall equally show you why you should go short (sell) during a pull up when you are swing trading a stock that has its price in a downtrend.

## Lookout for These Three

In every time frame, there is a pattern that can be traced if you know what to look for. And what we shall be looking at for a start is known as "stages." After that, we shall be looking out for "waves," and then we will begin to learn how to look for "trends." These are the first three patterns to look out for. So let's begin.

## Stages

Every stock in the market goes through four stages. And as a matter of fact, the entire market itself goes through these stages. The stages give you a very important message, and that is, they tell you when to buy a stock (go long), or when to sell a stock (go short), or when to keep your money (stay in cash). This brings to mind Kenny Roger's lines from his popular 1978 song *The Gambler* where it says, "*you've got to know when to hold 'em, know when to fold 'em, know when to walk away, know when to run.*" These famous lines also apply to the art of swing trading and trading stocks in general no matter what methods you choose to use.

All time frames do consist of the four stages – it doesn't matter how long the time frame is (a year or a quarter of a year) or how short the time frame is (a month or a day). A careful look at the chart for the time frame will reveal the four stages.

*Image source: www.stockcharts.com*

Understanding what stage a stock is currently in may take some practice (and it should because you are a beginner), but with time you should be able to pinpoint exactly what stage a stock is in by simply taking a look at the stock's price chart. Such mastery doesn't come by skipping this important knowledge. You must be committed to learning everything there is to be learned about swing trading for you to easily spot a stock's stage on a chart.

## First Stage

This stage happens immediately after a stock has been in a long period of a downtrend (please do remember that I am using "long" here as a relative term. If you are looking at a chart for one day, then "long" may mean a period of an hour. But "long" could mean two weeks if you are looking at a chart for one month). When a stock that has previously been heading downwards begins to move sideways to form a rather steady base, it indicates that the buyers of that stock are buying more of it than the sellers who previously dominated that stock. This is the first stage.

## Second Stage

At the second stage, the stock starts to take an upward trend. A lot of people still do not cash into this stage early enough because they feel it is still performing poorly. So they tend to wait a little more and usually miss this stage. There's a lot of money to be made at this stage for those who understand how to look out for it and seize the trend. If you understand how this stage works, you will amass as much as you could before the tide turns. And when the crowd begins to trade at this stage, you are already getting out of this stage because you know its movement is about to change.

### Third Stage

Similar to stage one, this stage goes sideways. There seems to be a balance between buyers and sellers, so there is mixed movement. However, this is the stage that most novices and those who are too fearful to come in. It is the stage where people who suffer from analysis paralysis try catching up, but it's too late.

### Fourth Stage

Stage four marks the downward trend of the stock. For those who are in the long (those who buy the stock), it is not a position they want to remain in. But inexperienced traders who are in the long still hold on a bit longer because they think it is just a slight dip or a correction of sorts. After all, from all indications, the stock still has solid fundamentals. Nevertheless, they find to their dismay that the downward trend is real and it's not a mere correction.

### Bottom Line

You can make money from the stages if you understand how they work. Basically, you should hold off trading (stay in cash) when the stock or the market is hovering around stage one. Stage two is where you really should be going long aggressively (buying). Do have it in mind that stage two is where novices hesitate for a bit too long to their own detriment. At stage three, hold off trading as you did at stage one. And in stage four, you should be going for the short position (selling) aggressively. Remember that at stage four most ignorant traders (and there is a lot of them) are focused on going long in the belief that the downtrend will not last.

All these sounds pretty simple, right? But in reality, it's not that quite simple especially for a beginner. There is something known as waves in each of these stages. In the next chapter, we shall take a quick look at waves.

**In this Chapter...**

You have learned the following:

- Stock movements have predictable patterns that show up on a chart, and which can be learned to help improve your chances of making better trade decisions and ultimately better profits.
- Technical analysis can be used to read these patterns so as to predict future patterns properly.
- In the stock market, you are rewarded with profits for correctly using technical analysis tools to predict price movements and punished for ignoring them.

- Tools for technical analysis are not 100 percent accurate. However, they are the key to a more successful trading experience.

- When prices begin to move higher than previous high prices and even when they fall, they are still higher than previous low positions; the price movement is in the uptrend.

- When prices begin to fall lower than previous high prices and fall lower than previous low positions, the price movement is in the downtrend.

- There are four stages in a stock movement. Stages tell you when to buy, sell, or hold your money.

- As a beginner, avoid trading in stages one and three. The market is going sideways and may not be healthy for a beginner in swing trading.

Seize the opportunity at stage two to make more profits.

# Chapter 3: The human mind and the stock market

Trades do not just happen on their own, neither do stocks move up or down of their own accord. Traders, that is, humans, determine how trades happen and what stocks go up and which comes down. We do this by how we feel – we buy or sell stocks based on our fears or greed or hope. All stock trends are driven by our feelings. This is why it is important to understand the mindset that drives the market.

Essentially, the action of buyers and sellers who exchange trades establish the price of a stock. The price of a stock will usually tilt upwards if there is more buying than selling. And of course, the reverse will be the case (a fall in price) if the action of sellers is greater than the action of buyers.

But what creates this often imbalance in the number of stocks bought and sold? It is the mindset or psychology behind why and how traders behave. The truth is that the market is saturated by people who do not have a plan. They enter and exit trades based on feelings or emotions of fear and greed.

Here's how you will know a person who has no plan or strategy (the number of years the person has spent trying their hands on trading doesn't matter); they are usually not sure if they should buy now or sell now? They are always not sure if they should take their profits now or if they should cut their losses. Why? There is no plan to tell them what to do? So they depend on their feelings. If they are making profits, they are happy, but their happiness is short-lived because they would not know whether to continue to ride the wave or take their profits because of fear of a sudden change in trend. If they are losing money, they feel sad because they do not know whether to exit or continue the trade perhaps they will be a change in trend. No plan means guesswork and gamble, simple.

**Mind Reading**

As a swing trader, one of your job descriptions is to read other trader's minds by looking at their behavior on the stock chart. The stock chart tells you if they are going to sell or buy. And they buy or sell based on the emotions of excitement or anxiety.

If traders are not interested in a stock, it shows up on the chart as hesitancy and you will see the volume of a stock going down (no much action from buyers and sellers). If there is an uneasy calm among the traders, the stock chart begins to show a drop in the momentum of buying or selling.

When traders are eager or excited, you will begin to notice a breakout pattern on the stock chart as traders are beginning to buy. And when traders become fearful, there is a rush to sell.

But why is there so much emotional attachment to trading? Why can't traders just get a handle on their emotions and buy at low prices, wait and watch, then sell at high prices? Why?

Well, the reason may not be too removed from what is known as social proof. This means acting in ways we perceive to be in keeping with what others are doing. The need to be doing what others are doing (even when we would want to do something else) drives us to blend with the majority. After all, if everyone is doing it, it must be right, right? Wrong! The fact that everyone is doing something doesn't make it right.

Now when you add to social proof one other factor called scarcity, then you will understand why humans do what they instinctively know they should not do. Why do you think antiques are very expensive? Because they are scarce! Have you not heard of limited editions of cars? Quite expensive eh? Well, now you get the gist of it. When people begin to perceive a stock as being scarce, they naturally get emotional and start rushing to buy it at very high prices. Most times, they rush into buying out of fear that the price will go up if they do not get it at the current price. So because everyone is buying and because the price may go up the very next moment, a lot of traders buy based on the emotion of fear.

Unfortunately, many times the prices do not go up as expected. In fact, sometimes, the opposite just happens. So buying low and selling high does a U-turn and becomes buy high and sell low.

This is the mindset behind price movements and you can see it repeat itself every now and again on the stock chart. It is human emotions driving the price movement. Learn to identify them and you would have mastered the psychology behind price movements.

## A Chart's Most Significant Price

What price means the most to you? What is the most vital price of all on a chart? Let me save you the time and energy and give you the simple answer. A chart's most significant price is the price that you paid!

And here's why.

Unless you have developed a certain level of discipline, your psyche is bound to be affected by price movements below or above the price you paid for a stock. For example, if you purchased a stock at $35 per share and a couple of days later, the stock begins to fall so quickly that it drops to $25, it is not the new price that actually gets you worried. It is the price at which you bought the stock ($35) that is giving you concern. The new price may be a perfect price to another trader who wants to trade in the opposite direction.

At the new price, your seemingly good strategies and all the tools and indicators are annoyances to you. You hope and pray and wait for a change. If at some point further down the line while you are still earnestly hoping, the price bounces back to $34, you are most likely to cut your losses and take whatever is left. But if it bounces as far up as $35.5, you will, by all means, grab the opportunity and get out of that position as fast as you can even with just less than a dollar per share profit.

This is what happens a lot of the time. And it happens to thousands of traders on the stock market. The most significant price has a way of making you take decisions that are far removed from your trading strategy unless of course you have self-discipline and have implemented measures to reduce your losses.

However, this also means that you should be motivated to give your plans the best thoughts so as to protect the most vital price of all – your price. Since it is the most important, and you won't want anything to impact negatively on it, you must learn how to not just keep it at a safe level, but to increase its value.

### Bottom Line

Trading real money is different from ordinary paper trading. The emotions are high and usually run haywire when trading real money. That is why it is a good practice to pen down your plans and strategies before you begin to trade. When your money is not at stake, you have the emotional control to write out a balanced plan. A swing trader who truly aims at succeeding must develop the discipline to stick to their plan during the actual trade.

When your emotions are high, go and do something else aside from swing trading. You are likely to make a hasty and irrational decision in an emotionally laden state of mind. You have a business plan for a reason, follow it.

But because a lot of traders do not have the discipline to follow through with their plans (that is even if they have one), it creates an avenue for you who is disciplined enough to make a profit – good profits.

**In this Chapter…**

You have learned the following:

- Stock price movements are a representation of the human emotion of hope, fear, greed, excitement.
- Many people trade the stock market without a strategic plan. It shows up in emotional trading.
- Learning how to read the stock chart tells you the minds and emotions of the traders.
- The emotions are difficult to control when you take your trading up a notch from trading paper to trading real money.

Get your strategies written down before attempting real money trading.

The most essential price on the chart is the amount you paid for a stock. Protect it by being emotionally detached when trading.

## Chapter 4: Charts

In the previous chapter, I mentioned the various mindsets which drive the market. That is exactly what you should be reading in a chart. The chart will tell you what the traders of a particular stock are feeling – fear, greed, indifferent, or uneasy. But before we start reading the charts, let us take a look at a few of the different charts available.

### *Bar Chart*

The bar chart is a series of bars with each individual bar showing the price range of a stock for a particular time frame. It is very easy to see a stock's price action on a bar chart and to uncover patterns.

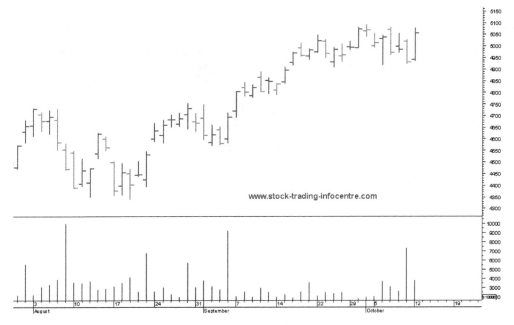

*Image source: http://www.stock-trading-infocentre.com/images/barchart.png*

## P & F Chart

On a P & F (point and figure) chart, stock price movements are represented by Xs and Os. Falling prices are depicted by an O while rising prices are represented by an X. This type of chart is well-suited for filtering out insignificant price movements.

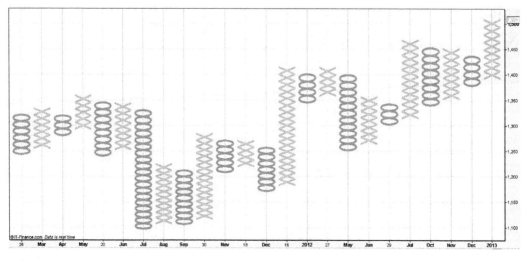

*Image source: http://www.binarytribune.com/wp-content/uploads/2014/02/Point-and-Figure-Chart-1.jpg*

## Line Chart

These are lines that show a stock's price action in a very simplified form. The beauty of the line chart is that it is presented simply on the chart without great details.

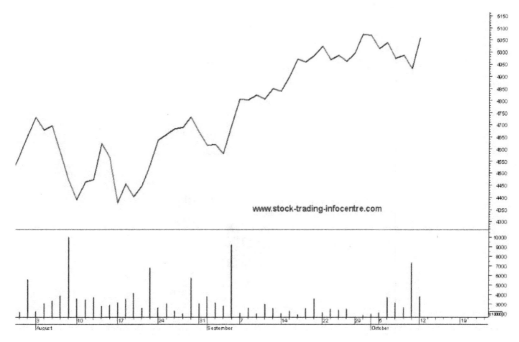

*Image source: http://www.stock-trading-infocentre.com/images/linechart.jpg*

### Candlestick Chart

The open, high, low, and close price of a stock for a specific time frame is clearly shown on a candlestick chart. The body of the candlestick which is usually filled or hollow shows the open and close ranges, while the shadows or the tails of the candlestick shows the price movements. The tails or wicks of the candle are at the top and bottom of the candlestick.

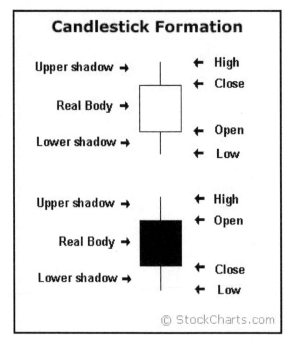

*Image source: www.stockcharts.com*

If the price at the close of a stock is higher than the price at the opening of that stock, the body of the candlestick will be hollow. And in that case, the top of the hollowed body will represent the closing price of the stock, while the bottom of the hollowed body will signify the opening price.

On the other hand, if the price of the stock closes lower than the opening price, the body of the candlestick will be filled. In such a case, the top of the filled body will represent the opening price of the stock, while the bottom of the filled body will denote the closing price.

A filled candlestick that closes lower than it opened signifies that sellers are on the aggressive side. And a hollow candlestick which closes higher than it opened signifies that buyers are on the aggressive side.

The candlestick is easier to read for many traders including beginners. Price action can be easily interpreted. This makes it a popular choice for most traders. However, it is important to note that while the candlestick is a very good tool, do not base all your swing trading judgment solely on this one tool.

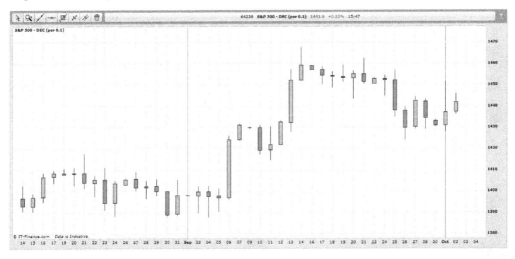

Image source: https://www.onlinefinancialmarkets.com/images/Candlestick-Chart.jpg

As a beginner, it is a good practice to pick one of the chart types and stick to it so as not to complicate things for yourself. In this swing trading guide; we shall focus on the candlestick chart because, in my opinion, this chart type is a tool you can use to read the minds of traders clearly. It has a way of laying bare before your very eyes the emotions that drive stock traders.

## The Candlestick

In this section, I shall devote ample space to discuss the candlestick since this is the major chart we shall be using.

Let me keep this as simple as it can be. The stock market is comprised of thousands of traders who are basically divided into those who are buying and those who are selling a particular stock. And the candlestick can clearly show you the behavior of the buyers and the sellers of any stock.

Note: During the formation of a candle, the open price remains the same but the other prices (high, low, and close) continue to change until the completion of the candlestick. This is so because prices are in action, that is, prices are constantly moving either up, down or sideways. The changes in the prices can also be reflected in the color of the candlestick during the formation stages.

Be aware also that candle color may vary depending on the charting programs used. While some may use green to indicate an upward price movement and red to represent a downward movement in price, other programs may choose to use white (hollow candle body) and black colors (filled candle body) to represent bullish and bearish signs respectively.

## Open

The first price traded within the time frame of the candlestick is known as the open. It is shown at the top or bottom of the candle's body. Usually, a green or white candlestick means an upward price movement, while a red or black candlestick represents a downward price movement.

## High

The highest price traded within the time frame of the candlestick is known as the high. It is represented on the candle by the wick or upper tail above the body. Usually, there will be no upper tail on the body of the candle if the open price was the highest price traded within the time frame of the candle's formation.

## Low

The lowest price traded within the time frame of the candlestick is called the low. It is pictured on the candle as the lower wick or the lower tail. When a candle has no lower tail, it shows that the open price was the lowest price traded within the time frame of the candle's formation.

## Close

The last price traded as the time frame of the candle completes is known as the close. It is shown at the top or bottom of the candle's body. Usually, a green or white candlestick means an upward price movement, while a red or black candlestick represents a downward price movement.

## *Give It a Try!*

Practice reading a candlestick chart. Here's what you can do right now. Get a demo trading account and adjust the time frame to five minutes selecting candlestick as the chart type. What will happen is that at every five minutes interval a new candlestick which represents the trades for the past five minutes is shown. You can play around with this for a couple of minutes to get a good handle on the general idea of candlesticks.

## Candle Ranges

The position of a stock price close is important because it tells you who was in charge of the trade – buyers or seller. This means when you see the price of a stock closing at the bottom of a range, you know that sellers were at the mercy of the buyers. The buyers were in charge of that trade. And when I say "in charge" I mean the sellers were eager to let go of their positions even as the buyers were only interested in buying the stock at a low price. This is a sign of falling prices.

On the other hand, when you see the price of a stock closing at the top of a range, you can be sure that the buyers were more than eager to buy the stocks at a higher price. This puts the sellers in charge. Even though the buyers appear busier, the sellers were actually in control of the stock price. This is a sign of rising prices.

But what about the length of the candles; why are some longer than the others? Simply put, a "long" candle shows a wider price range and is called a wide range candle. It signifies that there is aggressive or intensive selling or buying of a particular stock. And a "short" candle shows a narrow price range and is called a narrow range candle. It shows that price movements were very minimal and traders were more interested in strengthening their positions. We use wide and narrow to describe the candles so as not to confuse them with the long and short used to describe buying or selling positions.

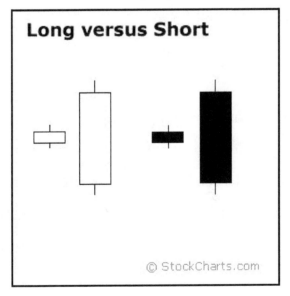

*Image source: www.stockcharts.com*

When white or hollow candles are longer, the length shows how higher the stock's closing price is above the opening price. This means that buyers were intensely buying the stock, consequently pushing the stock price to rise.

On the flip side, when a black or filled candle is longer, it shows how lower the stock's closing price is below the opening price. What this translates to is a fall in the price of the stock as sellers were intensely selling to exit their positions.

One huge tip that could help you is to remember that stocks have a tendency to gravitate towards the direction of candles with a wide range on the stock chart. In other words, if there is a downtrend on the stock chart, there is a higher tendency for the wide candles to be heading downwards meaning stock prices are following suit. Keep this in mind when studying a stock chart.

Recall that I just mentioned that wide range candles indicate that traders have a higher level of interest in a particular stock and narrow range candles signify lesser interest in the stock. Following this logic carefully, you can deduce that entering a trade when the interest is low and exiting when the interest becomes higher gives you a better chance at making higher profits.

## The Pluses of Using Candlesticks Chart

Other charts such as the bar chart and the lines do have their usefulness in analyzing stocks; however, the candlestick has some major advantages over them. I shall briefly highlight a few of the advantages of using the candlesticks chart.

- It is easier to see at a glance the messages of a candlestick chart. If you are completely new to trading, it might be a bit overwhelming to take in all the information about candlesticks and what each pattern means. But as soon as you get used to the meanings (which shouldn't be a long time), the messages standout as soon as you take a quick glance at the candlestick chart.

- Reversals can be easily detected using candlesticks. They forewarn of short-term reversals which a swing trader will find very interesting.

- Hollowed (or white) and filled (or black) candles can easily tell you stock trends within a particular time frame.

- Candlesticks can easily show you what is likely to set the pace for the next trading action. For example, if there is a wide range at the close, it is likely that the next day trading action will kick start on that same note.

**In this Chapter...**

You have learned the following:

- As a beginner to trading, choose only one type of chart and focus on it until you have mastered it before attempting to read other types of charts.

- The candlestick speaks more clearly to a beginner. Devout time to learn it.

- Practice how to read candlestick charts by setting the time frame on your practice account to five minutes. Watch and learn how the candles show you the open, high, low, and close of each time frame.

- Stocks have a tendency to move towards wide range candles on a chart.

Narrow range candles signify that traders' interest on the stock is low. This is a good time for you to enter trades. And look out for when interests are high to exit the trade. You make better profits this way.

# Chapter 5: Candlestick patterns

In this chapter, we are going to take a quick look at some of the candlestick patterns that are important to you as a beginner. Understand that no individual pattern alone can give you all the clues you are looking for, so as I earlier mentioned, be sure to combine whatever information you deduce from a pattern with other information from other tools as well. The aim is to get a balanced perspective before jumping into conclusion. As a side note, it is not important that you cram the names of these patterns. What is most important is to know the appearances or the shapes of these patterns and what they mean.

## Bullish Patterns

*Engulfing*

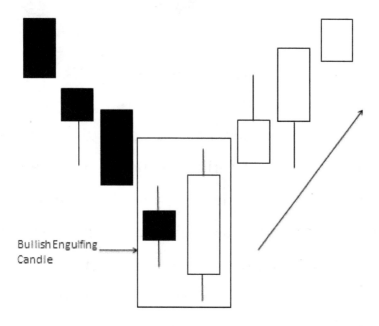

Bullish Engulfing Candle

*Image source: https://www.nasdaq.com/images/forex/education-bullish-engulfing-candles.png*

This bullish pattern occurs on a stock chart when a hollow or white large candle engulfs a previous smaller filled or black candle; hence the name engulfing. The bullish engulfing pattern often occurs in a downtrend and when it does, there is a high chance of a reversal from the downtrend (bearish trend) to an uptrend (bullish trend). This patterns shows up to signify that active traders as well as investors have had a change of mind about the value of a stock and are beginning to be aggressive about it. This is what usually leads to a reversal in the stock's trend.

*Doji*

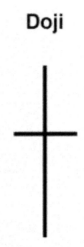

*Image source:*
*http://www.freeonlinetradingeducation.com/uploads/2/7/6/3/27639609/*
*__1421868008.png*

This bullish pattern often shows hesitancy or indecisiveness in the minds of the traders. Usually, the stock price remains the same for the entire time frame after it opens. It closes almost at the same opening price. When this happens, there is likely to be a reversal of the trend in the opposite direction because traders are more than likely to doubt the price's dominant trend. In a dominant downward direction, the question in the traders' minds would be something along the lines of "why is the price not going down?" and this could possibly result in buying rushing to buy and causing prices to rise. There is no one single candlestick that has the entire messages you need to make your trading decision, but the doji is a very significant candlestick you need to watch out for.

*Hammer*

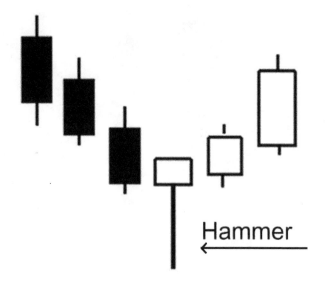

*Image source:*

*https://www.trendbibelen.no/images/help/indicator/h_CandlePatHammerBu*

*y.720x400.png*

This occurs when traders begin to short-sell a stock after it opens. However, before closing, buyers force a reversal and the price closes at the top of the range. Sometimes hammer patterns show up when there has been considerable orders placed for a stop loss.

*Piercing*

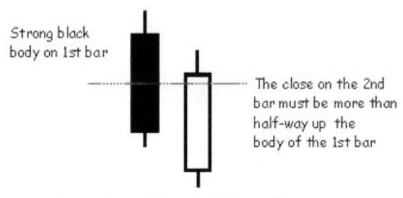

**Piercing Line - Reversal**

Strong black
body on 1st bar

The close on the 2nd
bar must be more than
half-way up the
body of the 1st bar

Reversal signal after a down-trend

*Image          source:          https://cdn-images-*
*1.medium.com/max/1600/0\*pABCGiNOoE_d5oVC.*

This pattern can also signify imminent reversal. From a previous trading period, there usually is a wide range black candle which closes at the bottom of a range or near the bottom, signifying that sellers have the upper hand. But in the next trading period, a wide range white candle closes at a position that is somewhere halfway into the previous candle. Short sellers in the previous trading period are at a loss when this occurs.

## *Harami*

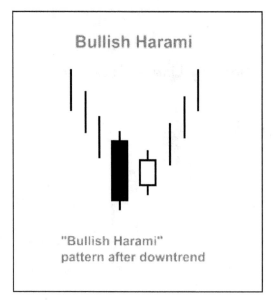

*Image source: https://c.mql5.com/18/2/bullish_harami_en.png*

Harami means pregnant in Japan; hence, the Harami pattern usually shows up as two candles with the smaller one nestled inside the larger one. It can easily be mistaken for the engulfing pattern, but there are not the same. The positions of the candles are opposite that of the engulfing pattern. Usually this pattern signifies a stop in preceding momentum. From a previous trading period, there usually is a wide range black candle which closes at the bottom of a range or near the bottom, signifying that sellers have the upper hand. However, in the next trading period, a narrow range white candle closes the period.

## Bearish Patterns

*Engulfing*

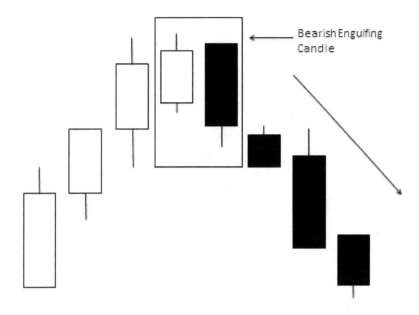

*Image source:* *https://www.nasdaq.com/images/forex/education-bearish-engulfing-candles.png*

This bearish pattern occurs on a stock chart when a filled or black candle engulfs a previous smaller hollow or white candle. The bearish engulfing pattern often occurs in an uptrend to signify a likely reversal to a bearish trend or downtrend.

*Doji Star*

## Bearish Doji Star

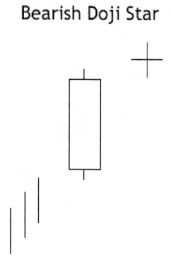

*Image source: http://thestockmarketwatch.com/learn/wp-content/uploads/2009/12/bearish-doji-star.gif*

The Doji Star is a bearish pattern that is formed by the appearance of a white wide range candle on the first day, and followed by a doji on the second day that gaps above the first day. The wigs of the dojiare not very long. This also signifies a possible reversal from an upward to a downward trend.

## Shooting Star

*Image source: https://ice3x.co.za/wp-content/uploads/2016/07/Trading-Elementary-School-Lesson-2-k.png*

This bearish candle pattern looks like an inverted hammer pattern. It occurs when a stock's price goes above the opening price during the trading period, but at the closing, it came lower than the opening price. This bearish candle pattern is a good sign that an uptrend is losing steam, therefore it is a good idea to consider entering short trades when you see this pattern.

*Dark Cloud Cover*

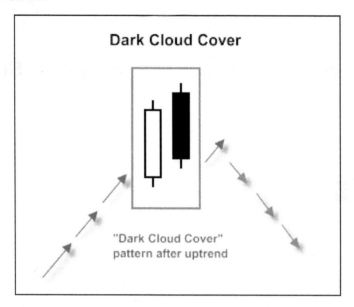

*Image source: https://c.mql5.com/18/1/dark_cloud_cover_en.png*

This bearish reversal pattern occurs when a filled (black) candle's opening price is above the closing price of a hollowed candle and is, at the same time, below the hollowed candle's midpoint.

*Harami*

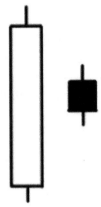

*Image source:*

*https://www.investopedia.com/thmb/8KI9SjY6yOd1efX3JG2Uv1Riw48=/24*

*7x273/filters:no_upscale()/img-5bfd703146e0fb0026964eef*

This two bar bearish candle pattern indicates a possible reversal to a downward trend. Obviously, an uptrend goes before a bearish Haramipattern occurs. Bearish Harami shows a hollow candle that is followed by a small filled candle. The opening price as well as the closing price of the small filled (black) candle has to be contained within the range of the hollow (white) candle.

## A Recap

Let me bring all of the above to a short close. I'll use a few of the candlestick patterns to drive home the lesson.

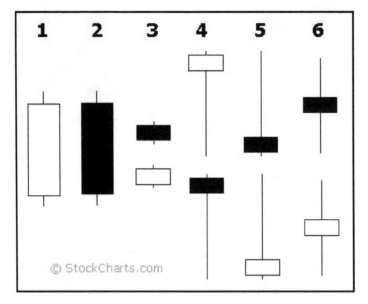

*Image source: www.stockcharts.com*

In summary:

- A wide range bullish candle signifies that buyers were actively buying and were therefore in charge of the trade during a larger part of the specified time frame.

- A wide range bearish candle means that sellers were vigorously selling and were more in charge of the trade for the most part of the trading duration.

- Narrow range candles shows that neither buyers nor sellers were too passionate about the stock therefore creating lesser impact on the opening price.

- A rather long tail at the bottom of a candle means that sellers were aggressive at the beginning of the time frame, however, before the close, buyers took the lead.

- A long tail at the top of a candle shows that buyers were tenaciously holding to their positions for a good part of the trading period. Nevertheless, sellers took over before the stock closed.

- When the body of a candle falls in between long upper and lower tails, it simply means that both buyers and sellers had an almost equal impact on the price of the stock. So trading appears balanced.

By now you should be able to look at a stock chart and, using what you have learned so far, understand exactly what the candlesticks are telling you.

**Using Two or More Candlesticks**

Basing your swing trading decision solely on the message of only one candlestick may not be a wise way to use candlesticks. Even if you do not fuse candlestick messages or signs with other tools, you should at least combine two or more candlesticks before taking any action.

**In this Chapter...**

You have learned the following:

- No individual candle alone can give you all the clues you need to make a killing.

- Do not use only one candlestick to form a trading opinion.

- Any time you see a doji, take particular note because the trend is very likely to reverse. Combine this signal with other chart analysis tools to make your trading decision.

The various candlestick patterns in the bullish and bearish markets give you a particular message. Learn them well.

## Chapter 6: Waves and trends

**Waves**

In explaining waves, I will use the Elliot wave pattern to show the behavior of stocks.

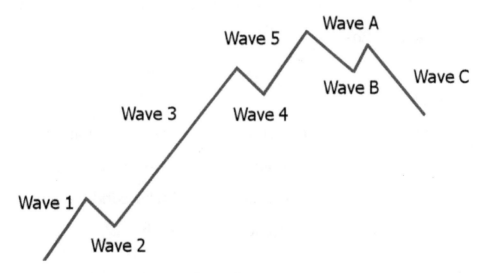

*Image source: www.swing-trade-stocks.com*

There is a motive phase of a stock's movement and there is also a corrective phase of the stock's movement all wrapped into the wave pattern. The pattern basically has five waves, but as a swing trader, your focus should be on the second wave structure.

*The motive phase*: the motive phase is the complete view of an upward trend.

*The corrective phase*: this corrects the upward trend of the stock movement. Correction simply means a slight decline that happens shortly after an upward movement.

### The First Wave

This is the beginning of a new upward trend or uptrend. It signals the first stage we discussed previously. To determine if this is truly the first wave, you should watch out for a retrace or a pullback shortly after this wave begins.

### The Second Wave

As soon as you notice a pullback (as shown in the diagram above), it is time to look for your entry point. You will use a candlestick chart to determine your entry point. Cashing in on this second wave ensures that you are coming in on the trend early enough.

### The Third Wave

This is the strongest and longest wave of the entire structure. When you learn how to get on board a stock as it is beginning the third wave (by noticing the pullback during the second wave), you will make much more profits in relatively short periods. The third wave is the cash cow and it is up to you to milk it and ride it for as long as the wave lasts.

## The Fourth Wave

This is a signal that the uptrend is over. For those who are just beginning to buy into the stock during this wave, they would have begun rather too late.

## The Fifth Wave

This signifies the final rush to buy before the downtrend begins in full. The stock movement is usually really slow at this point.

## Other Waves

The other waves (labeled a, b, c) are the actual start of the downtrend. Wave A is similar to the second wave (the pullback) but you will know the difference when it gets to Wave B because wave B is lower than the fifth wave. Wave C signals an official downtrend in force.

## Bottom Line

As a smart swing trader, you should go for the short position (sell) when the stock hits a downtrend at Wave C. Traders who hold on to the long position at Wave C (in the hope that Wave A is a retract or pullback) end up losing.

## Trend

Okay, we've looked at stages and waves. Now let's turn our attention to trends.

To put it simply, a trend is the relatively consistent price movement in one predominant direction within a particular time frame. These price movements could be either sideways, up, or down so long as they are fairly consistent for a considerable amount of time. Trends may last for as long as several months; a huge profit-making period for traders who can see the bigger picture.

## Countertrends

It is possible to have a countertrend within a predominant trend (the bigger picture). This is not just a pullback or a rally; it is period where a trend goes in the opposite direction of a major trend for as long as several weeks or months. However, its price movements eventually return to the major trend. This is good for you as a swing trader because you are not in the market for the long-haul. So you can make a profit from both the predominant trend (bigger picture) and from the countertrend.

## Short-term Trends

Within the predominant trend, there is also the possibility of having short-term trends which are super cool for swing traders. Short-term trends can sometimes last for as long as several days to weeks. But guess what: short-term trends are usually not apparent when you are looking at the bigger picture – the predominant trend. You need to zoom in closer to see them. So, take a look at any stock chart that shows a predominant trend for several months, but this time, magnify the chart to show you daily trends. You can zoom in closer to see hourly or shorter time periods. There you will find swing trading honeypots that are of no interest to the buy-and-hold investor, but which are goldmines to the swing trader!

*Trending Stocks*

As a beginner, if you really want to make money from swing trading over and over again, you should trade trending stocks (stocks that are in an uptrend or downtrend). And here is how to know a trending stock. A stock in an uptrend has higher highs and higher lows. In other words, a stock in the second stage is in an upward trend. Also, a stock in a downtrend has lower highs and lower lows. That is to say; fourth stage stocks are in a downward trend.

Generally, stocks are either in a trending phase or they are in a trading ranges phase. It has been roughly estimated that stocks are in the trending phase for about 30 percent of the time. The rest of the time, they are in the trading ranges phase.

Take a look at the chart below to see an example of a trending phase.

*Image source:*

*http://www.swing-trade-stocks.com/image-*

*files/xtrendexample.png.pagespeed.ic.OoQSQ2IfX6.png*

Now take a good look at another chart below to see if, as a beginner, you would prefer to trade during a trending ranges phase.

*Image source:*

*http://www.swing-trade-stocks.com/image-*

*files/xtradingrangeexample.png.pagespeed.ic.YJhr_hpAe9.png*

Ignorance is what makes people who are new to swing trading enter trades during the trading ranges phase. It is very risky because there is hardly a chance of predicting any trend up or down. Trading ranges usually occur during the first and third stages of a stock movement. Remember, we said that you should stay in cash (*hold 'em*) during these stages. One of the fastest ways to throw away your capital is to trade stocks when they are in the trading ranges phase.

## A Note About "Buying Cheap"

When stocks are falling excessively (in a critical downtrend), a swing trader may be tempted to go long excessively (buy larger amounts of stock) because falling price means cheap stocks. I would recommend that you should be very careful when attempting to buy into such stocks. If you must buy, you should utilize stop orders. Let me briefly explain why.

You see, in the stock market, as well as with every other aspect of life, "cheap stocks" usually have a tendency of eventually becoming cheaper. It may not happen all of the time, but it does happen. However, there is a possibility of cheaper stocks to rebound. But it may take a long time for cheaper stocks to bounce back up; time which a swing trader does not have. In other words, if a swing trader rushes into "buying cheap" he or she may end up amassing cheap stocks that no one will be interested in buying back. I believe that is not your aim for venturing into swing trading, yes?

### Bottom Line

Practice looking at charts and pinpointing whether they are in the trending or trade ranges phase. It is a huge mistake to go long or buy a stock that is heading in a downtrend simply because you notice a sudden upward price movement. If the stock is truly in a downtrend, then the sudden upward price movement is a rally that doesn't last. It usually quickly returns downward, and that is a great time to go short (sell). The opposite applies to an uptrend. Do not go short because you observe a pullback. It usually bounces back in a short while. The sudden downward price movement is an excellent time to go long (buy stocks) before the bounce back happens.

## Trend Lines and Trend Prediction

In order to use trends to your advantage, it is a good practice to learn how to draw trend lines on charts. This will help you to quickly recognize when a trend is about to deviate from its current path. Although this may not happen a hundred percent of the time, it is still a good way to help you trade more intelligently as a smart swing trader should.

To draw a trend line for an upward trend, follow these steps:

- Beginning at the left of the chart, look for the lowest price point.
- Look for a second lower point that can connect to the first point in a straight line without passing through price movements on the chart. Usually, the second lower point will be at a retrace or pullback.
- Now draw a straight line to connect the two points on the trend. Make sure that the line does not pass through the prices. You have drawn a speculative trend line. You still need one more point to confirm it.
- Look for a third low point that can connect with the straight line without breaking it. If you can find and draw this line, your uptrend is confirmed. When your trend line is complete, it will

appear as if the prices are finding a support level on an inclined base. (We shall discuss support level in subsequent chapters)

- Reverse the process to draw a trend line for a downtrend. This time, instead of looking for the lowest points, you should be looking for the highest points. And instead of looking for a pullback, you should be looking out for a rally. Remember that the line needs to touch at least two highest points to be regarded as a tentative trend line. And when the line touches a third point, the trend is confirmed. When you have successfully completed your trend line, it will appear as if the prices are bouncing off a resistance level on a slant line. (We shall discuss resistance level in subsequent chapters)

*Image source:*

*http://d.stockcharts.com/school/data/media/chart_school/chart_analysis/trend_lines/trendlines-5msft.png*

## *What to Do If A Trend Is Confirmed*

When you have confirmed an uptrend by drawing a trend line that touches three points, you should enter and remain in the long position (hold on to the stock) and remain vigilant for signs of line breaks. When the stock price breaks your trend line, it is likely that things are about to change. They may be a reversal in the trend or prices will begin to go sideways. Whatever the case, you do not want to wait and see. As a beginner who wants to be a smart swing trader, your best bet is to sell!

Note: As a beginner, you may not know how to use technical indicators (such as RSI, Stochastics, and CCI) to double check your trading decisions, but that is okay. You cannot learn everything all at once. Remember, we are concerned with the very basics of swing trading. As you advance in the trading business, you will learn more about technical indicators.

A break in the trend line (when prices cross the trend line) may indicate an imminent change in the trend. However, this may not always be true. In order to be close to accurate in predicting a change in trend, you need to learn how to use a three-step confirmation process. But before we go into that, let us take a look at few tips for using trend lines.

## Tips on Using Trend Lines

- When a trend line is steep, it indicates a somewhat less reliable trend line. Do not bother so much with steep trend lines.

- For a trend line to be reliable, it has to connect at least two low points on an uptrend, and two high points in a downtrend. When there are three touches to the trend line, then the trend line is confirmed as very reliable.

- When a stock continues to touch a trend line, it indicates a higher level of significance and reliability.

- Breaking a trend line is not a guarantee that the price movement will automatically change.

- Do not buy a stock solely because it is touching a trend line. Touching a trend line or even breaking it is only but one aspect in the trend prediction process.

## Predicting Trends Using the Three-Step Method

As I stated earlier, there is no 100 percent assurance with trading stocks no matter what sophisticated methods or dependable tools are available to you. However, there are methods that have been evolved to give up to 60 to 80 percent accuracy. The three-step method gives such accuracy. And trust me, that is huge in the world of swing trading.

Here are the three steps:

1. *First, there is a break in the trend line*: it is possible to have a trend line broken but the trend still continues moving in the current direction.

Although there may be no apparent change in direction, it is important to take note of the break and keep an eye on it.

2. *Secondly, a retest and failure follows*: the characteristic of an uptrend is higher highs, and higher lows. But when there is a break in the trend line, and then the uptrend does not continue to hit high highs and high lows, it has failed to meet the previous high test (retest and failure). The stock is currently not making higher highs neither is it making any lower lows. But it is still too early to confirm that there is a change in trend.

3. *Finally, there is a fall in price below a previous low*: when the stock falls below a prior low, it is now a confirmed change in trend. This is true because there is now a lower high and lower low. For a change in a downtrend, the reverse is applicable.

### Bottom Line

All this is useful to you as a swinger trader if you are careful to note when a stock starts breaking the trend line. Although you may still trade a stock that is touching or breaking the trade line, you need to be extra vigilant to observe if they meet the second step – the retest and failure step. If the stock follows the second step; there is a likelihood of the trend changing. Armed with this knowledge, you are better prepared to trade in the opposite direction when the trade eventually changes trend.

Equally, as a swing trader, you should look out for stocks that are just beginning a new trend and trade them. Stocks that are at the start of a new trend are likely to have explosive moves that you can make real profits from.

To be able to find stocks that are at the start of a new trend, you need to become familiar with moving averages. Also, for an easier way to identify the different stock stages, and the several waves, plus the trends, a good knowledge of moving averages is important.

**In this Chapter...**

You have learned the following:

- There are five waves for a stock price movement that indicates an uptrend and three other waves (waves a, b, and c) which starts an actual downtrend.

- Look for a retrace or a pullback in the stock wave. If it happens, that is the second wave. Enter a trade and ride the wave.

- When price movements continue in one direction for a considerable amount of time, it is known as a trend.

- A swing trader makes profits from a dominant trend as well as countertrends and short-term trends.

- You can set the stock chart to daily or hourly time frame to see short-term trends.

- How to make money over and over as a swing trader, trading trending stocks. As a beginner, avoid stocks that are in the trading ranges phase.

- Buying cheap may not always be a good idea.

- You need three touches to a trend line to confirm a trend. Enter a trade after confirming the trend line.

- When prices break trend lines, there is a possibility of a change in trend. You are a beginner without much experience in using other technical indicators in combination with trend lines. So get out of the trade as fast as you can before the trend changes.

- You can predict a change in trend using the three-step method.

Always trade stocks that are beginning a new trend. They usually have more explosive moves.

# Chapter 7: Other analysis tools

Technical indicators are good… but they are complex for a beginner. So do not bother so much about which to use or which is more reliable than the other. As a beginner, you need to stop beating on yourself for not understanding technical indicators. Also, resist the temptation for depending on one technical indicator to tell you exactly which stock to buy or sell.

Let us take a look at a few more good tools you could use for analyzing the stock and market to help you make informed decisions.

**Volumes**

The total number of shares that are bought and sold in a particular period is called a stock chart volume. It appears below a chart in the form of a histogram. One of the functions of a volume is that it indicates the level of interest traders have in a particular stock. It is like measuring the heartbeat of traders about a particular stock. Apparently, a high stock volume indicates a high level of interest and action going on with that stock, and a low stock volume indicates that traders are not too keen about that stock.

Another function of the stock volume is the indication of a stock's liquidity or illiquidity. That is to say, it tells traders how easy it will be to buy a particular stock (or not) or how easy it will be to sell a particular stock (or not).

This is common sense. Let us take a minute to consider the everyday physical market where goods and services are purchased. If there are fewer people interested in a particular good or service, it becomes difficult for those who have those goods to sell their products or get people to buy their goods and services.

This is what is known as illiquidity. On the other hand, if there are a lot of people who are in need of the goods and services, it becomes easy to trade those goods and services. The products will trade like crazy. That is what is known as liquidity of a product.

Now apply the same principle to your stock volume. The volume of the stock tells you the interest level of traders. That means you can accurately gauge the liquidity or illiquidity of the stock to know if you will get stuck with a stock (pun intended) after purchasing it, or if you can easily find and buyer after getting into the stock.

Nevertheless, all this is not to say that high stock volume automatically translates into a higher number of buyers versus sellers, while low stock volume means a higher number of sellers than buyers. Than can't be true. Buyers and sellers of a particular stock are always balanced. After all, no one buys if there are no sellers; neither does anyone sell if there are no buyers. The volume only shows if more traders are taking part in the buying and selling of a stock. That is not the same as buyers being more than sellers or sellers being more than buyers. Clear? Great!

## *Bottom Line*

Volumes are important because they give you a general idea of which stock is catching the attention of traders and which is not. Although you can successfully swing trade without painstakingly studying stock volumes, it is a good idea to understand what a stock's volume is on a chart to give you a good insight into what other traders think of the stock.

## Moving Averages

Moving averages is a great tool that helps you to determine the direction of a trend and also to quickly spot indicators that signify a change in the trend. There are lots of details about moving averages (how they are computed and constructed) that will not interest a beginner to swing trading. At best, they will simply bore you! One rule of thumb I would recommend to you as a beginner is to always look out for simplicity. When something becomes too complex, there is a greater chance of failing at it. So I will not bother you with the computational details of moving averages. You may wish to look them up and get acquainted with them after you become good at swing trading. For now, let us give our focus to this one main fact about moving averages: the line of a moving average indicates a stock's average price over a given period. It is that simple.

Basically, two types of moving averages have become very popular over the years and are commonly used by traders. They are SMA – Simple Moving Average, and the EMA – Exponential Moving Average. These can easily be used to identify likely resistance and support levels (more on support and resistance later).

## Simple Moving Averages versus Exponential Moving Averages

The simple moving averages (SMA) are glaringly dissimilar from the exponential moving averages (EMA). However, that does not translate into one being superior to the other. Simple moving averages depict a more precise reflection of price average for a whole period. This is why the simple moving averages are considered well tailored for determining support and resistance level of a trend. On the flip side, the exponential moving averages are characterized by less lag. This makes them more responsive to changes in price that occur more recently. This means that exponential moving averages are sure to move well ahead of the simple moving averages.

You could experiment with any of the two and find what works well for you. However, you also have the choice of combining the two on a single chart. And we will see how to do just that.

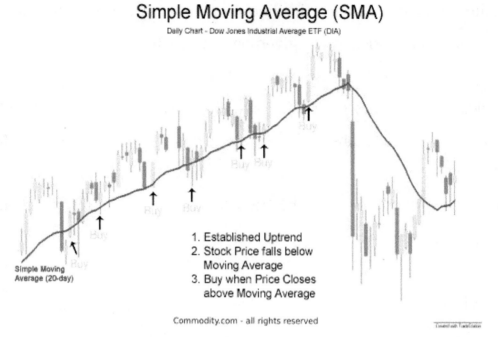

*Image source: https://commodity.com/wp-content/uploads/technical-analysis/MASimple20DIA.gif*

## How To Use Both Averages

Combining the simple moving averages with the exponential moving averages is a good way to maximize their benefits. Let us take a look at how to combine the two in the following example.

In this example, I shall use the 10-period SMA in combination with the 30-period EMA. One good advantage of combining a fast and a slow moving average is because once the fast average crosses the slow one, it is a high indicator of a possible change in trend. Take a look at this example.

*Image source: http://www.swing-trade-stocks.com/image-files/moving-averages.png*

The chart above is pretty simple to read. The 10-period SMA is positioned just above the 30 EMA in August while the trend is up. But as the 10-period SMA crosses down in mid-August, the trend also drops down. Notice that by mid-September there is still another cross by the 10-period SMA above the 30 EMA and the trend went back up and remains that way for a long time.

From the above we can deduce the following (pay close attention if you choose to use the 10-period SMA in combination with the 30-period EMA):

- When the 10-period SMA is *above* the 30-period EMA your trading emphasis should be ongoing long.

- When the 10-period SMA is *below* the 30-period EMA your trading emphasis should be ongoing short.

I am keeping this as simple as possible because I know this is a beginner's guide. What you need is the essentials, and that is what I am focused upon. Going into the nitty-gritty will spoil the fun for you as a beginner. Stick to the simple strategies for now and you will make good progress.

Please note:

- Moving averages work well when applied to trending stocks. When a stock is in the trading ranges phase, moving averages will do you no good.
- It is vital that there should be wide spaces between the two moving averages.
- The 10-period SMA has to be above the 30-period EMA before you go for long positions.
- The 10-period SMA has to be below the 30-period EMA before you go for short positions.
- It is compulsory for the two moving averages to slop upwards before you go for long positions.
- It is compulsory for the two moving averages to slop downwards before you go for short positions.

## Moving Averages: Advantages

Here are some of the advantages that come with using moving averages.

1. Moving averages helps you to easily build your skills to identify great openings for making good trades.

2. It helps you to trade in the direction of dominant market trends so that you can easily beat the odds.

3. It is a very simple method to identify market trends and the possibility of a breakout.

4. It provides a simple visual depiction of the prevailing market trend and the general price action of a specific time frame.

## Moving Averages: Disadvantages

As with all things that have advantages, there is sure to be some disadvantages. Here are a few disadvantages of using the moving averages.

1. There could be a possible false signal in the case of abrupt rise or fall in the price of a stock.

2. It only gives you a general overview of the trend plus the likely entry and exit points. However, you must be ready to make the call for the exact spot you wish to enter or exit a trade in a way that is beneficial for you.

3. Depending on the average charting, it can generate noise.

4. To get a good idea of the market position, the time period is very critical.

## *Testing Price Boundaries*

One other important use of moving averages is to determine support and resistance areas on a chart. The support and resistance are basically the limits or boundaries against which the rising and falling price movements of a stock are tested. The more often there is an attempted breach against these boundaries, the more likely there will be a breakout or a change in the direction of the trend (more about support and resistance in the next section).

## *Bottom Line*

Moving averages are a great market tool, but you must always have it in mind that they are a lagging indicator. Their function is mainly to confirm a trend that has been established already. You cannot use moving averages to accurately predict a trend. Nevertheless, you can use them as a yardstick to evaluate future movements in price.

## Support and Resistance

Take a good look at a chart. You'll notice there are some areas that buyers appear to be more dominant. This is known as demand because the buyers are significantly dominating the market, making the price of the stock to rise.

Certainly, if everyone is trying to buy a particular stock at the same time, it makes sense for the price to go up. When the demand for a stock is high, it shows up on a chart as support.

On the other hand, there are some areas on the chart where you'll notice that sellers are more in control. This is what is known as supply because the sellers are rushing out of their positions in the market, making the price of the stock they are selling to drop. Of course, when everyone is selling a stock, the value has nowhere to go but down. When the supply for a stock is high it shows up on a chart as resistance.

All of this simply means that support and resistance are key indicators for helping traders find out areas of demand and supply. Therefore, as a smart swing trader, the most sensible thing for you to do is to buy stocks during periods you have identified as support. Why you should do this is because, in all likelihood, traders who purchased the stock at the dying minute and then began to witness a downtrend in the stock will want to leave that position by breaking even. So they are likely to rush into selling.

And on the flip side, it is obvious you should sell the stocks during the periods you have identified as resistance. This is because many traders who did not get in on time while the stock was heading up have seen another opportunity and are most likely to rush into buying.

Nevertheless, you must be careful about buying at support and selling at resistance. Be sure to use more than one analysis tool before you attempt this so as not to encounter monumental failure. Remember, nothing is a hundred percent sure in trading stocks.

### What Novices Do Not Know

Furthermore, be aware that there are several types of support and resistance.

Looking at this from the long angle, a stock that drops back to a previous low is more worthy of your attention than a stock that drops back to a previous high.

Equally, from the short angle, a stock that moves up to a previous high should get more of your attention than a stock that moves up to a previous low.

But do you know what most novice traders do? They buy stocks when the stocks are running into resistance (when there is supply). And they sell their stock when it falls into support (when there is demand). This is completely backward and does not give you any meaningful profits from trading. For you to make money from swing trading, you should identify early when there is a period that presents an opportunity to buy and also the early signals to sell. Let the novices come in later after the major buying has been done and let them sell when the major selling is already over.

Smart swing traders are always on the lookout to make profits from novices because they are always there to buy from you (when there should be selling) and sell to you (when they should be buying). You have an edge because you are not guessing or following the crowd. You are implementing a perfectly laid out plan to make a profit. Your investment in acquiring the right trading knowledge will pay off if implemented correctly.

## Tips on Profiting from Support and Resistance

Now, let us look at a few tips on how you, a swing trader, can analyze the support and resistance levels of a stock chart to make good profits. Note that I am only referring to simple support and resistance in these tips. Support and resistance that occurs when a stock price falls or rises to touch a price level for a few days are referred to as simple support and resistance. When there is a repeated touch on a price level frequently, it is termed significant support and resistance level.

- More often than not, simple support and resistance happens at whole or round numbers. So, as you analyze your stock chart, it is a good practice to note at what round numbers the stock is finding support or running into resistance.

- Normally, horizontal lines on a chart can be used to define support and resistance levels. These lines will give you a visual representation of areas of aggressive buying and torrential selling. The slant trend lines on a downtrend can also be seen as a resistance level, and the inclined trend lines on an uptrend can also be seen as a support level.

- Another trend line that may not be very obvious at first is the moving averages. Sometimes when there is a downtrend, you will find a moving average becoming a resistance level at the top of the falling prices. And on the flip side, it is not out of place to find moving averages below rising prices in an uptrend providing support.

- When a resistance level is breached or broken, it is highly possible for the resistance to become the new support level.

- When a support level is breached or broken, it is highly possible for the support to become the new resistance level.

## What Indicators Mean to You as a Beginner

If you read most books on swing trading or trading in general, you will discover that indicators are somewhat sorted into two broad groups, namely: leading indicators and lagging indicators. While leading indicators are meant to lead price actions, lagging indicators follow price actions. These are awesome tools that can help an experienced trader. But you are a beginner at swing trading. The question you should be asking is how did these indicators come about? Leading indicators lead price action in what sense? Can there be any indicator drawn on a chart without a price action preceding it? Does that not effectively make the so-called leading indicator an actual lagging indicator when it comes to real-life application? Think about it.

The reason I bring this up, is to let you as a beginner take a breather from racking your brain in a bid to understand some of the complexities of technical indicators. Realize that whatever a technical indicator will tell you is right in front of you as a chart. So your first indicator is the chart. Learn how to read stock charts, and you would have learned a great deal even without a technical indicator.

Having said all of that, I am certainly not discounting the purpose or function of technical indicators. They have their place and, most importantly, their time. Learn the basics first –learn how to read charts – before delving into technical indicators. The time for technical indicators is a bit further down the road for you. And I have dedicated the whole of chapter 9 to technical indicators. So, my trading strategy is very simple: read the charts first, and then look at indicators for some form of confirmation of what you have deduced from the charts.

**In this Chapter...**

You have learned the following:

- Volumes on a stock chart tell you the interest level of traders on a particular stock.
- The liquidity or illiquidity of a stock shows up on the volume.

- Moving averages help you to quickly spot early signals for a change in the direction of a trend.

- SMA and EMA can be combined to give a better reading.

- Moving averages works better with trending stocks not trading ranges.

- Moving averages are lagging indicators, meaning they only confirm an already established trend.

- Demand means buyers are dominating a stock within a given time frame. This causes the price to go up.

- Supply means sellers are leaving their positions making prices to fall.

- Support and resistance levels help you to identify areas of demand and supply.

- Once broken, there is a high chance of support or resistance becoming the other.

- Trend lines and moving averages can also be seen as support and resistance levels.

Smart swing traders usually buy at a support level and sell at a resistance level. However, be careful when buying at a support because it could also tank! Remember, there are no 100 percent guarantees in trading stocks no matter the methods utilized.

# Chapter 8: Interpreting stock charts

Now, let us piece all of the patterns and all of the information about charts, trends, stages, waves, etc, together into charts and learn how to read them effectively. There is no way you could possibly succeed as a swing trader without knowing how to read charts. The vital information you need to know before letting your money go into any trade are all in the chart. The chart tells you if the risk is worth it.

Here is what you need to do to get yourself familiarized with reading stock charts. Look for stock charts online and print them out. Now look at each stock chart and try to determine the following:

What trend is the stock on the chart? Is it going up (uptrend) or is it going down (downtrend)? Is the stock price falling or is it rising? What is the current stage of the stock? Is it in the first, second, third, or fourth stage? Can you determine the support and resistance points? Are there any signs of a breach? Is the trend of the stock a strong one? When was the last breakout? Has there been any pullback or rally? Is this the beginning, middle, or the end of the trend?

Practice with a good number of stock charts and you will definitely get better. With time, you wouldn't have to force yourself to remember these questions – they will occur to you as you as soon as you look at any chart and the answers will come to you as fast as you can think of the questions.

Let me break down what you should be looking for as you practice reading stock charts. Remember, in this beginners guide, we are using only the candlestick stock chart.

### Look for the Stock Trend or Chart Pattern

Firstly, train yourself to quickly identify the general stock direction (uptrend or downtrend) on the stock chart. I would suggest that you should adjust your daily chart to show the chart patterns dating back to about 7 to 8 months. The chart pattern for that time frame should show you clearly the trend, stages, and waves of the stock. When you have successfully identified a trend, you are ready to look for the next important thing on the stock chart.

### Look for the Price Pattern

Secondly, try to identify the price pattern of the stock. What you are looking for on a stock chart that you have identified as having an uptrend is a pullback. If you have identified the chart pattern as a downtrend, then what you are looking for is a rally. So, you've identified a chart pattern (stock trend) and you have found a pullback or rally depending on the direction of the trend. Now you will need to find one more piece to solve the puzzle.

### Look for the Candlestick Pattern

Lastly, look at what the candlesticks are saying. In an uptrend, if the pullback you observed in the price pattern is really a pullback, when the trend comes back around (returns to the dominant trend) the candlestick that should follow in an ideal situation would be a bullish candlestick such as the piercing, hammer, or an engulfing candlestick pattern. In a downtrend, if the rally you observed in the price pattern is really a rally, when the price movement returns to the dominant trend, the dark cloud cover, engulfing, or a shooting star are the likely bearish candlestick pattern that will follow the rally.

When you can effectively combine these three parts of a stock chart, you would have successfully learned one major aspect of reading stock charts.

**In this Chapter...**

You have learned the following:

- Look at various stock charts to determine their trends, current stock stage, support and resistance levels, pullbacks and rallies.

- Reading a stock chart begins by finding the stock trend or the chart pattern.

- Next, find a price pattern by looking for a pullback or rally. Finally, listen to what the candlesticks are saying.

## Chapter 9: Master the swing trading technique

# Develop Your Trading Strategy

There is no perfect trading strategy; so stop searching for one. Moreover, you do not need a perfect trading strategy to make money from trading stocks. Ultimately, your trading strategy will be unique to you. However, as a beginner, you may need to lean a bit on an existing strategy in order to get the hang of it. With time, you can tweak things around to fit your particular trading style or build yours completely from scratch.

Here is a general idea you can use to build your own trading strategy.

*Preparation*

You could start preparing for your trade at the beginning of a new week. Find out what types of trade (short or long) you will want to focus on. You could use a technical indicator such as the moving averages to determine this. After that, take a look at a few financial columns or news, reports, etc. This will give you the general outlook of how stocks are performing and what the market is up to. Look at charts of various industries to see stock strengths and weaknesses, plus promising stocks. Be sure to write down whatever catches your attention in your trading notepad (you don't have one yet?), because in the heat of trading, most things you note mentally won't come to your mind.

## Finding Stocks

Begin to search for potential trades by looking for stocks that:

- Have a strong trend

- Have shown first pullbacks or rallies

- Are at a resistance or support level

- Are in the second or fourth stages

- Are repeatedly touching a support or resistance area

If you do not find a trade that you are comfortable with as a beginner, please do not trade. Remember, trading involves going long, short, or staying in cash. So, learn to stay in cash if there is nothing appealing for you to trade.

## Double Check

After you have found a trade, verify that the company whose stock you are about to trade is not going to release its earnings reports anytime soon. Trading a company's stock just before their earnings report is released can lead to a massive loss for you. So be sure to double check. Here's one way you could find out. Simply go to Yahoo Finance and type in the company's symbol. The date of the next earnings report will be shown.

## During Trades

All things checked and verified, start your trade. Do not give your attention to stock market news or other traders opinion during your own trades. Your attention needs to be only inone place: the stock chart. Ensure that you use trailing stops to closely follow your profits and that would be all you require during trades.

## Your Entry Strategy

Your money is at risk as soon as you enter a position to buy or sell a stock. So, you must be careful that you time your entry very well.

Your entry point should be at a swing point: a low swing point for buying, and a high swing point for selling.

A swing point is made up of three candles.

## Low Swing Point (for entering a long position – buying)

- Candle one goes low

- Candle two goes lower than candle one (lower low)

- Candle three goes higher than candle two (higher low)

Candle three indicates that sellers are no more aggressive. This is a precursor for a trend reversal. This is your cue to enter a long position.

*High Swing Point (for entering a short position – selling)*

- Candle one goes high

- Candle two goes higher than candle one (higher high)

- Candle three goes lower than candle two (lower high)

Candle three indicates that buyers are no more aggressive. This is a precursor for a trend reversal. This is your cue to enter a short position.

Take a look at this chart below.

*Image source: www.stockcharts.com*

## Successive Up Days or Down Days

Another way to enter a trade is to look for successive up days or down days. These are a lot easier to spot, but be sure that you are not entering the trade when the trend is about to end or reverse. Take a look at the chart below for a clearer understanding.

*Image source: www.stockcharts.com*

## Your Exit Strategy

You have read all the charts, and picked your stocks to trade and you have determined which market to trade on – in fact, you know exactly when to time your entry. But when do you exit a trade? When do you lock in profits? You see, as important as timing your entry is, if you neglect when to exit, you may not take any profits home after all.

You must plan well ahead of your entry how you intend to exit a trade. And remember that a plan is not a plan until it is written down. Following a plan in your head is the same as trading based on your emotions. It usually fails. Basically, there are three reasons why you should exit a trade, namely: when making profits, when losing money, and when you are not making or losing money.

Let us take a brief look at each of these reasons for exiting a trade.

### *Taking Your Profits*

Before you enter a trade, it is important to set a mechanism that tells you it is time to take your profits and exit the trade. Do not rely on some abstract feelings. Remember to be emotionally detached from your trade outcomes. That way, you will pay more attention to your previously set mechanism when it alerts you of an exit point. If you are greedy and wait too long, you may lose a substantial part of your profits. And if you are too fearful and quit too soon, you may equally lose a significant part of profits that should be yours. This boils down to emotional intelligence. The good news is that it can be developed. So if you intend to become a successful swing trader and you have determined that you do not have enough discipline to follow through with your plan, do not worry. You can learn how to do that as you take baby steps in swing trading.

When you buy or sell a stock, ensure that you have a stop loss point in mind. You can use that point to set a stop loss order, or you can click buy or sell when prices get to that point.

## Ending Your Losses

Make up your mind long before you enter any trade that you are going to cut your losses early enough before it digs a hole in your account that will require a lot of money to mend. Again, you have to set up a prior mechanism for identifying when to cut your losses. I strongly suggest that you use the trailing stops to cut losses. Set your losses to somewhere around 3% (or less) of your capital. Make your losses are as small as possible so you don't get all emotional about the loss.

Be on the lookout for repeated price attempts to breach a support or resistance. That is an indication of a possible breakout. Sticking to a losing position in the hope of it rebounding is abandoning your plans and listening to your emotions. In swing trading, hope doesn't give you profits. Most often than not, hope has an ironic way of crippling your account.

## Freeing Up Your Capital

Whether you choose to quickly exit a trade that is neither making you money nor making you lose money, or you choose to watch it for a few days, both choices are okay. The important thing is that before you enter the trade, you should make up your mind about how long you are willing to watch a trade that is generally lukewarm. Remember that you are in a type of trade that is considered as short-term. You don't have the whole month to wait for one position. If it is tying down your money, free up your capital and reinvest it in another stock or position.

**Trading Pullbacks and Rallies**

As earlier discussed, pullbacks and rallies are great opportunities to buy and sell stocks (in case you missed it, you can check it out at chapter 3).

Usually, when stock prices begin to move in an upward direction (an uptrend), they tend to briefly pullback. This presents you a good opportunity to buy at low risk and increases your chances of selling at a higher price later. On the reverse side, when stock prices begin to move in a downward direction (downtrend), they tend to briefly rally and offer you an excellent opportunity for shorting.

Here is something for you to consider as a beginner in swing trading. If all you do is simply stay in cash (that is, holding on to your money without trading) until you find excellent pullbacks and rallies, you will be making a wise beginner decision.

Think about it. It stands to reason that the best time to buy stocks at a great price is right after a recent occurrence of selling. It equally shows better judgment to short sell right after the occurrence of buying.

The best time to trade pullbacks and rallies is the first time they appear on a chart after a significant trend. So the first time you notice a pullback after a trend line is breached or broken, seize the opportunity. Be on the lookout for a pullback that happens immediately following a wide range candle. Buy or sell at that point.When you see a breakout, be ready to trade the first pullback after it. When a new high is set, wait for the first pullback. When it comes up, go in for the kill.

Let us look at the chart below to get a clearer picture of the above.

*Image source: www.stockcharts.com*

The first pullback after a significant downtrend offered those who were watchful an excellent opportunity to buy early.

Let us take a look at another beautiful example.

*Image source: www.stockcharts.com*

The pullback happened after a breakout. The trend line was breached or broken, so a smart swing trader will wait for the first pullback and seize the opportunity.

It is important that as you give thought to your trading strategy, you should include this type of scenarios in your setup scans. Trading first pullbacks (and rallies) are highly profitable and will definitely give you the type of boost you need as a beginner to swing trading. Keep an eye on them and milk them when they occur.

Buying pullbacks also mean buying into weakness and selling into strength. Buying into weakness means buying a stock as the price is falling instead of waiting for it to get to its lowest point before buying.

Flip that, and you get the meaning of selling into strength.

**You Cannot Win All Trades**

No, you can't. It doesn't matter what tools or magic formula you use. Remember that the stock market contains so many moving parts that are far beyond the control of any one individual or a body. Any of these moving parts could have a significant adverse effect on even the best technical indicators or analysis tools.

But you can win a lot of trades enough to make you good profits. The profits you make come from the ignorance or mistakes of other traders. In the stock market, you are either making mistakes or you are making profits. Unfortunately for most traders, they are making mistakes. Whether you will choose to make profits depends largely on if you will take your learning seriously to avoid the mistakes most novices make.

Some of these mistakes are depending 100% on technical analysis, being too afraid to lose, looking for a fail-proof system or trading magic formula, being emotional, etc. The truth is, not everyone is cutout to be a trader or a swing trader. However, a lot of people will give it a shot and eventually fail. It is from these failed attempts that you will make profits if you learn and apply what these other traders won't.

You will not win all your trades, but you will win a lot of your trades provided you do not buy and sell as the novices do. When do you time your buys? At the beginning of a pullback or when the crowd has said it is okay to buy? At what times do you sell? When you notice a rally or when major selling is almost over? You see, buying or selling too late is the hallmark of novices, which a lot of traders are, no matter how long they have spent trading. The number of years a trader spends trading the stock market does not necessarily make them experts. It is what you learn and apply that distinguishes you from the novices.

Stand apart by trading in the opposite direction of the crowd. Don't worry, expert and veteran traders don't usually trade in the direction of the crowd, so you are not making a mistake when you do so. Buy when the crowd is selling – the prices are a lot cheaper then. And of course, you know very well to sell when the crowd is buying, the price is a lot higher then because everyone wants to get the hot-selling stocks which you happen to have.

**Swing Trading is a Continuous Learning Process**

There are challenges you will encounter as you trade. You do not improve if you quit or if you stop only at what you have learned so far. Becoming a swing trader means you are going to keep learning on a continuous basis in order to bring on your A-game.

It is important to recognize the dynamism of the market. The market doesn't stay still for too long. For you to be anything close to successful in the art of swing trading, you must be ready to continue adapting to changes in rules, regulations, and laws. Additionally, new and exciting vehicles of investments keep springing up. Stay up to speed with new information about the market.

There is money to be made from swing trading, but you must be ready to do your part by continuously learning new ways to make money. You should see swing trading as an art of improving your trading skills rather than a way of making money. The money part is a natural result of making good trades. You cannot flop on your trades out of ignorance and expect to make money. It is not out of line to assume that the amount of profit you generate from swing trading is directly proportional to your swing trading skill level. The more you improve, the more profits flood your account. And you certainly cannot improve without keeping yourself abreast of up-to-date information about stocks, prices, markets, etc.

As part of your learning, you will encounter situations that will teach you better than any book the art of accepting losses. You may follow every single detail in your well mapped out strategy or plan, yet you will still lose a trade. It is not time to argue with the losses or stubbornly hold on to the position. Accept it. You have lost. It happens. Now dust yourself up and try again, this time, more intelligently.

Remember that you are a swing trader who is supposed to study the psychology of traders. You are supposed to leverage the emotional shortcomings of other traders and make profits. You cannot successfully do that if you have not mastered your own emotions. Continuing to trade with the aim of breaking even when you are losing is a gateway to financial disaster. Avoid it by all means.

I will not fail to add that you must shield yourself from the herd mentality. You must distinguish yourself from the trading crowd. Do not follow the crowd unless you have determined by yourself that they are towing the right direction (which is not a very common occurrence both in swing trading and any other aspect of life). And the reason why herd mentality is not good for you is because the herds do not think for themselves. They depend on one person's or one organization's opinion. These opinions were thought of by human traders (even if they used computerized tools to draw their conclusions). You are capable of reaching your own opinions too. Herd mentality is generated from the internet, message board, and even so-called guru analysts.

Nevertheless, do not discard time-tested facts about the market in the guise of shielding yourself from the herd mentality. That is why I would recommend that you find reliable sources of information so that you can digest them and draw your own conclusions.

**Finally, Learn Some Basic Money Management**

A lot of people win the lottery by chance (how else would you win a lottery if not by chance!), but they still become broke after a few weeks, months or a couple of years? Why is that so? They do not have basic money management skills. It doesn't matter how much money you make from the stock market (or from winning the lottery!), if you do not have money management skills, you are simply exposing yourself to trade like a gambler or someone buying a lottery ticket – you will begin trading in the hope that you will win (like a game of chance) because you are under pressure to make money you have previously lost due to bad money management policies.

**In this Chapter...**

You have learned the following:

- Develop your own unique strategy. None is perfect.

- Before you trade, make sure that you confirm that the company is not about to release their earnings report.

- A swing point is an excellent point to enter a long or short position.

- Successive up or down days are also another good entry point.

- Plan your exit strategy before you begin trading.

- Exiting a trade is as important as entering a trade.

- Set up your strategies for taking your profits, cutting your losses, and freeing up your capital.

- Look out for the first pullback (and rally) and trade them.

- Losing trades is inevitable, but you can win a lot of trades.

- How long you spend trading does not make you an expert trader. It is the application of time-tested methods that you learn that improves your trading skills.

- Do not follow the crowd. Trade in the opposite direction of the crowd.

- Buy when the crowd is selling. Too many sellers mean you will get the stock at a cheaper price.

- Sell when the crow is buying. Too many buyers mean your stock is scarce to come by, and the price will definitely be higher.

- You are in for a continuous learning experience. Quitting does not make you earn while you learn.

- Stay informed by keeping yourself abreast with the latest developments in the stock market especially as it relates to stocks you have interest in.

- Protect yourself from the herd mentality. Be disciplined. Have good money management policies.

## Chapter 10: Technical indicators

# Technical Indicator: What It Is

The OHLC (open, high, low, close) price of a stock over a period of time forms the price data of that stock or security. Now when the price data of a particular security is passed through a set of mathematical functions or formulas, a sequence of data points are created. This is what is known as a technical indicator. So to give it a proper definition: a technical indicator is a series or sequence of data points that are generated through the application of mathematical formulas to the price data of a particular security. Several other indices such as the volume of a stock may also be included into the formula to generate the data points.

I am going to save you the headache of how the formula is applied to the price data and all the computations involved in coming up with a technical indicator. All you need to know as a beginner is that technical indicators are displayed graphically on top or below the chart of a security or stock. And it is there to aid you in your market analysis – to compare the stock's chart with the information on the technical indicator. The more in agreement they are, the better decision you can make.

Before you go hunting for the perfect technical indicator that will show you all the good trades, be aware that these indicators are not 100 percent accurate all of the time. They can signal a false buy or sell alert. So be warned.

**Functions and What You Get From Technical Indicators**

Perhaps I should refresh your memory about moving averages. What did we say moving averages are used for? (Feel free to look back at chapter 4 to reacquaint yourself with moving averages.) We said the lines of a moving average indicate a stock's average price over a given period. So, they are basically indicators that show you the average price of a stock. Well, that's one thing you get from technical indicators.

While the stock chart shows you price action, technical indicators show you other information about the same stock from a different vantage point.

Basically, the functions of technical indicators are summarized below:

- *For Confirmation*: Throughout this guide, I have advised that you should not base your trading decisions solely on one tool. A technical indicator can serve as a tool that you use in confirming whatever you deduce from price actions on a chart. For example, when you observe that a stock has broken a support level, you could look at the OBV to confirm if there is a low reading to indicate that there is an actual weakness. OBV means On Balance Volume; it is a technical indicator.

- *For Calling Attention*: Technical indicators can draw the trader's attention to study price actions more carefully. It can prompt you to a variety of alerts that can really save you from some serious financial damage. For example, you may be prompted to look out for a break in support level when momentum is declining.

- *For Predicting Price Direction*: A technical indicator can also serve as a tool for predicting what side future prices will lean towards – up or down.

## Proper Use of Technical Indicators

- *No One Size Fits All*: Different stocks may cause the same indicator to behave differently. In using technical indicators, it is important to know that different indicators tend to work well for different stocks. With continuous practice and application, you will come to discover which indicator will serve you best for your chosen stocks.

- *To Indicate*: There is no single tool that has all the trading answers! Have I said that enough times yet? That is because it is of vital importance to keep that in mind. In that sense, it is important to note that one proper way to use a technical indicator is to see them as tools that only point to the likelihood of an outcome. They must be used in combination with price action. A technical indicator does not directly represent price action; what it does is to present you with information about its own generated or computed results from price data. There are times when a technical indicator will signal you to buy or sell, yet they could be very wrong. If you do not verify each signal with what the stock chart is telling you, it may lead to fatal trading mistakes. The bottom line is this: technical indicators aid you but they do not do the trading for you. Ultimately, you are the one who decides what and when to trade based on signals from indicators and other analysis.

- *Use Time Tested Indicators*: The proliferation of technical indicators seems to be on a constant rise. Some newer computer programs even provide users (traders) the choice of developing custom made indicators! But with all of the numerous new indicators available at our beck and call, it seems they do not offer anything too unique or new from others in existence before them. As a matter of fact, I would advise that as a beginner, you stick to time tested indicators to avoid being sent on a wild goose chase.

- *A Few Is Good Enough*: As mentioned above, there are several technical indicators available today. But you really do not need all of them. Heck! You do not even need more than three good technical indicators to succeed in a proper analysis. What matters is that you are well acquainted with the few you use. The fewer the number of indicators, the better you will learn and know how to use them.

- *A Few Complementary Indicators*: What would be the point of having three indicators that all function almost exactly the same way? That's a huge waste of time and resources. When you are picking out your few indicators, make sure that you select indicators that complement each other. That is to say, select indicators that perform functions that add to the functions of the other(s). If you decide to use only two indicators, for example, it doesn't make much sense to choose the Accumulation/Distribution Line and Chaikin Money Flow (CMF) as your only two technical indicators. Both of them perform the same function which is to show if money is coming in or going out of a stock by combining volume and price.

**Example of Technical Indicators**

There are very many technical indicators; however, I've listed below a few which you may find useful. You can research more to find the ones that best suit you. Generally, technical indicators are grouped into overlays and oscillators.

Overlays are technical indicators which are plotted on top of a chart above the stock price. They usually have the same scale as price. Examples include Pivot Points and Moving Averages.

On the other hand, oscillators are indicators that swing or fluctuate between set levels and are plotted below or above prices on a chart.

1. *Accumulation/Distribution Line*: This shows whether money is coming in or going out of a stock by combining volume and price.

2. *Average Directional Index (ADX)*: This shows whether a particular stock is oscillating or trending.

3. *Average True Range (ATR)*: This measures the volatility of a stock.

4. *Bollinger Bands*: This shows the lower and upper limits of price movements.

5. *Change Trend Meter (CTM)*: This measures the trend of a stock and scores the trend's strength using several indicators over a period of six-time frames.

6. *Chandelier Exit*: This can be used in setting up trailing stop-loss for all positions.

7. *Commodity Channel Index (CCI)*: Shows variation from the usual price of a stock.

8. *Correlation Coefficient*: Shows the level of relationship between two stocks or securities within a specific period.

9. *Decision Point Price Momentum Oscillator (PMO)*: This follows the rate of change of a stock closely.

10. *Ichimoku Cloud*: This defines resistance and support levels,

provide trading signals, measures momentum, and show the direction of a stock's trend.

11. *Moving Average Convergence/Divergence Oscillator (MACD)*: This is an oscillator that shows momentum based on the variation between two Exponential Moving Averages.

12. *Moving Averages*: These are overlays on a chart that display the average price of a stock over a given period.

13. *On Balance Volume (OBV)*: This shows whether money is coming in or going out of a stock by combining volume and price in a simple way.

14. *Pivot Points*: This is an overlay on a chart which displays reversal points above prices in a downtrend and below prices in the case of an uptrend.

15. *Relative Strength Index (RSI)*: Shows the strength of a stock's trend.

16. *Stochastic Oscillator*: Shows the performance of a stock's price in comparison with its past movement.

17. *Volume by Price*: This is an overlay on a chart which shows a horizontal histogram that displays the activities that occur at different price levels.

18. *Vortex Indicator*: Indicates the beginning of a new trend, and

also defines a current trend.

19. *Williams %R*: This indicator draws on Stochastics to find out oversold and overbought levels.

20. *Zig Zag*: This is an overlay on a chart that displays filtered price movements which are above a specific percentage.

**In this Chapter...**

You have learned the following:

- Technical indicators only indicate. They are not 100% accurate at all times.

- Technical indicators are used for confirming, calling attention, and predicting future price direction.

- Not all technical indicators suit all stocks or securities.

- Limit your use of technical indicators to a few dependable ones. Let your choice of indicators complement each other.

# Chapter 11: What to keep in mind as a swing trader

Here are a few trading tips I have found to be very useful for a swing trader. Remember them, and you will have yourself an amazing swing trading experience.

## *You Are A Beginner*

So you are done with studying this guide and you have mapped out your trading strategy. The best thing is to begin to trade like the professionals with both guns blazing, right? Wrong! You are not in competition with anyone; neither should you trade like a Warren Buffet wannabe. Take baby steps if not the market will deal you the types of hand it deals the professionals. Whether you can handle it is another question entirely.

## *Don't Go Against the Tide*

Remember when I said you should always trade trending stocks? Well, it is for the same reason that you should not go against the tide of a predominant trend. While it is often possible to make quick bucks from short-term trends in the opposite direction of the overall stock trend, that kind of trade is short-lived because the overall trend tide will definitely sweep over such insignificant oppositions.

You can use the S&P 500 index to measure the overall direction of the stock market. Armed with the overall trend of the market, you can best take informed decisions about short-term trading (swing trading) and maximize your profits. If the overall trend is bullish, you should go for long trades. And if the reverse is the case and the market is bearish, it will serve you better to look for short trades. Doing otherwise is going against the powerful tides of the overall market. You may not stand a chance against such pressure.

### *Use More than One Tool*

The truth is that there is no one single tool that can perform the ultimate swing trading magic and give you all the profits. Whether it is a technical analysis tool or a technical indicator, there just isn't one singular tool that can give you all the clues by itself. If there was, what then would be the point of all the rest of the tools?

When you trade, endeavor to combine your candlestick readings, with the messages from the moving averages or the volume, or even technical indicators like the MACD. They are all there to help you see what lies beneath the surface of the stock market.

### *"Like" and "Follow" Your Stocks*

Do you see how the social media bombards you with notifications about the pages or friends you liked and followed? That's because the social media applications are designed to keep you well-informed about the latest developments about your areas of interest. Now apply the same idea to the stock or group of stocks you choose to trade. Keep close tabs on them and follow all "notifications" about them in the form of financial news, earnings reports, etc.

While it is okay to hop from one promising stock to the other, it is advisable to maintain focus on your major stocks. Gradually add to your list any stock that performs well especially if they are volatile stocks.

Because swing trading can be comfortably done on a part-time basis does not mean you should treat it trivially and give it little attention. On the contrary, you should make it a habit to frequently look at the charts for your major stocks and stay informed about the happenings around the stock market.

*Expand Your Horizon*

You are a swing trader focused on short-term trades. True. But do not limit your trading to short-term charts. Look beyond the hourly and daily chart. Expand your swing trading horizon to include a larger time frame. Always zoom out far enough to look at time frames for perhaps a year or several months. Correlate that with weekly and daily charts to know if the messages are tending towards the same path.

*It Happens More Than Once*

History always has an ironic way of repeating itself not just on the grand stage of life, but also on the stock chart. Stock prices, like the humans who trade them, tend to have memories and replay themselves or behave in the same way nearly every time. Your job is to look for past price behaviors as they hit a certain level. Those past behaviors could give you insights as to how those stock prices will behave again when faced with similar levels. There is no magic to this. It is the way humans (most humans) are conditioned to behave. Remember, the stock market and price behaviors are simply a reflection of the human psyche.

### Stop Searching for the Holy Grail

Give up the search for a trading Holy Grail. There is none as far as swing trading is concerned. The time you will spend searching from one trading book to the other, or from one website to the other, is better spent learning how to analyze stock charts. You need to develop a solid self-discipline to stick to your guns when necessary and learn your lessons when the situation calls for it.

### Timing Your Entry

If you must make significant profits from swing trading, you must perfect your art of recognizing a trend at its early stages. The earlier you ride the wave of a trend, the better your chances of high profits and low risks.

If you are vigilant, you will know when a trend is likely to change so that you can be early enough to ride a new trend (or a reversal). When the market is oversaturated with buyers or sellers, there is likely to be a reversal.

## Find a Balance between Primary and Short-term Trends

I understand the need to "cut to the chase" by taking a look at the short-term chart, analyzing it, and make your swing trading decisions. But a balanced look at both the short-term trend and the primary trend is very important. Here's why. Short-term trends give you only a look at the pixels. The primary trend gives you a complete picture. But it is also a mistake to focus wholly on the primary trend, because even during a primary trend, there could be intermediate trends that are counter to the primary trend. As a matter of fact, you won't be a swing trader if you base your swing trading decisions solely on the primary chart trend. Remember you are looking for short-term swings. Nevertheless, the true swing trader is one who uses both the primary and short-term trends to make his or her trading decisions.

## Do Not Trade With an Attitude of Making Up for Previous Losses

You must learn to treat every trade as a stand-alone. When you encounter a loss (which is guaranteed!), learn your lessons and move on. Do not let it get to you; composure is vital if you must succeed. Go into each trade with fresh new insights, not with old wounds.

## Plan Before You Trade

What makes up a good plan for swing trading? Is it studying the stock charts and entering a trade at the most opportune time? Well, while timing your entry is part of a good plan, it still is not the only element of a good trading strategy.

Without a good plan, you are open to the temptation of trading on impulse. Don't get me wrong. Intuition is a good thing, but do also remember that gamblers who face huge losses listen to their intuitions too!

For your swing trading plan to be considered as good, it needs to clearly spell out when to enter a trade, that is to say, your plan should include what signals or trigger your decision to enter a trade. I have given a considerable amount of space in this guide to help you determine exactly when to enter a trade and when to stay clear of making trades (except if you just want to gamble!).

Secondly, your plan should state your limits. You need to give a limit order so that your broker will act accordingly. As a side note, you need to ask yourself at what point you would like to lock in profits. Do you want to continue riding the wave until the very last minute? Or would you want to take your profits and get out on time? Making profit has a way of making you abandon your trading plans. Greed is a precursor for all great losses.

Thirdly, your plan must clearly include a stop loss. If you ignore this and there is a reversal or a change of trend after you have entered a trade, you may end up losing your entire capital. In order to protect your money, it is best for you to set a stop-loss order before you execute a trade.

Fourthly, your plan should make room for additional buying. It is possible to enter a trade and later discover from all indicators and analysis (plus your intuition) that the trade could be better. In such cases, it would be good to add a few points to your initial position. I'll advise that you should be conservative about this though. For example, if your initial purchase was for 2,000 shares, adding a few more hundreds, say, 300 or 500 more could increase your profit substantially. Adding 2,000 more shares... well, that seems to me like greed beckoning on you!

Finally, for your plan to be considered a good one, it should include an exact re-entry level. If you have exited a position because you have heeded a warning signal but the reversal didn't pan out, instead the trend still continues getting stronger, at what point should you re-enter such trade?

Take the time to put all these down before executing a trade.

### *You Are Not Entitled To Anything*

Trading stocks is not a paid employment where you are remunerated for the number of hours you put into work. The market doesn't pay you for "working hard." No. It only pays you for being right. You've got to drop any entitlement mentality or paycheck mentality if you truly want to be a swing trader.

One of the things that will serve you well is your ability to take your mind off the profits and concentrate on improving your trading skills.

The profits are simply a reflection of how good you are becoming. Trading profits are not a representation of how long you work, but how well you work.

## What are the Odds?

Are the odds in your favor? How much are you putting on the line and for what returns? Always ask yourself: if I make this trade and win, how much do I stand to win? And if I lose, how much do I stand to lose? This will help you gauge if the risk is worth taking. Always aim to set a win/loss ratio that is acceptable to you for every trade. For example, you could aim to capture a profit of 10% and set your stop-loss order to about 3%. There is no hard and fast rule about this; whatever profit and loss ratio that is comfortable for you is fine.

## Are You Cutting Your Losses or Your Profits?

Sadly, the number of traders who cut their profits too soon outweighs those who let their profits run. The fear of the tides changing abruptly causes novice traders to take profits too soon. Ironically, when they are losing, it doesn't occur to them to cut their losses. Rather, the hope of the tides changing abruptly keeps them in a position they should have exited long ago. If you do your homework well, you will know when to let profits run without unnecessary fear.

## Don't Count Your Chicks Before They Are Hatched

Your trades are your eggs, count them. But never count your chicks before they are hatched! Do not go ahead and spend money you have not made in the hope that your trades will generate enough profits. Remember, swing trading is not the same as football betting where you can buy winning games ahead of a match outcome – there are no match fixes in the stock market.

### *Always Read the Handwriting on the Wall*

Although not all warning signals of impending reversals eventually turn out to be correct, it is important to heed those warnings. If you are attentive enough, you will soon learn in your journey into swing trading, that hardly does a great loss happens without first giving ample warnings. Unfortunately, not every trader is trained to read the handwriting on the wall.

### In this Chapter...

You have learned the following:

- Take baby steps as you begin your trading journey.

- Make sure your trades are usually in alignment with the overall trend of the stock market.

- Confirm your trading decisions with more than one tool.

- Closely monitor your group of core stocks.

- Prices behave in predictable patterns.

- Treat each trade you enter on its own merit. Do not try to regain a loss from a previous trade with the current trade.

- Develop a good plan that includes all the vital elements of strategic trading in it.

Swing trading is not the same as your 9 to 5 job. You only get paid when you are right.

# Chapter 12: Getting Started

Now that you are ready to begin swing trading, let us devout this chapter to the necessary steps that you can take to get you started. If you have not read the preceding chapters, I urge you to do so before taking any of the steps below, unless of course you are not a beginner to trading.

So I am proceeding in the assumption that you are a complete novice to trading in general and swing trading in particular. And I am assuming that you have read and understood (to some extent) the preceding chapters. Now, enough of the theories (although necessary) and let's get you started.

**Step 1: Determine Your Risk Capital**

Answer these important questions:

- How much do you want to use for your swing trading business?

- How much do you have as risk capital?

The amount of money you want to use for trading must be less than or equal to your risk capital. Your risk capital is money that has no living expenses attached to it. It is not meant for any debt repayment and it is not any money held in your retirement savings. You are free to use it for investments and you can stand to lose the money (even though that is not your goal). If you cannot afford to lose the money you want to use for swing trading, please do not proceed further. Forget the idea of trading until you have enough risk capital.

## Step 2: Choose a Broker

You do not trade the stock market from your bank account. You need someone who is licensed or a licensed agency called a stockbroker to do that for you. A stockbroker is an individual who is a professional at buying and selling stocks, commodities, shares, and other securities for retailers like you and for institutions or companies. A stockbroker does his or her business of buying and selling via stock exchange and sometimes over the counter and is paid a commission or a fee.

There are several online brokers all seeking for your attention. Your money is important to them, and their platform is important to you. You actually need them in order to trade stocks. But here's the thing: not all brokers are the same in terms of service delivery and their fees. I will leave it up to you to search for the broker that suits your particular style. Nevertheless, let me quickly show you the different types of brokers.

### *Money Managers*

These types of brokers handle everything for you – your trades, portfolio, etc. They give you updates on all aspects of your trading. The catch here is the management fees and the initial startup capital.

Many of them charge very high fees and their initial investment may be in the range of $100,000 and above.

## Full-Service Brokers

In addition to offering you stock buying and selling services, these types of brokers also offer you several plans regarding retirement, plus other investment advice. They provide awesome guidance about what stocks to trade. They are suitable for you if you intend to go into long term investments. Their fees are also on the high side compared to short-term brokers.

## Discount Brokers

These are the brokers that are more suitable for swing traders or short-term traders. Their commissions and fees are a lot cheaper than the full-service brokers. But keep in mind that they are not going to offer you any advice on what stocks to buy or trade, neither are they going to meddle in your retirement plans or any investment plans. You pay them and they buy or sell for you, period.

## Choose Online Brokers With Reliable Platforms

In choosing an online discount broker, be sure to scan through several options before making your final choice. Some factors to consider are how responsive the brokers are to your needs and whether their platform is reliable and well-known. Some of the renowned online brokers are Interactive Brokers, E-Trade, Trade Station, Fidelity, TD

Ameritrade, Scottrade, Charles Schwab, and Option House.

However, if you choose to go with a broker that is not well-known be sure to check that their platform is duly registered with SEC.

### Check Minimum Balance

Equally, before choosing a stockbroker, you should consider the minimum balance required to open and maintain a trading account with them. In some cases, when your trading account balance drops below the minimum balance, either due to loss or some other factor, some stockbrokers will charge you for a low account balance. So be sure to check several brokerages and compare fees, requirements, etc., before making your choice.

### Web-based versus Direct Access Brokers

Online stockbrokers are categorized into those who offer trading through a web browser, and those that require you to download third party software.

With a web-based stockbroker, you can simply log into the broker's website and enter your buy or sell order from your web browser. However, note that you may encounter quite a bit of delay with filling your orders because it may be routed through a third party.

The direct access brokers give you access to a market maker or ECN (Electronic Communication Networks) through an app. There is no interference from the brokers; you are dealing directly with the stock market. So you get to control the routing of your orders to the exchanges you wish to use. You have to download trading software apps for you to be able to execute trades directly. You will be charged fees and commissions, plus you may also be billed for access to ECN. If you choose to use direct access brokers, ensure that you check with your particular broker to know what their fees are.

## Step 3: Setup Your Trading Account

After you have determined which stockbroker to use, the next obvious thing to do is to set up your trading account with them.

### Sign Up

Go to the stockbroker's website and register or sign up to create a new trading account. The option to do this will be displayed as either "register," "signup" or "create account" in a conspicuous space on the stockbroker's homepage. You should have your email address handy as you may be required to use it or create a new username and password to be able to access your new trading account.

### Documentation

Depending on the stockbroker, you will be required to enter a number of personal information during your registration process such as your name, address, means of identification, and other personal information. You may be required to scan some documents too.

## Deposit Money into Your Trading Account

Obviously, you will need to make a deposit into your trading account before you can start trading. Use electronic fund transfer or any other form of deposit provided by your stockbroker to fund your newly created trading account.

## Tour the Platform

Get used to the trading platform by taking a tour or browsing through the features of the platform. Do not rush into trading simply because you have deposited money into your trading account. Get acquainted with the tools and the various pages on the platform first. Practice using the tools in a demo trade so that you are sure what each option means and how they are used in real money trade.

## Analyze Stocks

Use the knowledge you have acquired so far to search and analyze stocks. Take as much time as you need to do your findings. Remember all the cautions and warning you have read in this guide as you determine your first trade.

## Trade

When you are ready, enter your first order.

Congratulations! You have successfully made your first order. It doesn't matter whether you win or lose. What matters is that you have followed through and have the guts to put your knowledge into practice. Whatever the outcome of your trade, be sure that you will have a lot of other trades to make and learn from.

Happy swing trading!

**In this Chapter...**

You have learned the following:

- Find out if you have enough money set aside for stock trading. This money should be free from any living expenses and should not be a retirement savings.

- Locate several online stockbrokers to check out their fees, services, licensing, and minimum balance before choosing one.

- Register with the stockbroker of your choice via their website. Deposit funds and begin trading.

# Conclusion

I congratulate you on making the decision to learn swing trading. I encourage you to make this book your companion as you take your swing trading journey one step further from reading to actual trading. Do not stop at reading. Take the steps required to get started in swing trading. Do not be stuck in "analysis paralysis." Do not be afraid to fail; it is part of learning. And if you actually implement the tips and strategies in this book, your losses will be minimal while your profits will be pleasing to you (if you are not greedy).

As I mentioned earlier in the book, it is a good practice for beginners to treat swing trading as a part-time venture. Quitting your job to fully focus on swing trading as a beginner may place upon you enormous pressure that you may not be able to withstand. And you and I know what happens when you trade under pressure; your judgments are clouded by emotions of fear and greed, and you lose focus.

Pick one or two trades and begin swing trading. Practice with real money (an amount that won't cripple your account), and grow your expertise; we call that earning while you are learning.

If there was just one skill I would encourage you to master, it would be the art of reading price actions on a stock chart. Nothing is more important to you as a swing trader than that. Every other thing on the chart is minor in comparison to price movements. Learn it. Master it. And you'll be the better for it.

# Description

The market is ripe with opportunities only if you can recognize them and seize them at the right time. This book gives you the tools you can use to identify both the right opportunity and the right time to seize them. Every stock on the market shows you its trading patterns on a continuous basis. If you are diligent enough to recognize these somewhat hidden patterns (which are actually open for all traders who have learned how to see them); you would have created for yourself an opportunity that has a very low-risk and potentially high profit.

The truth is that swing trading does have the potential to make you good profits, but it is not meant for everyone. If you have carefully read through this book, you would be able to say for sure if swing trading is for you or not.

With the simple yet powerful tools I have exposed you to, you do not need to fear or doubt your ability to swing trades. Let me reiterate the need for discipline. Drawing out a plan to follow is good and fine, following it is a different ball game entirely. You need the discipline to follow your own plans. One of the huge differences between a successful swing trader and a novice is discipline. Your emotions are not your friend when it comes to swing trading. You need to set it aside and be very mechanical about your plans.

Some of the key areas covered in this book are:

- The basics of swing trading
- How the human mind affects trading
- Technical indicators
- Waves and trends

To be successful in swing trading, you need to achieve your goals, and to achieve the goals you set you need to have a positive mindset. Success requires definite goals and the commitment and desire to realize the goals. Success cannot be achieved overnight; it is paramount that you know that it is a time-consuming process that requires hard work and patience to be successful.

To be among the few who succeed in swing trading, you should know how to achieve your goals, and you must take the pursuit of success seriously. There are those who do not set goals at all but still hope to achieve the things they want- they certainly get some of the results they want but find most of their desires elusive because they do not have a plan. They pursue their goals by groping in the dark which is frustrating, uncertain and tiring.

Success begins with finding a purpose, then defining and identifying specific goals to help you attain the purpose, and then mapping out a detailed action plan to guide and help you achieve the purpose.

By following the steps in this book and going after your swing trading goals, you will develop and master the success elements you need to achieve your goals. Achieving your goals is not easy, and you will indeed be faced with some trying moments, however, through self-belief, positivity, and by following a clear action plan, you will have the commitment, focus, resilience and will to achieve everything you set out to do. Additionally, you will learn to apply the success tenets to overcome the inertia which often stifles goals even before you begin pursuing them.

# SWING TRADING

# ADVANCED COURSE

*David Lazarus*

## DISCLAIMER

The information contained within this eBook is strictly for educational purposes. If you wish to apply ideas contained in this eBook, you are taking full responsibility for your actions.

The author has made every effort to ensure the accuracy of the information within this book was correct at time of publication. The author does not assume and hereby disclaims any liability to any party for any loss, damage, or disruption caused by errors or omissions, whether such errors or omissions result from accident, negligence, or any other cause.

# ABOUT THIS BOOK

Puts, calls, strike prices, prices, derivatives, bear place spreads, and bull phone spreads -- the jargon is merely among the complex areas of options buying and selling. But don't allow some of it frighten you away.

Options can offer flexibility for traders at every degree and support them manage danger. listed below are the fundamentals of what options will be, why investors utilize them, and how to begin.

No real matter what you are doing in life there's always the first moment. Walking as a child, worries or starting a new job all belong to this category. That is correct of beginner's options buying and selling in the currency markets as well. Even though you have experience in stock trading you can't possibly know the distinction between a call up and a place; don't get bothered because this is not going to result in a pop quiz. What will happen is that people can look at options investing for beginners and present you a number of the basics to truly get you started. When you have never been subjected to options trading, here you are at your first time!

In options Trading for beginners, we are concerned with the basics, the fundamentals of a strong foundation in learning the stock options trade. Equipped with the proper knowledge, you can gain massive profits from stock options. It can be difficult for beginners in option trading to learn the exact difference between trading in the stock market and trading in the stock options market.

Because of the time limits set on each trade, many beginners in option trading have a common misconception that stock options are associated with significant risks. The time limit is often seen as a waste of assets. Options trading has proven to be profitable with those traders who go into it with a plan and the knowledge of effective leveraging techniques. Options tend to be chosen for the level of leverage versus the limited amount of risk.

# TABLE OF CONTENTS

# INTRODUCTION

Options will be conditional derivative agreements that allow purchasers of the accords (alternative holders) to get or sell off a security with a chosen price. option buyers priced an amount referred to as a "high quality" by sellers for this type of right. Should industry prices become unfavorable for option holders, they'll let the option expire worthless, therefore ensuring the deficits are not higher than the premium. On the other hand, option retailers assume higher risk compared to the option buyers, which explains why they require this premium.

Options can be bought like most various other asset groups with brokerage investment decision accounts.

Options are reliable since they can enhance a person's portfolio. They do that through added cash flow, protection, and also leverage. With regards to the situation, there's usually an option scenario befitting an investor's target. A simplified example of this would be employing options being a useful hedge against a declining currency markets to control downside losses. Alternatives could also be used to generate repeating income. Additionally, they are generally helpful for speculative purposes such for example wagering for the direction of a stock.

Options are being among the most popular cars for stock traders, because their price tag can move quickly, making (or getting rid of) big money fast. Options techniques can range between reasonably simple to highly complex, with several payoffs and in some cases odd titles.

An option is a contract to get or sell off a stock, typically 100 shares on the stock per agreement, in a pre-negotiated value and by way of a specific date.

Just as you can purchase a stock as you think the purchase price will rise or sell a stock once you think its price tag will drop, a option lets you bet which direction you think the price tag on a stock would go. But instead of shopping for or shorting the advantage outright, once you buy a option, you're investing in a contract which allows -- but doesn't obligate -- one to do a amount of things, like:

Buy or sell off shares of any share at an agreed-upon selling price (the "hit selling price") for a restricted time frame.

Sell the agreement to another buyer.

Let the alternative agreement expire and leave without further monetary obligation.

Trading options are of help for long-term buy-and-hold traders, too.

Options trading for beginners can be a daunting task. Words like delta, volatility and premium scare many investors. Are you looking to start the options trading market, following a few easy steps will make the task a bit more manageable?

With stocks and bonds, nothing like free launch. Options are the same. Options trading includes certain risks that the investor must know about before making an exchange. This is the reason, when trading options with a dealer, you more often than not observe a disclaimer like the accompanying:

"Significant: Options include risks and are not reasonable for everybody. Options trading can be theoretical in nature and convey generous risk of misfortune".

Options have a place with the more significant gathering of protections known as derivatives. A derivative's cost is reliant on or gotten from the cost of something different. For instance, wine is a derivative of grapes ketchup is a derivative of tomatoes, and a stock option is a derivative of a stock. Options are derivatives of money related protections—their worth relies upon the cost of some other asset. Instances of derivatives incorporate calls, puts, futures, advances, swaps, and home loan supported protections, among others.

Options are a particular sort of derivatives contracts. The fundamental protections can be stocks, records, ETFs or wares. With a derivatives contract, you don't legitimately claim the primary asset. Instead, you claim a related asset whose worth is influenced by changes in cost.

With an options contract, you reserve the option to purchase or sell an asset at a foreordained cost later on. At the point when that future point arrives, you will have the decision to practice the option or let it terminate.

Here's a model. Suppose the asset is selling for $110, an agreement giving you the privilege to purchase at $100 will have an inherent worth. As the expiration date draws near, the estimation of the options contract will change.

## Types of Options

Call Option - Option to buy the fundamental asset.

Put Option - Option to sell the fundamental asset.

Options Contract - The understanding between the author and the purchaser.

Vanilla Option - An ideal option with no extraordinary highlights, terms or conditions.

American Option - Option that can be practiced whenever before the expiration date.

European Option - Option that can be practiced uniquely on the expiration date.

Exotic Option - Any option with a mind boggling structure or result estimation.

## American and European Options

American options can be practiced whenever between the date of procurement and the expiration date. European options are not quite the same as American options in that they must traded toward the part of the arrangement on their expiration date. The differentiation among American and European options has nothing to do with topography, just with early work out. Numerous options on stock records are of the European kind. Since the privilege to practice early has some worth, an American option typically conveys a higher premium than a generally indistinguishable European option. This is because the early exercise highlight is attractive and directions a premium.

## American option

An American option is a put option or call option that can be practiced whenever before its expiration date.

How it functions/Example:

For instance, an investor holding an American option that lapses on the last Friday in March has the privilege to practice that option whenever at the very latest that date.

Since the option value moves in a state of harmony with the hidden asset, the estimation of the option may rise and fall on various occasions over the life of the agreement. The greater part of the options that exchange on real exchanges are American options.

With an American option, the holder can trust that the most effective cost will practice the option. He can exercise the option on any of the trading days up to the expiration date. Because of more noteworthy adaptability, American options are more profitable than European-style options, which must be traded at development.

## European option

An European option is a sort of put or call option that can be practiced uniquely on its expiration date.

How it functions/Example:

Assume an investor, John, purchases an European call option on March first that terminates on the third Friday in March. During the second seven day stretch of March, the estimation of the primary asset transcends the strike cost. The holder of an European option can't make the most of this fleeting chance to secure a benefit since the main date he can trade this option is on its expiration date.

Conversely, American options might be practiced whenever from the date of procurement until expiration. The holder of an American option may choose that the estimation of his option has arrived at its best point, regardless of whether development has not come. Such an option could then be sold before development.

The proprietor of an European option, then again, must hold up until development. In the model above, John may find that the European option is worth less at development than when he bought it. In the event that he held an American option, he might have the option to make a benefit prior in the life of the option.

European options more often than not exchange at a markdown to their American partners since there is just a solitary chance to practice the option. however, if the holder of the European option wouldn't like to hold up until the expiration date, he should close his situation by selling the option. These options exchange predominantly over the counter and are once in a while observed on the real exchanges

**Vanilla option**

A vanilla option alludes to an ordinary option with no uncommon highlights, terms, or conditions.

How it functions/Example:

Options arrive in an assortment of "flavors." A plain vanilla option offers the privilege to buy or sell a basic security by a specific date at a set strike cost. In contrast with other option structures, vanilla options are not extravagant or muddled. Such options might be outstanding in the business sectors, and simple to exchange.

Progressively, in any case, the term vanilla option is a general proportion of multifaceted nature, particularly when investors are thinking about different options and structures

Option structures might be mind boggling. Be that as it may, in options trading, at times, straightforward option structures might be justified. Note that vanilla options don't show lower execution or opportunity.

**Exotic option**

There are likewise exotic options, which are exotic because there may be a minor departure from the result profiles from the plain vanilla options. they can turn out to be entirely unexpected items all together with "optionality" implanted in them.

An exotic option is any option contract involving credits not regular to most contracts which result in confused valuation plans. It is something contrary to a plain vanilla option.

How it functions/Example:

Exotic options contain complex criteria influencing valuation and result. As a rule, these criteria are time-delicate and enable the holder to practice explicit inclinations at different focuses before the expiration date. Instances of exotic options incorporate Asian options (strike cost depends on the anticipated standard cost of the primary asset over a particular interim) and compound options (hidden asset is another option). Exotic options ought not be mistaken for plain vanilla options, which just contain a specific strike value, expiration date, and fundamental asset.

For instance, twofold options have a basic result structure that is resolved if the result occasion happens, paying little respect to the degree. Different kinds of exotic options incorporate thump out, thump in, hindrance options, lookback options, Asian options, and Bermudan options. Once more, exotic options are typically for expert derivatives dealers.

The complexities related with exotic options make them hard to exchange on a trade. Thus, most exotic options are exchanged over-the-counter (OTC) showcase.

## The two principle kinds of options

There are two distinct kinds of options, call options and put options. At the point when utilized effectively, options trading will make your methodology considerably more powerful. How about we plunge into the following area.

As we realize that Options are a kind of derivative security. An option is a derivative since its cost is intrinsically connected to the cost of something different. In the event that you purchase an options contract, it awards you the right, however not the commitment to purchase or sell a primary asset at a set cost before a specific date.

Regardless of their complexity, all options strategies are based on the two basic types of options: the call and the put. Call Options

Call options are money related contracts that give the option purchaser the right, yet not the commitment, to purchase a stock, security, product or other asset or instrument at a predetermined cost during a particular timespan. The stock, bond, or commodity is called the

hidden asset. A call purchaser benefits when the fundamental asset increments in value.

A call option might be appeared differently concerning a put, which gives the holder the privilege to sell the hidden asset at a predetermined cost before expiration.

**What is a Call Option?**

A Call Option gives you the privilege to buy an asset in the future. Whenever worked out, this buy will happen on a foreordained date. It will likewise happen at a foreordained worth. paraventureIn the event that you are uncertain about the future estimation of an asset, a call option can offer some assurance. Stock dealers generally buy call options. Be that as it may, they can likewise be found in numerous different markets. Actually, call options are the most ordinarily exchanged options contracts.

A call option gives the holder the privilege to purchase a stock, Think of a call option as a down-payment for a future purpose, With a call option, the buyer of the contract acquires the right to buy the underlying asset in the future at a predetermined price, called exercise price or strike price. A call option is known as the agreement between a buyer and a seller regarding the purchase of a stock at an agreed price up until a defined expiration date. The buyer has the right, but not the obligation, to exercise the call and buy the stock. The seller must deliver the stock if the option is exercised.

A hypothetical call option contract could give a buyer the right to buy 100 shares of a company for $100 each. In this case, $100 is what is referred to as the strike price. Until the option contract expires the option buyer has the right to those shares at that agreed price regardless of the stock market price. Any appreciation above that strike price represents profit for the buyer. If the price shoots up to $150 then the buyer has made a total profit of $5,000, less the cost of the option.

The call option buyer has to pay a fee known as the premium to the seller. In the case above, imagine the premium is $4. This means the premium total of $400 ($4 x 100 shares) would leave a profit of $4,600. However, if the stock instead declined in value, the buyer would have no reason to exercise the right to buy the stock for the higher cost. They would more than likely choose to allow the contract to expire and lose the $400. Or they could sell the option if it still has value, to avoid taking a full loss.

But this "full loss" is less than it seems. If you bought the underlying asset itself instead, say 100 shares for $100 each, even a $5 decline would see you lose more money. As this example shows, the option limits the risk.

In addition to the premium, commissions and fees can also add to the overall expense of options trading. That can be sizable.

Another example is ifa potential property holder sees another advancement going up. That individual may need the privilege to buy a home in the future, yet will just need to practice that privilege once specific improvements around the region are assembled.

The potential home purchaser would profit by the option of purchasing or not. Envision they can purchase a call option from the designer to purchase the home at state $400,000 anytime in the following three years.

The potential home purchaser needs to contribute an initial installment to secure that right.

Concerning an option, this expense is known as the premium. It is the cost of the option contract. In our home model, the store may be $20,000 that the purchaser pays the designer. Suppose two years have passed, and now the advancements are assembled, and zoning has been endorsed. The home purchaser trades the option and purchases the home for $400,000 because its the agreement acquired.

The market estimation of that home may have multiplied to $800,000. But since the up front installment secured a pre-decided value, the purchaser pays $400,000. Presently, in an other situation, state the zoning endorsement might not come doesn't until fourth year ration of this option. Currently, the home purchaser must compensation the market cost because the agreement has terminated. In either case, the designer keeps the first $20,000 gathered.

## What Is A Long Call Option?

When you have buy a call option, it means you have the right to purchase shares. It's referred to as being "long a call." Because a long call costs a fraction of the underlying stock price, there is more potential upside on a percentage basis than buying the underlying security itself.

## What Does Long Call Mean?

What is the meaning of long call? Long calls offer a critical development potential and investors acknowledge gains when the market value transcends the strike cost; for example, the value that the option is worked out. There is likewise an exceptional that investors pay to buy a long call, which is, really, the expense of the option understanding. At the point when investors expect or guess an ascent in the stock costs, they purchase a call option in light of the fact that the likelihood of the market going up is high.

Conversely, if the market value drops lower than the strike value, the long call holders lose the cash they paid to enter the option understanding in addition to the premium. In this manner, a long call limits risk to the sum paid for the call and has a boundless development potential.

## Model

Abis claims 250 portions of a development organization, which presently exchange at $105. Abis believes that the stock cost will increment on the grounds that the organization has finished a gainful arrangement with a focused firm. The market feels that this obtaining will support the gainfulness of the two organizations.

Abis needs to expand his situation in the stock; however he has no cash. To purchase another 100 offers would cost him $10,500. Consequently, he buys a long call with a strike cost of $130, expecting that the stock cost will transcend the strike cost before development, which is in 35 days. The option is evaluated at $3, so Abis pays $300 and purchases 100 portions of the basic stock.

In the event that the stock value ascends at $165, Abis has the privilege to trade his call option and purchase 100 offers for $130 and sell them in the open market for $165, along these lines understanding an increase of ($165 x 100) – ($130 x 100) = $3,500. In this way, his net benefit is $3,500 – $300 = $3,200

if the stock value unlikely drops to $125, Abis loses $300 that he paid for the long call.

## What Is A Short Call Option?

When a call option is been sold, you receive payment for the call and are obligated to sell shares of the underlying stock at the strike price until the expiration date. This is also known as writing or being short. While you can create income by selling call options via the premium, there is risk if the stock price rises above the strike price. And given the overall tendency of the stock market to go up, this risk is not insubstantial.

When you brief a call option, you're advertising it before you get it. That converts the whole transfer around, so you make money only when the alternative call price drops ahead of contract expiration.

It's much like shorting a inventory except you've got a deadline (once the contract expires).

Remember: additionally, you get a credit score back immediately once you short a phone. That credit can be your maximum revenue.

If the decision option is higher than the strike cost at expiration, after that, it's in the amount of money. That means the one who bought that call up option from you'll expect one to sell shares on the underlying stock to her or him at the strike price.

You will have to buy shares with the stock in order to complete that purchase. Because the phone option is the amount of money, you'll market those stocks for an instantaneous loss.

Remember: in the event, the stock rises dramatically; subsequently, you'll have a significant loss. A short call is a very dangerous approach because your damage is unlimited.

If the root stock remains below the affect price at agreement expiration, then your alternative expires worthless. You retain the prime you earned from sale of the decision and create a nice profit.

## What Is A Covered Call Option?

With short call options, consider the difference between covered and uncovered calls. The latter instrument is also called a naked call.

When your short call is covered, you already own the shares you are obliged to sell. The worst that can happen is that you are forced to sell your stock at a lower price. But even though they are being compensated with the premium, investors can find it tough psychologically if there is a big move in a stock they own when they know they will take none of the gains.

There are several benefits from this options trading approach for people who own stocks.

"In this case, the investor could be collecting income, while also defining an exit price (to sell the underlying at a predetermined price) and simultaneously partly offsetting a decline, should that occur,".

"Covered calls can allow investors to lower the cost basis of a long position since the income received from the sale effectively lowers the acquisition price."

An uncovered short call or naked call means you are betting on stock you do not even own. Here there is a theoretical potential for unlimited losses.

This is because you are obligated to sell shares. You might have to buy them on the open market at a much higher price and sell them for the lower agreed upon price of the option contract. The difference between those prices can end up being a sizable loss to your account.

## Why do traders use covered calls?

A covered call is employed by traders who are fundamentally bullish but believe the underlying asset will rise steadily, or not beyond a specific price point. Under these circumstances, the trader is able to make a profit from both the long position and the short call position. This enables the trader to secure a higher return than would be possible from holding the long position alone. If their bullish view is incorrect, the short call serves as a hedge to offset some of the trader's losses that are incurred as a result of the asset falling in value.

## How do covered calls work?

Covered calls work because a trader who currently holds a long position on an asset gives up their right to sell that asset at any time for the market value. Instead, under the obligations of a call option, they must sell the asset to the buyer at the expiry date for the strike price – so long as the buyer exercises their right to buy.

From the call seller's perspective, they can only be worried if the underlying asset price rises to levels higher than the strike, at which point the buyer can be expected to trade the option. However, if the sellers are already long on the underlying instrument, they would already be profiting from the upward move.

Buyers of calls will typically exercise their right to buy if the underlying price exceeds a pre-determined strike price at or before a given expiry date. If the underlying price does not reach this strike level, the buyer will likely not trade their option because the underlying asset will be cheaper on the open market.

## Covered call example

Let's suppose a trader owns 100 shares in company ABC, which they think have a strong chance of generating profit in the long term. But in the short term, they expect the share price to fall – or to not increase dramatically – from the current price of £50.

As a result, the trader decides to sell a call option on the same stock with a strike price of £60. They will earn a premium by selling this call option, but they will cap the total upside potential of their share investment at £60 – or a £10 profit per share.

In this example, let's assume that the premium for this call option is 100p per share. Since options are always traded in lots of 100 shares, the trader stands to receive a total premium of £100.

The trader will generate a profit for all gains up to a share price of £60, after which any additional profits will be offset by losses incurred on the short call option. This is because it is now above the stated strike, meaning the option is 'in-the-money'.

As a result, the maximum the trader stands to gain is the £100 premium, plus £10 profit per share. So, their total profit is capped at £1100 (for an underlying share price of £60 or higher) because they own 100 shares.

Now, if the share price rises to levels greater than £60, the trader will not realise these additional gains – or to be more accurate, gains in the long ABC position have been offset by losses on the short call.

However, for lesser upward movements – or drops in share price – the premium obtained by selling the call serves as a useful source of revenue, either to increase profits or to mitigate losses.

## Covered call Strategies

Here are some quick strategies you should use with covered telephone calls. Some connect with blue chips shares, others to high-risk organizations, and some for all those stocks that you expect minimal increases.

1. Boosting Dividends

Buying stocks and promoting options contracts decreases your adequate expense basis. Furthermore, you will nevertheless collect 100% on the dividends from firms who present these payments. Because of this, selling options agreements increase your dividend produce. Below can be an example:

You get Nutrisystem (NASDAQ: NTRI) stocks, which give quarterly dividends at $0.175 per show, at the current value of $14.24.

You then offer phone options that expire in 9 weeks with a affect price tag of $10 per show that are respected at $4.50.

You receive an instantaneous come back of $4.50, which reduces your net price per talk about to $9.74.

As explained in this book, share rates can fall practically 32%, from $14.24 for your net expense of $9.74, without the capital loss staying incurred.

Furthermore, at your brand-new cost groundwork of $9.74 per show, your yearly dividend yield increases from 5% to 7.2%. Therefore, while you have got limited your money increase upside, you also have significantly raised your dividend produce. This is a very useful strategy unless you think the actual stock price can make huge profit, or if you're pretty opposed to threat and desire to profit typically from dividends while developing a 32% hedge against dropping share prices.

2. Adding Income Steady stream to Funds Gains

Another solution to play covered phone calls is to established the strike value above the current price. You'll do this in the event that you expect share costs to appreciate reasonably. In so doing, you benefit from both a growth in share costs and the excess revenue from advertising the options. Beneath is an illustration:

You predict that stocks of Ford (NYSE: F), which now deals at $15.28, will rise over the up coming 3 months.

You own stocks at $15.28 each.

You offer a contact options agreement for $0.29 per talk about which will expire in a few months with a attack selling price of $17 per show.

If share rates rise, you're allowed to keep the capital gains around the $17 hit price tag, or $1.72 per show. Furthermore, you also acquire 29 cents per talk about of salary from selling the decision options contract. It didn't look much; nonetheless it can boost earnings by 7.6% on the year (predicated on annualizing the a few months call options agreement cost of 29 cents). Needless to say, your capital profits may also be capped if talk about prices create a huge function beyond the $17 reach price.

3. Hedging Chance with Volatile Stocks

Risk goes far up once you hold in volatile stocks. Obtaining call or set options for speculative buying and selling may also be high priced since options derive a lot of their benefit from volatility. When this happens, you can purchase the inventory and sell contact options which are "deep in the amount of money" to safeguard against a substantial decrease in inventory price tag. "Deep in the amount of money" identifies when the hit price is nicely below the actual price. Consequently, you involve some security against a downward slide and a decent upside increase. Consider this case in point to observe how it is completed:

Solar stocks include high possible but a correspondingly risky. One such inventory, Energy Conversion Products (NASDAQ: ENER), deals at $2.02 per present.

You get 100 stocks at $2.02 per show.

You offer a contact options contract which has a $1.00 affect value for $1.27 per present and expires in 21 a few months.

Your effective expense basis per present can be $0.75 per present.

Your maximum benefit is definitely $0.25 per talk about or the variation between your online cost as well as the strike price.

How is usually this top upside calculated? As your strike price is defined at $1.00, you might have necessarily offered the rights on your own inventory above this volume. To place this yet another way, you will preserve ownership around $1.00. If the price eventually ends up above $1.00, the options will undoubtedly be exercised. Your prospective reward may be the difference between your $0.75 of online cost along with the $1.00 of settlement once the options will be applied at any volume above this. Consequently, even if present prices slip to $1.00 (or perhaps a 50% shed from once you purchased it) plus the rights aren't exercised, you'll still built a 33% gain converting 75 cents into one money. This will be an excellent strategy if you are dedicated to a inventory that you think has a significant probability to suffer a substantial decrease in cost.

the covered contact strategy is common among long-term traders who want to amplify their go back on gives they own. In the event that you know very well what a covered call is and how you can properly put into action this options buying and selling strategy, it is possible to increase your inventory portfolio rapidly.

With a covered call, additionally, you get some drawback protection. However, the blissful luxury of experiencing this downside security includes a expense of capping the upside earnings probable on those lengthy shares.

# PUT OPTION

A Put Option offers you the right to market an asset in the foreseeable future. Like contact options, these agreements have predetermined rates and sell times. Put options and phone options tend to be purchased together to make a "hedged" posture. Below, we shall discuss the various forms of options sales. We shall then talk about how these product sales can be created into your buying and selling strategy.

Put option gives the holder the right to sell a stock. With a put option, the buyer acquires the right to sell the underlying asset in the future at the predetermined price. For clarity's sake, it is worth mentioning the difference between a call option and a put option. Basically, the latter is the exact opposite of the former. A put option gives the investor the option to sell a stock at an agreed price before or on a specified date. This can be used to protect your stock gains against a fall in price.

"If you are long a stock or an ETF that has risen in value, you may want to protect your gains," the Options Industry Council's Prosperi said. "One way to do so would be by purchasing a put, which is often referenced as similar to insurance."

Purchasing a PUT option on a stock gives the buyer the Option (But not the obligation) to sell a set stock at a fixed price until a set date.

Puts can be used as insurance against the price of stock you hold falling in price. If you bought some shares on a stock and they went up in price by purchasing a put option on the stock at the new price you have in effect locked in the price rise of the shares.

Put options provide owners the proper, however, not the obligation, to market a specified quantity of an underlying safety measures at a given price inside a specified timeframe.

Put options can be found on an array of assets, including securities, indexes, goods, and currencies.

Put option costs are influenced by the underlying property price and period decay.

## JUST HOW DO PUT OPTIONS FUNCTION?

A put option gets more valuable because the price of the actual stock depreciates per the strike selling price. Conversely, a set option manages to lose its value because the underlying stock raises. Because place options essentially give a short position within the underlying asset, they're useful for hedging purposes or even to speculate on downside price tag action. A defensive put can be used to make sure that losses within the underlying asset usually do not exceed a quantity, namely the attack price.

In general, the worthiness of a set option reduces as its time and energy to expiration approaches because of time decay, as the possibility of the stock dropping below the given strike price lowers. When a option loses its moment price, the intrinsic worth is left, which is equal to the difference between your strike price tag less the actual stock price tag. If a option has intrinsic value, it is in the money (ITM).

From the money (OTM) with the money set options haven't any intrinsic benefit because there will be no advantage of exercising the option. Investors could quick sell the inventory at the existing higher selling price, rather than training an from the money put option at an unhealthy strike price.

Time worth, or extrinsic worth, is reflected within the premium of the option. If the hit value of a set option is indeed $20, as well as the underlying is share is currently stock trading at $19, there's $1 of intrinsic benefit in the option. But the place option may swap for $1.35. The excess $0.35 is definitely time value because the underlying stock value could change prior to the option expires.

## Alternatives to Performing exercises a Put Option

The put owner, referred to as the "writer", doesn't need to hold a option until expiration, and neither will the option shopper. As the root stock price techniques, the high grade of the decision changes to mirror the recent main price movements. The option buyer can market their option anytime, either to lower their damage and recoup area of the prime (if OTM), or secure a income (if ITM).

Similarly, the option writer can perform a similar thing. In the event, the underlying's price is above the hit price they could do nothing as the option may expire worthlessly, plus they can keep the complete premium. If the underlying's price is usually approaching or shedding below the reach price, in order to avoid a significant reduction the option trader may simply choose the option back, obtaining them from the position. The loss or profit is the variation between the prime collected and prime paid to obtain from the position.

## Real World Types of Put Options

Assume an entrepreneur owns one set option in the SPDR S&P 500 ETF (SPY)--currently investing at $277.00--with a hit cost of $260 expiring in a single month. Because of this option, they compensated reduced of $0.72, or $72 ($0.72 x 100 gives).

The investor gets the right to promote 100 stocks of XYZ at a cost of $260 before expiration date in a single month, that is usually the 3rd Friday from the month, though it could be weekly.

If gives of SPY slide to $250 along with the investor exercises the option, the buyer could buy 100 stocks of SPY for $250 on the market and promote the shares for the option's article writer for $260 each. Therefore, the trader would create $1,000 (100 x ($260-$250)) for the put alternative, less the $72 price they covered the option. Online profit is certainly $1,000 - $72 = $928, much less any commission charges. The maximum damage on the industry is limited for the premium compensated, or $72. The maximum profit is accomplished if SPY comes to $0.

Contrary to an extended put option, a brief or written place option obligates an entrepreneur to take distribution, or purchase gives, of the root stock.

Assume a trader is bullish on SPY, that is currently investing at $277, and will not believe it'll tumble below $260 on the next 8 weeks. The buyer could collect reduced of $0.72 (x 100 stocks) by composing one put alternative on SPY, which has a strike cost of $260.

The option writer would collect a complete of $72 ($0.72 x 100). If SPY remains above the $260 punch price, the trader would keep carefully the premium collected because the options would expire from the money and become worthless. This is actually the maximum profit within the market: $72, or the top quality collected.

Conversely, if SPY techniques below $260, the entrepreneur is on for the hook for buying 100 gives at $260, even though the stock comes to $250, or $200, or lower. Regardless of what lengths the stock arrives, the put option trader is likely for purchasing gives at $260, signifying they experience theoretical threat of $260 per talk about or $26,000 per deal ($260 x 100 stocks) in the event the underlying stock comes to zero.

## Example Study: Buying a Put Option on a house

We have a house that is currently selling for $100,000.

We think the house prices may fall but do not want to sell the house this month, we approach a purchaser with a Contract (proposal).

Our Contract states that we will give the purchaser $1000 for the option (the right but not the obligation) to sell the house at the list price of $100,000.

The contract is valid for 30 days, and if we do not sell the house within that period the purchaser will keep the $1000, and there is no further commitment on either of our behalf.

We have in fact purchased the equivalent of a one month Put option on the property.

The contract is valid for 30 days, and if we do not sell the house within that period the purchaser will keep the $1000, and there is no further commitment on either of our behalf.

We have in fact purchased the equivalent of a one month Put option on the property.

o If the housing market soars (in the next 30 days) and the house is now valued at $110,000, we let our option expire worthless, and we can sell the house for $110,000.

$110,000 (Current Value) - $1000 (Option Price) - $100,000 (Initial Price) = $9000 (Our Profits).

o If the housing market crashes (in the next 30 days) and the house is now valued at $90,000, we can exercise our option and sell the house for $100,000.

$100,000 (Sale Price) - $1000 (Option Price) - $90,000 (Current Value) = $9000 (Our locked in value)

# CHAPTER 1

## OPTION TRADING TIPS AND STRATEGIES

As an option purchaser, your goal ought to be to buy options with the longest conceivable expiration, so as to give your exchange time to work out. On the other hand, when you are writing options, go for the shortest conceivable expiration so as to constrain your obligation.

Attempting to adjust the point above, when buying options, buying the least expensive potential ones may improve your odds of a beneficial exchange. Implied volatility of such modest options is probably going to be very low, and keeping in mind that this proposes the chances of a fruitful exchange are negligible, it is conceivable that implied volatility and henceforth the option are undervalued. Along these lines, if the exchange works out, the potential benefit can be gigantic. Buying options with a lower level of implied volatility might be desirable over buying those with an exceptionally abnormal state of implied volatility, as a result of the risk of a higher loss (higher premium paid) if the exchange doesn't work out.

There is an exchange off between strike costs and options expirations, as the previous model illustrated. An investigation of help and opposition levels, just as key up and coming occasions, (for example, a profit discharge), is valuable in figuring out which strike cost and expiration to utilize.

Comprehend the part to which the stock belongs. For instance, biotech stocks frequently exchange with double results when clinical preliminary consequences of a noteworthy medication are reported. Profoundly out of the money calls or puts can be obtained to exchange on these results, contingent upon whether one is bullish or bearish on the stock. Clearly, it would be amazingly risky to compose calls or puts on biotech stocks around such occasions, except if the degree of implied volatility is high to the point that the premium income earned makes up for this risk. By a similar token, it looks bad to purchase profoundly out of the money calls or puts on low-volatility divisions like utilities and telecoms.

Use options to exchange one-off occasions, for example, corporate restructurings and side projects, and repeating occasions like profit discharges. Stocks can display exceptionally unpredictable conduct around such circumstances, allowing the dealer of the shrewd options a chance to trade out. For example, buying modest out of the money calls before the income report on a stock that has been in an articulated droop, can be a profitable strategy if it figures out how to beat brought down desires and like this floods.

Fundamental option trading techniques for amateurs.

Merchants frequently bounce into trading options with small comprehension of options methodologies. There are numerous techniques accessible that farthest point risk and boost return. With a little exertion, merchants can figure out how to exploit the adaptability and power options offer. In light of this, we've put together this groundwork, which ought to shorten the expectation to absorb information and point you the correct way.

## Long Call strategy

This is the favored strategy for dealers who:

Are "bullish" or certain on a specific stock, ETF or file and need to restrain risk

Need to use leverage to exploit rising costs

Options are leveraged instruments, i.e., they enable dealers to intensify the advantage by risking littler sums than would some way, or another be required if trading the main assets itself.

A regular options contract on a stock controls 100 portions of the hidden security.

Assume a merchant needs to invest $5,000 in

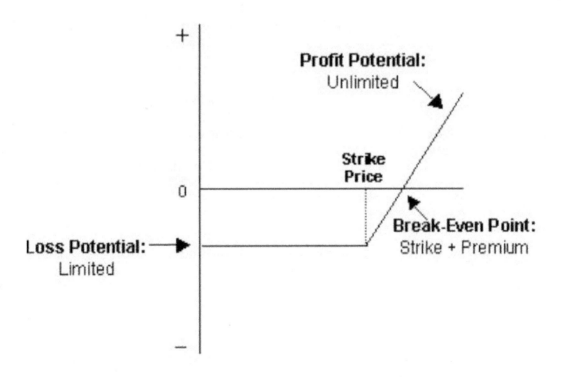

In this strategy, an investor will all the while purchase calls at a particular strike cost and sell a similar number of calls at a higher strike cost. Both call options will have a similar expiration and basic asset. This kind of vertical spread strategy is frequently utilized when an investor is bullish on the fundamental and anticipates a moderate ascent in the cost of the asset. As far as possible his/her upside on the exchange, however, diminishes the net premium spent contrasted with buying a stripped call option inside and out.

Bull Call Spread Options Strategy

strategy, so the dealer needs the stock to increment in cost so as to make a benefit on the exchange. The exchange off when putting on a bull call spread is that your upside is constrained, while your premium spent is diminished. If out and out calls are costly, one approach to counterbalance the high premium is by selling high strike calls against it.

A bull call spread is built this way.

## Buying Puts (Long Put)

This is the favored strategy for dealers who:

Are bearish on a specific stock, ETF or list, yet need to go out on a limb than with a short-selling strategy

Need to use leverage to exploit falling costs

A put option works the exact inverse way a call option does, with the put option picking up value as the cost of the basic abatements. While short-selling additionally enables a dealer to benefit from falling costs, the risk with a short position is boundless, as there is theoretically no restriction on how high a cost can rise. With a put option, if the basic ascents past the option's strike value, the option will lapse uselessly.

Risk/Reward: Potential loss is constrained to the premium paid for the options. The most extreme benefit from the position is topped since the basic cost can't dip under zero, yet similarly, as with a long call option, the put option leverages the broker's arrival.

At the point when to utilize it: A long put is a decent decision when you anticipate that the stock should fall primarily before the option lapses. On the off chance that the stock falls just a little beneath the strike value, the option might be in the money, yet may not restore the premium paid, giving you an overall deficit.

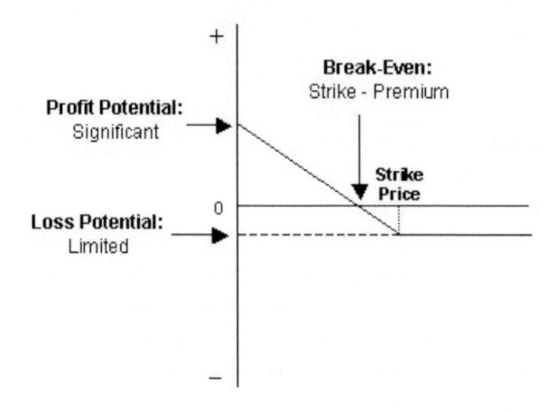

## Covered Call

This is the favored situation for merchants who:

Anticipate no change or a slight increment in the basic's cost

Are happy to constrain upside potential in return for some drawback insurance

Covered Call

With calls, one strategy is basically to purchase a stripped call option. You can likewise structure an essential covered call or purchase compose. This is a well known strategy since it produces income and lessens some risk of being long stock alone. The exchange off is that you should be happy to sell your offers at a set value: the short strike cost. To execute the strategy, you buy the basic stock as you regularly would, and all the while compose (or sell) a call option on those equivalent offers.

In this model, we are utilizing a call option on a stock, which speaks to 100 portions of stock for every call option. For each 100 portions of stock you get, you all the while sell 1 call option against it. It is alluded to as a covered call in light of the fact that if a stock rockets higher in value, your short call is covered by the long stock position. Investors may utilize this strategy when they have a short-term position in the stock and an unbiased feeling on its course. They may hope to produce income (through the closeout of the call premium), or ensure against a potential decrease in the hidden stock's value.

Covered Call Options Strategy

In the benefit and loss graph above, see how as the stock cost builds, the negative PROFIT AND LOSS from the call is counterbalanced by the long offers position. Since you get premium from selling the call, as the stock travels through the strike cost to the upside, the exceptional you got enable you to adequately sell your stock at a higher level than the strike value (strike + premium got). The covered call's PROFIT AND Loss-graph looks a great deal like a short bare put's PROFIT AND Loss-graph.

Risk/Reward: If the offer value transcends the strike cost before expiration, the short call option can be practiced, and the dealer should convey portions of the hidden at the option's strike cost, regardless of whether it is beneath the market cost. In return for this risk, a covered call strategy gives constrained drawback security as premium got when selling the call option.

At the point when to utilize it: A covered call can be a decent strategy to create income when you officially claim the stock and don't anticipate that the stock should rise fundamentally sooner rather than later. So the strategy can change your officially existing possessions into a wellspring of money. The covered call is prevalent with more seasoned investors who need the income, and it very well may be valuable in duty advantaged accounts where you may somehow, or another make good on regulatory obligations on the premium and capital additions if the stock is called.

**Short put**

This is the flipside of the long put, however here the merchant sells a put – alluded to as "going short" a put – and anticipates that the stock cost should be over the strike cost by expiration. In return for selling a put, the merchant gets a money premium, which is the best upside a short put can procure. On the off chance that the stock completes underneath the strike value, the broker must get it at the strike cost.

Model: Stock X is trading for $20 per share, and a put with a strike cost of $20 and expiration in four months is trading at $1. The agreement pays a premium of $100, or one contract * $1 * 100 offers spoke to per contract.

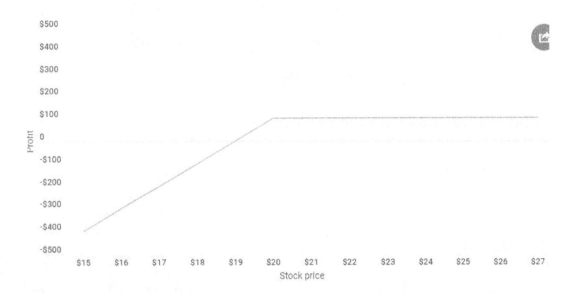

Reward/risk: In this model, the short put earns back the original investment at $19, or the strike cost less the premium got. Beneath $19, the short put costs the dealer $100 at each dollar decrease in cost, while above $20 the put merchant acquires the full $100 premium. Somewhere in the range of $19 and $20, the put merchant would gain a few; however, not the majority of the premium.

The upside on the short put is never more than the premium got, $100 here. Like the short call or covered call, the greatest profit for a short put is the thing that the vender gets forthright.

The drawback of a short put is the absolute value of the hidden stock less the premium got, and that would occur if the stock went to zero. In this model, the broker would need to purchase $2,000 of the stock (100 offers $20 strike cost); however this would be counterbalanced by the $100 premium got, for a complete loss of $1,900.

At the point when to utilize it: A short put is a decent strategy when you anticipate that the stock should transcend the strike cost by expiration. The stock should be just at or over the strike cost for the option to terminate useless, giving you a chance to keep the entire premium got. Your representative will need to ensure you have enough value in your record to purchase the stock if it's put to you. Numerous brokers will hold enough trade out their record to buy the stock if the put completes in the money.

**Married Put**

In a married put strategy, an investor buys an asset (in this model, portions of stock), and at the same time buys put options for a comparable number of offers. The holder of a put option has the option to sell stock at the strike cost. Each agreement is worth 100 offers. The explanation an investor would utilize this strategy is essentially to ensure their drawback risk when holding a stock. This strategy capacities simply like a protection arrangement, and builds up a value floor should the stock's value fall strongly.

A case of a married put would be if an investor purchases 100 portions of stock and gets one put option at the same time. This strategy is engaging in light of the fact that an investor is secured to the drawback should a negative occasion happen. Simultaneously, the investor would take an interest in the majority of the upside if the stock gains in value. The main drawback to this strategy happens if the stock doesn't fall, in which case the investor loses the premium paid for the put option.

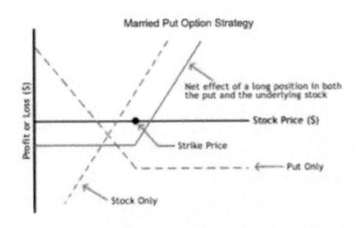

In the PROFIT AND Loss-graph over, the dashed line is the long stock position. With the long put and long stock positions consolidated, you can consider that to be the stock value falls; the losses are restricted. However, the stock takes an interest in upside over the premium spent on the put. The married put's PROFIT AND Loss-graph appears to be like a long call's PROFIT AND Loss-graph.

The most extreme upside of the married put is theoretically uncapped, as long as the stock keeps rising, less the expense of the put. The married put is a supported position; thus, the premium is the expense of safeguarding the stock and allowing it to ascend with constrained drawback.

The drawback of the married put is the expense of the premium paid. As the value of the stock position falls, the put increments in value, covering the decrease dollar for dollar. Due to this fence, the dealer just loses the expense of the option instead of the greater stock loss.

At the point when to utilize it: A married put can be a decent decision when you anticipate that a stock's cost should rise essentially before the option's expiration, yet you figure it might get an opportunity to fall fundamentally, as well. The married put enables you to hold the stock and appreciate the potential upside in the event that it rises, yet at the same time be covered from generous loss if the stock falls. For instance, a broker may anticipate news, for example, income, that may drive a stock up or down, and needs to be covered.

## Bear Put Spread

The bear put spread strategy is another type of vertical spread. In this strategy, the investor will all the while buy put options at a particular strike cost and sell a similar number of puts at a lower strike cost. The two options would be for the equivalent fundamental asset and have a similar expiration date. This strategy is utilized when the dealer is bearish and expects the hidden asset's cost to decrease. It offers both restricted losses and constrained increases.

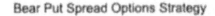

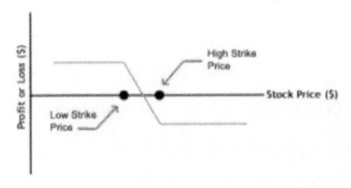

In the PROFIT AND Loss-graph above, you can see this is a bearish strategy, so you need the stock to fall so as to benefit. The exchange off when utilizing a bear put spread is that your upside is constrained; however, your premium spent is decreased. In the event that by and large puts are costly, one approach to balance the high premium is by selling lower strike puts against them. This is the way a bear put spread is built.

**Protective Collar**

A protective collar strategy is performed by buying an out-of-the-money put option and all the while writing an out-of-the-money call option for the equivalent fundamental asset and expiration. This strategy is regularly utilized by investors after a long position in a stock has encountered significant increases. This options mix enables investors to have drawback assurance (long puts to secure benefits), while having the exchange off of conceivably being committed to sell shares at a more expensive rate (selling higher = more benefit than at current stock levels).

A straightforward model would be if an investor is long 100 portions of IBM at $50 and IBM has ascended to $100 as of January first. The investor could build a protective collar by selling one IBM March fifteenth 105 call and all the while buying one IBM March 95 put. The dealer is ensured beneath $95 until March fifteenth, with the exchange off of conceivably having the commitment to sell his/her offers at $105.

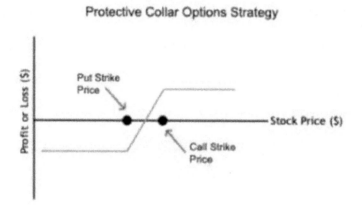

In the PROFIT AND Loss-graph above, you can see that the protective collar is a blend of a covered call and a long put. This is an unbiased exchange set-up, implying that you are secured in case of falling stock, however with the exchange off of having the potential commitment to sell your long stock at the short call strike. Once more, however, the investor ought to be glad to do as such, as they have effectively experienced gains in the hidden offers.

**Long Straddle**

A long straddle options strategy is the point at which an investor at the same time buys a call and put option on the equivalent hidden asset, with a similar strike cost and expiration date. An investor will frequently utilize this strategy when the individual in question accepts the cost of the basic asset will move essentially out of a range; however, it is uncertain of which heading the move will take. This strategy enables the investor to have the open door for theoretically boundless additions, while the greatest loss is restricted uniquely to the expense of the two options contracts joined.

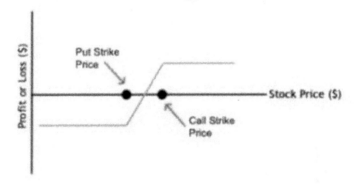

In the PROFIT AND Loss-graph above, notice how there are two breakeven points. This strategy becomes profitable when the stock makes a large move in one direction or the other. The investor doesn't care which direction the stock moves, only that it is a greater move than the total premium the investor paid for the structure.

**Long Call Butterfly Spread**

The majority of the methodologies so far have required a mix of two unique positions or contracts. In a long butterfly spread utilizing call options, an investor will join both a bull spread strategy and a bear spread strategy, and utilize three distinctive strike costs. All options are for the equivalent fundamental asset and expiration date.

For instance, a long butterfly spread can be developed by buying one in-the-money call option at a lower strike cost, while selling two at-the-money call options, and buying one out-of-the-money call option. A decent butterfly spread will have a similar wing widths. This model is called a "call fly" and results in a net charge. An investor would go into a long butterfly call spread when they think the stock won't move much by expiration.

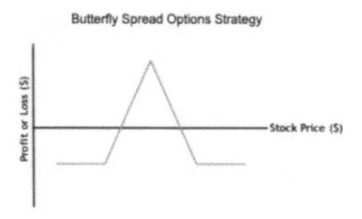

Butterfly Spread Options Strategy

In the PROFIT AND Loss-graph above, see how the greatest addition is made when the stock stays unaltered up until expiration (directly at the ATM strike). The further away the stock moves from the ATM strikes, the more noteworthy the negative change in PROFIT AND LOSS. Most extreme loss happens when the stock settles at the lower strike or beneath, or if the stock settles at or over the higher strike call. This strategy has both constrained upside and restricted drawback.

## Iron Condor

A much all the more intriguing strategy is the iron condor. In this strategy, the investor at the same time holds a bull put spread and a bear call spread. The iron condor is built by selling one out-of-the-money put and buying one out-of-the-money put of a lower strike (bull put spread), and selling one out-of-the-money call and buying one out-of-the-money call of a higher strike (bear call spread). All options have a similar expiration date and are on the equivalent fundamental asset. Typically, the put and call sides have a similar spread width. This trading strategy gains a net premium on the structure and is intended to exploit a stock encountering low volatility. Numerous brokers like this exchange for its apparent high likelihood of gaining a limited quantity of premium.

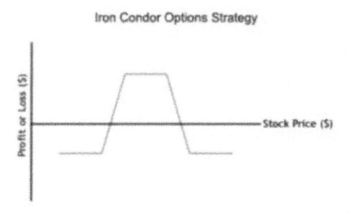

Iron Condor Options Strategy

In the PROFIT AND Loss-graph above, see how the most extreme addition is made when the stock stays in a generally wide trading extent, which would bring about the investor gaining the all out net credit got when developing the exchange. The further away the stock travels through the short strikes (lower for the put, higher for the call), the more prominent the loss up to the most extreme loss. Most extreme loss is generally altogether higher than the greatest addition, which naturally bodes well given that there is a higher likelihood of the structure completing with a little gain.

## Iron Butterfly

The last options strategy we will show is the iron butterfly. In this strategy, an investor will sell an at-the-money put and purchase an out-of-the-money put, while additionally selling an at-the-money call and buying an out-of-the-money call. All options have a similar expiration date and are on the equivalent hidden asset. Albeit like a butterfly spread, this strategy contrasts since it utilizes the two calls and puts, instead of either.

This strategy basically consolidates selling an at-the-money straddle and buying protective "wings." You can likewise think about the development as two spreads. It is entirely expected to have a similar width for the two spreads. The long out-of-the-money call secures against boundless drawback. The long out-of-the-money put shields against drawback from the short put strike to zero. Benefit and loss are both restricted inside a particular range, contingent upon the strike costs of the options utilized. Investors like this strategy for the income it produces and the higher likelihood of a little gain with a non-unpredictable stock.

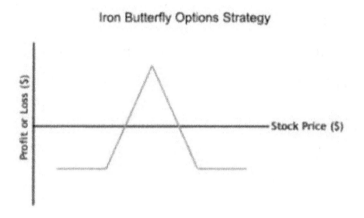

In the PROFIT AND Loss-graph above, see how the most extreme increase is made when the stock stays at the at-the-money strikes of the call and put sold. The most extreme increase is the complete net premium gotten. Greatest loss happens when the stock moves over the long call strike or beneath the long put strike.

**Married Put clarified**

A married put is the name given to an options trading strategy where an investor, holding a long position in a stock, buys an at-the-money put option on a similar stock to ensure against deterioration in the stock's cost.

The advantage is that the investor can lose a little yet constrained measure of money on the stock in the most exceedingly terrible situation, yet still partakes in any additions from value appreciation.

The drawback is that the put option costs a premium, and it is normally huge.

A married put might be diverged from a covered call.

This option strategy shields an investor from radical drops in the cost of the fundamental stock.

The expense of the option can make this strategy restrictive.

Put options shift in cost contingent upon the volatility of the hidden stock.

The strategy may function admirably for low-volatility stocks where investors are stressed over an unexpected declaration that would drastically change the cost.

**How a Married Put Works**

A married put also works to a protection approach for investors. It is a bullish strategy utilized when the investor is worried about potential close term vulnerabilities in the stock. By owning the stock with a protective put option, the investor still gets the advantages of stock possession, for example, accepting profits and reserving the option to cast a ballot. Conversely, simply owning a call option, while similarly as bullish as owning the stock, doesn't give similar advantages of stock possession.

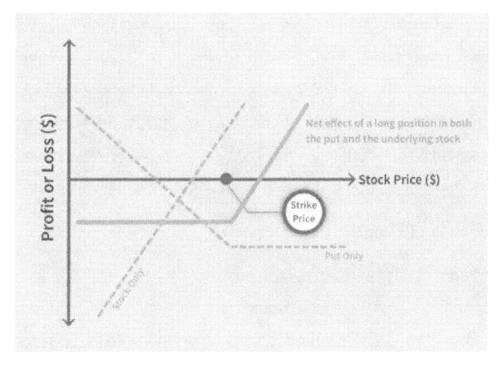

Both a married put and a long call have the equivalent boundless benefit potential, as there is no roof on the value energy about the fundamental stock. In any case, benefit is consistently lower than it would be for simply owning the stock, diminished by the expense or premium of the put option obtained. Coming to breakeven for the strategy happens when the basic stock ascents by the measure of the options premium paid. Anything over that sum is benefit.

The advantage of a married put is that there is presently a story under the stock restricting drawback risk. The floor is the distinction between the cost of the hidden stock, at the hour of the acquisition of the married put, and the strike cost of the put. Put another way, at the hour of the acquisition of the option, if the basic stock exchanged precisely at the strike value, the loss for the strategy is topped at precisely the cost paid for the option.

A married put is likewise viewed as an engineered long call since it has a similar benefit profile. The strategy has a likeness to buying a standard call option (without the hidden stock) in light of the fact that a similar dynamic is valid for both: restricted loss, boundless potential for benefit. The distinction between these procedures is just how considerably less capital is required in basically buying a long call.

## Married Put Example

Suppose a dealer purchases 100 portions of XYZ stock for $20 per offer and one XYZ $17.50 put for $0.50 (100 offers x $0.50 = $50). With this mix, they have acquired a stock situation with an expense of $20/share yet have additionally purchased a type of protection to ensure themselves in the event that the stock decays underneath $17.50 before the put's expiration. For a put to be considered "married," the put and the stock must be purchased around the same time, and the merchant must teach their expedite that the stock they have quite recently acquired will be conveyed if the put is worked out.

At the point when to Use a Married Put

As opposed to a benefit making strategy, a married put is a capital-protecting strategy. To be sure, the expense of the put bit of the strategy turns into an implicit expense. The put cost diminishes the benefit of the strategy, accepting the basic stock moves higher, by the expense of the option. In this manner, investors should utilize a married put as a protection strategy against close term vulnerability in a generally bullish stock, or as insurance against an unanticipated value breakdown.

More current investors profit by realizing that their losses in the stock are restricted. This can give them certainty as they become familiar with various investing procedures. Obviously, this security includes some major disadvantages, which incorporates the cost of the option, commissions, and conceivably different charges.

## Iron Condor

An iron condor is an options strategy made with four options comprising of two puts (one long and one short) and two calls (one long and one short), and four strike costs, all with a similar expiration date. The objective is to benefit from low volatility in the fundamental asset. At the end of the day, the iron condor procures the greatest benefit when the fundamental asset closes between the center strike costs at expiration.

The iron condor has a comparable result as a normal condor spread, however, utilizes the two calls and puts rather than just calls or just puts. Both the condor and the iron condor are expansions of the butterfly spread and iron butterfly, individually.

An iron condor is typically a nonpartisan strategy and benefits the most when the basic asset doesn't move much in spite of the fact that the strategy can be built with a bullish or bearish inclination.

The iron condor is made out of four options: a purchased put further OTM, and a sold put nearer to the money, and a purchased call further OTM and a sold call nearer to the money.

Benefit is topped at the premium got while the risk is likewise topped at the distinction between the purchased and sold call strikes and the purchased and sold put strikes (less the premium got).

## Understanding the Iron Condor

The strategy has restricted upside and drawback risk in light of the fact that the high and low strike options, the wings, secure against huge moves in either course. Due to this constrained risk, its benefit potential is additionally restricted. The commission can be a remarkable factor here, as there are four options included.

For this strategy, the merchant in a perfect world might want the majority of the options to terminate uselessly, which is just conceivable if the basic asset closes between the center two strike costs at expiration. There will probably be an expense to close the exchange in the event that it is effective. On the off chance that it isn't fruitful, the loss is as yet constrained.

NOTE: One approach to think about an iron condor is having a long strangle within a bigger, short strangle (or the other way around)

The development of the strategy is as per the following:

Get one out of the money (OTM) put with a strike cost beneath the present cost of the hidden asset. The out of the money put option will ensure against a critical drawback move to the hidden asset.

Sell one OTM or at the money (ATM) put with a strike value nearer to the present cost of the fundamental asset.

Sell one OTM or ATM call with a strike cost over the present cost of the basic asset.

Get one OTM call with a strike cost further over the present cost of the hidden asset. The out of the money call option will secure against a considerable upside move.

The options that are farther of the money, called the wings, are both long positions. Since both of these options are farther of the money, their premiums are lower than the two composed options, so there is a net credit to the record when putting the exchange.

By choosing diverse strike costs, it is conceivable to make the strategy lean bullish or bearish. For instance, if both the center strike costs are over the present cost of the fundamental asset, the broker trusts in a little ascent in its cost by expiration. Regardless it has constrained reward and restricted risk.

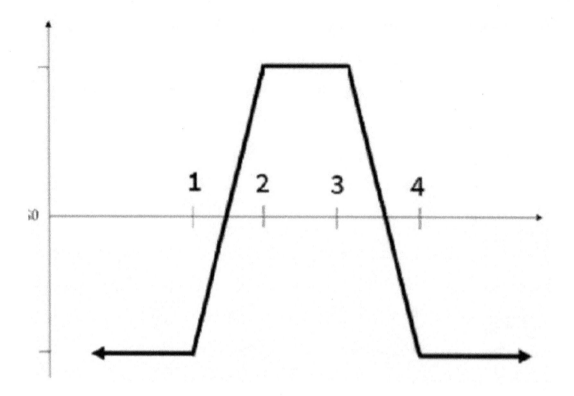

**Iron Condor Profits and Losses**

The most extreme benefit for an iron condor is the measure of premium, or credit, got for making the four-leg options position.

The most extreme loss is likewise topped. The greatest loss is the distinction between the long call and short call strikes, or the long put and short put strikes. Lessen the loss by the net credits got, however then add commissions to get the all out loss for the exchange.

The most extreme loss happens if the value moves over the long call strike (which is higher than the sold call strike) or underneath the long put strike (which is lower than the sold put strike).

example of an Iron Condor on a Stock

Accept that an investor trusts Apple Inc. (AAPL) will be generally level as far as cost throughout the following two months. They choose to actualize an iron condor. The stock is right now trading at $212.26. They sell a call with a $215 strike, which gives them $7.63 in premium. They purchase a call with a strike of $220, which costs them $5.35. The credit on these two legs is $2.28, or $228 for one contract (100 offers). The exchange is just half complete, however.

Also, the merchant sells a put with a strike of $210, bringing about a premium got of $7.20. They likewise purchase a put with a strike of $205, costing $5.52. The net credit on these two legs is $1.68 or $168 if trading one contract on each.

The complete credit for the position is $3.96 ($2.28 + $1.68), or $396. This is the most extreme benefit the broker can make. This most extreme benefit happens if every one of the options lapse useless, which means the cost must be somewhere in the range of $215 and $210 when expiration happens in two months. In the event that the cost is above $215 or beneath $210, the broker could at present make a decreased benefit, however, could likewise lose money.

The loss gets bigger if the cost of Apple stock methodologies the upper call strike ($220) or the lower put strike ($205). The most extreme loss happens if the cost of the stock exchanges above $220 or beneath $205.

Accept the stock at expiration is $225. This is over the upper call strike value, which means the broker is confronting the most extreme conceivable loss. The sold call is losing $10 ($225 - $215) while the purchased call is making $5 ($225 - $220). The puts terminate. The dealer loses $5, or $500 all out (100 offer contracts), yet they likewise got $396 in premiums. Along these lines, the loss is topped at $104 in addition to commissions.

Presently expect the cost of Apple rather dropped, however not beneath the lower put edge. It tumbles to $208. The short call is losing $2 ($208 - $210), or $200, while the long put terminates useless. The calls likewise lapse. The merchant loses $200 on the position yet got $396 in premium credits, accordingly, despite everything they make $196, less commission costs.

## Butterfly Spread

A butterfly spread is an options strategy joining bull and bear spreads, with a fixed risk and topped benefit. These spreads, including either four calls or four puts, are expected as a market-unbiased strategy and pay off the most if the fundamental doesn't move preceding option expiration.

There are different butterfly spreads, all utilizing four options.

All butterfly spreads utilize three diverse strike costs.

The upper and lower strike costs are equivalent good ways from the center, or at-the-money, strike cost.

Each kind of butterfly has a most extreme benefit and a greatest loss.

## Getting Butterflies

Butterfly spreads utilize four option contracts with a similar expiration yet three diverse strike costs: a higher strike value, an at-the-money strike cost, and a lower strike cost. The options with the higher and lower strike costs are a similar good ways from the at-the-money options. In the event that the at-the-money options have a strike cost of $60, the upper and lower options ought to have strike costs equivalent dollar sums above and underneath $60. At $55 and $65, for instance, as these strikes are both $5 away from $60.

Puts or calls can be utilized for a butterfly spread. Consolidating the options in different ways will make various sorts of butterfly spreads, each intended to either benefit from volatility or low volatility.

Long Call Butterfly

The long butterfly call spread is made by buying one in-the-money call option with a low strike value, writing two at-the-money call options, and buying one out-of-the-money call option with a higher strike cost. Net obligation is made when entering the exchange.

The most extreme benefit is accomplished if the cost of the fundamental at expiration is equivalent to the composed calls. The maximum benefit is equivalent to the strike of the composed option, less the strike of the lower call, premiums, and commissions paid. The most extreme loss is the underlying expense of the premiums paid, in addition to commissions.

**Short Call Butterfly**

The short butterfly spread is made by selling one in-the-money call option with a lower strike value, buying two at-the-money call options, and selling an out-of-the-money call option at a higher strike cost. A net credit is made when entering the position. This position expands its benefit if the cost of the hidden is above or the upper strike or underneath the lower strike at expiry.

The greatest benefit is equivalent to the underlying premium got, less the cost of commissions. The greatest loss is the strike cost of the purchased call short the lower strike cost, less the premiums got.

## Long Put Butterfly

The long put butterfly spread is made by buying one put with a lower strike value, selling two at-the-money puts, and buying a put with a higher strike cost. Net obligation is made when entering the position. Like the long call butterfly, this position has a greatest benefit when the hidden remains at the strike cost of the center options.

The most extreme benefit is equivalent to the higher strike value less the strike of the sold put, less the premium paid. The most extreme loss of the exchange is constrained to the underlying premiums and commissions paid.

## Short Put Butterfly

The short put butterfly spread is made by writing one out-of-the-money put option with a low strike value, buying two at-the-money puts, and writing an in-the-money put option at a higher strike cost. This strategy understands its most extreme benefit if the cost of the hidden is over the upper strike or underneath the lower strike cost at expiration.

The greatest benefit for the strategy is the premiums gotten. The most extreme loss is the higher strike value less the strike of the purchased put, less the premiums got.

## Iron Butterfly

The iron butterfly spread is made by buying an out-of-the-money put option with a lower strike value, writing an at-the-money put option, writing an at-the-money call option, and buying an out-of-the-money call option with a higher strike cost. The outcome is an exchange with a net credit that is most appropriate for lower volatility situations. The most extreme benefit happens if the fundamental remains at the center strike cost.

The most extreme benefit is the premiums gotten. The most extreme loss is the strike cost of the purchased call less the strike cost of the composed call, less the premiums got.

## Invert Iron Butterfly

The invert iron butterfly spread is made by writing an out-of-the-money put at a lower strike value, buying an at-the-money put, buying an at-the-money call, and writing an out-of-the-money call at a higher strike cost. This makes a net charge exchange that is most appropriate for high-volatility situations. Most extreme benefit happens when the cost of the fundamental moves above or beneath the upper or lower strike costs.

The strategy's risk is constrained to the premium paid to accomplish the position. The most extreme benefit is the strike cost of the composed call less the strike of the purchased call, less the premiums paid.

Example of a Long Call Butterfly

An investor accepts that Verizon stock, at present trading at $60 won't move fundamentally throughout the following a while. They actualize a long call butterfly spread to possibly benefit if the value stays where it is.

An investor composes two call options on Verizon at a strike cost of $60 and furthermore purchases two extra calls at $55 and $65.

In this situation, an investor would make the most extreme benefit if Verizon stock is evaluated at $60 at expiration. On the off chance that Verizon is beneath $55 at expiration, or above $65, the investor would understand their greatest loss, which would be the expense of buying the two wing call options (the higher and lower strike) diminished by the returns of selling the two center strike options.

On the off chance that the fundamental asset is estimated somewhere in the range of $55 and $65, a loss or benefit may happen. The measure of premium paid to enter the position is vital. Expect that it costs $2.50 to enter the position. In light of that, if Verizon is evaluated anyplace beneath $60 less $2.50, the position would encounter a loss. Similar remains constant if the fundamental asset were valued at $60 in addition to $2.50 at expiration. In this situation, the position would benefit if the fundamental asset is evaluated anyplace somewhere in the range of $57.50 and $62.50 at expiration.

This situation does exclude the expense of commissions, which can include when trading various options.

# CHAPTER 2

## IN THE MONEY (ITM)

ITM is a term that alludes to an option that has inherent value. ITM, in this manner, shows that an option has value in a strike value that is good in contrast with the predominant market cost of the fundamental asset:

An in the money call option implies the option holder has the chance to purchase the security beneath its present market cost.

An in the money put option implies the option holder can sell the security over its present market cost.

An option that is ITM doesn't really mean the dealer is making a benefit on the exchange. The cost of buying the option and any commission charges should likewise be considered. In the money, options might have appeared differently in relation to out of the money (OTM) options.

If the market cost is over the strike cost, then we can say a call option is in the money.

If the market cost is underneath the strike cost, then we can say a put option is in the money.

ITM options contracts tend to have higher premiums than different options that are not ITM.

# A Brief Overview

Investors who buy call options are bullish that the asset's cost will increment and close over the strike cost by the option's expiration date. Options are accessible to exchange for some money-related items, for example, bonds and products, at the same time, values are one of the most prominent for investors.

Options give the purchaser a chance—however not the commitment—of buying or selling the fundamental security at the agreement expressed strike cost, by the predefined expiration date. The strike cost is the exchange value or execution cost for the portions of the hidden security.

Options accompany a forthright charge cost—called the excellent—that investors pay to purchase the agreement. Different elements decide the exceptional's value. These variables incorporate the present market cost of the hidden security, time until the expiration date, and the value of the strike cost in relationship to the security's market cost. Typically, the top-notch demonstrates the value showcase members place on some random option. An option that has value will probably have a higher premium related with it versus one that has minimal possibility of profiting for an investor.

The two segments of options premium are natural and outward value. In the money, options have both characteristic and extraneous value, while out of the money options' premium contain just outward (time) value.

## NOTE: Explaining In The Money Call Options

Call options take into consideration the buying of the basic asset at a given cost before an expressed date. The exceptional becomes possibly the most important factor when deciding if an option is in the money or not, yet can be deciphered diversely relying upon the kind of option included. A call option is said to be in the money if the stock's present market cost is higher than the option's strike cost. The sum that an option is in the money is called the inborn value meaning the option is at any rate worth that sum.

For instance, a call option with a strike of $25 would be in the money if the fundamental stock was trading at $30 per share. What separates the strike and the present market cost is typically the measure of the premium for the option. Investors hoping to purchase a specific in the money call option will pay the premium or the spread between the strike and the market cost.

In any case, an investor holding a call option that is terminating in the money can practice it and gain the distinction between the strike cost and market cost. Regardless of whether the exchange was gainful or not relies upon the investors all out cost of buying the agreement and any commission to process that exchange.

It is critical to take note of that ITM doesn't mean the dealer is profiting. When buying an ITM option, the broker will require the option's value to move more distant into the money to make a benefit. As it were, investors buying call options need the stock cost to move sufficiently high with the goal that it, at any rate, takes care of the expense of the option's premium.

## Clarifying In The Money Put Options

While call options permit the acquisition of an asset, a put option achieves the contrary activity. Investors purchase these options contracts that enable them to sell the basic security at the strike cost when they anticipate that the value of the security should diminish. Put option purchasers are bearish on the development of the hidden security.

An in the money put option implies that the strike cost is over the market cost of the overarching business sector value. Holding an ITM put option at expiry for an investor implies the stock cost is beneath the strike cost and it's conceivable the option merits working out. A put option purchaser is trusting the stock's cost will fall far enough underneath the option's strike to in any event spread the expense of the premium for buying the put.

The closer the expiration date, the value of the put option will fall in a procedure known as time rot.

## Pros

Been in-the-money (ITM) at expiry for a call option holder gets an opportunity to make a benefit if the market cost is over the strike cost. An investor holding an in-the-money put option gets an opportunity to gain a benefit if the market cost is beneath the strike cost.

## Cons

In-the-money options are more costly than different options since investors pay for the benefit previously connected with the agreement.

Investors should likewise consider premium and commission costs to decide benefit from an in the money option.

## Different Considerations

At the point when the strike cost and market cost of the hidden security are equivalent, the option is called at the money (ATM). Options can likewise be out of the money, which means the strike cost isn't great to the market cost. Every OTM call option tends to have a higher strike cost than the market cost of the stock.

On the other hand, an OTM put option would have a lower strike cost than the market cost. An OTM option implies that the option still can't seem to profit on the grounds that the stock's rise hasn't moved enough to make the option productive. Accordingly, OTM options, for the most part, have lower premiums than ITM options.

In short, the measure of premium paid for an option depends on a huge piece of the degree an option is ITM, ATM, or OTM. Be that as it may, numerous different variables can influence the premium of an option, including how much the stock vacillates, called volatility, and the time until the expiration.

## Genuine Example of ITM Options

Let's say an investor operates a call option on Bank of America (BAC) stock with a strike cost of $30. The offers right now exchange at $33, making the agreement in the money. The call option enables the investor to purchase the stock for $30, and they could promptly sell the stock for $33, giving them a $3 per share contrast. Every option contract speaks to 100 offers, so the inherent value is $3 x 100 = $300.

On the off chance that the investor paid a premium of $3.50 for the call, they would not benefit from the exchange. He would have paid $350 ($3.50 x 100 = $350) while just picking up $300 on the contrast between the strike cost and market cost. As it were, he'd lose $50 on the exchange. Be that as it may, the option is as yet considered ITM in light of the fact that, at expiry, the option will have a value of $3 despite the fact that John's not winning a benefit.

Additionally, if the stock value tumbled from $33 to $29, the $30 strike value call is no longer ITM. It would be $1 OTM. It's essential to take note while the strike cost is fixed, the cost of the hidden asset will vacillate influencing the degree to which the option is in the money. An ITM option can move to ATM or even OTM before its expiration date.

# CHAPTER 3

## OUT OF THE MONEY (OTM)

This(OTM) is a term used to depict an option contract that just contains inborn value. These options will have a delta under 50.0.

Every OTM call option always has a strike value that is higher than the market cost of the hidden asset. On the other hand, an OTM put option has a strike value that is lower than the market cost of the hidden asset.

OTM options might be stood out from in the money (ITM) options.

Out of the money implies an option has no natural value, just extraneous value.

A call option is OTM if the hidden's cost is underneath the strike cost.

A put option is OTM if the hidden's cost is over the strike cost.

An option can likewise be in the money or at the money.

OTM options are more affordable than ITM or ATM options. This is on the grounds that ITM options have inborn value, and ATM options are near having inherent value.

### Option Basics

For a top-notch, stock options give the buyer the right, however not the commitment, to purchase or sell the hidden stock at a settled upon cost, known as the strike cost, before a settled upon date, known as the expiration date.

An option to purchase a basic asset is a call option, while an option to sell a hidden asset is a put option. A merchant may buy a call option in the event that they expect the basic asset's cost to surpass the strike cost before the expiration date. Alternately, a put option empowers the broker to benefit on a decrease in the asset's cost. Since they get their value from that of fundamental security, options are derivatives. An option can be OTM, ITM, or at the money (ATM). An ATM option is one where the strike cost and cost of the hidden are equivalent.

## Out of the Money Options

By figuring out where the present cost of the hidden is in connection to the strike cost of that option, you can tell if an option is out of the money. For a call option, if the fundamental cost is beneath the strike value, that option is OTM. For a put option, in the event that the hidden's cost is over the strike value, at that point that option is OTM. OTM option has no natural value, yet just has outward or time value. However, because it's out of the money doesn't mean a merchant can't make a benefit on that option. Every option has an expense, called the premium. A broker could have purchased an out of sight the money option, yet since the option is drawing nearer to being in the money (ITM). That option could wind up being worth more than the merchant paid for the option, despite the fact that it is right now out of the money. At expiry, however, an option is useless in the event that it is OTM. In this manner, if an option is OTM, the dealer should sell it preceding expiry so as to recover any extraneous value that is perhaps remaining.

Using a stock that is trading at $10, for example. If that stock, call options with strike costs above $10 would be OTM calls, while put options with strike costs underneath $10 would be OTM puts.

NOTE: TM options are not worth working out, on the grounds that the present market is offering an exchange level more engaging than the option's strike cost.

## Out of the Money Options Example

A merchant needs to purchase a call option on Vodafone stock. They pick a call option with a $20 strike cost. The option terminates in five months and expenses $0.50. This gives them the privilege to purchase 100 portions of the stock before the option terminates. The all-out expense of the option is $50 (100 offers * $0.50), in addition to an exchange commission. The stock is at present trading at $18.50.

After buying the option, there is no motivation to practice it in light of the fact that by practicing the option they need to pay $20 for the stock when they can as of now get it at a market cost of $18.50.

This option is OTM, yet that doesn't mean it is useless yet. The dealer simply paid $0.50 for the potential that the stock will acknowledge above $20 inside the following five months.

On the off chance that the option is OTM at expiry it is useless, however preceding expiry, that option will, in any case, have some extraneous value which is reflected in the premium or cost of the option. The cost of the hidden may never reach $20; however, the premium of the option may increment to $0.75 or $1 in the event that it draws near. Along these lines, the broker could even now harvest a benefit on the out of the month option itself by selling it at a higher premium than they paid for it. However, if the stock value moves to $22 — the option is presently ITM — it merits practicing the option. The option gives them the privilege to purchase at $20, and the present market cost is $22. The contrast between the strike cost and the present market cost is known as a natural value, which is $2.

For this situation, our merchant winds up with a net benefit or advantage. The option they paid $0.50 for is currently worth $2. They net $1.50 in benefit or preferred position.

Yet, imagine a scenario where the stock possibly encouraged to $20.25 when the option terminated. For this situation, the option is still ITM, yet the merchant really lost money. They paid $0.50 for the option; however, the option just has $0.25 of value currently, bringing about lost $0.25 ($0.50 - $0.25).

## Implied volatility

Implied volatility is a metric that catches the market's perspective on the probability of changes in a given security's cost. Investors can utilize it to extend future moves and market interest and frequently use it to value options contracts.

Implied volatility isn't equivalent to verifiable volatility, otherwise called acknowledged volatility or factual volatility. The valid volatility figure will quantify past market changes and their real outcomes.

Implied volatility is the market's estimate of cognitive development in a security's cost.

Implied volatility is regularly used to value options contracts: High implied volatility brings about options with higher premiums and the other way around.

Supply/request and time value are major deciding variables for figuring implied volatility.

Implied volatility increments in bearish markets and diminishes when the market is bullish.

Comprehension Implied Volatility

Implied volatility is the market's estimate of cognitive development in a security's cost. It is a measurement utilized by investors to assess future changes (volatility) of a security's cost dependent on certain prescient components. Implied volatility, indicated by the image σ (sigma), can frequently be believed to be an intermediary of market risk. It is usually communicated utilizing rates and standard deviations over a predefined time skyline.

At the point when applied to the stock market, implied volatility for the most part increments in bearish markets, when investors accept value costs will decay after some time. IV diminishes when the market is bullish, and investors agree that costs will ascend after some time. Bearish markets are viewed as unfortunate, consequently riskier, to most of the value investors.

Implied volatility doesn't anticipate the heading where the value change will continue. For instance, high volatility implies an enormous value swing, yet the cost could swing upward — extremely high — descending — exceptionally low — or vary between the two headings. Low volatility implies that the value likely won't make vast, erratic changes.

## Implied Volatility and Options

Implied volatility is one of the integral factors in the evaluating of options. Buying options contracts let the holder purchase or sell an asset at a particular cost during a pre-decided period. It approximates the future value of the option, and the option's present value is additionally contemplated. Options that posses high implied volatility will have higher premiums and the other way around.

It is imperative to recollect that implied volatility depends on likelihood. It is just a gauge of future costs as opposed to a sign of them. Although investors consider implied volatility when settling on venture options, and this reliance unavoidably has some effect on the costs themselves.

There is no certification that an option's cost will pursue the anticipated example. However, when thinking about speculation, it helps to consider the moves different investors are making with the option, and implied volatility is legitimately associated with the market conclusion, which thus influence option evaluating.

Implied volatility likewise influences the evaluating of non-option budgetary instruments, for example, a loan cost top, which confines the sum a financing cost on an item can be raised.

## Option Pricing Models and IV

Implied volatility can be controlled by utilizing an option evaluating model. It is the main factor in the model that isn't straightforwardly discernible in the market. Rather, the scientific option valuing model uses different components to decide implied volatility and the option's premium.

The Black-Scholes Model, a broadly utilized and surely understood options estimating model, factors in current stock value, options strike value, time until expiration (signified as a percent of a year), and sans risk financing costs. The Black-Scholes Model is brisk in figuring any number of option costs. In any case, it can't precisely ascertain American options, since it just considers the cost at an option's expiration date. American options are those that the proprietor may practice whenever up to and including the expiration day.

The Binomial Model utilizes a tree outline with volatility calculated in at each level, to demonstrate every conceivable way an option's cost can take, at that point works in reverse to decide one cost. The best part of this model is the fact that you can return to it anytime for the plausibility of early work out. Early trade is executing the agreement's activities at its strike cost before the agreement's expiration. Early practice occurs in American style options. In any case, the computations engaged with this model set aside a long effort to decide, so this model isn't the best in hurried circumstances.

## Components Affecting Implied Volatility

Similarly, likewise, with the market in general, implied volatility is dependent upon eccentric changes. Market interest are major deciding elements for implied volatility. At the point when an asset is in extreme interest, the value will increase generally. So does the implied volatility, which prompts a higher option premium because of the risky idea of the option.

The inverse is likewise valid. At the point when there is a lot of inventory yet insufficient market request, the implied volatility falls, and the option cost ends up less expensive.

Another premium impacting element is the time value of the option, or the measure of time until the option lapses. A short-dated option regularly brings about low implied volatility, though a long-dated option will, in general, bring about high implied volatility. The distinction lays in the measure of time left before the expiration of the agreement. Since there is a lengthier time, the cost has an all-encompassing period to move into a high-value level in contrast with the strike cost.

## Advantages and disadvantages of Using Implied Volatility

Implied volatility evaluates showcase notion. It assesses the size of the development an asset may take. Be that as it may, as referenced prior, it doesn't demonstrate the heading of the development. Option scholars will utilize figurings, including implied volatility to value options contracts. Likewise, numerous investors will take a gander at the IV when they pick speculation. During times of high volatility, they may put resources into more secure areas or items.

Implied volatility doesn't have a premise on the essentials fundamental the market assets, yet depends exclusively on cost. Additionally, unfriendly news or occasions, for example, wars or cataclysmic events may affect the implied volatility.

**Pros**

Evaluates advertise opinion, vulnerability

Help set options costs

Decides trading strategy

**Cons**

In light of on costs, not basics

Touchy to unforeseen variables, news occasions

Predicts development, yet not the course

Genuine Example

Brokers and investors use outlining to break down implied volatility. One particularly prominent instrument is the Chicago Board Options Exchange (CBOE) Volatility Index (VIX). (CBOE), the VIX is a continuous market file. The file uses value information from close dated, close the-money S&P 500 record options to extend desires for volatility throughout the following 30 days.

Investors can utilize the VIX to contrast various protections, or with check the stock market's volatility overall, and structure trading methodologies as needs be.

## How Options Work

As far as esteeming option contracts, it is basically about deciding the probabilities of future value occasions. For example, a call value goes up as the stock (fundamental) goes up. This is the way to understanding the overall value of options.

The less time there is until expiry, the less value an option will have. This is on the grounds that the odds of value move in the fundamental stock decrease as we move nearer to expiry. This is the reason an option is a squandering asset. If you purchase a one-month option that is out of the money, and the stock doesn't move, the option turns out to be less significant as time passes. Since time is a part to the cost of an option, a one-month option will be less significant than a three-month option. This is on the grounds that with additional time accessible, the likelihood of a cost move to support your increments, and the other way around.

In like manner, a similar option strike that lapses in a year will cost more than a similar strike for one month. This squandering highlight of options is a consequence of time rot. A similar option will be worthless tomorrow than it is today if the cost of the stock doesn't move.

Volatility additionally builds the cost of an option. This is because vulnerability pushes the chances of a result higher. In the event that the volatility of the basic asset increments, bigger cost swings increment the conceivable outcomes of generous moves both here and there. More prominent cost swings will expand the odds of an occasion happening. Along these lines, the more prominent the volatility, the more noteworthy the cost of the option. Options trading and volatility are intrinsically connected to one another along these lines.

Generally, U.S. exchange stock option contract is the option to purchase or sell 100 shares; that is the reason you should increase the agreement premium by 100 to get the aggregate sum you'll need to spend to purchase the call.

What happen to our option investment

September 1 September 21 Expiry Date

Stock Price $67 $78 $62

Option Price $3.15 $8.25 worthless

Contract Value $315 $825 $0

Paper Gain/Loss $0 $510 -$315

Most of the time, holders take their benefits by trading out (finishing off) their position. This implies option holders sell their options in the market, and journalists repurchase their situations to close. As indicated by the CBOE, just about 10% of options are worked out, 60% are exchanged (shut) out, and 30% terminate uselessly.

Fluctuations in option costs can be clarified by inherent value and outward value, which is otherwise called time value. An option's premium is the blend of its natural value and time value. Natural value is the in-the-money measure of an options contract, which, for a call option, is the sum over the strike value that the stock is trading. Time value speaks to the additional value an investor needs to pay for an option over the intrinsic value. This is the extraneous value or time value. Along these lines, the cost of the option in our model can be thought of as the accompanying:

Premium = Intrinsic Value + Time Value

$8.25 $8.00 $0.25

In actuality, options quite often exchange at some level over their inherent value, because the likelihood of an occurrence happening is rare or total zero, regardless of whether it is exceptionally improbable.

**Options Expiration & Liquidity**

Options can also be classified by their span. Short-term options are those that terminate for the most part inside a year. Long-term options with expirations more prominent than a year are named long-term value expectation protections or LEAPs. LEAPS are indistinguishable from customary options; they simply have longer spans.

Options can likewise be recognized by when their expiration date falls. Sets of options presently terminate week after week on every Friday, toward the part of the bargain, or even once a day. Record and ETF options likewise, in some cases, offer quarterly expiries.

## Options Tables

An ever-increasing number of merchants are discovering option information through online sources. While each source has its very own arrangement for showing the information, the key segments, by and large, incorporate the accompanying factors:

Volume (VLM) basically discloses to you what number of contracts of a specific option were exchanged during the most recent session.

The "offer" cost is the most recent value level at which a market member wishes to purchase a specific option.

The "ask" cost is the most recent cost offered by a market member to sell a specific option.

Implied Bid Volatility (IMPL BID VOL) can be thought of as the future vulnerability of value heading and speed. This value is determined by an option-evaluating model, for example, the Black-Scholes model and speaks to the degree of expected future volatility dependent on the present cost of the option.

Open Interest (OPTN OP) number shows the complete number of contracts of a specific option that have been opened. Open intrigue diminishes as open exchanges are shut.

Delta can be, For example, a 30-delta option has around a 30% possibility of terminating in-the-money.

Gamma (GMM) is the speed the option is moving in or out-of-the-money. Gamma can likewise be thought of as the development of the delta.

Vega is a Greek value that demonstrates the sum by which the cost of the option would be required to change dependent on a one-point change in implied volatility.

Theta is the Greek value that demonstrates how much value an option will lose with the section of one day's time.

The "strike cost" is the cost at which the purchaser of the option can purchase or sell the fundamental security on the off chance that he/she practices the option.

## Motivations to Trade Options

Investors and brokers embrace option trading either to support open situations (for instance, buying puts to fence a long position, or buying calls to support a short position) or to hypothesize on likely value developments of a basic asset.

## Speculation

Speculation is a bet on future value bearing. An examiner may think the cost of a stock will go up, maybe dependent on central examination or specialized investigation. An examiner may purchase the stock or purchase a call option on the stock. Guessing with a call option—rather than buying the stock by and large—is alluring to certain merchants since options give influence. An out-of-the-money call option may just cost a couple of dollars or even pennies contrasted with the maximum of a $100 stock.

The greatest advantage of utilizing options is that of influence. For instance, say an investor has $900 to use on a specific exchange and wants the most value for-the-money. The investor is bullish in the short term on XYZ Inc. In this way, expect XYZ is trading at $90. Our investor can purchase a limit of 10 portions of XYZ. Be that as it may, XYZ likewise has three-month calls accessible with a strike cost of $95 for an expense $3. Presently, rather than buying the offers, the investor purchases three call option contracts. Buying three call options will cost $900 (3 contracts x 100 offers x $3).

Shortly before the call options lapse, assume XYZ is trading at $103, and the calls are trading at $8, so, all in all, the investor sells the calls. Here's how the arrival on venture piles up for each situation.

Through and through acquisition of XYZ shares at $90: Profit = $13 per share x 10 offers = $130 = 14.4% return ($130/$900).

Acquisition of three $95 call option contracts: Profit = $8 x 100 x 3 contracts = $2,400 short premium paid of $900 = $1500 = 166.7% return ($1,500/$900).

Obviously, the risk with buying the calls as opposed to the offers is that if XYZ had not exchanged above $95 by option expiration, the calls would have lapsed useless and all $900 would be lost. Truth be told, XYZ needed to exchange at $98 ($95 strike cost + $3 premium paid), or about 9% higher from its cost when the calls were acquired, for the exchange just to breakeven. At the point when the intermediary's expense to put the exchange is likewise added to the condition, to be beneficial, the stock would need to exchange much higher.

These situations accept that the broker held till expiration. That isn't required with American options. Whenever before expiry, the merchant could have offered the option to secure a benefit. Or if it looked like the stock was not going to move over the strike value, they could sell the option for its residual time value to diminish the misfortune. For instance, the merchant paid $3 for the options, yet over the long haul, if the stock value stays beneath the strike value, those options may drop to $1. The merchant could sell the three contracts for $1, getting $300 of the first $900 back and staying away from a complete misfortune.

The investor could likewise practice the call options as opposed to offering them to book

Benefits/losses, however, practicing the calls would require the investor to think of a significant whole of money to purchase the number of shares their contracts speak to. For the situation over, that would require buying 300 offers at $95.

## Hedging

Options were truly imagined for hedging purposes. Hedging with options is intended to lessen risk at a sensible expense. Here, we can consider utilizing options like a protection strategy. Similarly, as you protect your home or vehicle, options can be utilized to safeguard your ventures against a downturn.

Envision that you need to purchase innovation stocks. Be that as it may, you additionally need to confine misfortunes. By utilizing put options, you could restrict your drawback risk and appreciate all the upside in a savvy way. For short dealers, call options can be utilized to constrain misfortunes assuming incorrectly particularly during a short crush.

Adaptability with novel methodologies. There's a wide assortment of option systems that can be performed on numerous kinds of fundamental protections, similar to stocks, Indexes, and ETFs. So whether your standpoint is bullish, bearish, or unbiased, a strategy can work to support you if your estimate is right.

Reasons why options might be proper devices for an investor to think about utilizing, which can be abridged as:

• Portfolio and market risk mitigation

- Salary age

- Stock substitution

- Saddle influence

- Take an interest in the market with restricted risk.

- Modify techniques with objective results

## Risk mitigation

Risk mitigation is a key thought in an investor's portfolio. By obtaining a put option, an investor can shield his fundamental value holding from unfriendly value developments. The expense of this is the option premium paid by the purchaser of the option. Remember that options have an expiration date, so the investor may need to move her option position forward, or on the other hand, buy another put when the past one has lapsed.

The expense of the option can be balanced by buying pretty much value assurance. An at-the-money option (that is with exercise/strike cost at the market cost of the fundamental value) will typically be more costly than an out-of-the-money option (that is, with an activity cost underneath that of the market cost of the basic asset).

## Protective Put

Buy 100 shares XYZ at $42.00

Buy 1 60-day XYZ 40 put at $1.55

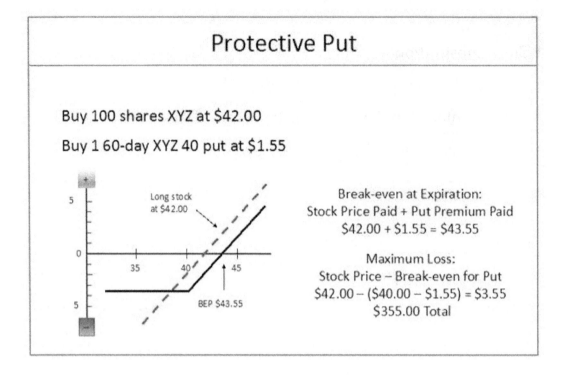

Long stock at $42.00

35    40    45

BEP $43.55

Break-even at Expiration:
Stock Price Paid + Put Premium Paid
$42.00 + $1.55 = $43.55

Maximum Loss:
Stock Price – Break-even for Put
$42.00 – ($40.00 – $1.55) = $3.55
$355.00 Total

## Income generation

Options can assist the investor with increasing his income from his stock or trade exchanged store (ETF) portfolio. There are two different ways to approach this: the secured call and the purchase compose.

For the secured call, the investor is as of now holding stock and accepts that its cost will stay enduring, or rise somewhat. The person in question composes a call against the stock he is holding. The strike cost of the call sold directs the farthest point to which he will profit on the upside.

In the model demonstrated as follows, the investor has sold a 55 call. On the off chance that the hidden value ascends past 55, at that point, the option he has sold can be practiced by the counterparty, and the basic stock obtained. The call vender has still gotten the premium for writing the option.

If the fundamental value remains beneath 55, at that point, the stockholder will get the premium and furthermore proceed to possess the hidden stock. On the off chance that the value falls, at that point, the call option sold won't be traded, and the premium got will balance, either entirely or halfway, the fall in the stock's cost.

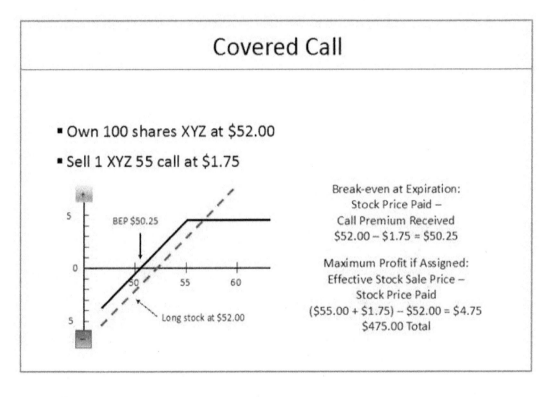

The purchase compose is like the covered call; however, the acquisition of the stock or ETF and the closeout of the call option are done simultaneously. The investor for this situation is seeking after the call offered to be worked out, in this manner, verifying the highest profit for the strategy, and after that to rehash the activity with another stock.

## Stock substitution

Buying stock altogether includes paying for it. Utilizing a call option rather enables the investor to take an interest in the market at a much lower cost in the short term, just as the long term with LEAPS.

Keep in mind, in any case, that an option has a constrained life expectancy and after that lapses. Keep in mind likewise that stockholders on the record before the ex-profit date are qualified for other income, for example, the profits, call option purchasers are most certainly not.

Not every single basic stock or ETFs have an option accessible on them, in which case a few investors may try to coordinate a fundamental stock with an option on a comparative stock, which they accept to offer a sensible fit.

## Harness leverage

Call option purchasers don't get profits or other money disseminations, in contrast to stockholders. In any case, they do pick up the advantage of leverage if their option sees on the market is right.

If an investor purchases a call option and the fundamental value ascends past the activity cost (or on account of a put option buyer, falls underneath the activity value), at that point, she will profit by leverage.

# Leverage: Call Buying Example

## Buy 60 strike call at $3.00

compared with

## Buy 100 shares at $60.00

| Stock Price at Expiration | Long 60 Call Net Profit/(Loss) | Long Call % Profit/(Loss) | Long Stock Profit/(Loss) Per Share | Long Stock % Profit/(Loss) |
|---|---|---|---|---|
| $70.00 | $7.00 | 233% | $10.00 | 17% |
| $65.00 | $2.00 | 67% | $5.00 | 8% |
| $60.00 | ($3.00) | (100%) | 0 | 0 |
| $55.00 | ($3.00) | (100%) | ($5.00) | (8%) |
| $50.00 | ($3.00) | (100%) | ($10.00) | (17%) |

The table above depletes various results for a stockholder and a call purchaser. If the hidden value climbs in value, at that point, the call purchaser gets a higher rate return on the money she has invested in buying the call than if she had purchased the stock or ETF outright.

The only setback for the investor is if the foreseen up-ward movement doesn't occur, her investment will be decreased, conceivably to zero. The basic stock or ETF holder appreciates a lower rate return at an ascent in the cost of the hidden value; however, she additionally encounters a lower loss as communicated as a level of her unique investment if the fundamental descends.

Additionally, holding a stock or ETF doesn't have a period breaking point, and profits for stockholders on record preceding the ex-profit date will at present be gotten paying little mind to the cost if the primary pay a profit.

Invest with restricted risk

Buying calls or puts enables investors to situate themselves for a foreseen market move by paying the option's premium to the option's dealer. The most that they can lose is the premium, which could, in any case, be all their investment reserves.

The experience of option purchasers stands out from the case for the dealers of calls and puts. Once more, option venders will have their own directional view on the market. On account of the put dealer, she will trust that costs will rise so she can keep the premium at expiration and maybe offer another put to create more income or purchase the hidden on account of a practiced put.

On account of the call merchant, he will trust that the costs will stay level underneath the call strike cost. If the market doesn't move as envisioned, at that point the option will be practiced, and the call merchant will be obliged to sell the basic on account of a practiced call. This will include a money cost that might be significant, just somewhat balanced by the premium got.

# CHAPTER 4

## THE BASICS OF OPTION TRADING PRICES

Options are contracts that give option purchasers the privilege to purchase or sell a security at a foreordained cost at the latest a predefined day. The cost of an option, called the premium, is made out of various factors. Options merchants should know about these factors so they can settle on an educated option about when to exchange an option.

When acquiring an options contract, the most excellent driver of results is the main stock's value development. A call purchaser needs the stock to rise, while a put purchaser needs it to fall. However, there's another dimension to the cost of an option than that! How about we dive further into why an option costs, what it does, and why the value of the option changes.

Options costs, known as premiums, are made out of the entirety of its intrinsic and extrinsic value.

Intrinsic value is the measure of money gotten promptly if an option were traded and the hidden discarded at market costs, it is determined as the current basic cost less the strike cost.

The extrinsic value of an option is what surpasses the option's premium over its intrinsic value - it is made out of a probabilistic component impacted primarily during volatility and expiration.

In-the-money options posses both the intrinsic and extrinsic value components, while out-of-the-money options just have extrinsic value.

## Intrinsic Value

The option's premium is comprised of two sections: intrinsic value and extrinsic value (once in a while known as the option's time value). Intrinsic value is the amount of the premium that comprised of the value contrast between the present stock cost and the strike cost. For example, accept you possess a call option on a stock that is at current trading at $49 per share. The strike cost of the option is $45, and the option premium is $5. Since the stock is presently $4 more than the strike's value, at that point $4 of the $5 premium is involved intrinsic value, which implies that the rest of the dollar must be comprised of extrinsic value.

We can likewise make sense of the amount we need the stock to move so as to benefit by including the cost of the premium to the strike cost: $5 + $45 = $50. Our make back the initial investment point is $50, which means the stock must move above $50 before we can benefit.

Options with intrinsic value are called in the money (ITM), and options with just extrinsic value are called out of the money (OTM).

Options with progressively extrinsic value are less delicate to the stock's value development while options with a ton of intrinsic value are more in a state of harmony with the stock cost. An option's affectability to the basic stock's development is called delta.

1.0 of delta tells investors that the option might probably upset dollar for dollar with the stock, though a delta of 0.6 methods the option will move roughly 60 pennies for each dollar the stock moves.

The delta for puts is spoken to as a negative number, which exhibits the opposite relationship of the put contrasted with the stock development. A put with a delta of - 0.4 should bring 40 pennies up in value if the stock drops $1.

## Extrinsic Value

Extrinsic value is frequently alluded to as time value; however, that is just incompletely right. It is additionally made out of implied volatility that changes as interest for options vacillates. There are likewise impacts from loan fees and stock profits.

Time value is the bit of the premium over the intrinsic value that an option purchaser pays for the benefit of owning the agreement for a specific period. After some time, the time value gets littler as the option expiration date draws nearer — the farther the expiry date, the additional time premium an option purchaser will pay for. The closer to expiration an agreement turns into, the quicker the time value liquefies.

Time value is estimated by the Greek letter theta. Option purchasers need to have exceptionally proficient market timing since theta consumes the premium. A typical mix-up option investors make is enabling a gainful exchange to sit long enough that theta diminishes the benefits significantly.

For instance, a broker may purchase an option at $1, and see it increment to $5. Of the $5 premium, just $4 is intrinsic value. If the stock cost doesn't move any further, the premium of the option will gradually corrupt to $4 at expiry. An unmistakable leave strategy ought to be set before buying an option.

Implied volatility, otherwise called vega, can expand the option premium if brokers anticipate volatility. High volatility expands the opportunity of a stock moving past the strike cost, so option dealers will request a more expensive rate for the options they are selling.

This is the reason surely understood occasions like income are frequently less productive for option purchasers than initially envisioned. While a significant move in the stock may happen, option costs usually are very high before such occasions which balances the potential increases.

On the other side, when a stock is quiet, option costs will in general fall, making them moderately modest to purchase. Albeit, except if volatility extends once more, the option will remain decent, practically ruling out benefit.

# CHAPTER 5

## CHOOSING THE RIGHT OPTION

Here are some expansive rules that should enable you to choose which sorts of options to exchange.

Bullish or bearish

Is it true that you are bullish or bearish on the stock, segment, or the broad market that you wish to exchange? Provided that this is true, would you say you are wildly, modestly, or only a touch bullish/bearish? Making this assurance will enable you to choose which option strategy to utilize, what strike cost to utilize, and what expiration to go for. Suppose you are wildly bullish on theoretical stock ZYX, an innovation stock that is trading at $46.

**Volatility**

Is the market quiet or very unstable? What about Stock ZYX? If the implied volatility for ZYX isn't high (say 20%), at that point it might be a smart thought to purchase calls on the stock since such calls could be moderately modest.

**Strike Price and Expiration**

As you are wildly bullish on ZYX, you ought to be alright with buying out of the money calls. Expect you would prefer not to spend more than $0.50 per call option and have a decision of going for two-month calls with a strike cost of $49 accessible for $0.50, or three-month calls with a strike cost of $50 available for $0.47. You choose to go with the last since you accept the somewhat higher strike cost is more than counterbalanced by the additional month to expiration.

Imagine a scenario in which you were just marginally bullish on ZYX, and its implied volatility of 45% was multiple times that of the general market. For this situation, you could consider writing close term puts to catch premium income, as opposed to buying calls as in the prior occasion.

# CHAPTER 6

## THE BASICS OF OPTIONS TRADING PROFITABILITY

Options dealers can benefit by being an option purchaser or an option author. Options take into account potential benefit during both unstable occasions, and when the market is calm or less erratic. This is conceivable because the costs of assets like stocks, currencies, and wares are continually moving, and regardless of what the economic situations are, there is an options methodology that can exploit it.

Options contracts and systems utilizing them have characterized benefit and misfortune, profit, and losses profiles for seeing how a lot of cash you will make or lose.

The maximum benefit you can get from selling an option is the cost of the premium gathered, however regularly there is boundless drawback potential.

When you buy an option, your upside can be boundless, and the most you can lose is the expense of the options premium.

Contingent upon the options methodology utilized, an individual stands to benefit from any number of economic situations from bull and bear to sideways advertises.

Options spreads will remain in general top both potential benefits just as misfortunes.

**Essentials of Option Profitability**

A call option purchaser stands to make a benefit if the fundamental asset, suppose a stock, transcends the strike cost before expiry. A put option purchaser makes a benefit if the value falls beneath the strike cost before the expiration. The definite measure of benefit relies upon the distinction between the stock cost and the option strike cost toward the end or when the option position ends.

A call option essayist stands to make a benefit if the basic stock remains underneath the strike cost. When writing a put option, the merchant can only benefit if the value stays over the strike cost. An option author's benefit is constrained to the superior they get for writing the option (which is the option purchaser's expense). Option journalists are additionally called option merchants.

## Option Buying versus Writing

An option purchaser can make a generous quantifiable profit if the options exchange works out. This is on the grounds that a stock cost can move altogether past the strike cost.

An option writer makes a relatively littler return if the option exchange is gainful. This is on the grounds that the writer's addition is constrained to the premium, regardless of how much the stock moves. So why compose options? Since the chances are typically overwhelmingly on the option author. An examination in the late 1990s, by the Chicago Mercantile Exchange (CME), found that somewhat over 75% of all options held to expiration lapsed uselessly.

This examination bars option places that were finished off or practiced before expiration. All things being equal, for each option contract that was in the money(ITM) at shutting, Provided that this is true, would you say you are there were three that were out of the money (OTM) and in this way, useless is a quite important measurement.

## Evaluating Risk Tolerance

Here's a simple test to assess your risk tolerance to decide if you are in an ideal situation being an option purchaser or an option author. Suppose you can purchase or compose 10 call option contracts, with the cost of each call at $0.50. Each agreement typically has 100 offers as the fundamental asset, so 10 contracts would cost $500 ($0.50 x 100 x 10 contracts).

However, if you purchase 10 call option contracts, you pay $500, and that is the most extreme misfortune that you can cause. In any case, your potential benefit is theoretically boundless. So what's the trick? The probability of the exchange being gainful isn't high. While this likelihood relies upon the inferred unpredictability of the call option and the timeframe staying to expiration, suppose it 25%.

Then again, in the event that you compose 10 call option contracts, your most extreme benefit is the measure of the superior salary, or $500, while your losses are theoretically boundless. Be that as it may, the chances of the options exchange being gainful are primarily to support you, at 75%.

So would you risk $500, realizing that you have a 75% shot of losing your venture and a 25% possibility of making a benefit? Or then again would you want to make a limit of $500, realizing that you have a 75% shot of keeping the whole sum or part of it, yet have a 25% possibility of the exchange being a losing one?

The response to those inquiries will give you a thought of your risk resilience and whether you are in an ideal situation being an option purchaser or option author.

It is imperative to remember that these are the general measurements that apply to all options, yet on specific occasions, it might be progressively advantageous to be an option writer or a purchaser in a particular asset. Utilizing the correct strategy at the perfect time could change these chances altogether.

### Option Strategies Risk/Reward

While calls and puts can be joined in different changes to frame complex options techniques, how about we assess the risk/reward of the four most essential strategy.

### Buying a Call

This is the essential option strategy. It is a moderately okay strategy since the most considerable loss is confined to the premium paid to purchase the call, while the most extreme reward is possibly boundless. Although, as expressed prior, the chances of the exchange being entirely beneficial are typically genuinely low. "Generally safe" expect that the complete expense of the option speaks to a little level of the broker's capital. Risking all capital on a solitary call option would make it a risky exchange since all the cash could be lost if the option terminates useless.

## Buying a Put

This is another strategy with generally okay, yet the conceivably high compensate if the exchange works out. Buying puts is a practical option in contrast to the riskier strategy of short selling the fundamental asset. Puts can likewise be purchased to support drawback risk in a portfolio. But since value records typically pattern higher after some time, which implies that stocks by and large will in general advance more frequently than they decay, the risk/remunerate profile of the put purchaser is marginally less ideal than that of a call purchaser.

## Writing a Put

Put writing is a favored strategy of cutting edge options brokers since, in the direst outcome imaginable, the stock is appointed to the put author (they need to purchase the stock), while the most ideal situation is that the writer holds everything of the option premium. The greatest risk of put writing is that the essayist may wind up paying a lot for a stock on the off chance that it in this manner tanks. The risk/remunerate profile of put writing is more ominous than that of put or call buying since the most extreme reward rises to the premium got, yet the greatest misfortune is a lot higher. All things considered, as talked about previously, the likelihood of having the option to make a benefit is higher.

## Writing a Call

Call writing comes in two structures, secured and stripped. Secured call writing is another most loved strategy of middle of the road to cutting edge option dealers, and is commonly used to create additional salary from a portfolio. It includes writing calls on stocks held inside the portfolio. Revealed or stripped call writing is the select area of risk-tolerant, sophisticated options merchants, as it has a risk profile like that of a short deal in stock. The most extreme reward in call writing is equivalent to the premium gotten. The greatest risk with a secured call strategy is that the basic stock will be "called away." With exposed call writing, the most extreme misfortune is theoretically boundless, similarly for what it's worth with a short deal.

## Options Spreads

As a rule, brokers or investors will join options utilizing a spread strategy, buying at least one options to sell at least one distinct options. Spreading will balance the premium paid on the grounds that the sold option premium will net against the options premium bought. Besides, the risk and return profiles of a spread will top out the potential benefit or misfortune. Spreads can be made to exploit almost any foreseen value activity and can run from the easy to the complex. Similarly, as with individual options, any spread strategy can be either purchased or sold.

## Credit Spread And Debit Spread: The Difference?

During trading or investing in options, there are several option spread strategies that one could employ—a spread being the purchase and sale of different options on the same underlying as a package.

While we can classify spreads in various ways, one standard dimension is to ask whether or not the strategy is a credit spread or a debit spread. Credit spreads, or net credit spreads, are spread strategies that involve net receipts of premiums, whereas debit spreads include net payments of premiums.

An option spread is a strategy that involves the simultaneous buying and selling of options on the same underlying asset.

A credit spread includes selling a high-premium option while obtaining a low-premium option in a similar class or of a related security, bringing about credit to the merchant's record.

A charge spread includes buying a high-premium option while selling a low-premium option in a similar class or of a related security, bringing about a charge from the broker's record.

## Credit Spreads

A credit spread includes selling, or writing, a high-premium option, and at the same time buying a lower premium option. The premium got from the composed option is higher than the premium paid for the long option, bringing about a premium credited into the merchant or investor's record when the position is opened. Whenever merchants or investors utilize a credit spread strategy, the most extreme benefit they get is the net premium. The credit spread outcomes in a profit when the options' spreads limited.

For instance, a broker actualizes a credit spread strategy by writing one March call option with a strike cost of $30 for $3 and all the while buying one March call option at $40 for $1. Since the typical multiplier on a value option is 100, the net premium got is $200 for the exchange. Moreover, the merchant will benefit if the spread strategy limits.

A bearish trader expects stock prices to decrease, and, therefore, buys call options (long call) at a specific strike price and sells (short call) the same number of call options within the same class and with the same expiration at a lower strike price. In contrast, bullish traders expect stock prices to rise, and therefore, buy call options at a certain strike price and sell the same number of call options within the same class and with the same expiration at a higher strike price.

**Debit Spreads**

Conversely, a debit spread—most often used by beginners to options strategies—involves buying an option with a higher premium and simultaneously selling an option with a lower premium, where the premium paid for the long option of the spread is more than the premium received from the written option.

Unlike a credit spread, a debit spread results in a premium debited, or paid, from the trader's or investor's account when the position is opened. Debit spreads are primarily used to offset the costs associated with owning long options positions.

For example, a trader buys one May put option with a strike price of $20 for $5 and simultaneously sells one May put option with a strike price of $10 for $1. Therefore, he paid $4, or $400 for the trade. If the trade is out of the money, his max loss is reduced to $400, as opposed to $500 if he only bought the put option.

## Straddle

A straddle is a neutral options strategy that involves simultaneously buying both a put option and a call option for the underlying security with the same strike price and the same expiration date.

A trader will profit from a long straddle when the price of the security rises or falls from the strike price by an amount more than the total cost of the premium paid. The profit potential is virtually unlimited, so long as the price of the underlying security moves very sharply.

A straddle is an options strategy involving the purchase of both a put and call option for the same expiration date and strike price on the same underlying.

The strategy is profitable only when the stock either rises or falls from the strike price by more than the total premium paid.

A straddle implies what the expected volatility and trading range of a security may be by the expiration date.

## Understanding Straddles

More broadly, straddle strategies in finance refer to two separate transactions which both involve the same underlying security, with the two-component transactions offsetting one another. Investors tend to employ a straddle when they anticipate a significant move in a stock's price but are unsure about whether the price will move up or down

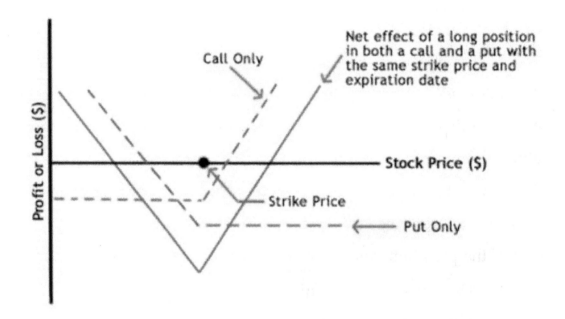

A straddle can give a broker two noteworthy intimations about what the options market thinks about a stock. First is the unpredictability the market is anticipating from the security. Second is the standard trading scope of the stock by the expiration date.

## Putting Together a Straddle

To decide the expense of making a straddle, one must include the cost of the put and the call together. For instance, if a dealer accepts that a stock may rise or tumble from its present cost of $55 following income on March 1, they could make a straddle. The merchant would hope to buy one put and one call at the $55 strike with an expiration date of March 15. To decide the expense of making the straddle, the broker would include the cost of one March 15 $55 call and one March 15 $55 put. In the event that both the calls and the puts exchange for $2.50 each, the total cost or premium paid would be $5.00 for the two contracts.

The premium paid proposes that the stock would need to rise or fall by 9% from the $55 strike cost to gain a benefit by March 15. The sum the stock is relied upon to rise-or-fall is a proportion of the future anticipated unpredictability of the stock. To decide how much the stock needs to rise or fall, partition the premium paid by the strike value, which is $5/$55, or 9%.

**Finding the Trading Range**

To decide the normal trading scope of the stock, one would include or subtract the $5 premium to or from the $55 strike cost. For this situation, it makes a trading scope of $50 to $60. In the event that the stock exchanged inside the zone of $50 to $60, the merchant would lose a portion of their cash; however, not every last bit of it. It is just conceivable to acquire a benefit if the stock ascents or falls outside of the $50 to $60 zone.

**Winning a Profit**

In the event that the stock tumbled to $48, the calls would be worth $0, while the puts would be worth $7 at expiration. That would convey a benefit of $2 to the merchant. Be that as it may, if the stock went to $57, the calls would be worth $2, and the puts would be worth zero, giving the dealer lost $3. The most desired outcome could be derived on the point at which the stock value remains at or close to the strike cost.

## True Example

The options market was inferring that AMD's stock could rise or fall 20% from the $26 strike cost at 06,10,2018 for expiration on November 16, since it cost $5.10 to get one put and call. It put the stock in a trading scope of $20.90 to $31.15. After seven days, the detailed organization outcomes and offers dove from $22.70 to $19.27 on October 25. For this situation, the dealer would have earned a benefit because the stock fell outside of the range, surpassing the superior expense of buying the puts and calls.

## Strike Price

A strike cost is the set cost at which a derivative contract can be purchased or sold when it is worked out. For call options, the strike cost is the place the option holder can purchase the security; for put options, the strike cost is the cost at which the security can be sold.

Strike cost is otherwise called the activity cost.

Strike cost is the cost at which a derivative contract can be purchased or sold (worked out).

Derivatives are monetary items whose value is based (inferred) on the hidden asset, typically another money related instrument.

The strike cost, otherwise called the activity cost, is the most significant determinant of option value.

## Understanding Strike Prices

Strike costs are utilized in derivatives (for the most part options) trading. Derivatives are monetary items whose value is based (determined) on the fundamental asset, typically another money related instrument. The strike cost is a key variable of call and put options. For instance, the purchaser of a stock option call would have the right, yet not the commitment, to purchase that stock in the future at the strike cost. Thus, the purchaser of a stock option put would have the right, yet not the commitment, to sell that stock in the future at the strike cost.

The strike. or on the other hand exercise cost, is the most significant determinant of option value. Strike costs are built up when an agreement is first composed. It tells the investor what value the basic asset must reach before the option is in-the-cash (ITM). Strike costs are standardized, which means they are at fixed dollar sums, for example, $31, $32, $33, $102.50, $105, etc.

The value distinction between the hidden stock cost and the strike cost decides an option's value. For purchasers of a call option, if the strike cost is over the unknown stock value, the option is out of the cash (OTM). For this situation, the option doesn't have inherent value; however, it might, in any case, have a value dependent on instability and time until expiration as both of these two components could put the option in cash in the future. Alternately, If the hidden stock cost is over the strike value, the option will have characteristic value and be in cash.

A purchaser of a put option will be in the cash when the basic stock cost is beneath the strike cost and be out of the money when the hidden stock cost is over the strike cost. Once more, an OTM option won't have inherent value, yet it might, in any case, have a value dependent on the unpredictability of the hidden asset and the time left until option expiration.

**Strike Price Example**

Expect, there are two option contracts. One is a call option with a $100 strike cost. The other is a call option with a $150 strike cost. The present cost of the hidden stock is $145. Expect both call options are the equivalent; the main contrast is the strike cost.

At expiration, the principal contract is worth $45. That is, it is in cash by $45. This is on the grounds that the stock is trading $45 higher than the strike cost.

The subsequent contract is out of the cash by $5. On the off chance that the cost of the hidden asset is underneath the call's strike cost at expiration, the option lapses useless.

On the off chance that we have two put options, both going to lapse, and one has a strike cost of $40 and different has a strike cost of $50, we can look to the present stock cost to see which option has value. On the off chance that the basic stock is trading at $45, the $50 put option has a $5 value. This is on the grounds that the hidden stock is beneath the strike cost of the put.

The $40 put option has no value, in light of the fact that the basic stock is over the strike cost. Recall that put options enable the option purchaser to sell at the strike cost. There is no point utilizing the option to sell at $40 when they can sell at $45 in the stock market. In this manner, the $40 strike value put is useless at expiration.

## Expiration Date? (Derivatives)

An expiration date in derivatives is the latest day that derivative contracts, for example, options or futures, are substantial. At the most recent this day, investors will have officially chosen how to manage their lapsing position.

Before an option terminates, its proprietors can practice the option, close the situation to understand their benefit or losses or let the agreement lapse useless.

The expiration date for derivatives is the last date on which the derivative is substantial. After that time, the agreement has lapsed.

Contingent upon the kind of derivative, the expiration date can bring about different results.

Option proprietors can practice the option (and acknowledge benefits or misfortunes) or let it lapse useless.

Futures contract proprietors can move over the agreement to a future date or close their position and take conveyance of the asset or item.

## Essentials of Expiration Dates

Expiration dates, and what they speak to, shift dependent on the derivative being exchanged. The expiration date for recorded stock options in the United States is regularly the third Friday of the agreement month or the month that the agreement terminates. On months that the Friday falls on a vacation, the expiration date is on a Thursday preceding the third Friday. When an options or futures contract passes its expiration date, the agreement is invalid. The most recent day to exchange value options is the Friday preceding expiry. In this way, merchants must choose how to manage their options by this last trading day.

A few options have a programmed exercise arrangement. These options are automatically practiced in the event that they are on the money(OTM) at the hour of expiry. On the off chance that a broker doesn't need the option to be worked out, they should finish off or roll the situation by the last trading day.

Record options additionally terminate on the third Friday of the month, and this is likewise the last trading day for American style list options. For European style record options, the previous trading is typically the day preceding expiration.

**Expiration and Option Value**

When all is said in done, the longer a stock needs to expiration, the additional time it needs to arrive at its strike cost and in this way the extra time value it has.

There are two sorts of options, calls, and puts. Calls give the holder the right, however not the commitment, to purchase a stock on the off chance that it arrives at a specific strike cost by the expiration date. Puts give the holder the right, yet not the commitment, to sell a stock in the event that it arrives at a specific strike cost by the expiration date.

This is the reason the expiration date is so critical to options merchants. The idea of time is at the core of what gives options their value. After the put or call lapses, time value doesn't exist. At the end of the day, when the derivative terminates, the investor doesn't hold any rights that accompany owning the call or put.

NOTE: The expiration time of an options contract is the date and time when it is rendered invalid and void. It is more explicit than the expiration date and ought not to be mistaken for the last time to exchange that option.

## Expiration and Futures Value

Futures are not quite the same as options in that even an out of the cash futures contract (losing position) holds value after expiry. For instance, an oil contract speaks to barrels of oil. On the off chance that a dealer retains that agreement until expiry, it is on the grounds that they either need to purchase (they purchased the agreement) or sells (they sold the agreement) the oil that the agreement speaks to. Subsequently, the futures contract doesn't terminate uselessly, and the gatherings included are subject to one another to satisfy their part of the arrangement. Those that don't have any desire to at risk to fulfill contract must roll or close their situations at the latest the last trading day.

Futures dealers holding the terminating contract should close it at the very latest expiration, regularly called the "last trading day," to understand their benefit or misfortune. On the other hand, they can hold the agreement and request that their merchant purchase/sell the basic asset that the agreement speaks to. Retail dealers don't typically do this; however, organizations do. For instance, an oil maker utilizing futures contracts to sell oil can sell their tanker. Futures brokers can likewise "roll" their position. This is an end of their present exchange, and a prompt reinstitution of the exchange an agreement that is farther from expiry.

Strangle

A strangle is an options strategy where the investor holds a situation in both a call and a put option with various strike costs, however with a similar expiration date and basic asset. A strangle is a decent strategy on the off chance that you figure the hidden security will encounter an enormous value development sooner rather than later yet are uncertain of the course. In any case, it is productive for the most part if the asset swings solidly in cost.

A strangle is like a straddle, yet utilizes options at various strike costs, while a straddle utilizes a call and put at a similar strike cost.

A strangle is a prominent options strategy that includes holding both a call and a put on the equivalent basic asset.

A strangle covers investors who figure an asset will move dramatically; however, are uncertain of the course.

A strangle is gainful just if the hidden asset swings firmly in cost.

How Does a Strangle Work?

Strangles come in two structures:

In a long strangle — the more typical strategy — the investor at the same time purchases an out-of-the-cash call and an out-of-the-cash put option. The call option's strike cost is higher than the basic asset's present market cost, while the put has a strike value that is lower than the asset's market cost. This strategy has huge benefit potential since the call option has theoretically significant upside if the basic asset ascends in cost, while the put option can benefit if the basic asset falls. The risk on the exchange is constrained to the premium paid for the two options.

An investor doing a short strangle all the while sells an out-of-the-cash put and an out-of-the-cash call. This methodology is an unbiased strategy with restricted benefit potential. A short strangle benefits when the cost of the hidden stock exchanges a thin extend between the breakeven focuses. The most extreme benefit is comparable to the net premium got for writing the two options, less trading expenses.

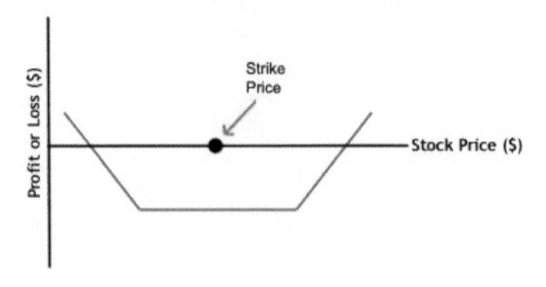

## A Strangle vs a Straddle

Strangles and straddles are comparative options systems that enable investors to benefit from enormous moves to the upside or drawback. Nonetheless, a long straddle includes all the while buying at the money call and put options – where the strike cost is indistinguishable from the basic asset's market cost – as opposed to out-of-the-money options. A short straddle is like a short strangle, with constrained benefit potential that is identical to the premium gathered from writing the at the money call and put options.

With the straddle, the investor benefits when the cost of the security rises or tumbles from the strike cost just by a sum more than the complete expense of the premium. So it doesn't require as enormous a value bounce. Buying a strangle is commonly more affordable than a straddle—however, it conveys more serious risk on the grounds that the basic asset needs to make a greater move to produce a benefit.

**Pros**

Advantages from asset's value move in either course

Less expensive than different options methodologies, similar to straddles

Boundless benefit potential

**Cons**

Requires a huge change in asset's cost

May convey more risk than different methodologies.

### Certifiable Example of a Strangle

To outline, suppose that Starbucks (SBUX) is right now trading at US$50 per share. To utilize the strangle option strategy, a merchant goes into two option positions, one call and one put. The call has a strike of $52, and the premium is $3, for a complete expense of $300 ($3 x 100 offers). The put option has a strike cost of $48, and the premium is $2.85, for a complete expense of $285 ($2.85 x 100 offers). The two options have a similar expiration date.

In the event that the cost of the stock remains somewhere in the range of $48 and $52 over the life of the option, the misfortune to the dealer will be $585, which is the all-out expense of the two option contracts ($300 + $285).

Be that as it may, suppose Starbucks' stock encounters some volatility. In the event that the cost of the offers winds up at $40, the call option will terminate uselessly, and the misfortune will be $300 for that option. Be that as it may, the put option has picked up value and delivers a benefit of $715 ($1,000 less the underlying option cost of $285) for that option. Subsequently, the all-out addition to the merchant is $415 ($715 benefit - $300 misfortune).

In the event that the value ascends to $55, the put option lapses useless and brings about lost $285. The call option gets a benefit of $200 ($500 value - $300 cost). At the point when the misfortune from the put option is figured in, the exchange acquires lost $85 ($200 benefit - $285) in light of the fact that the value move wasn't huge enough to make up for the expense of the options. The employable idea is the move being huge enough. On the off chance that Starbucks had risen $10 in cost, to $60 per share, the absolute addition would have again been $415 ($1000 value - $300 for call option premium - $285 for a lapsed put option).

## Option Premium

An option premium is the present market cost of an option contract. It is in this way the salary gotten by the vendor (author) of an option contract to another gathering. In-the-money option premiums are made out of two elements: natural and outward value. Out-of-the-money options' premiums comprise exclusively of extraneous value.

For stock options, the premium is cited as a dollar sum for each offer, and most contracts speak to the responsibility of 100 offers.

The premium on an option is its cost in the market.

Option premium will comprise of outward, or time value for out-of-the-money contracts and both inherent and extraneous value for in-the-money options.

An option's top-notch will by and large be more noteworthy given more opportunity to expiration and additionally more prominent inferred volatility.

## Understanding Option Premium

Investors who compose, which intends to sell for this situation, calls or puts use option premiums as a wellspring of current pay in accordance with a more extensive venture strategy to fence all or a part of a portfolio. Option costs cited on a trade, for example, the Chicago Board Options Exchange (CBOE), are considered premiums when in doubt, on the grounds that the options themselves have no fundamental value.

The segments of an option premium incorporate its natural value, its time value, and the inferred volatility of the basic asset. The nearer the expiration date of the option draws near, the time value will edge consistently nearer to $0, while the natural value will intently speak to the distinction between the fundamental security's cost and the strike cost of the agreement.

## Elements of Option Premium

The fundamental variables influencing an option's cost are the basic security's cost, moneyness, valuable existence of the option, and inferred volatility. As the cost of the basic security changes, the option premium changes. As the fundamental security's cost builds, the premium of a call option increments, yet the premium of a put option diminishes. As the fundamental security's cost abatements, the premium of a put option increments, and the inverse are valid for call options.

The moneyness influences the option's premium since it shows the distance away the basic security cost is from the predefined strike cost. As an option turns out to be further in-the-money, the option's premium ordinarily increments. On the other hand, the option premium reductions as the option turn out to be farther of-the-money. For instance, as an option turns out to be farther of-the-money, the option premium loses inborn value, and the value stems essentially from the time value.

The time until expiration, or the helpful life, influences the time value bit of the option's premium. As the expiration date, the option's top-notch stems principally from the natural value. For instance, profound out-of-the-money options that are lapsing in one trading day would regularly be worth $0, or near $0.

## Suggested Volatility and Option Price

Suggested volatility is gotten from the option's value, which is connected to an option's evaluating model to demonstrate how unpredictable a stock's cost might be in the future. Additionally, it influences the outward value bit of option premiums. In the event that investors are long options, an expansion in inferred volatility would add to the value. This is on the grounds that the more prominent the volatility of the fundamental asset, the more shots the option has of completing in-the-money. The inverse is valid whenever inferred volatility diminishes.

For instance, expect an investor is long one call option with an annualized suggested volatility of 20%. In this manner, if the inferred volatility increments to half during the option's life, the call option premium would acknowledge in value. An option's vega is its adjustment in premium given a 1% change in inferred volatility.

# CHAPTER 7

## USING OPTIONS FOR SPECULATION

Options contracts offer purchasers the chance to acquire huge introduction to a stock at a moderately little cost. Utilized in segregation, they can give huge additions if a stock ascents. In any case, they can likewise bring about a 100% loss of premium, if the call option terminates useless because of the fundamental stock value neglecting to move over the strike cost. The advantage of buying call options is that risk is constantly topped at the premium paid for the option.

Investors may likewise purchase and sell diverse call options at the same time, making a call spread. These will top both the potential benefit and loss from the strategy, yet are more savvy at times than a solitary call option since the premium gathered from one option's deal counterbalances the premium paid for the other.

Utilizing Options for Tax Management

Investors, in some cases, use options to change portfolio assignments without really buying or selling the hidden security.

For instance, an investor may claim 100 portions of XYZ stock and might be at risk for a huge undiscovered capital addition. Not having any desire to trigger a taxable occasion, investors may utilize options to diminish the introduction to the basic security without really selling it. While gains from call and put options are additionally taxable, their treatment by the IRS is progressively intricate in view of the different sorts and assortments of options. For the situation over, the main expense to the investor for taking part in this strategy is simply the expense of the options contract.

## Spreads and Combinations

Spreads utilize at least two options places of a similar class. They join having a market feeling (speculation) with constraining losses (hedging). Spreads regularly limit potential upside also. However, these methodologies can, in any case, be alluring since they typically cost less when contrasted with a solitary options leg. Vertical spreads include offering one option to purchase another. For the most part, the subsequent option is a similar kind and same expiration, yet an alternate strike.

A bull call spread, or bull call vertical spread, is made by buying a call and all the while selling another call with a higher strike cost and a similar expiration. The spread is beneficial if the hidden asset increments in cost; however, the upside is restricted because of the short call strike. The advantage, in any case, is that selling the higher strike call diminishes the expense of buying the lower one. So also, a bear put spread, or bear put vertical spread, includes buying a put and selling a second put with a lower strike and a similar expiration. In the event that you purchase and sell options with various expirations, it is known as a schedule spread or time spread.

Combinations are exchanges developed with both a call and a put. There is a unique sort of combination known as a "manufactured." The purpose of an engineered is to make an options position that acts as a basic asset, however without really controlling the asset. Why not simply purchase the stock? Perhaps some legitimate or administrative explanation limits you from owning it. Be that as it may, you might be permitted to make an engineered position utilizing options.

Since options costs can be displayed mathematically with a model, for example, the Black-Scholes, huge numbers of the risks related to options can likewise be demonstrated and comprehended. This specific component of options really makes them seemingly less risky than other asset classes, or possibly permits the risks related with options to be comprehended and assessed. Individual risks have been doled out Greek letter names, and are now and again alluded to just as "the Greeks."

# CHAPTER 8

## HOW TO START TRADING OPTIONS

Options don't generally move the manner in which stocks do, and you'll need to find out about what makes them extraordinary.

Likewise, don't be in a surge, consider paper trading while you start the instruction procedure. Options can move quick, and they can move against you in the event that you don't comprehend their subtleties.

Beginning in options can be troublesome. There are a lot of moving parts occurring inside options, and there is a bounty of data promptly accessible. The issue is it is regularly hard to make sense of what data to trust and what data you should start at.

Your initial step will be to get a few asset books, that why I set up this book with sufficient data to kick you off. Since you have a thought of what is happening, you need a spot to exchange, so finding an intermediary is an unquestionable requirement.

Finding Your Option Broker

Finding a merchant is a basic piece of trading. Through your representative, you will enter your exchanges and track your positions. With every one of the brokers out there which do you pick? Would it be advisable for you to go with the handle that has the best commissions or maybe the expedite that has the best option instruments? To begin with, suppose that you are not married to your agent. Who you pick presently doesn't need to be who you end up inside the long term. Discover one to meet your present objectives and proceed onward when your objectives change, and you are never again being satisfied.

As an option youngster, it might appear as though a smart thought to go with a handle that has unrivaled option trading apparatuses. In any case, you won't have the option to exploit those apparatuses for a long while so instruments ought not to sit as your most astounding need. What you have to concentrate on are low commissions and unwavering quality. As you learn you are going to make, many dumb slip-ups and those mix-ups don't have to cost you a ton. You likewise don't need high commissions raising your breakeven costs and make it hard to produce a benefit. A dependable intermediary is only a need. Modest commissions are nothing worth mentioning on the off chance that you can't sign in to exchange anything in light of the fact that your dealer is down.

Brokers need you to have an essential comprehension of stocks and investments. As such, they need you to comprehend the risks engaged with trading. A few brokers might need to see your fluid assets and your absolute total assets as well. Trading options is a risky business. This is the reason you need an intermediary to begin.

As you search for a business firm, don't put together your option with respect to commission charges alone. Rather, take a gander at the 10,000 foot view. As a starting investor, you need a strong business firm. You need great client assistance, just like a lot of training as you come. While inquiring about brokers, think about the accompanying inquiries:

What sorts of help do they offer? Is everything on the web? Would you be able to call a live individual on the off chance that you have questions?

Do they offer research on stocks and options?

What sort of direction do they give? Will they walk you through your exchanges?

Do they have platforms specifically for novices?

It's right to say that they are genuine? However, do your homework well before giving over your money to ensure you are utilizing a reputable trading stage and that installment strategies will be secure.

Finding the correct merchant can mean the distinction among progress and disappointment in options trading.

## Tips for Choosing an Options Broker

Options trading can be convoluted. However, if you pick your options dealer with consideration, you'll rapidly ace how to lead inquire about, place exchanges and track positions.

Here's our recommendation on finding an expedite that offers the administration and the record includes that best serve your options trading needs.

## 1. Search for free training

In case you're new to options trading or need to grow your trading procedures, finding a facilitate that has assets for teaching clients is an unquestionable requirement. That training can come in numerous structures, including:

Online options trading courses.

Live or recorded online classes.

One-on-one direction on the web or by telephone

Eye to eye gatherings with a bigger handle that has branches the nation over.

It's a smart thought to spend some time in understudy driver mode and absorb as much training and guidance as you can. Stunningly better, if a dealer offers a reenacted variant of its options trading stage, test-drive the procedure with a paper trading account before putting any genuine money on hold.

## 2. Put your agent's client support to the test

Solid client support ought to be a high need, especially for more current options merchants. It's likewise significant for the individuals who are exchanging brokers or leading complex exchanges they may need assistance with.

Think about what sort of get in touch with you like. Live online talk? Email? Telephone support? Does the agent have a committed trading work area on call? What hours is it staffed? Is specialized help accessible every minute of every day or just weekdays? Shouldn't something be said about delegates who can address inquiries regarding your record?

Indeed, even before you apply for a record, connect and pose a few inquiries to check whether the appropriate responses and reaction time are good.

## 3. Ensure the trading stage is anything but difficult to utilize

Options trading platforms come in all shapes and sizes. They can be web-or programming based, work area or online just, have separate platforms for essential and propelled trading, offer full or incomplete versatile usefulness or a mix of the abovementioned.

Visit an agent's site and search for a guided voyage through its foundation and apparatuses. Screen captures, and video instructional exercises are pleasant, however evaluating a merchant's reenacted trading stage, on the off chance that it has one, will give you the best feeling of whether the intermediary is a solid match.

A few interesting points:

Is the stage structure easy to use or do you need to chase and peck to discover what you need?

How simple is it to put an exchange?

Could the stage do the things you need, such as making cautions dependent on explicit criteria or giving you a chance to round out an exchange ticket advance to submit later?

Will you need portable access to the full suite of administrations when you're in a hurry, or will a pared-down adaptation of the stage do the trick?

How solid is the site, and how rapidly are requests executed? This is a high need if your strategy includes rapidly entering and leaving positions.

Does the specialist charge a month to month or yearly stage expense? Assuming this is the case, are there approaches to get the expense postponed, for example, keeping a base record equalization or directing a specific number of exchanges during a particular period?

## 4. Survey the expansiveness, profundity and cost of information and instruments

Information and research are an options merchant's soul. A portion of the nuts and bolts to search for:

An as often as possible updated statements feed.

Fundamental graphing to help pick your entrance and leave focuses.

The capacity to examine an exchange's potential risks and rewards (most extreme upside and greatest drawback).

Screening devices.

Those wandering into further developed trading methodologies may require further expository and exchange displaying apparatuses, for example, adjustable screeners; the capacity to assemble, test, track and back-test trading systems; and continuous market information from various suppliers.

Verify whether the extravagant stuff costs extra. For instance, most brokers give free deferred statements, falling 20 minutes behind market information, yet charge an expense for a constant feed. Also, some star level apparatuses might be accessible just to clients who meet month to month or quarterly trading action or record balance essentials.

## 5. Try not to gauge the cost of commissions too intensely

There's an explanation bonus expenses are lower on our rundown. Cost isn't all that matters, and it's positively not as significant as the different things we've covered. But since commissions give an advantageous one next to the other correlation, they regularly are the principal things individuals see when picking an options specialist.

A couple of things to think about how much brokers charge to exchange options:

The two segments of an options trading commission are the base rate, basically equivalent to the thing as the trading commission that investors pay when they purchase a stock, and the per-contract expense. Commissions typically go from $3 to $9.99 per exchange; contract expenses keep running from 15 pennies to $1.25 or more.

A few brokers pack the trading commission and the per-contract expense into a solitary level charge.

A few brokers additionally offer limited commissions dependent on trading recurrence, volume or normal record balance — the meaning of "high volume" or "dynamic merchant" shifts by the investor.

In case you're new to options trading or utilize the strategy just sparingly you'll be well-served by picking either an expedite that offers a solitary level rate to exchange or one that charges a commission in addition to per-contract expense. In case you're an increasingly dynamic merchant, you should survey your trading rhythm to check whether a layered evaluating plan would set aside your cash.

Obviously, the less you pay in charges, the more benefit you keep. However, we should put things in context: Platform expenses, information expenses, inertia charges and fill-in-the-clear charges can occur without much of a stretch counterbalance the reserve funds you may get from going with an expedite that charges a couple of bucks less for commissions.

There's another potential issue in the event that you base your option exclusively on commissions. Rebate brokers can charge absolute bottom costs since they give just no frills platforms or attach additional expenses for information and apparatuses. Then again, at a portion of the bigger, increasingly settled brokers you'll pay higher commissions, however in return you get free access to all the data you have to perform due to perseverance.

## Best Options Trading Brokers and Platforms

Options trading has turned out to be amazingly prominent with retail investors in the course of recent years. Our best options brokers have an abundance of instruments, including portfolio margining, that help you measure and oversee risk as you figure out which exchanges to put. They likewise incorporate significant instruction that encourages you to develop in modernity as an options dealer. Here are our top brokers in the business for options trading:

- TD AMERITRADE (THINKORSWIM)
- ROBINHOOD
- E-TRADE
- INTERACTIVE BROKERS
- TRADESTATION
- ALLY INVEST
- CHARLES SCHWAB (STREETSMART PLATFORMS)
- LIGHTSPEED

## TD Ameritrade (thinkorswim)

TD Ameritrade takes the top spot in this positioning gratitude to a combination of sensible evaluating, brilliant fledgling assets, and a best in class trading stage that functions admirably for specialists and expert dealers. Regardless of where you are in your options trading venture, TD Ameritrade has something for everybody.

Exchanges at TD Ameritrade cost $6.95 per exchange in addition to $0.75 pennies per contract. There is no record least. The site offers a present advancement where you get 60 days of without commission value, ETF, and options exchanges with a store of $3,000 or more. You get extra rewards with bigger opening stores.

Novices have a wide scope of assets that are incredible for options and other investing and trading techniques. For master merchants, the Think or Swim stage gives you Wall Street quality at a Main Street cost.

The thinkorswim stage is most appropriate for further developed options dealers, with an assortment of options option devices and risk management. You can assemble your very own specialized examinations from more than 500 markers in both the downloadable stage and its going with portable application.

TD Ameritrade likewise got honors for Best Overall Online Brokers, Best for Day Trading, Best Web Trading Platforms, Best for Beginners, Best for ETFs, Best for Roth IRAs, Best for IRAs and Best Stock Trading Apps.

**Pros**

Top notch training, including live content on TDAmeritradeNetwork.com

Practice options trading systems utilizing a trading test system

thinkorswim stage has dynamite apparatuses for choosing options systems

Gushing information accessible on all platforms

**Cons**

Higher than normal commissions and per-contract expense

Extremely high edge rates

The intricacy of the thinkorswim stage makes a few highlights hard to discover

Having options devices spread more than two unique platforms is awkward

## Robinhood

You can't get less expensive than free. While some expert dealers are not content with how exchanges are taken care of and handled at Robinhood, it is a great stage for amateurs, to begin with, less risk. With no trading expense, you can purchase and sell options without risking anything over your underlying investment.

Robinhood is a web-first stage, and it doesn't offer much with regards to instruction and research apparatuses. In any case, if you read a book on options and need to attempt your hand as a pro, Robinhood can positively deal with your needs.

Robinhood additionally offers without commission stock exchanges, ETFs, a predetermined number of cryptocurrencies, and a set number of ADRs (American Depository Receipts — a sort of stock posting in the US for an outside organization). Since it is versatile first, it offers incredible continuous warnings for investments and exchanges on the stage.

## ETRADE (Power ETRADE)

ETrade is the most established online financier, and it has a long history of supporting both apprentice and master level brokers.

Through its committed OptionsHouse stage, you can locate a wide scope of information and research instruments. Those incorporate devices to manufacture propelled options chains and trading stepping stools.

While it is a rebate financier, commissions are not the most minimal on the rundown. Exchanges cost $6.95 in addition to $0.75 pennies per contract. Be that as it may, a few limits apply for high volume dealers. Value and list options drop to $4.95 per exchange and $0.50 pennies per contract with at least 30 exchanges for each quarter.

With another record that gets an equalization of $10,000 or more, you'll get up to $600 in free exchanges and 60 days of sans commission exchanges. That is a really decent arrangement to kick you off. With ETrade and others, generally, consider how exchange charges cut into your benefits after some time.

Despite the fact that you approach an abundance of investigation and research on the great E*TRADE stage, you'll need to flip over to discover those highlights.

ETRADE additionally got honors for Best Web Trading Platforms, Best for ETFs, Best Stock Trading Apps, Best for Roth IRAs, Best for IRAs, and Best for Beginners.

**Pros**

Graphing and estimating devices in the Power E*Trade stage are option

Adjustable options chains and trading stepping stools

Visit merchants meet all requirements for lower base commissions

THE SOUL OF BUSINESS ONLINE [9 IN 1] BY DAVID LAZARUS

## Cons

Higher-than-normal commissions and per-contract charge

High edge rates

Multi-leg spreads bring about an extra base commission charge

## Interactive Brokers

This broker had a long-standing reputation for low costs, a troublesome stage and horrible administration that obliged hyperactive merchants. However, that reputation has changed so much in the last three to four years as the firm sought after less dynamic and less complex clients. The organization's Trader Workstation stage, accessible as either a downloadable bundle or a site, has turned out to be friendlier and increasingly adaptable. Their portable applications are intended to work with least composing, rather, using haggles directions.

A generally new highlight, IBot, gives you a chance to pose inquiries in plain English and get a brisk answer, instead of burrowing around the stage. For instance, you can ask IBot to show a specific strike and expiry date by composing (or saying) "Show options chain for GOOG for the following three expirations."

Options brokers can set up a spread rapidly and move it to a future expiry with only two or three ticks. IB's Probability Lab gives you a chance to reproduce a potential exchange before utilizing genuine money.

You can just show spilling cites on each gadget in turn, so in the event that you have the site up on your computer and, at that point sign in to your portable application, one stage will be automatically limited to depiction cites. Records with under $100,000 in assets pay a base expense of $10/month and may need to pay extra charges for continuous information. The web adaptation of Trader Workstation does not have a portion of the highlights in the downloadable stage; however all watchlists and alarms are shared.

Interactive Brokers additionally got honors for Best Overall Online Brokers, Best for International Stock Trading, Best for Low Costs, Best for Penny Stocks, and Best for Day Trading.

**Pros**

No record least and no per-leg base expense

Edge rates are the most minimal of all brokers overviewed

Many options-arranged exercises

**Cons**

Gushing statements show on each gadget in turn

Client support is improving yet, at the same time has a reputation for being lazy.

## TradeStation

TradeStation began as a product organization for merchants, and despite the fact that it has developed after some time, it has maintained its underlying trading standards. In the event that you need proficient information and fast exchange execution on a specialist level stage, TradeStation is an extraordinary decision.

TradeStation charges $5 per exchange in addition to $0.50 pennies per contract. Be that as it may, it additionally offers unbundled and per-contract evaluating. Expert and high-volume dealers may improve the level rate cost of $1 per contract rather than the base + per contract expense most financiers charge.

While it doesn't offer as much for novice merchants and new brokers, you could have a family office or business portfolio on TradeStation without any issues. Truth be told, its instruments are so great it offers a significant number of them for a charge to proficient investors with records at different brokers. With a functioning record at TradeStation, you get those apparatuses for nothing. Simply be careful the base $2,000 parity or five exchanges for every year to maintain a strategic distance from a $95 yearly record expense.

## Ally invest

Ally Invest is another minimal effort business best known for its cousin Ally Bank. Like the bank, Ally Invest offers a straightforward and low-charge business lineup. Exchanges are $4.95 each in addition to $0.65 pennies per contract. There is no record least. With a present advancement, you can get up to $3,500 reward money relying upon the size of your store.

You can begin with a low investment to become familiar with Ally without stressing over huge least adjusts or charges. Be that as it may, even some increasingly experienced brokers will be content with the low costs and a wide scope of administrations intended for option merchants.

Features incorporate an incredible trading stage and important graphs, information, and examination to enable you to assemble your options trading strategy. In the realm of markdown financiers, you can't generally take the value of a merchant from its trading expenses. At Ally, that is surely the situation.

## Lightspeed

Lightspeed is a specialist intended to address the issues of experienced and exceptionally dynamic options brokers. Lightspeed gives a committed options-trading stage (Livevol X) and a few options diagnostic devices –, for example, verifiable options Greeks and slants information – not offered by different brokers. A variety of scanners in the Lightspeed Trader stage helps spot trading openings, and the stage's progressed diagramming highlights are very adaptable.

For portfolio investigation, you can bunch your situations by basic image, which enables productive merchants to figure out which procedures are working. You'll likewise discover a benefit and-loss risk graph for complex methodologies. The stage performed very well during the ongoing trading floods.

Versatile and electronic applications, be that as it may, don't permit futures trading or direct market get to. This isn't a fitting stage for new options brokers.

Lightspeed likewise got honors for the best when it comes to low Costs and Best for Day Trading.

**Pros**

per-contract commissions rate is very low (with no per-leg base charge)

Staggering request execution programming produces value improvement

Livevol X stage has no month to month charge

**Cons**

High parity required to open a record

Lightspeed Trader stage has a base $100/month charge

Restricted instructive contributions


## Charles Schwab (StreetSmart platforms)

Charles Schwab conveys an inside and out incredible involvement with fantastic client support. When you open another record, exchanges are $.95 each in addition to $0.65 pennies per contract. First-time customers get 500 sans commission exchanges for a long time when you store $100,000 or more in another record.

Schwab offers better than expected research and training contributions. It additionally gives you a generally excellent stage for trading on work area, web, and versatile. Indeed, even outside of options, it is extraordinary compared to other by and large financiers for a wide scope of investing and trading needs.

With the enormous library of instructive and research content, you can enter the fast options trading world with your eyes wide open to the risks and openings. All things considered, the aggressive expenses and quality trading platforms make it a commendable consideration for even the most experienced dealers. Records require a $1,000 least to get to options trading.

This is a decent stage for the rising options broker, with a lot of help and instruction. The expenses are on the low side too. For progressively refined options dealers, a device demonstrates how a speculative exchange would influence your edge balance.

Charles Schwab likewise got honors for Best Overall Online Brokers, Best Web Trading Platforms, Best for International Trading, Best for Penny Stocks, Best for Beginners, Best for Roth IRAs, Best for IRAs, Best for ETFs, and Best Stock Trading Apps.

**Pros**

The Idea Hub in the StreetSmart platforms shows noteworthy trading thoughts

Options-situated trading exercises that develop with you

A wide exhibit of asset classes can be exchanged on any of the accessible platforms

**Cons**

The multiplication of platforms disperses options determination devices in better places

Altering portfolio examination pages to show options-explicit execution is awkward

Edge rates are higher than normal

## Tastyworks

A stage worked for regular options merchants, tastyworks is the business ally to tastytrade, a cheeky budgetary news and instruction stage. There are three different ways to get to the stage: a ground-breaking downloadable bundle, a site, and versatile applications. The firm charges commissions just for opening a position, urging their clients to escape level exchanges and

There are a couple of more fancy odds and ends in the downloadable rendition; however, the others aren't missing much. The majority of the apparatuses are intended to get you concentrated on liquidity, likelihood, and volatility. This financier opened in January 2017, so it's not burdened with heritage frameworks that hinder huge numbers of the more seasoned businesses. Executions are quick, and the expenses are low, especially with the evaluating change declared in July 2018 that tops value option exchange commissions at $10 per leg. Despite the fact that a newcomer to options trading may be initially awkward, the individuals who comprehend the fundamental ideas will value the substance and highlights.

tastyworks likewise got honors for Best for Day Trading and Best for Low Costs.

**Pros**

Entirely steady stage

Every one of the apparatuses are open from a solitary page

The stage is centered around derivatives trading

**Cons**

Newcomers might be overpowered

Some asset classes are inaccessible

Restricted portfolio examination

## Opening an options trading account

Before you can even begin, you need to clear a couple of obstacles. Due to the measure of capital required and the multifaceted nature of foreseeing numerous moving parts, brokers need to discover more about a potential investor before granting them a consent slip to begin trading options.

Brokerage firms screen potential options dealers to evaluate their trading knowledge, their comprehension of the risks in options and their budgetary readiness.

Opening a brokerage record doesn't mean you can begin trading options. Despite everything, you need endorsement before you can even fire thinking of a strategy. Brokerage firms rate their customers on a scale.

The regular scale runs 1 to 5. Yet, a few spots, similar to Charles Schwab, take a shot at their own scale. As a rule, the scales go from low to high in this technique:

Covered calls

Purchase calls and puts

Spreads

Uncovered calls/puts

Each level is aggregate. On the off chance that you are appraised at Level 2, you can likewise exchange whatever Level 1 can exchange. The higher you proceed onward the scale, the more you can exchange. Your affirmed level relies upon an assortment of components:

Money related destinations: Are you attempting to develop your income or keep up your capital?

Investment goals, for example, income, development, capital conservation or speculation

Involvement in the market: Are you a prepared dealer? What sorts of protections have you purchased/sold? Have you at any point purchased/sold options previously? What number of exchanges do you make every year?

Trading background, including your insight into investing, to what extent you've been trading stocks or options, what number of exchanges you make every year and the size of your exchanges

Risk resistance: Do you have strong work? It is safe to say that you are risking the majority of your capital or only a small amount of it? Brokers may even get some information about your yearly income and absolute total assets. They need a strong thought of the risks you are happy to take. Individual budgetary data, including total fluid assets (or investments effectively sold for money), yearly income, all out total assets and work data

This data enables brokers to choose which option trading level suits you. Each trading level permits a particular kind of options exchanges. Be that as it may, the permitted exchanges at each level could change by agent. Approach your agent for a rundown of each level so you can see where you stand.

## Sorts OF OPTIONS

Most of options exchanged on the market are list or individual security options. The options anticipate either how a noteworthy file, similar to the S&P 500 will do or how a particular basic stock will perform. These are the fundamental exchanges.

However, it's additionally conceivable to exchange ETF and forex options. ETFs track a particular market fragment, for instance, precious stones. On the off chance that you have an enthusiasm for the precious stones market, you could exchange ETF options this market fragment. You can likewise expand your risks and purchase options on the forex market.

## PUT YOUR PREDICTORS' CAP ON

When you comprehend the essentials of options trading, it's a great opportunity to decide. It begins with foreseeing a stock's heading.

There are three center components you ought to consider.

What do you figure the stock will do?

You should decide whether you think the stock will go up or down. This will help decide the correct strategy for options trading.

On the off chance that you foresee the stock cost will build, you'll purchase a call. This gives you the right (not the commitment) to purchase the stock at the strike cost. When the stock's market cost surpasses your strike value, you are in the money. You'll purchase the stock at the lower strike cost and sell it at the higher market cost. You benefit is the distinction short any commissions paid.

On the off chance that you anticipate the stock cost will diminish, you'll purchase a put. This gives you the right (not the commitment) to sell the stock at the strike cost. When the stock's market cost is beneath your strike value, you are in the money. You could purchase the stock at the lower market cost and afterward sell it at the higher strike cost. The distinction short commission paid is your benefit.

In the event that the stock's market cost doesn't move like you figured, the option could lapse "out of the money." If you purchased a call and the stock's market cost didn't surpass the strike cost at expiration, it's out of the money. In the event that you purchased a put, and the stock's market cost surpasses the strike value, it's out of the money. These are the real risks associated with buying options.

What amount do you figure the stock cost will change?

This will enable you to decide the correct strike cost.

Picking the correct strike cost isn't as overpowering as it appears. The strike costs are institutionalized. You'll see an assortment of accessible strike costs; however, they will consistently be in explicit augmentations. The common additions incorporate $1, $5, and $10. Occasionally, you may likewise observe $2.50 increases. The institutionalized additions remove a little mystery from the procedure.

A call is "in the money" when the market cost is higher than the call's strike cost.

A put is "in the money" when the market cost is lower than the put's strike cost.

what extent do you think it will take the stock's cost to move?

This is the place taking a gander at the stock's chronicled examples satisfies. Realizing the stock's history can give you a thought of when/on the off chance that you figure the stock's cost will change.

You can just browse the accessible expiration dates. Be that as it may, you can generically decide to what extent you think a stock will take to change.

On the off chance that you think a stock will change in the short-term, you could consider a month to month expiration, regardless of whether 1, 3, or a half year.

In the event that you think a stock will take more time to transform, you could consider a yearly expiration.

Specialized ANALYSIS

Anticipating an option's future requires a touch of specialized examination. You'll need to comprehend the accompanying:

Bolster levels: This is the stock's normal "depressed spot." Relying on the stock to go underneath this point could be risky.

Opposition levels: This is the stock's regular "high point." Relying on the stock to go over this point could be risky.

Volume: As you track the stock's history, you'll need to take a gander at the volume behind it. The more offers exchanged at a specific value, the more probable it's a pattern. Depending on low volumes could lead you off course.

You can become familiar with these levels by perusing the stock's graph designs. Take a gander at its history, concentrating on explicit examples. Your brokerage firm should enable you to get familiar with these components, and that's just the beginning, especially as another options merchant.

Concentrating on these variables will enable you to decide whether you should purchase/sell a put or call; the strike cost; and the expiration date.

For instance, if you think stock costs are going to build, you need to purchase a call. This gives you the privilege to purchase the stock of the basic protections at the strike cost. This ought to be beneath the market value. You would then make a benefit.

Then again, if you figure stock costs may fall, you'd purchase a put. This gives you an agreement to sell the stock at a more expensive rate than the market value.

Foreseeing the expansion/decline requires research and learning, however. This is the place the correct merchant proves to be useful.

They'll give you the exploration you have to choose. What did the stock do historically? What are the general sentiments towards the stock today? You'll likewise need to comprehend the stock's implied volatility. Your agent can enable you to comprehend the risks in question.

Finally, you'll have to pick an expiration date. The farther the expiration date, the more prominent the time value of the option. As such, the longer the stock needs to increment or reduction, contingent upon what you're seeking after to make a benefit. Keep in mind, the longer the expiration, the more prominent the premium.

## Setting your first trading on options

Setting your first options exchange isn't as hard as it might appear. You'll never learn until you do it so how about we stroll through putting your first exchange bit by bit at this moment.

Toward the part of the arrangement instructional exercise, include your remarks and let me know whether you think this was useful in kicking you off or not.

firstly: Login To Your Brokerage Account

I accept that you as of now have an extraordinary specialist and can either login on the web or download a work area application. In any case, to put a trade, you have to gain admittance to the market.

I'll be utilizing TD Ameritrade (thinkorswim) for this down to earth manage

### Next: Discover The "order" or "trade" Page

A few brokers will have tabs or pages where every one of the orders are finished. Discover this page - it's most likely unmistakably named since they need you trading.

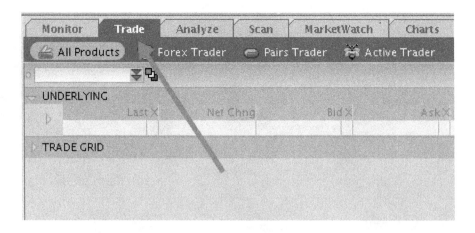

## Next: Draw Up A Stock/ETF Quote

Type in a ticker image to draw up the live market cites for the stock/ETF you might want to trade options on. In this model, I'll simply utilize AAPL for Apple Stock.

## Next: Quest For The Options Quote Table

When the statements start spilling in, there will be both the "basic" and "options" cites. Pick the options.

## Next: Pick Your Expiration Month

Presently you need to choose with the month you need to trade; the front month or close to month. Front month options are the following month terminate. For our situation, these will be March.

## Next: Select Your Strike Price

Down the center of the valuing table will be all the distinctive strike costs for the two Calls and Puts. Look down and pick the strike value that you need.

| ROC | Bid X | Ask X | Exp | Strike | Bid X | Ask X | Mark |
|-----|-------|-------|-----|--------|-------|-------|------|
| N/A | 27.75 A | 28.00 X | MAR 12 | 495 | 8.05 A | 8.15 A | 8.10 |
| N/A | 24.45 N | 24.60 C | MAR 12 | 500 | 9.70 X | 9.80 A | 9.75 |
| N/A | 21.30 A | 21.50 X | MAR 12 | 505 | 11.55 X | 11.70 X | 11.625 |
| N/A | 18.45 X | 18.55 Q | MAR 12 | 510 | 13.70 Q | 13.80 Q | 13.75 |
| N/A | 15.80 X | 15.90 X | MAR 12 | 515 | 16.00 A | 16.20 X | 16.10 |
| N/A | 13.50 A | 13.60 Q | MAR 12 | 520 | 18.65 X | 18.80 A | 18.725 |
| N/A | 11.30 X | 11.40 W | MAR 12 | 525 | 21.55 X | 21.70 X | 21.625 |
| N/A | 9.50 N | 9.60 Q | MAR 12 | 530 | 24.65 X | 24.90 X | 24.775 |
| N/A | 7.90 X | 8.00 C | MAR 12 | 535 | 28.10 A | 28.30 A | 28.20 |

## Next: Pick Either "Call" or "Put."

Typically, the Calls will be recorded on the left and the Puts on the privilege in the header. Locate the side of the trade you need to be on and hit the offered/request that statements draw up the genuine order structure for the option. Keep in mind that BID = Sell and ASK = Buy

| Net Chng (kts) | Bid X | Ask X | Exp | Strike | Bid X | Ask X | Last X |
|------|-------|-------|-----|--------|-------|-------|--------|
| +6.80 | 27.75 A | 28.00 X | MAR 12 | 495 | 8.05 A | 8.15 A | 8.15 A |
| +6.36 | 24.45 N | 24.60 C | MAR 12 | 500 | 9.70 X | 9.80 A | 9.80 C |
| +5.45 | 21.30 A | 21.50 X | MAR 12 | 505 | 11.55 X | 11.70 X | 11.60 A |
| +4.80 | 18.45 X | 18.55 Q | MAR 12 | 510 | 13.70 Q | 13.80 Q | 13.70 Q |
| +3.55 | 15.80 X | 15.90 X | MAR 12 | 515 | 16.00 A | 16.20 X | 16.15 A |
| +3.60 | 13.50 A | 13.60 Q | MAR 12 | 520 | 18.65 X | 18.80 A | 18.80 A |
| +2.97 | 11.30 X | 11.40 W | MAR 12 | 525 | 21.55 X | 21.70 X | 21.65 N |
| +2.45 | 9.50 N | 9.60 Q | MAR 12 | 530 | 24.65 X | 24.90 X | 24.70 A |
| +2.01 | 7.90 X | 8.00 C | MAR 12 | 535 | 28.10 A | 28.30 A | 28.85 C |

## Next: Enter The Quantity

Basic enough right, simply enter the quantity of contracts you need to trade.

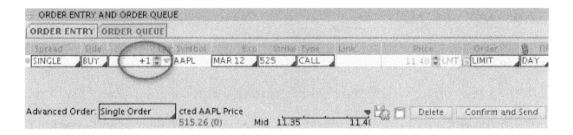

## Next: Set You Desired Price

Again set the cost to what you need to pay for the option.

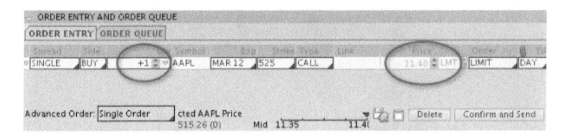

## Next: Pick The Order Type

The order type is a further developed element that I've covered in other video instructional exercises. For our motivations, we are going to utilize a LIMIT order that pegs the value we are happy to pay the value we enter.

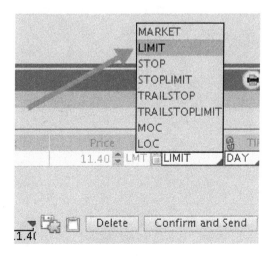

## Next: DAY or GTC?

This will decide to what extent the order will remain open if it's not filled. Day orders unmistakably remain open only the day and automatically drop at the market close. GTC orders are "Great Til Cancelled" which means they will remain open and working until they are filled, or you drop it yourself.

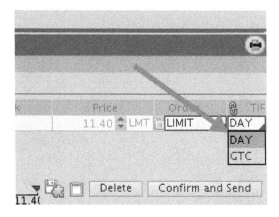

## Next: Confirm and Send!

Take 1 moment and go over your order again ensuring that everything is right. Ensure you are entering the correct cost and amount. Only a brief period checking your orders will spare you a large number of dollars every year.

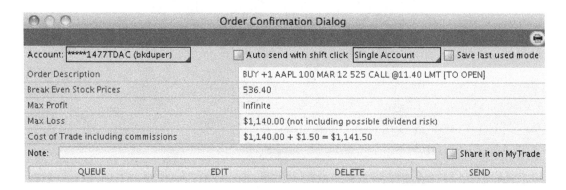

That is it; You just place your first options trade, wasn't that simpler than you think?

## CONCLUSION

Options trading might seem frustrating, but they're clear to see once you learn a few tips. Investor portfolios are often constructed with different asset sessions. These could be stocks and shares, bonds, ETFs, and also mutual funds. Options are another property class, so when used correctly, they provide several benefits that stock trading and ETFs only cannot.

## Do not go yet; One last thing to do

If you enjoyed this book or found it useful I'd be very grateful if you'd post a short review on it. Your support really does make a difference and I read all the reviews personally so I can get your feedback and make this book even better.

Thanks again for your support!

# DAY TRADING FOR BEGINNERS

*David Lazarus*

# Table of Contents

# CHAPTER 1:

# STARTING OUT WITH DAY TRADING AND

# FOREX

## STARTING OUT WITH DAY TRADING AND FOREX

The forex (FX) market features a lot of parallels to your equity areas; nonetheless, you'll find some crucial differences. This article will explain to you those distinctions which help you get begun in forex exchanging.

If you've chosen to take a stab at forex exchanging, accessibility to money marketplaces has not recently been much easier with a wide selection of online brokerage systems offering everything from place trading to futures and CFDs.

## KEY TAKEAWAYS

- Before you settle on a forex dealer, carry off the because of diligence while making sure you are selecting the best choice for your self.
- Search for low spreads and fees from a supplier in a well-regulated jurisdiction which provides a collection of methods and access to leverage, among various other factors.
- When you've chosen your agent, study up on standard forex strategies and how exactly to properly analyze money markets.
- You might want to focus on a demo account to test your own strategy out and backtest before risking real cash into the market.

### Choosing a Forex Broker

There's a lot of forex brokers to select from, just like in almost any other market. Check out situations to take into consideration:

## Lower spreads help you save cash!

Low Develops. The spread, calculated in "pips," will be the distinction between the cost from which a currency can be bought and the cost at that it may be sold at virtually any part of DAY. Forex brokers don't recharge a commission, thus this distinction is the way they create money. In comparing brokers, you will find that the difference in advances in forex is actually as great whilst the difference in commissions in the stock field.

## Be sure your agent is backed by regulatory organizations and a trustworthy institution!

High-Quality Institution. Unlike money agents, forex brokers are normally associated with big banks or lending establishments because of the large quantities of money required (control they must supply). Additionally, forex brokers ought to be authorized together with the Futures Commission Merchant (FCM) and managed by the Commodity Futures Trading Commission (CFTC). You can easily discover this along with other financial information and statistics about a forex brokerage on its site, the site of its mother or father company or through the Financial business Regulatory Authority's BrokerCheck website.

## Obtain the resources you will need to succeed!

Extensive Tools and Analysis. Forex agents offer a lot of different trading platforms for their customers – just like brokers various other markets. These trading and investing systems often function real-DAY charts, technical evaluation resources, real-DAY development, and data and even support for trading techniques. Before committing to your broker, end up being yes to request complimentary studies to evaluate different trading platforms. Agents usually, in addition, offer technical and fundamental information, monetary calendars and different study.

## Leverage your own bets!

A number of Leverage Options. Leverage is required in forex because the cost deviations (the resources of revenue) are generally just fractions of a penny. Influence conveyed as a ratio between total capital available to actual money will be the amount of cash a broker will lend you for trading. For instance, a proportion of 100:1 means the broker would give you $100 for virtually any $1 of genuine capital. Many brokerages provide just as much as 250:1. Recall, reduced leverage means a lower threat of a margin call, but additionally lower bang for the money (and vice-versa).

If you've got limited money, be sure your broker offers high control through a margin membership. If money is certainly not an issue, any specialist with a large assortment of influence possibilities needs to do. a range of options allows you vary the actual quantity of danger you may be happy to take. For instance, much less leverage (and thus less danger) can be preferable for extremely volatile (exotic) money sets.

**Be sure the broker utilizes the proper influence, resources, and services in accordance with your quantity of capital.**

Account Types. Numerous brokers supply two or a lot more kinds of accounts. The littlest membership is referred to as a mini account and needs you to exchange with at least of, state, $250, offering a large amount of influence (which you want so as to make cash because of these measurements of preliminary money). The standard membership allows you to trade at a number of different leverages, however, it calls for at least $2,000. Finally, premium records, which often require significantly higher levels of capital, allow you to make use of various amounts of control and often supply added resources and services.

### Broker Actions in order to prevent in Forex Trading and investing

Sniping or searching. Sniping and hunting – described as prematurely purchasing or selling near preset points – are generally unsuitable functions determined by brokers to improve revenue. Unfortunately, truly the only option to determine the agents which do this and the ones that don't is to speak with guy traders. There's no blacklist or organization that reports such activity.

Strict Margin Guidelines. Whenever you will be exchanging with lent money, the agent has a suppose in how a lot of threat you take. As a result, your broker can invest in or sell at their own discretion, which is often a bad thing for you personally. Let's imagine you have got a margin account, and your position takes diving before rebounding to all-DAY levels. Even though you have actually sufficient money to pay for, some agents will liquidate your situation on a margin phone call at that low. This activity on their part can price you a significant quantity of money.

Make sure to perform thorough due diligence prior to choosing a broker! Once you have decided, applying for a forex membership is actually similar to obtaining an equity membership. The actual only real significant distinction is that for forex accounts, you may be necessary to signal a margin arrangement. This arrangement states you are trading with lent money, and, like these, the broker has just the right to intervene in your own positions to protect its passions. Having said that, as soon as you sign up and fund your account, you will be prepared to trade.

## Defining a Simple Forex Investing Technique

Technical evaluation and fundamental analysis tend to be a couple of oft-used strategies in the forex market. Technical evaluation is actually the most popular method used by individual forex dealers, which we'll explain in further detail below.

## Fundamental Analysis

If you believe it's hard to appreciate one company, attempt valuing an entire nation! Fundamental evaluation when you look at the forex industry is really intricate, and is often made use of and then anticipate long-expression styles; however, some traders carry out exchange quick-term purely on news produces. You'll find a lot of fundamental indicators of currency values released at lots of different DAYs such as for example:

- Non-farm Payrolls
- Purchasing Executives Index (PMI)
- Consumer Price Index (CPI)

- Retail Sales
- Long-Lasting Goods

These accounts are generally perhaps not truly the only fundamental elements to view. You'll find also several group meetings in which estimates and commentary can affect marketplaces equally as much as any report. These conferences are generally often called to discuss interest costs, inflation, and other problems that affect money valuations. Even adjustments in the text when handling particular issues — the Federal Reserve chairman's statements on interest rates, for example — can cause market volatility. Therefore, two important meetings for forex dealers to see are the Federal Open marketplace panel and Humphrey Hawkins Hearings.

Simply reading through the accounts and examining the discourse can really help forex fundamental analysts gain a far better comprehension of long-term market trends and enable short-term traders to make money from extraordinary events. If you decide to stick to a fundamental strategy, make sure to hold an economic calendar handy after all instances so you understand when these reports are released. Your broker may, in addition, give real-DAY access to this kind of information.

## Technical Analysis

Technical analysts for the forex assess price trends, comparable for their counterparts during the money marketplaces. The just key distinction between complex evaluation in forex and technical analysis inequities will be the schedule, as forex areas are available twenty-four hours each day. As an end result, some forms of complex analysis that factor in DAY must certainly be changed to factor within the 24-hour forex market. They're probably the most common types of complex analysis utilized in forex:

- The Elliott Surf
- Fibonacci Studies
- Parabolic SAR
- Pivot factors

A lot of technical analysts combine these scientific studies to make more accurate forecasts. (i.e., the common rehearse of mixing the Fibonacci studies with Elliott Waves.) other individuals produce trading and investing systems to continuously track down similar purchasing and marketing circumstances.

## Finding Your Forex Trading Strategy

The majority of successful traders develop an approach and best it over DAY. Some focus on one particular research or calculation, while other people use wide spectrum evaluation to determine their particular investments.

Many experts advise trying a mixture of both fundamental and specialized evaluation so as to make long-term projections and discover entryway and exit areas. Having said that, it will be the specific investor who needs to determine what is best suited for him or the woman (most frequently through learning from mistakes) in the long run.

## Fx Investing Factors to Keep In Mind

Open a trial membership and paper trade until you'll be able to create a steady revenue. Many people get into the forex marketplace and quickly lose serious cash because of taking on also a lot of leverage. It is necessary to spend some DAY and learn how to exchange properly before committing capital.

Trade without emotion. Don't hold "mental" stop-loss points if you don't have the capability to execute them on DAY. Constantly established your stop-loss and take-profit factors to carry out automatically, and don't change them unless absolutely necessary.

The tendency can be a friend. If you are going resistant to the trend, be sure you've got a good cause. That is because you have a higher possibility of success in trading and investing with the trend considering that the forex market tends to move around in that direction as compared to various other.

## The Base Line

The forex marketplace is the biggest market in the field, and people have become increasingly enthusiastic about plying their particular trade in FX. Nevertheless, there tend to be numerous factors to get into membership before you begin investing, such as for example being certain your broker fulfills specific criteria and realizing an investing strategy that works for you. One option to learn how to trade forex will be start-up a demonstration membership and attempt it away.

Like beginning any profession, there's a great deal to discover when you're a day trading newbie. Here are some ideas to steer you in the right direction while you start your journey. These suggestions will bring you established up utilizing the proper equipment and computer software, assist you to choose what to trade and when to trade, explain to you just how much capital you require, how to handle the threat, and just how to practice an exchanging approach successfully.

## Choosing every single day investing Market

As a novice day individual, chances are you'll currently have a market in head that you like to trade. A day trader's job is to look for a repeating pattern (or that repeats sufficient to generate a profit) and after that take advantage of it.

Stocks tend to be the shares of the businesses, such as Walmart (WMT) and Apple (AAPL). During the forex market, you're buying and selling currencies, like the euro and US dollar (EUR/USD). There's a large variety of futures readily available to trade, and futures are often dependent on commodities or spiders. In the futures industry, you can trade crude oil, gold or S&P 500 motions.

One industry isn't much better than another. It boils down to what you would like to exchange, and what you'll be able to manage. The forex marketplace requires the least capital to day trade. You could get started with as little as a few hundred dollars, although beginning with at the very least $500 is recommended.

Working particular futures markets, such as for instance the S&P 500 E-mini (ES), that will be a hugely popular DAY trading futures contract, requires just $1,000 to get going. Starting with a minimum of $2,500 is advised, however.

Stocks require a minimum of $25,000 to visit trade, generating all of them a much more capital-intensive option. While even more capital is needed to visit trade stocks, that doesn't create it a much better or worse marketplace as compared to others. But without having $25,000 to trade (and cannot keep your membership above $25,000), then shares likely aren't the greatest day working marketplace for you. If you have actually a lot more than $25,000 after that shares tend to be a feasible DAY buying and selling market.

All markets supply exceptional profit capacity. Therefore it usually will come down to exactly how a lot of money you have to get started. Choose a market, that way you can start concentrating your own education on that market, and maybe not throwing away your DAY finding out things about some other marketplaces which might not be of support in your selected market.

Don't you will need to learn all the markets as soon as. This will break down your attention and creating money can take much longer. Once you know to generate income in one market, it is a lot easier to adjust to discover other markets. So, be a client. You have no need to learn all the markets at once. You can easily learn different markets later on if you want.

**Gear and Software for DAY Trading Newbies**

**Today trade you need a couple of basic methods:**

- A pc or laptop computer. Having two monitors is preferable, but not necessary. The computer will need to have sufficient memory and a quick enough processor that whenever you operate the exchanging system (discussed afterward) there's no lagging or crashes. You don't need a leading-of-the-line pc, however, you do not want to inexpensive off either. Software and computers are continuously changing, thus be sure your computer is keeping up with the DAYs. A slow computer system can be costly when DAY trading and investing, particularly in the event it crashes when you are in investments, causes you to overlook positions, or its slowness triggers you to receive stuck in trades.

- A trustworthy and fairly quick internet connection. Day traders ought to be using at least a Cable or ADSL type internet hookup. Rates change across these kinds of services, so shoot for at least a mid-range internet package. The slowest speed provided by your internet supplier may perform some work, however, if you have got several internet pages and apps running (which use the online world), you might observe your trading and the investing system isn't updating as fast as it should and therefore can cause issues (find out above). Focus on a mid-range net bundle, and give it a try. You can easily always adjust your net rate later if required. If your internet goes down a good deal, that's an issue. See if there's a much more reliable internet provider. Day investing isn't recommended with a sporadic internet connection.

- A trading platform suitable for your market and magnificence of day investing. If you're only starting, locating the most perfect platform isn't your ultimate goal. Download numerous exchanging systems and attempt them out. Since you will be a beginner, you'll not have a well-developed investing style, however. For that reason, your own exchanging system may someDAYs improve throughout your work, or perhaps you may change exactly how it is established to support your exchanging advancement. NinaTrader is a popular day trading system for futures and forex traders. You'll find a lot of inventory trading and investing systems. Ultimately, check out a couple of that your broker offers and see which you like best.

- A broker. Your broker centers your own trades, and in exchange charges you a payment or fee on your positions. Day dealers would like to concentrate on low-fee agents since large commission costs can destroy the profitability of a day trading strategy. That said, the cheapest charge broker isn't always well. You desire a broker that'll be there to offer support if you have got an issue. A few cents added on a percentage is actually worth it in the event that the company can conserve you 100s or hundreds of bucks whenever you have got a computer crisis and cannot obtain out of your trades. Major banks, while these people provide trading accounts, generally aren't the greatest option for DAY traders. Costs are usually greater at major finance companies, and more compact brokers will typically offer a lot more customizable fee and commission frameworks to DAY traders.

## When you should Day Trade

As a day trader, both as a beginner and a pro, your own life is focused around consistency. One of the ways to create reliability will be trading during the exact same hours each DAY.

While many DAY traders trade for a whole regular session (9:30 a.m. to 4 p.m. EST, for instance, when it comes to the United States inventory market), the majority of the sole trader for a section of a single day. Trading only 2 to 3 many hours a day is actually very usual among day dealers. Here are the hours you will want to focus on.

- For stocks, the optimum DAY for day investing will be the very first one to a couple of hours following the open, together with final DAY prior to the near. 9:30 a.m. to 11:30 a.m. EST is actually a two DAY duration you need to obtain great at trading and investing. This is actually the most volatile period of the DAY, offering the most significant cost techniques and many revenue potentials. The final hour of the day, 3 p.m. to 4 p.m. EST is also typically a great DAY for trading and investing, as some substantial movements happen then also. If you just want to trade for a DAY or two, trade the morning session.

- For DAY exchanging futures, around the available is actually a fantastic DAY for you day trade. Productive futures see some investing activity night and day, therefore good day trading opportunities generally start a bit earlier compared to the stock exchange. If day investing futures concentration on working between 8:30 a.m. and 11 a.m. EST. Futures markets have actually formal closes at various DAYs, however, the last hour of investing in a futures contract additionally typically supplies considerable techniques for day traders to cash in on.
- The forex industry investments 24-hours just about every day during the few days. The EURUSD is actually the preferred DAY investing match. It typically considers by far the most volatility between 0600 and 1700 GMT. Day traders should exchange within these several hours. 1200 to 1500 GMT generally views the greatest price techniques, therefore this is a hugely popular and energetic DAY for day dealers. During this period both London while these markets are open, dealing with the euro and also the US buck.

As each and everyday trader, you don't have to trade all day long. You will probably find a lot more consistency by just trading two to 3 hours a DAY.

## Control Your Day Trading Danger

You've picked a market, have equipment and software setup, and someDAYs understand what is perfect for day investing. Just before also start believing about exchanging, you should know simple tips to control danger. Day traders should control risk in two ways: trade danger and day-to-day threat.

- Trade threat is just how much you will be prepared to take a chance of on every trade. If at all possible, risk 1% or less of the capital for each trade. This is achieved by selecting an entry point after which setting a stop reduction, which will obtain you out of the trade if it starts heading to a lot against you. The danger is also affected by exactly how big of a situation you are taking, consequently, learn how to just how to calculate the correct situation size for shares, forex, or futures. Factoring your situation dimensions, your own entry price, and your end loss price, not one trade should expose you to more than a 1% loss in capital.

- In addition, control your own day-to-day risk. Just like you do not desire a single trade resulting in a lot of damage to your bank account (hence the 1% rule), you additionally don't want eventually to damage your own week or month. Therefore, establish a daily reduction limit. One chance is actually to create it at 3% of the capital. If you should be risking 1% or significantly less on every trade, you'd require to shed three trades or higher (with no winners) to get rid of 3%. With a sound method, that shouldn't happen very frequently. As soon as you strike your daily cap, stop trading for any DAY. When you are regularly profitable, set your daily loss restriction equal to your average winning day. For instance, if you usually make $500 on winning DAYs, then chances are you are enabled to get rid of $500 on losing days. If you drop significantly more than that, end investing. The logic is the fact that we would like to keep daily losings small to ensure the loss can end up being quickly recouped by a typical winning day.

## Exercising Techniques For DAY Trading Newbies

When you begin, don't you will need to discover everything about trading at once. You never require to understand all of it. As a day individual, you merely require one approach which you implement more than over and over.

Just about every day trader's job is to find a repeating design (or that repeats enough to create an income) after which make use of it.

You have no need for a college education or specialist designation, nor do you want to review through 100s of publications, to accomplish that.

Get a hold of one method that provides a method for entry, placing an end reduction and getting profits. After that, get to work with applying that strategy in a trial account.

For forex and futures traders, among the best how to exercise is utilizing the NinjaTrader Replay function, which allows you to trade historic DAYs as though you had been trading in actual DAY.

This implies you can easily practice all the DAY if you wish, even if the market is shut.

No matter what marketplace you trade, available a trial account and begin training your approach. Understanding a method isn't the very same to be in a position to carry out it. No two days are exactly the same in the marketplaces, therefore it takes training to be ready to see the trade configurations and be able to execute the positions without hesitation. Rehearse for at least three months before trading actual money. Merely when you've got at minimum three several months in a line of profitable demonstration functionality should you change to stay exchanging.

Remain dedicated to that single strategy, and only investing the market you chose, just throughout the DAY you have got chosen to exchange.

## From Demo to Alive Trading

The majority of traders observe a deterioration in performance from once they turn from demo trading to live exchanging. Demo trading and investing is a beneficial practice ground for deciding if an approach is viable, however, it can't imitate the particular market exactly, nor does it generate the emotional chaos many dealers confront once they put real cash in the range.

Thus, if you see that your particular exchanging isn't going really well when you start to live (compared to the demonstration), understand that this is actually normal.

Start utilizing the smallest situation size feasible when you to begin with beginning real DAY trading since this helps relieve some stress and anxiety of losing huge amounts of money.

While you become comfier investing genuine money, enhance your situation size up to the 1% limit discussed above. Also, continuously bring your concentration returning to what you've got practiced and applying your methods exactly. Focusing on accuracy and execution may help dilute a few of the powerful emotions that may negatively influence your trading.

## Final Keyword for DAY Trading Novices

Choose a market you are interested in and that can afford to exchange. Subsequently, set yourself up with just the right gear and software. Select a period of day which you will day trade, and just trade during that DAY; typically the greatest day trading instances are around significant marketplace openings and closings.

Control your risk, on each trade and each day. Then, exercise a strategy over and over once more. You never have to know everything to exchange earnings. You have to be in a position to put into action one strategy that makes cash.

Focus on winning with one approach before trying to find out others. Hone your capabilities in a demonstration account, but know that it is really not exactly like real trading. Whenever you turn to buy and selling with real money, a bumpy ride is actually common for a number of months. Focus on accuracy and implementation to steady your nerves.

# CHAPTER 2:

# HOW FAR MONEY YOU OUGHT TO START DAY INVESTING?

## HOW MUCH MONEY YOU OUGHT TO BEGIN DAY TRADING?

"How much capital do I have to start day trading?" is just about the most generally asked questions I receive from individuals who wish to begin day trading shares, forex, or futures markets.

Just how much money you'll need depends on the model of trading that you want to do, for which you trade, and the marketplace you trade (stocks, forex or futures).

### Day investing needs in the US and Abroad for Stock Traders

To DAY trade US shares, you will need to keep free account stability of $25,000 or much more. Begin with at least $30,000 if you intend in order to make significantly more than 4-day trades per trading week. 4 DAY trades or even more per week offers you "day individual position" and you're subject to your $25,000 minimal membership balance. If your own membership drops below $25,000 you won't be able to day trade unless you replenish your account to significantly more than $25,000. This is actually why it's recommended you begin with over $25,000, to provide your self a buffer over and over the minimum need.

You may possibly be able today to exchange other international areas without this membership minimal. If the nation you're in, or desire to exchange, doesn't call for the $25,000 minimal account balance, it is strongly suggested you continue to deposit at least $10,000 to your day exchanging account. With more compact accounts than this, commissions and fees will considerably erode or erase profits made. On bigger reports, the prices of trading and investing have actually significantly less of an effect.

One of the typical mistakes dealers make is getting under-capitalized. Dropping trades and DAYs occur, also into the best dealers. After taking losses you still need to have sufficient money to hold trading.

we recommend risking 1% or less of your money on a trade. The danger is described as the difference between the entry price and your stop loss cost, increased by the number of shares of have. For instance, you purchase an inventory at $10, place a stop loss at $9.75, and simply take 500 shares (position dimensions). Your own danger is actually $0.25 x 500 = $125. To make positions such as this you need $12,500 in your bank account, as $125 is 1% of the account ($12,500). That will be the minimal membership size you may need with this trade, but in the US, you will be required to have $25,000 to visit trade. That means you may be ready to take a chance of as much as $250 per trade, and still remain inside the 1% risk guideline.

For lots more on stock trading needs within the United States, read through this pamphlet from the Securities and Exchange Commission (SEC). Here you will find the main points within the pamphlet:

Minimal Equity necessity: The minimum money required for a customer that is a pattern day trader is actually $25,000 [four-day trades per week]. This $25,000 necessity must be deposited into the customer's account prior to virtually any day exchanging tasks and must be preserved all of the DAY. A consumer cannot meet this $25,000 requirement by cross-guaranteeing separate reports. Each day investing membership is needed to meet the $25,000 requirement independently, using only the financial resources offered in that account.

If a customer's membership comes underneath the $25,000 need, the consumer will likely not be allowed to visit trade until the customer builds up money or securities into the membership to bring back the account into the $25,000 minimum equity degree.

DAY Trading Purchasing Power: a client that is specified as a pattern DAY dealer may exchange as much as four occasions the customer's upkeep margin excessive as of the close of the company of the previous day for money securities. If a buyer exceeds this day investing purchasing power limitation, the customer's broker-dealer will issue a per day trading margin call. The client provides five company days to satisfy their or the woman margin call, during that the customer's day trading buying power is restricted to two DAYs the customer's servicing margin extra predicated on the customer's daily utter trading determination for money securities. If the client does maybe not satisfy the margin phone call because of the 5th company day, a single day trading account will end up being constrained to trading just on a money readily available basis for 90 days or through to the call is fulfilled.

The "buying energy" part above is actually a small complicated to understand, however, it is basically stating that all of us marketplace day dealers can control their day trading capital up to 4:1, so a $30,000 account actually allows your day trader to keep up to $120,000 in DAY investing positions. Brokers have their own leverage rules and could offer much less margin than the 4:1 max.

## Investment Needed To Day Trade Fx

In the forex market, accounts to be opened for smaller levels of money since it is not a topic to your same legislation as stocks. Forex supplies leverage up to 50:1 (higher in some nations). Increased leverage means increased risk and reward. To figure out exactly how much leverage you want, find out How a lot Fx Leverage.

The international Exchange (Fx) marketplace is based on the parallel purchasing of one currency and the attempting to sell off some other. Currencies are readily available for trade twenty-four hours a day, 5 days a week. Becoming that the money marketplace is the biggest market in the world, with a daily quantity of $5 trillion being purchased and offered, the liquidity makes it an appealing day trading choice.

Accounts may be opened for very little as $100, but you'll like to start with at the very least $500 to become in a position to place DAY trades with proper end loss amounts.

With that amount of cash you aren't going which will make a living through the marketplaces. Though, you may make a couple of dollars a DAY which will increase your membership over DAY.

If you'd like an income from forex DAY trading, start with a minimum of $1000, and ideally $3,000 to $5,000. This quantity enables you to potentially start building month-to-month earnings, that will be what many DAY dealers are after. To get more, find out Just how much revenue Do I have to Trade Fx?

## Investment Involved in DAY Trade Futures

Futures contracts are common because futures day traders don't want to keep the $25,000 membership minimal that's required of United States inventory day dealers.

Futures contracts tend to be exchanged on all kinds of products, such as for instance petroleum, silver, natural gas, and stock indexes.

To DAY trade futures the majority of agents only require at least a deposit of $1,000. In an effort to visit trade an E-mini S&P 500 (ES) futures contract–one from the popular futures contracts for day exchanging–most agents require you have actually at the very least $400 or $500 of offered capital in your bank account to take a single contract trade. This is known as day trading margin.

## Opening a free account with only $1,000 isn't recommended.

Start a futures account with a minimum of $8,000 or higher if DAY trading ES futures. For various other futures agreements, your dealer might need additional margin, so you may decide to begin day investing with at the very least $10,000 to provide you with some flexibility in what you could exchange.

Utilizing a risk-controlled strategy you can begin to develop an earnings off of $8,000, while nevertheless only risking about 1% of this account per trade.

## Final Word On Exactly How A Lot Of Money It Requires to Day Trade

Day investing shares are capital intensive, as you'll require to preserve at least a $25,000 membership stability for all of our shares. Make certain you deposit significantly more than this to provide your self a buffer. Trip underneath the minimum balance and you can't day trade.

Forex supplies a much less capital rigorous option to day trade. While the money prerequisite is actually much less, beginning with at least $1,000 or even more is suggested.

For futures trading, if you trade an agreement like ES, begin with $8,000 or higher. Each contract has different margin requirements, therefore if marketing different contracts focus on $10,000 for some flexibility.

Before risking actual capital and making a deposit with a broker, produce a trading plan and check it over in a demo membership. Be lucrative for at least a couple several months in a row before opening a real day exchanging account. This gives you DAY for you see for which you need improvements.

# CHAPTER 3:

# PERSONAL EXCHANGING

## SOCIAL EXCHANGING

Spending in financial markets such as for instance shares, Forex and cryptocurrencies need extensive knowledge and knowledge. You have to be up-to-date with news events affecting the company globe, and also have actually the ability to read charts, statistics reports and comprehend trends.

If you are lacking this capacity, odds are you may lose your own money in the marketplace. It's unfortunate that lots of people continue steadily to lose their particular difficult earned cash in the financial marketplaces mainly because they have actually little knowledge of how to and when to invest. Social exchanging comes in handy in cubing such challenges.

### So, What Exactly Is Personal Investing?

Social trading works a lot more or less like a personal circle. Really the only distinction is actually that instead of revealing selfies or lunch pictures, on a trading network people express trading ideas. Right here traders connect, watch exchanging outcomes of additional specialists and brainstorm on industry scenarios in real DAY.

As an investor or less experienced individual, in social trading your financial trading choices are derived from some other proficient investors created financial content gathered from different trustworthy platforms. Easily put, once you identify a profitable trader and you also like their investing strategy, you can begin following them and copy their trades.

### Do you know the advantages of personal Trading and investing?

### Well, a number of the benefits of Social Trading include:

• Fast accessibility to dependable trading and investing information

Social Trading platforms cut down on the procedure of looking for reliable trading info by giving extensive info from specialist traders over the world. You additionally have to connect with the skilled traders regarding the programs like one-on-one Tutorage.

• Fast grasping of the trading and investing marketplace

Personal Trading platforms reduce the extent and cost of getting an expert buyer by permitting you to learn from experienced people, efficiently and quickly.

• Receiving while nonetheless learning

Social Trading platforms enable you to learn from experienced people, in which you are free to understand just how to navigate the trading industry but still earn some cash by copying their trades. Consequently, you don't have to wait patiently until such DAY you have got all the desired knowledge to help you start making.

• Develop trading and investing community of buyers

Personal trading systems build an area of buyers, in which you have to have interaction with other investors and share information, while also collaborating on various ventures. It became an internet system, you'll be able to access trading information from anyplace in the field easily and quickly as long as you have got the net.

## Popular Systems for Personal Trading

Today that you know just what personal trading can be nice as some of the benefits, what about you understand a small about platforms you can make use of for Social Trading.

Contained in this posting, we all shall explore both conventional social trading systems along with modern/crypto personal trading platforms:

## 1. Spiking

www.spiking.io

Spiking has got to its credit the very first technology exchanging application created to aid the average buyer to comprehend the nitty-gritty of this investing industry. The proven real-DAY revisions assist the investor in ascertaining the reason why when it comes to a spike in the exchanging market. It will help the typical dealer follow the Big dealers like Warren Buffett, as these people trade on the inventory market, aiding the investor in making informed decisions fairly than relying on impulse. This has around 170,000 advanced investors along with it correct today.

The present app may be installed on Google Enjoy and Application Store.

**One of the keys functions of this app include:**

- See exactly what shares are active in NASDAQ, Dow Jones, NYSE, AMEX, S&P, and others
- All American inventory market cost updates, news feeds, and price notifications
- Get notified whenever buddies buy or sell inventory possibilities
- Track sophisticated traders real-DAY

Spiking is actually a management method using Blockchain Spike Protocol to enable you, as a trader, to find and stick to industry whales with the goal of learning or collaborating together with them. Right here, whales relate to seasoned dealers, large holders of cryptocurrency tokens, exploration pools or essential managers of companies owning cryptocurrency tokens.

Spiking will collaborate with leading sharks to offer you, as a trader, a Certified Clever investor (CST) program that can enable you to discover about trading and investing in cryptocurrencies. Additionally, you will have the ability to collect and confirm information regarding sharks. And through its Spike Protocol, it will likely be able to validate all trading deals to ensure there is actually no falsification of data.

It will probably, in addition, use Spike Tokens as a reward incentive as well as all transactions on the protocol. As a trader, you'll be able to shell out for the CST program with Spike Tokens. Additionally, if you graduate through the program as a leading student or you receive chosen whilst the top teacher in the CST program, you're going to be compensated in Tokens. The tokens will essentially allow customers to gain access to the Spiking system and its services.

## 2. eToro

https://www.etoro.com

eToro is a system allowing users to talk about and access each additional information and trading activities like on social communities.

The platform has actually attributed these types of Information Feed, duplicate Trading and demo accounts for users. The News Feed element enables users to keep track of and manually replicate their own recommended dealers, while the duplicate exchanging element immediately does the coping for users. The demo account is actually totally free and endless for users, and additionally, they can try most of the eToro trading and investing and social attributes.

## 3. TradingView

https://www.tradingview.com/

TradingView is a cloud along with a web-based personal investing program for Futures and Fx traders. It gives extraordinary charting resources and social elements for beginners and advanced dealers to review and share investing ideas.

Through a forum setting, the working platform enables users to adhere to, copy as effectively exchange tips with other like-minded traders. Dealers talk to their unique peers and with additional advanced dealers on the present market conditions. The talks are in real DAY.

Dealers release their exchanging tips, and they have feedback or opinions of their dealers trading the same tool. The target here is promoting each other to prosper as traders by sharing ideas and witnessing exactly what other people are generally undertaking.

## 4. Covesting

https://covesting.io/

Covesting is a Blockchain and intelligent agreement based system that allows novice investors to connect with skilled traders to earn income into the crypto market. Here, as an investor, you could generate earnings in the crypto market by simply duplicating exchanging methods from proficient dealers automatically. You get to pick the trader to content from in accordance with his/her strategy and level of trading skill.

On the platform, as an investor, you are free to see and choose skilled cryptocurrency dealers relating to their investing strategy, which matches your income aim. Before you pick an experienced trader, you will get a summary of each skilled trader's strategy, read their exchanging strategies evaluations, accessibility history of the real-DAY trading method. Therefore you will be ready to know, before picking, the best-skilled investor to complement your own profit goal. And because the skilled traders are many, you can decide to sign up for as many specialist dealers while you want.

But it's not just beginner traders who gain benefit from the platform; professional dealers benefit too through profit from profit sharing from an investor.

## Final word

To place up, we now have learned that social exchanging enables free of charge flow and access to details to assist people to make well-informed investment decisions through leveraging in the power for the community.

Personal Trading platforms supply novices strategies exactly where they can very quickly and efficiently trade when you look at the crypto marketplace without having the anxiety about beginners' failures. Needless to say, they don't totally eradicate failure, however, they reduce the chances of failure.

Since personal trading platforms cater both for beginners and professionals, they create a reliable trading area, which allows you to make revenue while you learn.

# CHAPTER 4:

# AN INTRO TO DAY TRADING AND INVESTING TOGETHER WITH TIPS METHODS OF MAKE MONEY IN THE MARKET

## Just What Is Day Trading?

The meaning of "day trading" is the buying and selling of a security in one exchanging day. If you're day trading online you are going to close over the position prior to the marketplaces close throughout the day to secure your profits. You may possibly also enter and leave several trades during just one trading session.

Agents on the event have actually various meanings for 'active' or day traders. Their particular viewpoint is frequently based on the number of positions a client opens up or closes within a month or year. Some brands also relate to 'hyper-active dealers' – a step beyond the 'active trader'.

DAY trading is actually normally completed by utilizing trading methods of capitalizing on tiny cost moves in high-liquidity shares or currencies. The purpose of DayTrading.com will provide you an introduction to DAY trading basics and just what it takes to help you allow it to be as every single day trader. From scalping a few pips profit in mins on a forex trade to trading development events on stocks or indices – we explain just how.

## Just What Can End Up Being Traded?

The absolute most financially rewarding and popular day trading areas today tend to be:
• Forex – The foreign exchange currency market is the world's most common and fluid.

The pure volume of forex trading tends to make it attractive today dealers. There are generally multiple short-term options in a hot currency pair, and a unique amount of liquidity to ensure opening and shutting positions is actually quick and slick. Much more suitable for technical evaluation, there are various other ways to trade currency exchange. In inclusion, forex has no main marketplace. This indicates dealers can create investments six days a few days, 24 hours a day. They provide a fantastic starting point for entryway level or aspiring traders with complete DAY tasks. Dealers in the Australian Continent might be specifically enthusiastic about working the AUD USD set.

• Stocks – actual shares in specific companies, regular and Leveraged ETFs (an "Exchange Traded Fund" retains numerous stocks or commodities and is actually traded like just one stock), futures, and inventory options.

Trading shares intraday offers various options than a traditional 'buy and hold' strategy. Speculating on stock rates via CFDs or distributed gambling, for instance, hostile dealers can benefit from slipping prices also. Margin or control, in addition, lower the capital necessary to open up a situation. So you are able to take a place from the latest news launch, item statement or monetary report – along with technical indications.

• Cryptocurrencies – The two hottest currently are Bitcoin and Ethereum.

The financial vehicle of the moment. Amazing development has viewed cryptos attract many brand new investors. Agents are generally additionally guaranteeing retail accessibility to these areas is actually significantly less complicated. Having a view on any of the new blockchain-based currencies is actually getting simplified all the DAY. Obstacles to entry are now almost nil, so whether you're a bull or a keep, today will be the DAY.

• Binary Alternatives – The simplest and most foreseeable approach, while the timing and come back on a successful trade are known in advance.

Regulating changes are generally pending, in accordance with the sector maturing, these products are now offered by huge developed brand names. The only question for you is actually – will the asset increase in value, or otherwise not? With the downside limited to your measurements of the trade, and the possible commission understood in sophisticated, understanding binaries is simple enough. They provide various techniques of trading and investing, and can play a role in any day trader's everyday portfolio.

• Futures – The future price of an item or safety.

• Commodities – Oil and organic gas, meals things, metals, and minerals

If you're S&P 500 DAY investing, you'll be getting and selling the shares of organizations, such as Starbucks and Adobe. During the day investing forex marketplace, you'll be trading currencies, for instance, the Euro, U.S buck and GBP. Within the futures marketplace, typically according to commodities and spiders, you are able to trade everything from silver to cocoa.

Index funds often take place in financial information these DAYs, but they are sluggish financial vehicles that make all of them unsuitable for daily trades. They have actually, but, recently been shown to be great for long-term trading plans.

Another raising area of great interest during the payday trading world is actually a digital currency. DAY trading with Bitcoin, LiteCoin, Ethereum along other altcoins currencies is actually an expanding company. With lots of volatility, potential eye-popping comes back and a volatile future, day exchanging in cryptocurrency could be an interesting method to follow.

**Obtaining Started**

Recent research reveals a rise when you look at the wide range of day trading newbies. But unlike the short-expression exchanging from the past, today's traders are generally wiser and much better updated, to some extent because of trader academies, classes, and resources, such as trading programs. Daytrading.com exists to assist inexperienced dealers who have educated and avoided mistakes while being able to visit trade.

DAY trading 101 – have to grips with trading shares or forex real DAY using a demo membership first, these people can give you indispensable trading tips. These free trading simulators give you the chance to discover before you decide to put real money on the line. They, in addition, offer hands-on training in how to choose stocks.

It also means changing out the television along with other passions for academic guides and online methods. Find out about strategy to get an in-depth knowledge of the complex trading world. DayTrading.com is the perfect novices guide to day trading online.

## Books for Beginners

- 'Day trading and swing trading the money market', Kathy Lein
- 'Day Trading And Investing for Dummies', Ann Logue

Both guides give you the standard day trading rules to stay by. You'll in addition benefit from suggestions about stock picks, plus creative method ideas. As Benjamin Franklin highlighted, 'financial investment in knowledge will pay the greatest interest'.
While the 'for dummies' line of books tend to be very available, it'll be beneficial to broaden the depth of exchanging literary works you try – A lot more on day trading books

## Activities And Technical Review

DAY trading and investing chart habits paint an obvious image of the trading task which enables you to discover people's motivations. These people could highlight s&p day trading signals for instance, such as for example volatility, which can help you anticipate potential cost motions.
The 2 most popular day investing chart patterns are reversals and continuations. Whilst the former indicates a development will change as soon as completed, the second suggests the trend continues to rise. Understanding these trading patterns, as well as 'triangles', 'head and shoulders', 'cup and handle', 'wedges' and lots more, will all turn you into much better well informed when considering using your trading strategies.

## Day Investing Strategies

Mind over to web pages like Reddit and you'll see many trading dummies who will frequently fall in the approach hurdle, bringing the very first momentum examples they see and losing money kept, right and middle. Savvy dealers will employ day dealing techniques in forex, grain futures and something else they're trading in, to provide them an advantage over the marketplace. That very small side can end up being all that separates successful day traders from losers.

You'll find a number of DAY trading strategies and methods out truth be told there, but all will depend on precise data, thoroughly laid out in maps and spreadsheets. Options consist of:

- Sway trading
- Scalping
- Exchanging zones
- Trading and investing in the amount
- Arbitrage trading and investing
- An easy DAY trading exit strategy
- Utilizing news

It is actually people who stick religiously to their own small-expression trading strategies, principles and details that produce the greatest outcomes. As well numerous minor losses add up after a while.

**Trading And Investing Accounts**

The component of your day trading setup will include selecting an investing membership. There's a multitude of various membership possibilities available to you, however, you want to find one that meets your specific requirements.

- **Money account** – DAY trading with a money membership (also referred to as without margin), will enable one to only exchange the capital you have got in your membership. This limits the possible profits, however, it also inhibits you from losing more than you'll be able to afford.
- **Margin account** – This kind account enables you to borrow cash from your agent. This will allow you to bolster your own potential profits, but additionally has the risk of better losses and rules to adhere to. If you would like begin day trading with no minimum this isn't the choice for your needs. Many brokerage organizations will insist you lay all the way down a minimum investment before you could start exchanging on margin. You can easily, in addition, enjoy a

margin telephone call, where your own broker requires a higher deposit to protect potential losses.

The broker's number has more in-depth informative data on membership choices, such as DAY trading cash and margin accounts. We, in addition, explore expert and VIP reports in-depth on the membership types page.

## Language

Learn the trading and investing lingo and language and you'll unlock the home to an entire number of investing keys. Below we have actually collated the main basic jargon, to create an easy to comprehend day exchanging glossary.

## General

- **Leverage price** – this will be the rate your broker will grow your deposit by, providing you with getting power.
- **Computerized trading** – Automated trading systems are generally products that will instantly type in and leave trades predicated on a pre-programmed group of regulations and standards. Also, they are known as algorithmic trading systems, marketing robots, or simply bots.
- **Original market Offering (IPO)** – This is when an organization offers a fixed number of stocks to the market to boost money.
- **Float** – This is just how a lot of shares are generally accessible to trade. If an organization emits 10,000 stocks in the preliminary IPO, the float would be 10,000.
- **Beta** – This numeric value steps the fluctuation of an inventory against alterations in the marketplace.
- **Cent shares** – They're any shares exchanging below $5 a share.
- **Profit/Loss proportion** – Based on a portion basis, this is basically the way of measuring a system's ability to come up with profit rather than reduction.

- **Entry points** – This is basically the cost at which you purchase and enter your place.
- **Exit factors** – This is actually the cost at which you promote and exit your own position.
- **Bull/Bullish** – By taking a bullish position DAY investing you expect the inventory to go up.
- **Bear/Bearish** – If you're taking a bearish position you anticipate the stock to get down.
- **Market developments** – This is basically the basic direction protection is proceeding over an offered DAY period.
- **Hotkeys** – These pre-programmed keys enable you to enter and leave trades swiftly, making all of them perfect if you will need to exit a dropping position right as you possibly can.

**Charts, Graphs, Patterns & Technique**

- Support amount – This will be the cost level in which the demand is potent sufficient that it prevents the decrease in price past it.
- Resistance amount – This will be the cost level in which the need is strong enough that selling the security will eliminate the escalation in cost.
- Transferring Averages – these people give you with vital buy and sell indicators. Whilst they won't tell you in advance if modification is imminent, they're going to confirm if an existing pattern is however in movement. Make use of all of them properly and you can tap into a potentially profitable development.
- Relative energy Index (RSI) – applied to compare gains and losings over a particular duration, it will measure the speed and modification of the cost motions of security. Various other words, it gives an evaluation of the power of a security's current cost performance. DAY trading tip – this list shall help you determine oversold and overbought problems in the investing of a valuable asset, making it possible for you to steer obvious of prospective issues.

- Transferring Normal Convergence Divergence (MACD) – This technical signal determines the real difference between an instrument's two great going averages. Making use of MACD can provide you straightforward invest in and sell trading indicators, which makes it popular amongst beginners.
- Bollinger Bands – They measure the 'high' and 'low' of a cost in relationship to prior trades. They may be able to help with routine identification and allow you to arrive at systematic investing decisions.
- Vix – This ticker symbol for the Chicago Board Alternatives Exchange (CBOE), demonstrates the estimated volatility on top of the next thirty day period.
- Stochastics – Stochastic will be the point on the existing price in connection to a budget range over DAY. The approach will forecast when costs are likely to turn by contrasting the closing cost of safety to its budget range.

If you stumble across a term or phrase that leaves you scratching your mind, refer right back to this DAY trading dictionary and possibilities are you'll get a quick and easy description.

Read the glossary for definitions of several more words and ideas.

## DAY Trading vs The Options

Yes, you've got day trading, but with choices like swing trading, standard trading and automation – how carry out you understand which to utilize?

- Sway trading – Swing traders usually create their own play over several DAYs or also days, rendering it various to day investing. It can nevertheless be a great technique when it comes to a trader who would like to broaden.
- Traditional investing – Traditional trading is actually an extended game and looks to put cash in popular assets such as for example stocks, bonds, and real property for long-term value understanding. Reasonable investment returns over an entire 12 months are into the 5-7% range. Unless

THE SOUL OF BUSINESS ONLINE [9 IN 1] BY DAVID LAZARUS

you're already wealthy and can spend millions, conventional trading comes back also little to make most of a distinction on a daily basis. Nonetheless, the smart individual will also invest long-term.

- Robo-advisors – An increasing amount of individuals are turning to robot-advisors. You merely chose an investing profile, next punch in your own amount of risk and period of DAY for investing. After that, an algorithm will do all of the weighty training. This will be usually a long-term trading program and too sluggish for daily utilize.

DAY trading vs long-term investing tends to be two completely different games. They might require entirely different techniques and mindsets. Before you decide to dive into one, think about how many days you have, and how rapidly you need to find out results. All of us suggest having long-term trading propose to enhance your everyday positions.

## Day Trading And Investing For a Living

So you would you like to work complete DAY from the house and possess an independent trading way of life? If that's the case, you should be aware that turning component DAY working into a lucrative work with a liveable salary calls for specialist tools and gear to provide you the necessary side. You might also need to be self-disciplined, patient and treat it like any proficient job. Becoming the own boss and deciding the very own work hours tend to be fantastic benefits if you succeed.

## Analytic Program

Whilst it will come with a significant price tag, DAY traders who depend on specialized signals will rely more on software than on news. Whether you make use of Windows or Mac computer, just the right trading software will have:

- Automatic Pattern Recognition – Identifies flags, stations, along with other indicative patterns,

- Hereditary and Neural apps – Profit from neural systems and genetic algorithms to higher anticipate future price movements.
- Broker integration – With direct links to brokerages, you are able to automatically execute trades, the removal of psychological distractions and streamlining the execution procedure.
- Backtesting – pertains to strategies to previous positions to show exactly how these people would have performed. This allows dealers to higher comprehend exactly how particular trading methods may execute during the future.
- Multiple development sources – Online newsfeeds and radio news notifications play a vital part in DAY investing. As Kofi Annan rightly asserted in probably the most sensible working quotes, 'knowledge is power'. The greater amount of you understand, the quicker you'll be able to respond, and the quicker you can react, the more day exchanging profits you may make.

## Psychology

If you are trading as a career you must grasp the emotions. When you are generally dipping inside and out of various hot stocks, you have to produce swift choices. The thrill of those choices can also lead to some dealers obtaining a trading dependency. To stop that and also to make intelligent decisions, follow these well-known day trading guidelines:

- **Managing worry** – Also the supposedly greatest stocks can begin plummeting. Anxiety then establishes in and many buyers liquidate their holdings. Today whilst they prevent losings, they even wave good-bye to possible gains. Recognizing that fear is actually a normal response enables you to definitely maintain focus and respond rationally.
- **'Pigs get slaughtered'** – whenever you're in a winning place, understanding whenever to leave before you receive whipsawed or blown out of the place isn't effortless. Dealing

with your very own avarice is a hurdle, but one you must get over.

Becoming present and self-disciplined is really important if you wish to become successful when you look at the DAY trading globe. Identifying your own psychological pitfalls and separating the feelings is actually vital.

## Knowledge

DayTrading.com is available because we could perhaps not discover a reliable day investing school, college, academy, or institute that operates courses where you could obtain an all-inclusive day trading education. This web site ought to be your primary manual whenever finding out how to day trade, but needless to say there are other resources available to you to accentuate the material:

- Podcasts
- Blog Sites
- Online DAY investing classes
- Practice game applications
- Publications
- Ebooks
- Audiobooks
- Seminars
- Journals
- Message boards like Discord
- Discussion Boards
- Chat rooms (always cost-free)
- Updates
- Pdf manuals

For the ideal amount of income, you can even obtain your own personal DAY trading mentor, that may be truth be told there to coach you every step of this way. Opt when it comes to learning methods that finest satisfy your specific requirements, and recall, knowledge is actually energy. The 'Day Trading For Dummies' books are generally not the only option!

## 7 Ways To Success

Whether you're trying to find jobs you can do from home, or perhaps you wish to begin day trading as an interest, follow these seven essentials.

## 1. Setting up

The greater begin you allow yourself, the better the chances of very early success. That indicates whenever you're sat at your desk, looking at your monitors with fingers dancing across your keyboard, you're looking at the best sources of data. That implies having the greatest investing platform for your Mac computer or PC laptop/desktop, having a quick and dependable asset scanner and live flow, and software that won't crash at a crucial minute.

## 2. Ensure that stays simple

This is particularly vital at the start. You may be enthusiastic about s&p 500, mutual funds, relationship futures, Nasdaq, Nasdaq futures, blue-chip stocks, equities, or the Dax 30, but first of all focus on only one. Get proficient at earning money from just one market/security before you decide to branch away. The other marketplaces will wait for you personally.

## 3. Be sensible

The flicks might have managed to get look effortless, but don't be misled. Actually, your day trading gurus in college devote several hours. You won't end up being asked to join that hedge fund after reading through simply one Bitcoin guide. You ought to purchase those trading books from Amazon, grab that spy pdf guide, and discover how it all operates.

## 4. Threat management

This will be probably the most essential lessons you can discover. You need to adopt a money management method that permits you to exchange regularly. Is day investing really worth it if you'll be broke because of the end regarding the first thirty days?

History has shown that a lot of successful traders never chance significantly more than 1% of the account stability on just one trade. Thus, if you had $25000 in your bank account, you'd only risk $250 on just one trade. Constantly sit down with a calculator and run the amounts just before entering a position.

## 5. Keep a record

One of the day exchanging basics is actually to help keep a tracking spreadsheet with detailed earnings research. If you'll be able to rapidly seem back and see for which you went wrong, you can identify spaces and address any pitfalls, minimizing losings the next DAY.

## 6. Timing

Just like the whole world is actually separated into groups of people located in different DAY areas, thus are the markets. If you begin trading in the Cac 40 at 11:00 ET, you may find you've missed the best entry signals of the day currently, minimizing your potential conclusion of daily earnings. Therefore, if you need to end up being at the top, you have to seriously modify your own working hours.

## 7. Sensible decision making

Whenever you begin DAY trading you'll have actually a host of difficult decisions to create. In the event, you are utilizing Robinhood? What about day trading on Coinbase? Have you got just the right desk setup? Exactly where are you able to locate a shine layout? Exactly how do you really create a watch number? The significance of all of these questions and a great deal more is explained in detail over the extensive pages on this internet site.

There are also more in-depth and detailed classes within our very top suggestions.

## Taxes

The tax scenario for day traders is actually completely centered on for which country the trader is "tax resident". Furthermore, a prominent advantage these as Bitcoin is actually so brand-new that tax laws have never but fully caught up – is it money or an item?

The way you are going to be taxed can also depend on the specific circumstances. For instance, within the UK the HMRC are recognized to address DAY trading tasks from 3 different perspectives:

- Speculative/similar to betting tasks – Day trading income would likely be totally free from income taxation, company income tax, and capital benefits taxation.
- Substantial self-employed trading task – expected to end up being topic to business taxation.
- Significant tasks of a personal buyer – Gains and losses would fall underneath the remit associated with the capital gains tax program. Paying just business tax would be highly unlawful and open you up to serious financial penalties.

Because of the fluctuations in the DAY investing task, you can fall into any three categories over the course of a few years. Even though you don't need a license, it's important you carefully monitor your own trades, seek income tax guidance, and stay within laws and regulations when processing your tax statements.

Check the help guide to Day Trading Taxes for much more detailed information on income tax rules and revealing.

**Just How Much Money Will You Produce?**

An overriding aspect in your pros and cons listing is probably the vow of riches. We've all seen tales of day exchanging millionaires who started trading in just 1000 dollars, but soon struck the jackpot and mastered the markets. Whilst, needless to say, they are doing exist, the fact is, profits may differ hugely.

Generating a living day trading depends on the dedication, the discipline, and your strategy. Most of which you'll be able to find in-depth informative data on across this website.

The real DAY trading question then, does it actually work? If you're willing to spend enough DAY and energy, then for you, it could very well perform.

# CHAPTER 5:

# THE RIGHT EMOTIONAL MINDSET TO HAVE

For some, trading and investing will come right down to indications, inventory screeners, and economic accounts.

Very few traders elevate their particular online game sufficient to comprehend the essential importance of noise psychological state. In this short article, we will reach a wide range of topics related to day trading therapy and tips on how to use these tools to keep in control of this game.

## #1 - Patience

One of these toughest things to learn whenever day trading is perseverance. [1] when the market starts you will notice the level 2 flashing green and reddish and alerts going down.

If you're not coming from a destination of discipline, the market has actually a way of sucking you into trades without the permission. I'm sure, you will be taking the trigger, but it is just like the marketplace places a hypnotic trance over you and you find your self jumping into investments too quickly.

You've got to locate an approach for looking at most of the activity, yet not having any action until the great setup materializes.

A genuine test for you will be a glance at your own finally 3 months of trading information and find out if you'll find eventually in which you failed to place a trade.

If you're unable to find eventually, then you're likely forcing the problem.

## #2 - Understand the Herd

Have you ever viewed the tv series The Walking inactive? Effectively during the show, you'll find these herds, which are mobs of zombies that move in unison as these people march towards their own then person dinner.

It's unfortunate to state, but dealers are not any much better than these mindless creatures every so often.

As a trader, you ought to end up being in a position to recognize the thoughts of different traders on a macro degree. These feelings can present themselves when you look at the form of worry and greed (which we touch upon then) and so are illustrated from the chart. I simply composed a piece on two-cent stock guide habits which walkthrough in detail the boom and bust period through the day period.

Simply bear in mind a number of personal beings can continue to be insanely bullish more than the offer signal you may be acquiring from your Williams %roentgen indicator.

Learn to have the feeling of the herd in inclusion in comprehending the specialized setups.

## #3 - Understand the Psychology of worry and Greed

Fear within the stock areas is whenever investors shun risk and seek safety in possessions with reduced yields. The general thinking here is that the investor is just too worried to invest their particular cash for worry that they would finish up shedding their particular capital instead of making any profits.

Fear can additionally show up as investors just worry sell actually if the inventory is well below fair value.

Worry and Green rounds as observed in the CBOE Volatility Index

Greed into the stock markets, on the other side hand, is when traders find higher returns regardless of this risk. This means they tend to be just getting into a position or using as well much control in hopes of making huge returns.

These feelings happen during the extensive marketplace but can also creep up on you as an individual investor.

## Greed

The fact not discussed is really what happens to you mentally after greed or concern holds ahold of you.

If you've been showing greedy conduct and winning, this is probably a lot of dangerous mixtures. This will push one to exchange with dimensions along with small to no care. What do you really believe will occur? That's suitable, a blow-up trade.

## Fear

Worry will be the exact face-to-face, where it shows itself in your capability to carry out trades. [2] This is often by means of maybe not taking a situation or incapable of close a losing position.

## Just how to overcome these Emotions

## Meditation

The one remedy for those two emotions is actually meditation and a lot of it. There isn't any acquiring out from both of these, very please don't tell your self you have every little thing under control.

## #4 - Cut the displays Off

Will you be done trading when it comes to DAY? If yes, then reduce your displays off. The sheer fatigue of trading all day very long can injure your performance as well as your nature.
Take the DAY to get outside and breathe within the fresh atmosphere. Pick up a hobby, but first and foremost reduce the displays off.

## #5 - Prevent the Huge Blow Up DAYs

## Explosion

If you should be brand-new to trading, do not fret about how a lot of cash you are able to make. Merely focus on without having big losing trades and large dropping DAYs.
Beyond the cash, the psychological effect will last very well beyond the finishing bell.
So, have a look at each trade initially on just how much you'll be able to to lose versus how much you possibly can make.

## #6 - Try not to Add to burning opportunities [3]

You'll find DAYs in past DAYs where we have actually bought a breakout and the stock rolls more than. So, everything I believed ended up being a breakout now becomes a pullback trade.

we should, to begin with, honor my own stop and if the stop is perhaps not hit, sell the stock out near my entry to minimize my danger.

But performed I actually do this? Nope. we would wait for then support level down or even for some anxiety to kick-in after which double my place.

Today, you'll find occasions in which the stock becomes right back to my own initial entry point and I'm up big.

There are also other DAYs where I recently breakeven on the trade.

Each of these makes me really feel like I am toying with the market.

But then the inevitable occurs. The inventory continues reduced and a small manageable loss gets a life-changing occasion.

"The greatest enemy of the individual is fear. He who is actually afraid loses." That's the basic thesis of "Tradingpsychologie", a 2012 German book on trading and investing therapy that was received with fantastic enthusiasm. Lots of audience and reviewers commented this was the greatest book on the topic that these people had ever read or that it was the first that ended up being of every actual usage.

The book's author, Norman Welz, is a psychologist and reporter that created a keen interest when you look at the inventory industry in addition to associated therapy. Their specialty is trading therapy, a topic upon which he has got not just substantial experience but in addition some special ideas. Among other situations, he trains dealers to create their minds in the right way.

Welz stresses that exactly what differentiates both their function and his book from the huge literature in the field will be the importance of applied investing therapy. It is actually well known that traders need self-discipline, but accepting this concept is in fact not enough to allow investors to work in the appropriate fashion.

### It's Really All into the Notice

The substance of the issue is that many men and women like and need security in all its forms, but "trading will be the most vulnerable business you may be in," claims Welz. The man argues that hardly any other occupation makes therefore numerous and these intense emotions and reflects a lot of your characters. The guy goes as far as to state that stock market activities personify money: "we don't just trade assets and money, we all get to be the money," according to Welz.

To trade effectively, the proper mindset is essential. However, there's nothing more difficult than divorcing ourselves through the multitude of aspects that have created all of our mindsets when you look at the very first spot and therefore influence how our minds work. We are generally affected by moms and dads, family members, good friends, the planet, society, the mass media, publications and much more. Because of the DAY, we begin trading and investing, a few of these influences tend to correct trading habits that are generally often impaired or suboptimal. Attempting to change these patterns is someplace between difficult and frightening.

## How exactly to Develop an exchanging Brain

## How Come Traders Neglect Psychology?

To be able to comprehend Welz's approach, it is important to understand the pervading character of therapy and the mind. While the idea that therapy is essential to your stock marketplace is nothing brand new, Welz believes that trading is literally 100% therapy. Without a mind, we all could never evaluate monetary threats or recognize trends. "No brain, no inventory market trading," states Welz. Emotional strength is actually therefore absolutely fundamental to exchanging success. Furthermore, about 95% of your measures are subconscious mind, so we often tend to replicate our actions over as well as over again. All too usually, this replication suggests repeating not the right or even disastrous programs of motion.

To aid this assertion, Welz relates to research for which 120 traders had been provided a method that had shown its intrinsic importance statistically in 19 of these previous 20 many years. After a test 12 months, it ended up being apparent that 119 among these dealers were unsuccessful with the system because their particular mental inclinations brought all of them astray. All but one trader met with the incorrect mental procedures. "Success comes from the head," states Welz. The program ended up being good, however, the attitudes and therapy with that the dealers applied that system was not.

Many traders are guys, who tend to consider that psychology is not what actually does matter. They believe that what does matter, rather, are simplistic notions to be coldly rational, very well informed and experienced. Relating to Welz, nevertheless, rationality, information, and knowledge don't help if the mind is perhaps not correctly set and tuned. So what can we perform to get all of our thoughts and subconscious to act correctly?

## Welz's Approach

Welz deals with the minds of dealers through the subconscious mind and hypnosis. Students are placed into trustworthy spirits additionally the needed competencies are anchored in subconscious mind areas of the mind. When this process sounds a bit odd, start thinking about this: For lots of years, Welz has actually helped people overcome their unique fears and obstructions, enabling them to win sporting titles and even to secure an Olympic triumph. Also, he's got helped dealers to make cash through triggering the correct mental energy, determination and, therefore, conduct. He stresses that each individual provides unique mental bridges and obstacles that have to be entered or conquered in purchase to guarantee success.

"Trading self-discipline" arrives from modifying one's conduct in the desired path and conquering the psychological opposition and fear that generally get in the way. Particularly relating to investing, Welz believes that "you'll find armies of resistance." The trading brain, in fact, entails the integration of the proper financial investment and marketplace information with just the right psychological capabilities. It's not too the most common skills are generally insignificant, it is merely which they usually have overridden because of the wrong emotional and behavioral patterns.

Powerful exchanging, therefore, requires personality customization. Relating to Welz, "people who are not happy to attempt this should not really bother with trading." Those who focus just on the so-called logical components of charts and styles, including all those habits like "flags, triangles and channels or prevents and exchanging selections," will ultimately flounder on the wide variety of emotions that certainly come into play and actually dominate the marketplaces.

The above, clarifies Welz, is "the ultra-short model" of their theory, but indeed the substance of the issue. Plus, he feels that anybody can come to be a trader and get over their or her fears. Given that individuals are generally maybe not scientifically ill, these people can resolve those fundamental anxieties when they are truly willing to function on themselves. In inclusion, they need a good feeling and grasp on the truth if success will be the outcome. Of program, economic understanding, and skills, information and research all, however, perform key roles.

Nonetheless, it's hard to function getting the truth to be told there. Welz believes that individuals shouldn't believe they're able to "begin with a mini-account and stay from their income as an expert trader within six many months." It takes DAY and commitment. Welz thinks that when this wasn't the case, the streets would be full of Ferraris and Porsches.

## The Base Line

The basic role of trader therapy has a tendency to end up being underestimated and too much emphasis placed on the technical side. While both are essential, it is perhaps the right frame of mind that differentiates successful from not successful dealers. But, finding out the specialized components of trading and investing is much more clear-cut than buying a top-notch trading and investing head. The latter usually involves functioning intensely on one's own character traits and eradicating entrenched behavioral patterns. This technique is quite difficult and needs dedication, some DAY, usually, the help of an experienced coach. Nonetheless, the outcomes are particularly most likely to experience dividends.

# CHAPTER 6:

# STACKING UP MONEY AND RAISING THE FUNDS

## The Problems of Earning Profits by Day Investing

Whenever you glance at a cost chart—whether it is for a stock, overseas money set, or futures contract—it seems like it ought to be pretty simple to generate income. Typically, whenever DAY dealers first get begun, these people focus their unique attention from the huge movements and imagine, "easily had gotten in truth be told there, I really could are making a lot of money."

Adopting these types of perspectives can direct a lot of individuals to imagine day trading is reasonably effortless and a brief way to riches. Day trading can offer substantial revenue once you know exactly how to go about it. But, for most of us, the necessary quantities of DAY invested learning and training prevent all of them from gaining enough experience to come to be consistently successful with their positions.

## Day Trading And Investing Triumph Speed

It's an obstacle to switching a revenue through DAY trading, and although every DAY trader thinks they may be able to make cash, about 95 percent of the people who attempt day trading end up getting a net reduction. You can improve your own odds of successful trading by comprehending the potential risks that can result in losses and also by acquiring beyond the assumption that day trading is actually easy.

## The requirement for a Robust Process

The major reason traders lose money will be the lack of a solid trading approach. Simply appearing at a chart in hindsight is actually maybe not a very good way to produce a successful program. If you develop a strong strategy, it can be utilized in just about all market circumstances and can actually inform you when to stay from the market due to the fact circumstances tend to be perhaps not advantageous.

A very good strategy will help prepare you to definitely just take action before a profitable opportunity occurs, perhaps not after. The aim of your strategy should always be to discover patterns and trends that point out exchanging options that could deliver good comes back. Without doing that research, your results might be largely determined by opportunity.

## Taking DAY to Exercise

A lot of novice dealers fail to realize that DAY exchanging takes an effective bargain of the DAY to find out. Setting up a few hours of research without regularly committing DAY for your DAY trading and investing won't make someone an effective investor.

You'll need to rehearse day dealing while maintaining another job unless you have cash established separately to cover your expenditures for a couple of many months or higher. It is extremely uncommon for day traders to produce earnings correct whenever they get going. Most DAY dealers don't see their attempts lead to sufficient profits to pay themselves any kind of income for at the very least 6 months to a year from their start day.

## Whims of the Market

Many issues and situations add to putting some market hard to assess and navigate. Bringing the DAY for you to find out and comprehend exactly what causes changes in investing activity can better make one to reply to those changes.

- Learn to manage your own financial threat if you create an incorrect summary about the direction of a trade, by putting an end reduction on your trade. Think of it as placing a limit to assist mitigate how much money you may lose while pursuing trading options.
- Realize that you can't usually obtain the specific price you prefer when exchanging, particularly with industry instructions. The weighty trading activity might press a cost out from your own exact target before you react. You'll be

able to pick to miss what might still be a good trade or accept the less-than-ideal market cost. Both options will dramatically reduce the theoretical earnings on the trade. Even though you utilize limit orders, you could get loaded for sole component of the order on winning trades (the marketplace runs out before filling the whole purchase) but end up with total opportunities on your own losers (the pricing is transferring against you, so, sadly, you always obtain your full order).

- Realize that the marketplace is written entirely of other individuals attempting to make cash or fend down losings (hedgers). Individuals who are very proficient at a trading appearance to make use of the orders which are put by inexperienced dealers. Veteran dealers try to find prices they think let them control some perspective when you look at the advantage that others have ignored which will provide a good entryway or escape point for them.

## Greed and Fear

The person's desires and intentions of day traders can considerably influence the effects of their attempts. A little bit of success can result in unethical actions that stray from developed trading and investing plan. These can add taking activity too before long, holding to a successful gain for too much DAY, or maybe not cutting losings quickly enough in a losing trade.

Fear can likewise result in day dealers to keep back also much when a chance is within the generating. These people might also sell in a panic in response to busting news without taking into consideration all of the different aspects at play. Forming a strong trading approach has the massive advantage of trying to keep you focused on your own results without having to be swayed by emotions.

Day exchanging is just one of the many popular trading styles in the Fx market. Nevertheless, becoming an effective day dealer entails a good deal of bloodstream, sweating, and rips if you don't follow some important guidelines and don't handle your risk correctly.

In this short article, we'll discuss what must be done in order to become a successful day trader. Probably the most preferred day trading and investing techniques and how exactly to enhance your trading and investing abilities by continuing to keep an easy trading record.

**Thus, what exactly are the various Fx trading styles?**

The very first thing you may need to understand is that DAY trading isn't just one kind of trading and investing style.

It's maybe not a trading and investing strategy on its very own, as it doesn't reveal you simple tips to open up a trade, were established the escape areas, when to result in a trade or just how much to take a chance of.

It is merely a method of trading. This means that you'll find 100s of DAY trading strategies that you are able to switch between and nonetheless be a DAY trader.

To totally comprehend day exchanging, let's quickly get through the other a lot of popular trading styles in Forex trading – Scalping, swing investing and position investing.

- **Scalping** – This is actually the fastest and a lot of exciting investing design of all. Scalpers start a big number of trades in just one DAY, keep all of them open for a small duration of some DAY you will need to shut them in an income. Since scalping involves pulling the cause several DAYs during an investing day, trading expenses may be quite large and consume up a large part of the overall day-to-day earnings.
- **Swing trading** – slowly than scalping and day trading, sway trading suits diligent and self-disciplined dealers that can wait for a number of days for trading and investing opportunity. Swing traders aim to catch the "swings" in the industry, up-moves and down-moves that may keep going for a number of days.

Being a longer-term exchanging style, sway traders typically incorporate basics in their analysis and employ specialized analysis to get involved with trade and to create their unique escape levels.

- **Position trading** – Position trading is definitely a long-term trading design where trades are someDAYs used available for months or even years. Situation dealers depend on fundamental analysis to locate overvalued and undervalued currencies and also to determine trends in macro-economic variables that could lead to long-lasting styles.

Position traders have to be well-educated on money fundamentals, extremely patient and in a position to withstand large cost fluctuations (i.e. have a large investing account.) One benefit of place investing is actually that trading prices are almost non-existent in comparison to the possible revenue.

## Day Trading And Investing: A Fast-Paced Trading Style

So much, we've covered the main areas of scalping, swing exchanging and position trading. Day investing is yet another trading and investing style that suits perfectly in between scalping and swing trading.

Day dealers open a couple of positions per few days and attempt to shut all of them by the end of the trading and investing DAY, making either revenue or loss. DAY traders prevent keeping their trades in a single day, as news this is certainly published overnight may affect a position and change the price.

Many day traders analyze the market when you look at the day. They choose whether to go very long or quite short on a currency pair. But, dealers who stick to a DAY trading style want to take note that making a trade unmonitored throughout the DAY can be really dangerous, as intraday marketplace volatility (e.g. after a GDP development launch) may quickly switch the cost against you.

FINRA (The Financial Industry Regulatory Authority) describes a pattern DAY trader as "any customer which executes four or higher 'day trades' within five business DAYs, provided that the amount of day trades signifies more than six percent of the customer's total trades in the margin make up that very same five business day period.

Consumers should keep in mind that this rule is at least requirement and that some broker-dealers make use of a somewhat broader description in determining whether a client qualifies as a "pattern day trader."

Dealers that trade shares with a DAY trading approach have to be mindful of FINRA's rule since numerous stock brokers require at least deposit with a minimum of $25.000 for a trader that is flagged as a "pattern day trader." Up to now, there aren't any unique needs whenever DAY trading Forex.

There is a lot of DAY working strategies available to you, and almost all of them may be grouped into one of several next types:

- **Trend-following:** Trend-following techniques are perhaps the absolute most wide-spread day trading approach, and that's for a good reason – it works. Trend-following refers to riding the development so long as it lasts. You enter very long as soon as the trend is up, and quick as soon as the trend is down.
- **Counter-pattern trading**: Counter-trend trading refers to trading against the trend. This approach is very high-risk and must remain to the many knowledgeable DAY traders available to you. Generally, in a counter-trend method, a trader goes short during uptrends and very long during downtrends in an effort to profit from price-corrections (counter-trend moves).
- **Breakout trading:** Trading breakouts is a well-known DAY trading strategy, especially among retail Fx dealers. Breakout dealers desire to get a breakout associated with price above or below an important support/resistance amount, chart pattern or just about any other price-structure. Volatility can be very high immediately during the breakout point, which is the primary reason why day dealers grab the benefit of pending purchases to get into a trade as soon as a breakout happens.

### Just how can Dealers Make Money DAY Trading?

Using a well-defined trading approach is actually simply one side associated with money in DAY trading. Without risk management, even the greatest trading approach will at some point strike your bank account. You want to define your risk-per-trade and reward-to-risk ratios of configurations that you would you like to simply take to be able to allow it to be in the long run.

- **Hazard administration** – Risk administration is a set of rules which are developed that will help you increase your membership and get away from large losses. You will need to maintain a risk-per-trade (total risk on any solitary trade) equal to about 2% of the total trading membership dimensions, and a reward-to-risk ratio (ratio amongst the possible revenue plus the potential lack of trade) of approximately 2:1. Because of this, you'll stay in the video game even during a losing move.
- **Riding the Momentum** – Since day trading is a relatively short-term trading design, there requires to be a sufficient activity when you look at the market to be able to help make a revenue. Traders live on volatility, and investing sluggish markets with very little activity will only boost your trading and investing costs. Try to choose a volatile money pair when day trading and find breakouts because soon as they occur (with purchase prevent and market stop pending orders, for instance.)
- **Trade tracking** – final yet not least, it's very important to keep track of your own investments whenever day trading and investing. Also, the smallest improvement in market belief may cause a trade to get against you, making you with a reduction. Prevent trading during essential development produces as areas can get quite unstable soon after a release.

### Simple tips to insert into on a daily basis Trade?

As mentioned previously, most day exchanging strategies may be grouped into three primary types: trend-following, counter-trend trading and investing and breakout investing. Now let's learn how exactly to type it into a day trade, the best place to spot your own stop-loss and profit goals, and just how to manage positions that are already open.

### Trend-following techniques

Lots of DAY traders love to adhere to the tendency. In a trend-following strategy, you would type in very long as soon as the trend is up and short as soon as the trend is actually down. The optimum DAY to enter into a trend-following trade is actually right after the completion of a price-correction. You don't want to brief a downtrend when the cost has recently fallen to a big extent, or get long in an uptrend as soon as the pricing is already overbought.

To master trend-following, you ought to comprehend how trades develop. An uptrend is created when the cost makes consecutive higher levels and greater lows, with every higher large pushing the cost more than the earlier high. The greatest DAY for you to enter into a trade is actually just at the base of a larger low – that's the level where dealers who've missed the trend are prepared to join the group and where traders who're currently very long are generally contributing to their positions.

Comparable to uptrends, downtrends are generally formed as soon as the price helps make successive lower lows and lower highs. Here, the optimum DAY to short is actually right after an innovative new reduced high provides formed – this is when new dealers will jump into the downtrend using the small roles and where traders who're currently short will add to their roles.

The guide here shows an uptrend in the EURUSD pair with a soaring channel applied to the guide. Points (2) show levels for which you could type in lengthy, while points (1) are possible earnings targets. You should position your own stop-loss right below the rising channel or below the greater low.

## Counter-trend trading and investing strategies

Counter-trend trading is a day trading method that adopts the opposite approach to trend-following.

In a counter-pattern trade, an individual would get resistant to the established trend to be able to catch price-corrections. If you're taking a look again during the data above, you'll see that the uptrend didn't get up in a straight line. As an alternative, the price types so-called corrections at levels where many market participants are generally closing their unique extended orders and take profits (points marked

(1)). Thus, a counter-trend trader would generally get quite short in areas (1) and take profits at a reduced channel range.

The issue because of this approach is that it's riskier than trend-following and has now a lower profit capacity. On the various other sides, incorporating a trend-following and a counter-pattern exchanging strategy permits a trader to take more trades, in both the path of the well-known trend and on the contrary path. However, counter-trend trading should simply be carried out by experienced dealers.

## Get a review of the following guide.

A trader could get into a quick place at point (1) following the price made a fake breakout into the upside. His income goal could be established at a crucial Fibonacci degree (these types of given that 38.2%), proven at point (2). Following the cost rejects the 38.2% Fib level, the individual could enter into a long position and drive the pattern. This way, he would create an income both on the up- and down-moves. A stop-loss ought to be placed simply preceding point (1).

## Breakout trading methods

Finally, breakout traders are day dealers that aim to profit from outbreaks out of important complex levels, support and weight traces and guide habits. Breakouts are often adopted by a solid move and increased volatility, which makes breakout trading a prominent way to visit trade in the Forex market.

Pending requests are a very good tool whenever trading breakouts. By placing buy prevents or sell stops at the breakout degree, you don't have to wait for the real breakout to happen in purchase to open a trade. The pending order will immediately induce a market purchase when the cost reaches the amount given in the pending order. This will help to catch the initial market volatility and boosts the profit potential.

The information above shows a standard breakout trade mainly based on a symmetrical triangle. You can type in into the course from the breakout correct at a breakout point or after the cost completes a pullback towards the damaged triangle line, found by line (1). an end loss should be put just underneath the recent low (2), in addition to earnings target, shown by line (3), should be equal to the height associated with the pattern projected from the breakout point.

## Day Trading with little to no Revenue: is actually Its potential?

Lots of brand new dealers tend to be drawn to the Fx market as a result of the reduced minimum deposit requirements and the large leverage supplied by Fx brokers. This means traders with exchanging membership measurements of $100 can, in theory, manage an extremely big market place whenever exchanging on leverage. For instance, an influence ratio of 100:1 enables a trader to open up a trade worth $10,000 with just $100 of trading money.

## Watch: power: could it be a trader's friend?

This means DAY trading is achievable with little to no money. However, if you are thinking to begin trading and investing with a little amount of money, constantly hold attention on the free margin as it can drop quite quickly considering the number of investments whenever DAY investing. Your free of charge margin equals the equity minus the total margin made use of on all your valuable available positions. Your own investing platform should always be able to calculate this instantly.

In addition, bear in head that trading on extremely high leverage is actually risky. Leverage increases both your profits and losses. That's exactly why you should usually respect your threat administration and simply risk a little quantity of the money on any individual trade. Your position dimensions should rely on the dimensions of the stop-loss level.

## How come Day Trading So Hard?

Similar to trading in basic, day trading and investing is not easy to learn. In reality, shorter-term investing types, such as for instance scalping and day trading, tend to be often a lot more hard to learn than longer-term trading and investing types.

Many of the rules that apply to longer-term trading, in addition, apply to DAY trading, technical amounts work exactly the same and data habits tend to be analyzed in an identical way across all

DAYframes. However, day traders intend to make trading and investing choices a great deal faster since they're trading and investing in short-term DAYframes. There's no room to double-guess an entry, analyze the market in-depth and let feelings hinder your investing choices.

If you need to become a successful day investor, you must have an in-depth trading strategy and stick to it most of the DAY. Also, attempt first to master a longer-term investing style before acquiring your own feet damp in day investing. a popular mistake among beginners will start exchanging on extremely brief DAYframes after which go to longer-term trading and investing afterward on.

**Exactly how to Avoid Common Errors Whenever Day Trading**

Day trading and investing is perhaps not simple. Follow these points and abstain from creating typical errors of traders' new today exchanging. Only start day trading and investing after you've built an investing strategy, have actually a successful trading approach and strict danger management rules in location.

- **Have a Trading Plan** – A trading plan operates like a roadway chart in exchanging. It contains your strategy, entry and exit factors, entry causes, simple tips to manage losings and when you should shut a profitable trade, to mention a couple of points. an exchanging plan ought to be created in writing, so you're able to quickly return to it if the trading overall performance begins to deteriorate.
- **Build a Robust Trading Strategy** – the investment strategy should be part of a well-written trading program. Good trading methods should be powerful and describe how to evaluate the marketplace to find trading and investing possibilities. It should also consist of rules when you should enter a trade and in which to spot your own stop-loss and take-profit degrees.
- **Respect Risk Management** – Managing your own trading threat will be the ultimate road to success. Even the greatest exchanging strategy and approach won't be of much assistance if you don't take control of your losings and

control your own cash. Determine the maximum quantity you would like to risk on any single trade plus the reward-to-take a chance of proportion of possible positions you wish to take.

- **Keep a Trading Journal** – If you wish to improve your investing overall performance, maintaining a trading record is actually a great way to achieve that. an exchanging log consists of journal entries that consist of the exchanged instrument, entryway, and exit prices, the DAY and DAY you got the trade, the cause you pulled the trigger and its results. You need to do routine retrospectives of your diary entries and try to learn from your past mistakes, i.e. losing trades.

- **Monitor the Trades** – Day trading is a short-term trading style and keeping track of your trades should be a component of the everyday routine. Since day traders have fairly tight escape points, actually the smallest improvement in marketplace senDAYnt can result in a dropping trade. If a trade doesn't perform, just near it. There'll be many other trading possibilities along with the means.

- **Stick to an Fx Calendar** – News accounts, statements, labor marketplace statistics, inflation costs and other important produces can have a significant impact on the market. In the event the investments aren't predicated on principles, you will need to stay away from making a trade open during important development produces. After an Fx diary has to be part of your own market evaluation.

## EAs, Robots, and Signs in Day Trading: Carry Out They Function?

All DAY investing strategies described preceding tend to be mainly based on pure price action. Nonetheless, you can successfully apply signs to them to improve the success price of investments, confirm a setup or filter through them.

The RSI is actually a prominent sign among DAY traders. This momentum indication steps the magnitude of new price-moves and recognizes overbought and oversold industry conditions. Whenever the worth of the RSI sign moves above 70, this signals an overbought market (consider selling). Similarly, as soon as the value regarding the RSI moves below 30, it suggests an oversold market (consider purchasing).

However, the RSI can remain overbought or oversold for a long DAY during powerful uptrends and downtrends, respectively. That's something you must carry in mind.

Some traders use EAs (Expert experts) and investing robots, but their unique functionality can effortlessly transform during significant shifts when you look at the marketplace environment. Trend-following EAs function great in popular markets but provide plenty of phony indicators whenever marketplaces are varying. If you're using an EA or robot in your trading, you have to be really careful and keep track of your positions a lot more active than when trading on the own.

## DAY Trading Some Other Areas: Shares and Cryptocurrencies

Besides the money industry, dealers can additionally visit trade other financial areas, such as for instance stocks or cryptocurrencies. However, be aware that various financial markets may behave differently and consider adjusting and fine-tuning your trading and investing strategy to suit the dynamics of other marketplaces.

DAY trading shares may additionally require a larger investing account (structure day traders have to have at least $25,000 in their accounts), numerous illiquid stocks form gaps into the price at the beginning of an innovative new exchanging treatment and trading instances tend to be also different. In addition, many brokers have actually various leverage percentages for inventory exchanging.

Simply like stocks, cryptocurrencies may be effectively traded with a DAY trading and investing method by adjusting your recent trading method and threat management regulations. Bear in brain that cryptocurrencies can be rather volatile in certain cases, which makes having rigorous risk administration guidelines even much more vital. Prevent exchanging in DAYs of a future hand or any other important events that may change the cost of cryptocurrencies.

## Greatest DAY to DAY Trade

The optimum DAY to put a day trade is actually whenever the marketplace is by far the most liquid. This will dramatically reduce trading and investing expenses by keeping spreads tight, reduce slippage that could move the cost against both you and raise the overall rate of success of your positions.

In Forex, the absolute most liquid marketplace several hours are often the unique York together with London session, especially when those two trading sessions overlap. The after graphic shows the open marketplace hours of each Forex investing program as well as their overlaps.

# CHAPTER 7:

# THE 7 RULES OF DAY TRADING

Most individuals who are generally interested in mastering simple tips to become profitable traders need only invest a couple of minutes online before reading through such expressions as "plan your trade; trade your plan" and "keep your losings down." for brand new traders, these tidbits of data can seem much more like a distraction than any actionable advice. New traders often would like to understand how to create up their maps so these people can hurry upwards and create cash.

To be a success in trading, one requirement to comprehend the significance of and adhere to a ready of tried-and-true regulations which have guided all types of traders, with a variety of investing membership dimensions.

Each guideline by yourself is actually important, however when these people work collectively the consequences are generally potent. Investing by using these principles can significantly improve the chances of succeeding in the areas.

## KEY TAKEAWAYS

- DAY investing is just profitable whenever dealers take it seriously and carry out their investigation.
- DAY trading is actually a job, perhaps not an interest or passing fad of a payday. Deal with it as such — be persistent, concentrated, objective, and detach thoughts.
- Here we provide some fundamental ideas and know-how to be a profitable day trader.

### Guideline 1: Always Use a Trading Arrange

A trading and investing plan is actually a created set of rules that specifies a trader's entry, escape and money administration conditions. Making use of a trading plan enables dealers for this, although it is a DAY-consuming venture.

With today's technology, it's very easy to check a trading concept before risking a real income. Referred to as backtesting, this practice applies to deal ideas to historical information, enables traders to decide if a trading strategy is viable, and in addition shows the span regarding the plan's reason. As soon as program features been designed and backtesting shows great outcomes, the program can end up being utilized in real investing. The trick let me reveal to stick towards the strategy. Having trades outside the trading plan, even if they come out to be winners, is actually considered bad trading and damages any expectancy the program might have had.

## Tip 2: Treat Trading Like a Company

To be able to end up being prosperous, one must address exchanging as a complete- or part-DAY business—not as a hobby or a task. As a passion, where no real dedication to learning is actually generated, trading can be quite expensive. As a task, it may be irritating while there is no regular paycheck. Exchanging is actually a company and incurs costs, losses, fees, anxiety, anxiety, and threat. As an investor, you are basically a little company manager and must perform your own investigation and strategize to optimize your business's perspective.

## Guideline 3: Use Technology to Your Advantage

Trading and investing is a competitive company, and it is secure to assume the individual sitting on the opposite side of a trade is getting the total benefit of innovation. Charting platforms enable dealers an infinite assortment of techniques for looking at and studying the markets. Backtesting an idea on historical data before risking any cash can help to save an investing membership, not to ever mention anxiety and frustration. Getting market updates with smartphones permits people to keep track of trades virtually everywhere. Even innovation that nowadays all of us grab for issued, like high-speed internet connections, can significantly increase exchanging functionality.

Making use of technology to your advantage, and keeping existing with available technological advances, may be enjoyable and rewarding in trading and investing.

## Guideline 4: Protect The Exchanging Capital

Saving cash to finance an exchanging membership may take a few years and a lot of energy. It can end up being also a lot more difficult (or impossible) another DAY around. It is necessary to keep in mind that safeguarding your own investment capital is actually maybe not synonymous with perhaps not having any losing trades. All dealers have actually dropping investments; that is a component from the business. Protecting money entails perhaps not taking any unneeded threats and doing everything you can to preserve your own trading company.

## Rule 5: Become a college student of the marketplaces

Really feel of it as continuing education—traders have to remain dedicated to learning much more each DAY. Because so many principles carry prerequisite knowledge, it is actually vital to keep in mind that understanding the areas, and most of their intricacies, is an ongoing, lifelong process.

The hard analysis permits dealers to learn the main points, like exactly what the various monetary reports mean. Focus and observance allow traders to gain instinct and discover the subtleties; this is exactly what helps traders comprehend just how those economic accounts affect the marketplace these are typically trading.

World politics, activities, economies—even the weather—all have a visible impact on the markets. The marketplace environment is actually dynamic. The greater the number of traders understand the past and recent areas, the better ready they'll be to handle the future.

## Rule 6: Possibility Only What You Are Able To Manage to Shed

Tip No.4 mentions that funding a trading account can be an extended process. Before a trader begins using real money, it's crucial that all the cash within the account be genuinely expendable. If it isn't, the dealer should hold saving until it's.

It should go without saying that the cash in an exchanging account should not be allocated for the children's school university fees or paying the mortgage. Traders must never ever enable on their own to imagine these people are just "borrowing" money from all of these other essential requirements. One must certainly be ready to lose most of the cash allocated to a trading membership.

Losing profits is actually traumatic sufficient; it is additionally a lot more therefore if it is money which should have actually never ever been risked, to begin with.

## Tip 7: create a Trading Methodology predicated on details

Taking the DAY to create a sound trading methodology is really worth the effort. It could be tempting to think during the "so easy it's like printing cash" trading and investing cons that are prevalent on the internet. But insights, perhaps not emotions or hope, ought to be the determination behind developing an investing plan.

Dealers who aren't in a rush to learn usually have actually an easier DAY sifting through all of the data available on the internet. Think about this: if you decided to begin a new career, more than probably you'd want to examine at a college or institution for around a year or two before you were qualified to even apply for a place during the brand-new field. Expect that discovering simple tips to exchange needs at least exactly the same period of DAY and factually driven research and research.

## Rule 8: Usually Use an Avoid Reduction

A stop loss is a predetermined quantity of risk that a trader is happy to accept with each trade. The end loss may be either a buck quantity or percentage, but either method limits the trader's coverage during a trade. Utilizing an end loss may take a few of the feeling out of trading since we know that we're going to merely shed X amount on virtually any trade.

Ignoring a stop reduction, just because it results in a winning trade, is bad rehearse. Exiting with a stop loss, and thereby having a dropping trade, is actually nonetheless good trading and investing if it falls in the investing plan's rules. While the preference will leave all trades with earnings, it's not reasonable. Using a protective end reduction will help ensure which our losings and our risk are limited.

## Guideline 9: Know When to cease investing

There are two main reasons to prevent exchanging: an inadequate trading strategy, and a useless investor.

Inadequate trading and investing programs reveal much better losings than anticipated in historical testing. Marketplaces may have changed, volatility within a particular exchanging instrument may have lessened, or the trading program just is certainly not performing along with predicted. One will benefit from remaining unemotional and businesslike. It could be DAY to reevaluate the trading strategy and make a couple of modifications or to begin over with a brand new exchanging plan. a not successful trading plan is actually an issue that has to be solved. It isn't necessarily the termination of the trading company.

A useless trader is a person who is not able to stick to his or the woman trading program. Outside stresses, bad habits and absence of actual tasks can all play a role in this issue. A trader which is certainly not in top situation for trading should give consideration to a break to cope with any personal issues, be it wellness or tension or other things that prohibit the investor from becoming good. After any issues and issues have actually been dealt with, the dealer can continue.

## Rule 10: Keep Trading And Investing in Attitude

It is actually important to remain focused on the top picture when trading and investing. A shedding trade should not surprise us — it's an integral part of the exchange. Likewise, a winning trade is actually simply one step along the path to profitable trading. It will be the cumulative profits that create a difference. Once a trader takes wins and losings as an element of the business, emotions will reduce an impact on trading and investing functionality. This is not to say that we cannot end up being excited about an especially fruitful trade, but we must remember that a losing trade is certainly not considerably down.

Setting sensible targets is a vital part of trying to keep exchanging in point of view. If a trader has a tiny trading account, he or she should not anticipate to take in huge returns. A 10% return on a $10,000 membership is very distinct from a 10% return on a $1,000,000 investing membership. Function with just what you have got, and remain sensible.

## Summary

Understanding the significance of each of these trading rules, and the way they work collectively can really help traders establish a feasible trading business. Trading is actually a tough function, and traders that have actually the control and persistence to follow these guidelines can improve their unique chances of success in a really competitive field.

# CHAPTER 8:

# DIFFERENT SORTS OF INVESTING

Fundamental trading is actually a method where individual centers on company-specific occasions to identify which stock to buy and when you should invest in it. Trading and investing on fundamentals is a lot more closely connected with a buy-and-hold approach rather than short-term trading. You'll find, however, specific instances exactly where trading and investing on fundamentals can generate significant revenue in a short duration.

## Numerous kinds of Dealers

Before we focus on fundamental trading, here's a breakdown of the major kinds of money investing:

- **Scalping**: A scalper is someone who makes dozens or hundreds of trades a day in a try to "scalp" a tiny profit from each trade by exploiting the bid-ask scatter.
- **Momentum Trading:** Momentum traders seek shares that are moving significantly in a single direction in large volumes. These dealers try to drive the impetus to your desired earnings.
- **Technical Trading:** Complex traders focus on maps and graphs. They study contours on inventory or index graphs for signs of convergence or divergence that might indicate buy or offer indicators.
- **Fundamental Trading:** Fundamentalists trade companies dependent on fundamental evaluation, which examines corporate activities, particularly real or anticipated profits research, stock splits, reorganizations, or acquisitions.
- **Swing exchanging:** Swing traders are fundamental traders who hold their particular positions much longer than just one DAY. Many fundamentalists are actually sway trading and investing since alterations in business basics typically

require several days or also weeks to produce a cost motion adequate for the trader to state a reasonable income.

Beginner traders might experiment with every one of these methods, however, they should ultimately settle on just one market matching their unique trading knowledge and knowledge with a method to which they are generally determined to dedicate additional research, knowledge, and practice.

## Fundamental Information and Investing

Many money investors know a lot of common monetary data utilized in the fundamental evaluation such as profits per share (EPS), revenue, and cash movement. These quantitative factors feature any numbers located on a company's earnings report, cash flow statement, or balance sheet. They may be able additionally to include the results of financial percentages such as for instance return-on-equity (ROE) and financial obligation to equity (D/E). Fundamental traders may utilize this quantitative information to determine investing options if, for example, a business issue earnings results that catch the marketplace by shock.

Two of the most closely watched fundamental factors for dealers and investors everywhere are generally profits notices and analyst improvements and downgrades. Getting an edge on such information, nonetheless, is actually tough since there are generally literally an incredible number of eyes on Wall Street searching for the very exact same advantage.

## Earnings Announcements

A lot of important elements of earnings announcements will be the pre-announcement phase—the amount of DAY whenever a company problem a declaration stating whether or not it will meet, exceed, or fail to satisfy earnings objectives. Trades often take place quickly after these types of an announcement because a short-term impetus opportunity will most likely end up being available.

## Analyst Upgrades and Downgrades

Similarly, analyst upgrades and downgrades may provide short-term trading and investing possibility, specifically whenever a notable specialist unexpectedly downgrades an inventory. The cost action contained in this situation can be comparable to a stone shedding from a cliff so that the investor must certainly be quick and nimble together with small selling.

Income notices and analyst ratings are generally additionally closely connected with energy trading. Momentum traders seem for unexpected activities that can cause an inventory to trade a big number of stocks and go steadily either upwards or down.

The essential investor is often a lot more concerned with obtaining info on speculative activities that the remainder market may lack. To keep one action ahead for the marketplace, smart traders can typically use their understanding of traditional trading and investing habits that occur during the introduction of stock breaks, purchases, takeovers, and reorganizations.

## Stock Breaks

When a $20 stock splits 2-for-1, the company's market capitalization really does maybe not change, but the business today has twice the sheer number of shares outstanding each at a $10 inventory price. Lots of investors think that since people are going to be much more willing to acquire a $10 stock than these people would a $20 stock, a stock split portends a rise in the company's market capitalization. Nevertheless, do not forget that this fundamentally does not change the worth of the business.

To trade stock splits successfully, an investor must, above all, correctly identify the phase at which the stock is presently trading. History has confirmed that a wide range of certain trading patterns happens both before and after a split announcement. Price admiration and, for that reason, short-term purchasing opportunities will generally occur within the pre-announcement period and the pre-split run-up and cost depreciation (shorting opportunities) will occur in the post-announcement despair and post-split depression. By determining these four phases correctly, a split investor can actually trade-in and from the very same stock at minimum four different occasions before and following the split with perhaps plenty more intraday or actually hour-by-hour trades.

## Acquisitions, Takeovers, and Much More

The old saying "buy from the rumor, promote on the headlines," can be applied to those trading in purchases, takeovers, and reorganizations. In these instances, a stock will most likely enjoy extreme price increases in the conjecture period prior to the function and considerable decreases instantly following the occasion are actually announced.

That mentioned, the old investor's adage "market on development" has to be skilled significantly for the smart trader. A trader's game is to be one action prior to the market. Thus, the trader is actually improbable to get stock in a speculative phase and keep it all the way to the actual statement. The trader is actually concerned with capturing a few of the momenta in the speculative phase and could trade inside and outside of the exact same stock several instances given that rumormongers get to operate. The trader may keep an extended position during the day and short into the mid-day being ever watchful of charts and Level 2 data for signs of whenever to improve the place.

When the particular statement is made, the trader will most likely are able to short the stock of the obtaining organization right away after it issues the development of its intention to obtain, thus ending the speculative excitement prior to the announcement. Rarely is an exchange statement observed favorably, thus shorting a company that is performing the buying is actually a twofold sound strategy?

By contrast, a corporate reorganization is likely to be looked at favorably if it was maybe not expected because of the market and when the inventory had already been on a long-term slide due to internal corporate troubles. If a panel of administrators all of a sudden ousts an unpopular CEO, for instance, an inventory may display short-term ascending motion in celebration associated with the news.

Trading the inventory of a takeover target is actually a special instance since a takeover offer will have a connected price per share. A trader should end up being cautious to prevent getting stuck holding stock at or near the offer price because shares will generally not go significantly during the short term once these people find their own narrow array near the prospective. Specifically, within the instance of a reported takeover, the best investment opportunities would be in the speculative phase (or the duration whenever a rumored price per share for the takeover present will generate actual price activity).

Rumor and conjecture are high-risk trading propositions, specifically when it comes to purchases, takeovers, and reorganizations. These events create severe stock-price volatility. However, as a result of the prospective for quick cost motions, these events also possibly act as the essential profitable fundamental trading options offered.

## The Base Line

A lot of exchanging strategists utilize innovative types for trading opportunities associated with events top upwards to and next earnings announcements, expert upgrades and downgrades, stock splits, acquisitions, takeovers, and reorganizations. These charts resemble the maps made use of in specialized evaluation but lack numerical class. The charts are generally simple pattern maps. These people exhibit traditional habits of trading and investing behaviors that take place near to those activities, which patterns are generally used as guides for forecasts on short-term movements in ours.

If fundamental dealers properly determine the present position of stocks and consequent price moves that are going to take place, these people stand a high probability of performing successful positions. Trading on basics can be high-risk in cases of excitement and hype, but the smart trader can mitigate risk simply by using traditional patterns to guide their own short-term trading. In short, buyers should do their research before jumping in.

# CHAPTER 9:

# DAY TRADING CRYPTO

Very you are reasoning about making your work and getting a full-DAY day working cryptocurrency specialist? Well before you do, we feel you should read my own guide first!

Day trading and investing cryptocurrency isn't for everybody so there is a great deal to consider if you're wanting to get going. In reality, it's estimated that virtually 95% of all DAY traders ultimately fail.

In my own "Day exchanging Cryptocurrency" manual, I am about to inform you anything you must know. This will begin by explaining just exactly what DAY trading is, followed by the things you want to consider.

After that, if you are still interested, I am then going to explain to you how exactly to get going!

Because of the conclusion of reading my own guide from beginning to end, you will have got all the details you may need to choose if DAY exchanging cryptocurrency suits you.

What exactly are you currently waiting around for? Let's start by finding a way exactly what DAY trading is actually!

## Day Trading Cryptocurrency: What Exactly Is Day Trading?

Whenever folks chat about trading, they're talking about purchasing and marketing a resource with the goal of creating a revenue. For instance, in real-world stock exchanges, people trade a myriad of things. This could easily include stocks and shares like Apple, currencies like U.S. Dollars, and also metals these as silver and gold.

Whatever is actually being exchanged, the aim is actually the same. Purchase a valuable asset and next offer it for longer than you paid for it! This is precisely exactly the same as investing cryptocurrency.

You'll find different sorts of trading goals, which are generally normally split into short-term exchanging and long-term investing. This is certainly determined by how very long you love to hold an asset before you sell it.

Day exchanging is actually extremely short-term trading, and it can suggest keeping an advantage for just a couple of seconds, to a few of several hours. The concept is that you sell your asset prior to the conclusion regarding the day, looking to make a tiny, but quick profit. Let's take a quick have to look at a good example of two cryptocurrency day positions.

**Sample 1:**

1. Peter buys some Ripple (XRP) as the man believes the cost will rise in another couple of minutes as it's got just recently been revealed when you look at the news that a huge U.S. bank will probably be utilizing it for their intercontinental repayments.
2. The guy buys 1000 XRP at a cost of $0.80
3. As a lot of other individuals are now trying to get it, the pricing is going up.
4. 10 moments afterward, the price tag on XRP happens to be $0.816 and Peter's features decided he desires to market to create a fast profit.
5. Peter can make a 2% profit, which amounts to $16 – not bad for only a couple of minutes "work"!

**Example 2:**

1. John buys some EOS (EOS) as he happens to be learning the charts and it appears just like the cost is certainly going to help keep going up.
2. The man buys 100 EOS at a cost of $17.
3. The cost continues to get up, achieving $24 in only a couple of hours, however, it then starts to get back down.
4. John carries their EOS at a cost of $21.
5. John tends to make a profit of just over 23%, which sums to only over $391!

But, it's vital to keep in mind that the above two trades tend to be illustrations of a successful prediction. On another DAY, the prices could have effortlessly gone the other means, which may have intended that both Peter and John lost cash.

The key concept is that whenever DAY trading, you try to find opportunities that will make a fast income. If you are generally considering keeping to a cryptocurrency for a longer DAY, that is called long-term trading.

Fun fact: A buzzword you'll hear a lot into the crypto space is actually 'HODL'. This really is a misspelling of the term 'hold', as someone when produced a typo in a forum and it also has since trapped around as a crypto-community tendency. It literally simply methods to hold money or token for quite a few years and resist trying to sell it. There are a variety of methods that individuals use nowadays trade, but the main two are mainly based on either conjecture or chart evaluation.

The conjecture is whenever a trader feels a price is certainly going upwards or down as a result of a particular event. In the above example of Peter, he bought Ripple because he noticed a positive development story. There was clearly no promise that the cost would get up, but he speculated this would end up being predicated on his or her own viewpoint.

Some other DAY trading cryptocurrency methods frequently made use of is chart evaluation. This is when dealers learn the cost movement of a specific cryptocurrency and attempt to imagine which way it is certainly going, mainly based on historical cost moves. When examining charts, you can look at how a cost moves every few seconds, moments or also many hours.

So now you understand how it operates, the then part of my own "Day Trading and investing Cryptocurrency" guide is certainly going to check at what you should understand before acquiring started.

## DAY Trading Cryptocurrency: What You Should Know First

In the above section, I quickly mentioned just what DAY trading cryptocurrency really is and a few of the crypto trading techniques people utilize. This section is certainly going to speak about the mental side of investing, that is possibly the most significant thing to start thinking about.

## Volatility

First of all, you'll find one significant distinction between DAY exchanging cryptocurrency and DAY trading and investing real-world assets. The main reason for this might be volatility. Volatility occurs when the cost of a valuable asset moves up or down really quickly, which means it can often be a good success for the individual or alternatively a great failure.

For instance, if you had been DAY marketing shares regarding the NYSE (New York inventory Exchange), it is extremely unlikely that the costs would change that much in a twenty-four-hour duration. Simply because these are generally safe businesses which have been functioning for quite some DAY. Of training course, rates nevertheless get up or down, but compared to cryptocurrencies, it would normally only be by a small quantity.

Conversely, the prices of cryptocurrencies are particularly volatile. It's perhaps not strange for any cost of money to rise or fall by a lot more than 10%-50% in a solitary DAY. In a few conditions, even more. For instance, in February 2018, a cryptocurrency called E-Coin increased in worth by significantly more than 4000% in only 24 several hours, only to fall straight right back right down to in which it started.

Anyone who bought the coin towards the beginning of the day would be making plenty of money, however, the individuals that bought it at its highest cost could have lost almost all their financial investment.

## Accepting losses

The E-Coin example is why you should comprehend that day trading Bitcoin along with other cryptocurrencies will likely not always go-to strategy. You need to be ready to recognize losings once they happen since this is a component of trading. Perhaps the many successful traders during the world create losses since it is difficult to always make the proper prediction.

Remember, you need to never ever attempt to "chase" your losses.

Chasing losings will be the work in which an investor experiences a bad loss and they try to make it back if you take truly large risks.

This is regarded as the key factor in why the greater part of traders is unsuccessful. You've got to take which you can certainly make losings at some point!

## Exercise tends to make perfect

If you're wanting to even feel about depositing funds into your exchanging account, it's important which you exercise first. Although none of the main cryptocurrency exchanges offer a demo membership, a great spot to start would end up being Coins2Learn.

Coins2Learn provides trading and investing simulation that enables you to exchange making use of fake money. The program is truly good for newbies and they even supply tips and just how to be successful.

You are able to access their site by clicking this backlink!

When you have a far better comprehension of the way the markets work, the next action will be doing the actual thing. Although making use of a demonstration simulation is great for being able trading works, it doesn't prepare you for real-world losses.

This is the reason why you should start off with really low amounts. In fact, the amounts should not be any larger than you really can afford to lose. At this DAY of the DAY trading cryptocurrency career, you will be learning about the levels and lows regarding the markets and a lot of importantly, boosting your capabilities and understanding.

## Goals

When you have actually decided out the way the marketplaces work and you also feel you are prepared to begin investing with a real income, at this point you have to establish yourself some objectives. This is vital just like you are preparing to perform this as your part-DAY or full-DAY task, you have to have expectations as to just how a lot you hope to produce.

As we talked about previously, day traders turn to make quick, short-term increases, which may be reduced than 1% per trade. These dealers will have a tremendously large "bankroll", which means that they can nevertheless create decent money even in the event that percentage gains are small.

Observe: A bankroll will be the total quantity of cash that trade has actually readily available to them.

Experienced traders will hardly ever take a chance of significantly more than 1% of their unique total bankroll. This means if you've got

$1,000 to invest, you never spot more than $10 on each trade. Although this feels like a little amount, in the long term, this will shield you against going broke.

This will additionally enable you to build a continuous revenue by growing your general bankroll extended-expression.

## Stop losings

Another essential element to DAY trading and investing cryptocurrency is that you set your self an end reduction. A stop-loss occurs when you enter a price that you need to instantly exit your trade.

For instance, if you purchased Ethereum at a cost of $700, you could set your self an end reduction of 10%. This indicates that when the cost of Ethereum moved down to $630, the program would immediately sell your financial investment. This protects away from you an abrupt decrease in price, or you had been perhaps not at your computer to do it your self.

You may also do a "limit sell order", which means your own trade can end up being instantly shut when your money strikes a particular higher cost. Whenever we used the above Ethereum instance, you could set a 10% restriction sell order, which may suggest that when the cost reached $770, the program would immediately close your trade.

## Consider an alternative

Now you know about most of those things that might prevent you against becoming an effective day investor, you should keep in mind that this isn't the just choice. If you believe that you simply will not have the emotional need, DAY or patience to be a day investor, you can usually think about long-term investing as an alternative.

Long-term trading is actually much less stressful, as when you buy a coin you can easily leave it to grow over an extended period of DAY. For instance, if you purchased some Dash coins in very early 2017 when they certainly were well worth about $15 each after which waited until December of the identical year when they hit over $1,500, you'd are making a profit of 10,000%!

This might have been accomplished without you having to remain at your pc all day long to inspect for any price motions. You can easily also use the same investing strategies too, such as for instance setting stop-losses or market limit-orders.

Nevertheless, if you're specific that you need to be a cryptocurrency DAY investor, then the next component of my own guide is certainly going to demonstrate you exactly how to get going!

DAY Trading And Investing Cryptocurrency: How Exactly To Get Started

Now you understand what DAY investing cryptocurrency calls for because very well as what you want to consider, I'm now likely to explain to you just how to get going!

The initial step whenever looking at simple tips to day trade cryptocurrency will demand you to get a hold of a great exchange. A cryptocurrency exchange enables one to purchase and offer coins 24 hours a day. You should think about what kind of cryptocurrencies you tend to be looking to get involved in.

If you're looking to day trade full DAY, then it's effectively well worth choosing a trade who has a lot of difference pairings noted.

Note: A pairing is the two coins that are being exchanged. For instance, if you thought that the cost of Ethereum would increase up against the cost of Bitcoin, you then would have to find a BTC/ETH pairing!

It's also essential to locate a change that includes lots of exchangeability. This will ensure which you can usually end up being matched with a consumer or vendor, normally, you may not have the ability to shut your own trade as soon as the pricing is slipping!

An excellent location to begin would end up being Binance, as they've got hundreds of trading and investing sets offered and in addition, they get one of the biggest tradings and investing volumes in the marketplace. To get a hold of over extra information on setting up a free account at Binance, see my own guide here!

When you have opened a membership with an exchange, it's DAY to put some funds. The majority of cryptocurrency exchanges try not to allow you to deposit using a debit/credit card or bank membership, however, some do.

In the event that trade that you wish to use will perhaps not take real-world money deposits, then chances are you can very first get to Coinbase to purchase some Bitcoin or Ethereum and after that transfer it around. To discover out even more details exactly how to purchase a cryptocurrency at Coinbase utilizing a debit/credit card, see my own guide here!

Be sure to look at exactly how much you're planning to deposit. Never ever overlook that the cryptocurrency markets are actually volatile, therefore there's always a chance you can get rid of your whole financial investment. Begin off with smaller amounts first.

When you are set up and you've got deposited some funds, take a while to comprehend the various attributes on the investing display. Every exchange will have a piece of information, so it is actually a smart idea to learn to assess pricing moves.

There's a very good beginner's guidebook at CryptoPotatoe, just who demonstrates to you exactly how to read maps and then how to assess pricing developments. You'll be able to visit their free guidebook here. As you certainly will see within the preceding screenshot, the trader is wanting at the pricing motion of USD/BTC. The green bars suggest that the price has gone upwards, while the red bars mean that the cost has eliminated down.

Mastering how these resources tasks are vital as it's going to enable you to identify when there is a great possibility that a coin is actually going to rise or fall. Nevertheless, as soon as once again, there is not an assurance that your forecast is going to be suitable, therefore usually be sure to are ready to exit a trade if situations go poorly!

## Conclusion

That's the termination of my "Day investing Cryptocurrency" guide! we know We have given you a lot and a lot of info, but we believe it is important for you to definitely understand most of the potential risks involved.

If you have read my guide from beginning to complete, you really need to now understand whether DAY trading and investing is best for your needs, as well as how to trade Bitcoin, and exactly how to exchange cryptocurrency as a whole.

While you have probably observed, there are tons of actions to consider before you start your exchanging career. In fact, it's going to take a very lengthy DAY just before you tend to be able to trade successfully just like you carry out things properly, you will have to build situations up gradually.

Actually, though losses are generally never ever an excellent thing, when you are doing experience them in your own very early DAYs of trading, it will probably assist you to learn never to result in the very same mistake once again!

Therefore what do you believe about DAY trading cryptocurrency? Will it be something you will consider, or do you really like the sound of long-term investing rather? You will want to commit plenty of days if you may be likely to do so, however, it can be really worth it once you've made very first million!

Just make sure you never devote more than you can easily manage to drop and therefore you never chase the losings.

## Just How To Trade Cryptocurrency

Scared of missing out on out? The following is a quick propose to enable you to get trading and investing cryptocurrency easily;

1. Determine if you would like to own the cryptocurrency, or just have a hunch that it's worth will go up or down.
   a. if you would like to acquire the currency, you require an exchange – attempt Hodly – It is a simple, easy to use software
   b. If you would like to speculate in the cost, you need a broker. Look at the list above or use the agent web page for a complete list.
2. Fund your own membership
3. Purchase the Cryptocurrency you wish or open a trade on its price.

Congratulations, you are generally today a cryptocurrency dealer! Remember, you can operate through the acquisition or purchase of cryptocurrencies on a dealer demonstration account. Unfortunately, you cannot practice on a trade.

Investing crypto generally revolves around speculating on its price, instead of owning some of the real coins. As a result, agents offering forex and CFDs tend to be normally a much easier introduction for beginners, as compared to the alternative of purchasing real money via an exchange.

## Just how to Examine Brokers

Which cryptocurrency platform you decide to-do the investing in is among the many essential choices you'll make. The exchange will work as an electronic budget for your cryptocurrencies, so don't dive in without considering the factors below first.

Some brokers specialize in crypto trades, others less thus. Other individuals offer specific products. IQ Choice, for instance, delivers traditional crypto trading via Fx or CFDs – but also supply cryptocurrency multipliers. These supply enhanced control and as a consequence risk and reward. Innovative items like these may be the distinction whenever beginning a free account cryptocurrency day investing.

## Apps & Program

DAY traders have to be continuously tuned in, as responding just a couple of mere seconds belated to large news activities could result in the distinction between profit and reduction. That's why numerous agents today offer easy to use cryptocurrency cellular apps, making sure you can stay up to date whether you are really on the practice, or producing your own sixth coffee of the day.

The cryptocurrency trading and investing system you subscribe to will likely be for which you invest a lot of days each day, thus seek out one that suits your investing design and requirements. Exchanges like Coinbase offer in-depth platforms, because of their Global Digital resource Exchange (GDAX). It is always really worth establishing up a trial account first to ensure the change has the technical methods and sources you'll need.

## Safety

Constantly check reviews to ensure the cryptocurrency trade is secure. If your bank account is hacked as well as your digital money transported out, they'll be eliminated permanently. Therefore whilst secure and intricate credentials tend to be half the battle, the different half may be battled by the trading computer software.

## Fees

Each trade supplies different percentage rates and fee structures. As a DAY trader making a high volume of trades, just a limited difference in prices can seriously lower into income. You'll find three main fees to compare:

- **Exchange fees** – this can be just how much you'll be billed to make use of their unique cryptocurrency software. What currency and coins you're trading can impact the rate.
- **Trade fees** – This is how much you'll be billed to exchange between currencies to their change. A marker fee is actually the price of making an offer to the market. A taker fee will be the price of taking an offer from somebody.
- **Deposit & Withdrawal charges** – this is certainly how a lot of you'll be charged whenever you need to deposit and withdraw cash from the change. You'll usually see it's more affordable to put your resources. Also, hold in your mind some exchanges don't enable credit score rating notes. Making use of debit/credit will usually arrive with a 3.99% charge, a lender account will generally incur a 1.5% fee.

## Final Word On Brokers

This isn't a decision to simply take softly. Do the maths, read reviews and trial the change and software very first. Coinbase is widely considered as just about the most trusted exchanges, but trading cryptocurrency on Bittrex is also a sensible option. CEX.IO, Coinmama, Kraken, and Bitstamp are also popular possibilities.

## Market Rates

## Cryptocurrency Trading For Beginners

Before you choose an agent and test different platforms, you'll find a couple of straightforward things to get the head around first.

Comprehension and accepting these three things give you the greatest possibility of succeeding whenever you move into the crypto trading field.

- **Find out what's growing** – Bitcoin, Ethereum and Litecoin top the list for tradability and simplicity of utilizing. However, you'll find also Zcash, Das, Ripple, Monero and several more to hold an attention on. Carry out the research and discover completely what's on the upwards and concentrate your focus there.
- **Embrace volatility** – Cryptocurrencies are notoriously volatile. The price tag on Bitcoin, for instance, went from $3,000 down to $2,000 after which leaped up to almost $5,000, all within 3 months in 2017. Whilst this suggests danger is high, it additionally means the possibility for revenue is great too. It's always practical to examine the volatility associated with the exchange you decide to go with.
- **Understand blockchain** – You don't need to understand the technical difficulties, but a basic comprehension may help you reply to news and announcements that will help you forecast future price motions. It is actually essentially a continually growing list of safe records (hinders). Cryptography obtains the relationships after which stores all of them publicly. These people act as a general public ledger, cutting out intermediaries such as banks.

## Purses

If you'd like to possess the particular cryptocurrency, rather than speculate on the cost, you ought to store it.

There are generally a large variety of budget suppliers, but you'll find also threats utilizing lesser-known budget companies or exchanges. All of us suggest a service called Hodly, which is actually backed by managed brokers:

## Strategy

Once you've decided on a dealer, received common along with your system and funded your bank account, it's DAY for you to start trading and investing. You'll require to use a very good approach lined up with an effective cash management method to create earnings. Here is actually a good example of a clear-cut cryptocurrency strategy.

## Swing Trading And Investing

This straightforward strategy simply calls for vigilance. The concept is you hold close attention out for a correction in development after which catch the 'swing' out of the correction and straight back into the tendency. A correction is actually simple when candle lights or cost bars overlap. You'll find popular costs go quickly, but corrections, conversely, will likely not.

Let's say on your cryptocurrency chart at 250-minute candles, the thing is 25 candles where the cost continues to be within a 100 point assortment. In the event that price contracted to a daily action of merely 20 areas, you'd be honestly curious and aware. You should see lots of overlap. This says to you there is a substantial possibility the pricing is heading to continue into the pattern.

You really need to then sell whenever the very first candle moved below the contracting selection of the earlier several candles, and you could place a stop at by far the newest small move large. It's quick, clear-cut and effective.

## Tips

Despite having just the right dealer, software, money, and approach, you'll find a wide range of general tips that can help enhance your margin of profit and reduce losings. Listed here are some helpful cryptocurrency ideas to bear in your mind.

## Utilize News

Short-term cryptocurrencies are incredibly responsive to pertinent development. Whenever news these types of as federal government rules or perhaps the hacking of a cryptocurrency change comes through, prices tend to plummet.

On the other hand, if a large company announces they'll end up being integrating the utilization of a currency into their particular company, rates can climb up quickly. If you're conscious of any news and can react rapidly, you'll have actually an edge throughout the other countries in the industry.

## Technical Assessment

Analyze historical price maps to determine informing patterns. The record has actually a practice of repeating itself, if you can hone in on a design you could possibly anticipate potential price motions, providing you with the advantage you need to make an intraday profit. To get more information on pinpointing and making use of habits, see here.

## Study Metrics

This is one of the most significant cryptocurrency tips. By looking at the wide variety of wallets vs the number of energetic wallets and the present exchanging volume, you can easily try to give a particular currency a current value. Then you can create well-informed decisions dependent on today's marketplace cost. The more precise your forecasts, the greater the possibility of income.

## Trade On Margin

If you anticipate a specific cost move, trading on margin will permit you to acquire money to enhance your possible profit in the event the prediction materializes. Exchanges have different margin demands and supply varying costs, therefore performing the research initiative is actually advisable. Bitfinex and Huobi are a couple of a lot more popular margin platforms.

Bear in mind, Trading or speculating using margin rises the dimensions of potential losings, along with the possible profit.

## Rules & Taxes

The digital marketplace is fairly brand-new, so countries and governing bodies are scrambling to carry in cryptocurrency fees and rules to manage these new currencies. If you're not mindful among these before starting investing, you may possibly find yourself in a spot of costly bother advance along with the range.

## Rules

Lots of governments are generally unsure of things to class cryptocurrencies as, currency or property. The U.S in 2014 introduced cryptocurrency investing rules that mean digital currencies will fall beneath the umbrella of residential property. Traders will then be classed as traders and can need to conform to complex revealing needs. Facts that could be discovered by going to the IRS observe 2014-21.

## Fees

In addition to the opportunity of challenging revealing procedures, brand-new rules can additionally influence the income tax responsibilities. The U.S, the 'property' ruling means the income will today be considered as capital benefits income tax (15%), instead of normal earnings tax (up to 25%). Each countries cryptocurrency taxation needs are very different, and numerous will alter as these people adjust to your changing industry. Before starting trading, perform your research and discover what sort of income tax you'll pay and just how much.

## Spiders

If you've currently got a method that really works, next to a cryptocurrency trading and investing robot may be worth taking into consideration. When you've programmed the strategy, the bot is certain to get to work, automatically performing investments whenever the pre-determined criteria tend to be met. There are two benefits to this.

First of all, it will help save you serious DAY. You won't need to look at charts throughout the day, hunting for opportunities. Trade delivery rates should be boosted as no manual inputting will be required.

Secondly, the automatic software program permits you to exchange across numerous currencies and possessions at a DAY. This means greater potential revenue and all without you having to do any hefty training.

## Dangers

Having said that, bots aren't all ordinary sailing. If you desire to avoid losing your income to computer system collisions and unforeseen market activities then you'll definitely, however, require to keep track of the bot to a level.

These people can additionally be costly. Whilst there are several choices like BTC Robot that provide cost-free 60-day studies, you certainly will generally be charged a month-to-month subscription cost that will consume into your profit. They're able to additionally end up being expensive to set up if you need to send someone to program your own bot. On top of this, you'll want to pay to have your robot updated as the market changes.

So, whilst bots can really help increase your conclusion of day cryptocurrency income, you'll find no complimentary rides in life and you have to be conscious of the risks. Perhaps next, they're the greatest resource whenever you currently have an established and effective approach, that can just end up being computerized.

## Education

The most useful cryptocurrency trading guide you'll be able to get on is the only you can give yourself, with a demonstration membership. Firstly, you are you going to obtain the opportunity to test your possible brokerage and system before you purchase.

Secondly, these are generally the most wonderful destination to correct blunders and create your art. You'll usually end up being trading with artificial money, therefore mistakes won't expense you the difficult earned capital. As soon as you've trialed your strategy and ironed through any creases, subsequently, start executing positions with real cash.

Online there are also a variety of cryptocurrency intraday trading classes, plus a myriad of books and ebooks. The greater amount of information you digest the much better ready you'll be, while the better chance you'll have of sustaining an advantage over the marketplace.

## Crucial Areas

Really feel of the as your guidebook to DAY trading cryptocurrency and you'll avoid almost all of the obstacles lots of traders fall down at. Whenever choosing your own broker and system, consider the simplicity of use, security in addition to their fee construction. You'll find a wide range of techniques you can use for trading and investing cryptocurrency in 2017. Whichever one you decide for, generate sure technical analysis and the news play vital functions. Finally, keep conscious of regional variations in rules and fees, you don't would you like to drop profit to unanticipated laws.

# CHAPTER 10:

# TECHNICAL AND FUNDAMENTAL ANALYSIS

Technical analysis will be the study of past market data to predict the direction of potential price movements. The strategy is regarded as a subset of security analysis alongside fundamental evaluation. Right here all of us glance at exactly how to utilize technical analysis in DAY trading.

It often contrasts with fundamental analysis, which can be utilized both on a microeconomic and macroeconomic level. Micro-level fundamental analysis consists of the study of profits, expenses, income, possessions and debts, money construction, and "soft" areas (quality of administration team, competitive position).

Macro-level fundamental evaluation involves the study or forecasting of economic development, rising cost of living, credit rounds, interest rate trends, money streams between countries, labor and reference utilization and their cyclicality, demographic developments, main bank, and political procedures and behavior, geopolitical things, consumer and business trends, and "soft" information (age.g., senDAYnt or confidence surveys).

Some dealers may focus on a single or the other while some will employ both strategies to tell their trading and trading choices.

The majority of big banking companies and brokerages have actually groups that focus on both fundamental and specialized evaluation. As a whole, the more quality information one requires to improve the chances of becoming appropriate, the better one's trading and investing effects are usually.

Technical analysts are generally often called chartists, which reflects the usage charts showing cost and volume information to determine trends and patterns to evaluate securities. Price habits can add support, resistance, trendlines, candlestick patterns (age.g., mind and shoulders, reversals), transferring averages, and specialized signals.

For Advanced charting functions, which make technical analysis much easier to implement, we advise TradingView.

## Presumptions in Technical Analysis

Although some traders and investors utilize both fundamental and specialized analysis, most often tend to fall into one camp or some other or at least rely on a single far a lot more seriously in creating trading and investing decisions.

Technical experts depend on the methodology because of two main values – (1) cost record has a tendency to be cyclical and (2) prices, amount, and volatility tend to work in specific trends.

## Let's get through each independently:

## Industry Cyclicality

Human instinct getting exactly what it is, with commonly shared behavioral characteristics, industry record provides a propensity to repeat alone. The series of occasions is certainly not likely to repeat itself completely, however, the patterns tend to be typically comparable. These could use the type of long-term or short-term cost behavior.

During the long-term, business cycles tend to be naturally at risk of repeating by themselves, as pushed by credit score rating booms where debt goes up unsustainably above earnings for a period and at some point leads to monetary discomfort if not adequate money is actually accessible to service these financial obligations. This has a tendency to result in sluggish progressive increases in stocks along with other "risk-on" investments (age.g., carry trading) during expansion and a razor-sharp fall upon an economic downturn.

Technicians implicitly think that market participants tend to be inclined to repeat the conduct of history because of its collective, patterned character. If conduct is definitely repeatable, this implies that it could be acknowledged by looking at the previous price and amount of information and familiar with predict potential price patterns. If traders can locate opportunities where behavior is probably to be duplicated, they can identify trades in which the risk/reward runs in their particular favor.

Hence, there's the built-in expectation in complex analysis that a market's cost discounts all information influencing a specific market. While fundamental events influence financial areas, such as for instance development and economic data, if these details have already been or promptly reflected in asset prices upon launch, the specialized analysis will instead focus on pinpointing cost styles and the degree to which market participants value certain information.

For instance, if all of us CPI inflation information arrived in a tenth of a proportion more than exactly what was being priced into the marketplace before the development launch, we could back out exactly how hypersensitive the marketplace will be that details by watching exactly how asset prices react immediately following.

If me inventory futures go down X%, the US dollar directory improves Y%, together with 10-year US Treasury produce increase Z%, we are able to obtain a sense based on how many monetary inputs affect specific marketplaces. Knowing these sensitivities can end up being important for stress assessment purposes as a type of danger management. For illustration, if rising prices had been to unexpectedly move upwards by 1%, we can make use of data factors regarding surprise inflation indication to decide the way the collection may be influenced.

## Cost, Volume, and Volatility Operate in Distinct Trends

Another assumption behind technical analysis (and all sorts of securities analysis a lot more broadly) is the fact that cost does not move relating to a "random walk", or based on to no evident or logical pattern. Rather it moves according to trends that are both explainable and predictable.

For instance, if we all glance at a chart associated with the EUR/USD from mid-2013 to mid-2017, we can find out exactly how specialized evaluation played a task by looking at help and resistance inside the context of the trend. Following the euro started depreciating resistant to me a dollar because of a divergence in the financial plan in mid-2014, specialized analysts might have chosen to take small trades on a pullback to opposition levels in the context for the downtrend (designated with arrows in the picture below). Following the trend had faded and the marketplace inserted into consolidation, a technician may have chosen to relax and play the range and started using longs at help while shutting any pre-existing brief positions.

## Attributes

Originally, the technical analysis had been mostly a case of "reading the tape" or interpreting the successive circulation and magnitude of price and amount information through a stock ticker. As personal computers grew to be a lot more extensive in the seventies, information was created into data form and grew to be a technician's standard point of research.

The popularity of information habits and club (or later candlestick) evaluation had been the most typical form of analysis, followed closely by regression analysis, going averages, and cost correlations. Today, the number of technical indicators are a lot more numerous. Anyone with coding knowledge relevant to the software system can transform cost or amount information into a specific indicator of great interest.

Though technical analysis by yourself are not able to wholly or precisely predict the future, it is helpful to determine trends, behavioral proclivities, and prospective mismatches in supply and need where trading possibilities could arise.

## Analytical Techniques

There are several techniques to address complex evaluation. The most basic technique is through a standard candlestick price guide, which demonstrates price history as well as the purchasing and trying to sell characteristics of cost within a specific period.

## (Weekly candlestick cost data of this S&P 500)

Others use a cost chart along with technical indicators or use particular forms of complex evaluation, such as for instance Elliott trend theory or harmonics, to create trade concepts. Some usage elements of a number of different methods. In one DAY, traders must resist the concept of "information excess" or cluttering charts with many indicators and lines that it starts to adversely affect one's capability to check the chart.

Dealers may take a subjective view of their exchanging phone calls, preventing the requirement to trade based on a restrictive rules-mainly based method because of the uniqueness of every scenario.

Other people may get into trades merely when particular rules evenly implement to improve the objectivity of the investing and get away from emotional biases from affecting its efficiency.

## Forms of Charts

### Candlestick

Candlestick maps tend to be the most typical form of charting in today's software. Green (or at DAY's white) is normally familiar with depict bullish candle lights, where the current price is greater than the orifice price. Red (or someDAYs black) is actually popular for bearish candles, exactly where current pricing is below the beginning cost.
It shows the exact distance between opening and finishing prices (the body of this candle) and the total everyday selection (from the very top from the wick to the bottom of this wick).
(Candlesticks revealing up and down motion when you look at the S&P 500 index)

### Open-High Low-Close

A candlestick chart is actually comparable to an open-high-low-close data, also referred to as a club chart. But alternatively of the human body from the candle displaying the real difference amongst the open and near cost, these amounts are represented by horizontal tick markings. The opening price tick factors to the remaining (to demonstrate that it originated from the last) even though the other cost tick points on the right.

### Line

A range guide connects information points making use of a line, typically from the finishing cost of each period of DAY.

### Area

An area chart is actually essentially exactly the same as a line chart, aided by the location under it shaded. This is mostly completed to more quickly visualize the price movement in accordance with a range of data.

## Heiken-Ashi

Heiken-Ashi charts make use of candlesticks whilst the potting medium, but take a different mathematical system of cost. Rather than the common treatment of candles converted from basic open-high-low-close criteria, rates are smoothed too much better indicate trending price action with respect to this method:

- Open = (Open of previous bar + Close of previous bar) / 2
- Near = (Open + High + Minimal + Close) / 4
- High = Highest of High, start, or Close
- Low = cheapest of Low, Open, or near

## Common Terms And Conditions

**Average true range** – The array over a certain period of DAY, typically every day.

**Breakout** – When cost breaches a segment of help or weight, frequently because of a notable surge in purchasing or selling volume.

**Cycle** – DAYs where price action is anticipated to adhere to a particular pattern.

**Dead cat bounce** – When cost diminishes in a down industry, there could be an uptick in price where buyers come in believing the advantage is inexpensive or selling overdone. However, whenever sellers force the market down more, the temporary purchasing spell arrives to be referred to as a dead pet bounce.

**Dow theory** – Studies the relationship between the Dow Jones Industrial Average (an index comprised of 30 United States multinational conglomerates) and Dow Jones transport Average. Advocates for the theory suggest that when one of all of the trends in a specific way, the additional is expected to follow. Many traders monitor the transportation sector offered it can shed insight into the health of this economic climate. A large amount of product shipments and deals is actually indicative that the economy is actually on a sound footing. An identical indication will be the Baltic Dry Index.

**Doji** – A candle type distinguished by little if any modification amongst the available and near price, showing indecision in the marketplace.

**Elliott trend theory** – Elliott trend theory implies that marketplaces run through cyclical intervals of optimism and pessimism that may be forecast and therefore ripe for trading options.

**Fibonacci percentages** – Numbers used as a guide to determine support and resistance.

**Harmonics** – Harmonic exchanging is dependent on the idea that cost habits repeat on their own and turning areas into the marketplace can be recognized through Fibonacci sequences.

**Momentum** – The price of modification of cost with regard to DAY.

**Cost activity** – The movement of price, as graphically represented through a chart of a specific industry.

**Weight** – A cost amount in which a preponderance of offer instructions can be located, creating price to bounce from the level down. Enough buying activity, typically from the increased amount, is frequently required to break it.

**Retracement** – A reverse into the direction of the prevailing pattern, likely to end up being temporary, often to a standard of support or resistance.

**Support** – A price amount where a higher magnitude of purchase orders can be put, causing the price to jump off the level upward. The degree will likely not hold if there's sufficient selling activity outweighing the purchasing task.

**Trend** – cost movement that persists in one single course for an elongated DAY period.

## Technical Evaluation Indicators

Technical indicators involve some mathematical or arithmetical shift of cost and/or volume data to provide mathematical descriptions of up/down movement, support, and weight degrees, momentum, trend, deviations from a central tendency, ratio(s), correlation(s), among various other delineations. Some signs additionally describe senDAYnt, such as short interest, implied volatility, put/call ratios, "fear" or "greed", and so on.

Technical indicators get into a couple of major categories, including price-based, volume-based, breadth, overlays, and non-chart based.

## Price-based

**Average Directional Index (ADX)** – Measures tendency energy on an absolute value basis.

**Regular Directional Movement rank (ADXR)** – steps the price of modification in a development.

**Product Channel Index (CCI)** – Identifies brand-new trends or cyclical problems.

**Coppock Curve** – Momentum sign, initially supposed to recognize soles in stock indices as an element of a long-term trading strategy.

**MACD** – Plots the relationship between two individual moving averages; designed as a momentum-following indicator.

**Momentum** – The rate of modification in cost with respect to DAY.

**Transferring Average** – A weighted average of prices to indicate the pattern over a show of values.

**Relative energy Index (RSI)** – Momentum oscillator standardized to a 0-100 scale designed to determine the price of change over a given DAY period.

**Stochastic Oscillator** – demonstrates the present price of the security or directory family member towards the high and low prices from a user-defined range. Used to determine overbought and oversold marketplace conditions.

**Trix** – Combines to reveal trends and momentum.

**Volume-based**

**Funds Flow Index** – steps the flow of money into and out of an inventory over a specific duration.

**Negative quantity Index** – Designed to understand when the "smart cash" is active, under the expectation that the smart cash is actually the majority of energetic on low-volume days rather than as active on high-volume DAYs. The indicator focuses on the day-to-day level when the volume is actually down from the previous day.

**On-Balance Volume** – Uses volume to anticipate subsequent changes in cost. Proponents of the indicator spot credence into the idea that when amount changes with a weak effect in the stock, the cost action is most likely to follow.

**Positive quantity Index** – Typically made use of alongside the negative amount index, the indicator is actually created to show whenever institutional people are many active beneath the assumption they're most more likely to buy or market whenever the volume is reduced. Concentrates on DAYs when quantity is actually up from the earlier DAY.

**Williams** Accumulation/Distribution – appears at divergences between protection (or index) cost and volume movement. This was designed to identify whenever dealers tend to be gathering (buying) or dispersing (selling). For instance, whenever cost tends to make a brand new low, as well as the indicator, does not additionally make a unique low, this could be used as a sign that accumulation (purchasing) is occurring.

## Depth

Breadth signals decide how strong or superficial an industry move is actually.

**Advance-Decline Line** – Measures how lots of stocks advanced (gained in value) in an index versus the number of shares that dropped (missing value). If a directory has acquired at price but just 30% regarding the stocks tend to be up but 70% are down or natural, that's an indication that the purchasing is actually very likely only occurring in particular sectors instead of being positive toward the whole industry.

If 98% of the shares are up but only 2% are down or natural at an open of the market, it's a sign that the marketplace may be much more trendless and "reversion to your mean" DAY investing techniques could become more effective. However, if a lopsided advance/decline continues, it could indicate that the marketplace could be trending.

**Arms Index (aka TRIN)** – Combines the number of shares improving or decreasing through its amount relating to the method:

(# of improving stocks / # of decreasing stocks) / (quantity of advancing stocks/amount of decreasing shares) a worth below 1 is thought about bullish; a value above 1 is regarded as bearish. Volume is actually calculated in the number of shares exchanged rather than the buck amounts, which is a central flaw in the indicator (favors reduced price-per-share stocks, which can trade in higher quantity). It's nonetheless still displayed on the flooring from the New York inventory Exchange.

**McClellan Oscillator** – Takes a ratio of the stocks improving minus the shares declining in an index and makes use of two individual weighted averages to show up at a value. Finest utilized when price together with the oscillator is generally diverging. For instance, when pricing is making a new low however the oscillator is making a new large, this could represent a getting opportunity. However, when the price is making a new large however the oscillator is making a new reduced, this could represent a marketing opportunity.

## Overlays

Overlay signals are positioned throughout the original cost chart.

**Bollinger Bands** – Uses an easy moving average and plots two contours two regular deviations above and below it to form a range. Often made use of by dealers using a hostile reversion approach where cost going above or underneath the groups is actually "stretched" and possibly anticipated to return back inside the bands.

**Channel** – Two synchronous trend outlines established to imagine a consolidation routine of a specific direction. A breakout above or below a station may be interpreted as an indication of an innovative new trend and a potential trading chance.

**Fibonacci Lines** – a device for help and opposition generally produced by plotting the signal through the large and reduced of a current trend.

**Ichimoku Cloud** – Designed to be an "all-in-one" indicator that provides support and resistance, momentum, trend, and stimulates trading and investing signals.

**Going typical** – A trend line that changes predicated on brand new cost inputs. For instance, a 50-day basic transferring average would portray the average cost of the last 50 exchanging days. Rapid transferring averages weight the range a lot more heavily toward new prices.

**Parabolic SAR** – meant to find short-term reversal patterns into the industry. Generally just advised for popular areas.

**Pivot details** – values of service and resistance determined from yesterday's available, large, low and close. Typically used by DAY dealers to locate potential reverse degrees when you look at the marketplace.

**Trend range** – A sloped range formed from two or more peaks or troughs on the cost guide. A rest above or below a tendency line might be indicative of a breakout.

## Non-Chart Based

Maybe not all complex analysis is dependent on charting or arithmetical changes of cost. Some technical analysts depend on senDAYnt-based surveys from buyers and businesses to evaluate where the price might be going.

When investor belief is powerful one way or some other, surveys may work as a contrarian indicator. If the market is very optimistic, this might end up being used as a signal that almost everybody is completely used and a couple of buyers stay regarding the sidelines to force prices up further. This might suggest that costs are more willing to trend down. Or at the minimum, the danger associated with getting a buyer is actually larger than if the belief had been slanted the other way.

# CHAPTER 11:

# DIFFERENT EXCHANGING TYPES

## The Four Principal Trading Designs

Dependent on your individual preferences, you'll find four major exchanging designs that could be employed to exchange the Forex marketplace.

Each design has its strengths and disadvantages, very be sure that you choose the only that best suits your own mental traits or perhaps you won't have the ability to make the most from your trading.

The primary trading types are generally scalping, day trading, sway trading and position trading.

## Scalping

Scalping is considered the most dynamic exchanging style in the list, as it entails beginning multiple trades in the day and closing them right after. Scalpers like fast-paced trading plus they don't wish to wait all day or days for a trade setup to create. That's the reason why scalpers trade on quick-term DAY-frames, for instance, the 1-minute or 5-minute ones.

## Day Trading

DAY exchanging is founded on greater DAY-frames, these types of as the 1-hour or 4-hour DAYframes. Day traders aim to keep their own trades for the whole trading DAY and often close their trades by the end associated with the DAY. US-based brokers will usually flag you as a day-trader if you place at least three positions a day for five consecutive DAYs. We'll soon include the key methods that day traders make use of to trade the marketplace.

## Swing Trading And Investing

Sway trading is dependent on longer-term DAYframes and trades are usually used available for a couple of days. Unlike day traders, swing traders are generally subjected to overnight market risks which could switch their own positions against all of them. It's not unusual that sway traders hold their particular investments over the weekend.

## Position Trading And Investing

Finally, position investing will be the longest-term exchanging style in all of our record. Place traders hold their own positions for months or even many years. Since fundamentals perform a crucial role over such long DAY-frames, place traders want to have a good knowledge of business economics and market dynamics that impact change rates.

## Day Trading And Investing Skills

Now that you are really common using the primary trading styles and know the primary characteristics of DAY trading, it's DAY for you to find out exactly how DAY dealers exchange the market. There are three main day-trading techniques, all of these have a proven track-record: (1) breakout trading, (2) trend-following and (3) counter-trend trading.

**Let's describe every one of them with instances.**

### #1 Breakout Trading

As the title suggests, breakout investing is dependent on catching the buying or offering momentum right after a breakout happens. Breakout traders usually depend on chart patterns and trendlines to evaluate the market and wait for the price to split above or below vital specialized degrees.

Since breakout traders wish to capture the breakout as soon as it occurs, they often use pending orders placed simply above or below the possible breakout point. Using pending requests is actually also DAY-efficient, as you don't need to wait in front of your own screen to start the trade – the pending orders will be automatically executed when the cost reaches the pre-specified degree.

The chart above shows a typical breakout trade setup predicated on a bullish wedge guide routine. Breakout traders ought to be up-to-date on essential industry improvements, as development can often trigger the rest of important complex amounts.

## #2 Trend-Following Trading

The next popular day-trading strategy is actually according to trend-following. Exchanging doesn't need to be complex, and trend-following positions are arguably the easiest and a lot of rewarding of all of the. Bill Dunn is actually a famous trend-following trader exactly who made significantly comes back in the US dollar vs. Japanese yen pair over 1995, simply through the use of a trend-following method.

Through the use of trendlines, Dunn grabbed both the downtrend in very early 1995 in addition to after uptrend throughout the Summer of the identical year within the USD/JPY pair.

Trend-following dealers use simple technical resources such as for example trendlines and channels to identify the present tendency and spot development-reversals. As soon as the price reaches near to a trendline, and also the following cost-action programs that the trendline is respected, development-after traders would enter in the direction for the development.

The data above shows an easy trend-following setup. Since the pricing is forming consecutive higher levels and higher lows, that are characteristics of an uptrend, a trend-following individual would wait for the price to reach towards the rising trendline and open up a lengthy place in the event that trendline demonstrates to keep.

## Browse:

Awesome help guide to Candlestick Patterns (You'll end up being astonished!)
Make Certain You Can Recognize Candlestick Charts
Benefits and Negatives of Automated Trading Methods

## Counter-Trend Exchanging

Final yet not minimum, counter-trend trading is actually additionally a prominent day trading method. However, because this DAY trading style involves starting trades into the opposite course of the fundamental pattern, counter-trend trades are normally riskier than their breakout of pattern-following alternatives.

Counter-trend traders usually use mean-reverting strategies to start a trade. Essentially, the cost can makeups and downs even when the marketplace is popular, and this type of individual wishes to just take benefit of the moves.

If the cost moves also much up during an uptrend, counter-trend dealers will turn to brief the money pair. Similarly, in the event that price moves also much down during a downtrend, these traders will aim to invest in the currency pair.

Alternatively, counter-trend traders can make use of Fibonacci tools to evaluate the extent of a modification additionally the possible profit target. The adhering to data demonstrates just how to make use of Fibonacci retracements to enter a counter-trend trade based on price corrections.

Strong uptrends and downtrends usually find assistance at the lower Fib proportions, like the 23.6% and 38.2% degrees. Weaker trends may correct most of the means to the 61.8% Fibonacci amount.

## Closing Statement

DAY trading is a popular trading design in the Forex industry. It allows traders to place positions within the morning, keep all of them in the day and close them because of the conclusion of the exchanging day, understanding whether these people produced a profit or a loss when it comes today. While DAY trading isn't as fast-paced as scalping, it permits placing more positions during a few days than swing dealers would do, and of course situation dealers.

There are generally three main DAY trading methods: breakout trading, trend-following trading, and counter-trend exchanging. While trend-following trades tend to be normally the simplest and a lot of worthwhile of these three, your trading functionality eventually depends on your experience and market understanding.

# STOCK MARKET INVESTING FOR BEGINNERS

*David Lazarus*

# Table Of Contents:

# Chapter One:  Introduction To Stock Market

In all actuality WE ARE ALL financial specialists. At the point when we hear the word financial specialists, we may think about a high-flying Wall-Street broker in a blue-stick striped suit. That is unquestionably one sort of financial specialist, yet so is the entrepreneur, the family attempting to put something aside for their children's school, and the understudy attempting to scrape up enough quarters to have supper. We as a whole need to deal with the cash we make, and we as a whole would like to wind up with however much cash as could reasonably be expected. The subject of building riches throughout your life will truly come down to two inquiries?

1) Are you ready to spare every year?

2) When you spare, where do you put the cash?

**Theoretical**

We should accept that you're 20 years of age and just accepting an occupation as a freeman, your youth dream (what child wouldn't like to be a freeman, right?). Your pay is pitiful, yet you make the objective to spare $1,000 dollars every year and put it in a retirement account.

You work and put something aside for the following 50 years until you resign.

Does it truly make a difference where I put that cash, I mean it's just a thousand bucks per year? Well you have a few choices, how about we assess.

1). Te bank account (also called the "Under the Mattress" approach). Te most effortless and "most secure" thing is you could simply placed the cash in real money. Pleasant and safe! It will never leave and it won't go all over. Normal Annual Return: 0%
Sum Accumulated in 50 Years: $50,000

2). Bonds or Real Estate. The vast majority state that they get the greater part of their retirement assets from putting resources into their home and watching it increment in esteem. Or then again contributing in bonds. Both of these alternatives will develop in accordance with expansion, which by and large is about 3% every year. Normal Annual Return: 3%. Sum Accumulated in 50 Years: $116,000

3). Te Stock Market. Frightening, isn't that so? It goes here and there. There are times when it can decrease by 20% in a brief timeframe, inciting frenzy and frightening features. Yet, after some time, the financial exchange develops with how quick enterprises develop. In each multi year time span, the securities exchange procures you 8-10% returns. Truth be told, in the course of the only remaining century, the S&P 500 (the biggest 500 organizations in the US) have returned 9.8% every year.

Normal Annual Return: 9.8% Amount Accumulated in 50 Years: $1,359,199

So does it truly make a difference where you put your cash? Uh, better believe it! It has a significant effect. Truth be told, the more cash that you can place in the financial exchange early, the more the amplifying effect of "accruing funds" or "intensifying" can work in support of you.

"Accruing funds is the eighth miracle of the world" - Albert Einstein

Presently, I recognize what you're thinking. On the off chance that going from 3% to 10% return gets me an additional million dollars, what does getting a 20% return do? Warren Buffett, the unbelievable financial specialist, for instance earned 30% return over a time of 30 years. (called the acclaimed "30/30").

4). Beating the Market. This isn't simple, it isn't for everybody, except suppose you take a couple of hours out of each week, and you get your work done, and put resources into some uncommon organizations through the financial exchange, and win an exceptional 20% return for each year. This is an extremely exceptional yield (even

12% every year is a serious accomplishment) yet allows simply accept that you're great at discovering incredible stocks.

Normal Annual Return: 20%

Sum Accumulated in 50 Years: $109,826,119 (Yes, that is over $100 million dollars)

That is a gigantic fortune for a freeman sparing just $1k every year. Thus, presently you know why you heard your father's companion gloating that he "beat the market" on his venture portfolio a year ago. Te contrast somewhere in the range of 3% and 10% may appear to be little, however it has a significant effect towards building riches.

Beginning Early

Accumulated dividends is an incredible efect, and the EARLIER you start contributing the more it will work for you. Consider the model above with the freeman, however as opposed to beginning to spare at 20 years of age, rather he begins to spare at 40 years of age. Rather than resigning with $1.3 million he will resign with just $190k. Take a gander at the outcomes beneath expecting he puts resources into the securities exchange:

Begun sparing $1,000 every year at

at Age 40 = $190,773 (at age 70)

at Age 30 = $535,682 (at age 70)

at Age 20 = $1,359,199 (at age 70)

And afterward, suppose you join Young Investors Society and start contributing when you're 15 years of age. What does an additional 5 years get you?at Age 15 = $2,224,948 (at age 70)

Notice that the diference is right around a million dollars diference in the event that you start just

5 years sooner!

In rundown, the TWO CRITICAL FACTORS of COMPOUND INTEREST are:

5). Acquire a High Return (for example the financial exchange)

6). Start Early

Furthermore, recall that, we're all speculators, regardless!

# WHAT DOES IT REALLY MEAN TO INVEST IN THE STOCK MARKET?

Questions:

1. What is a "stock"?

2. What is the securities exchange?

The accompanying connection is an incredible video clarifying a "stock" and the "financial exchange", if it's not too much trouble survey Lesson 1 (What is the Stock Market) and Lesson 2 (What are Stocks) done by our accomplice, Wall Street Survivor.

You can see from this that putting resources into the financial exchange is "not kidding business," simultaneously it tends to be a fun game. Always remember that when you purchase partakes in an organization, you become one of its proprietors!

Inquiries TO CONSIDER:

1. I'm not catching it's meaning to purchase a "stock"?

2. For what reason does the Stock Market go all over?

$190k. Take a gander at the outcomes beneath accepting he puts resources into the securities exchange:

Begun sparing $1,000 every year at

at Age 40 = $190,773 (at age 70)

at Age 30 = $535,682 (at age 70)

at Age 20 = $1,359,199 (at age 70)

And afterward, suppose you join Young Investors Society and start contributing when you're 15 years of age. What does an additional 5 years get you? at Age 15 = $2,224,948 (at age 70)

Notice that the thing that matters is very nearly a million dollars contrast in the event that you start just

5 years sooner!

In synopsis, the TWO CRITICAL FACTORS of COMPOUND INTEREST are:

5). Acquire a High Return (for example the financial exchange)

6). Start Early

Furthermore, recall that, we're all financial specialists, in any case!

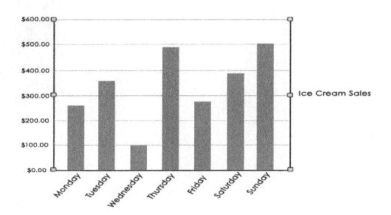

# Chapter Two: Choosing A Brokerage

## WHAT DOES IT REALLY MEAN TO INVEST IN THE STOCK MARKET?

Questions:

1. What is a "stock"?

2. What is the securities exchange?

The accompanying connection is an incredible video clarifying a "stock" and the "securities exchange", it would be ideal if you survey Lesson 1 (What is the Stock Market) and Lesson 2 (What are Stocks) done by our accomplice, Wall Street Survivor.

You can see from this that putting resources into the securities exchange is "not kidding business," simultaneously it very well may be a fun game. Always remember that when you purchase partakes in an organization, you become one of its proprietors!

Inquiries TO CONSIDER:

1. I don't get it is meaning to purchase a "stock"?

## 2. For what reason does the Stock Market go here and there?

All organizations have proprietors. A little organization began by a solitary individual may have just that person as the single proprietor. Te huge companies that have stock (shares that are exchanged by the overall population) have numerous proprietors.

To improve and sort out the purchasing and selling of these offers by the general open, organizations utilize the securities exchange. Indeed, US government guidelines necessitate that an organization, when it arrives at a specific number of proprietors, must open up to the world. This is to permit its now huge number of proprietors to have the option to purchase and sell their portions of stock in the organization all the more effectively.

Simply consider it along these lines. We should imagine that your kin or a dear companion is beginning a little organization. The person is doing truly well, yet needs more cash (money) to grow. The person in question requests that you become a section proprietor in the business by contributing a portion of your investment funds. You concur. OK attempt to sell your proprietorship in the organization only a couple of days after the fact? In all probability not! It ought to be something very similar when you choose to purchase an open organization's stock. The main genuine distinction is that your kin's or companion's organization is a privately owned business with only two investors, though there are a lot more proprietors in an open organization with shares in the "financial exchange."

"Without a sparing confidence later on, nobody could ever contribute by any means. To be a financial specialist, you should be a devotee to a superior tomorrow" Benjamin Graham.

Action: FIND THE STOCK

Putting resources into a stock is purchasing a bit of the organization.

Search the web to coordinate the brands with the organization (stock) that claims it. What stock ticker (model AAPL for Apple) okay purchase in the event that you needed to put resources into the development of the accompanying items?

ESPN

Spoils

YouTube

BEATING THE MARKET

To begin, let me acquaint you with Warren Buffett. Mr. Buffett has been the absolute best financial specialist since the late 1950s.

We should set the stage. It is 1984. As of late, there had emerged a developing agreement that the securities exchange was completely productive, called

"Effective Market Theory." Basically, scholastics and speculators were pronouncing it incomprehensible for somebody to reliably pick stocks that would beat the general market normal, in light of the fact that everything was evaluated in as of now. Columbia Business School facilitated an epic discussion as a challenge between Michael Jensen, an educator from the University of Rochester and one of the main voices of the Efficient

Market Theory versus Warren Buffett, acclaimed stock-picker. Jensen went first. He contended that on the off chance that you flipped a coin multiple times, there would be somebody that happened to get heads multiple times in succession, yet that didn't imply that that individual had expertise. He considered picking stocks a "coin flip".

At that point Buffett talked. He said "we should envision that we had a coin flipping challenge. What's more, that obviously we could have some fortunate champs and washouts. In any case, at that point, how about we expect that every one of the victors shared something for all intents and purpose.

Consider the possibility that every one of the victors of the coin-flipping challenge originated from Omaha, or had an uncommon procedure. Wouldn't you be interested to discover what made this high grouping of victors? Bufett then experienced the venture execution of nine fruitful financial specialists that just so happened to all training a similar procedure and all had similar educators, Benjamin Graham and David Dodd. He called them "The Super speculators of Graham-and Doddsville." Buffett was unequivocally pronounced the victor after his mind blowing discourse. Nobody could question the numbers or the rationale. The reasonable end is that you can be fruitful in picking stocks, and it requires following the speculation standards of Graham and Dodd and Buffett.

Buffett references Benjamin Graham and David L. Dodd. Together Graham and Dodd composed Security Analysis in 1934. This book, still in print after a few versions, has affected numerous incredible financial specialists since the absolute first production. Furthermore, Benjamin Graham composed The Intelligent Investor in 1949. Mr. Buffett first read this book in 1950 and thinks about it, "by a long shot the best book on contributing at any point composed." Benjamin Graham is viewed as the dad of significant worth contributing thus we start here. As you read the article, make a note of the key ideas that are referenced. Some are rehashed a few times.

Inquiries TO CONSIDER:

1. What are the regular qualities of effective financial specialists?

2. On the off chance that there is an unmistakable formula for venture achievement, for what reason do you suspect as much few individuals tail it?

THE SEVEN GOLDEN RULES

Being fruitful at anything requires adhering to a lot of rules. Great rules are the aggregation of many years of knowledge summarized into the couple of parts that truly matter. Effective football players win since they dodge punishments and on account of the manner in which they train. Effective understudies get An's a result of the manner in which they study.

Putting resources into the financial exchange is the same, then again, actually when you prevail with regards to contributing you profit - a great deal of cash. Take Warren Buffett for instance; he began with $10,000 and transformed it into a total assets of $60,000,000,000 (That's 60 BILLION!) . Yet, he's not the only one. Dwindle Lynch, Bill Ruane,

Walter Schloss, Bill Miller, Charlie Munger, Joel Greenblatt, and numerous others created comparative exceptional speculation returns, reliably, over a long haul time skyline. Each fruitful reserve chief's style was marginally unique, yet on the off chance that you study them each cautiously you'll begin to see significant designs. We added these examples into Seven Golden Rules.

In this way, right away, here are the Seven Golden Rules of Successful Investing with the goal that you can pound it in the financial exchange.

Attempting to time the financial exchange or gambling everything to "twofold your cash in a year" is, best case scenario hypothesizing, at the very least betting. You should simply take your cash to Vegas and lose it there. Tose who can effectively explore the financial exchange are not theorists or card sharks, they are speculators. Financial specialists realize they can beat the market since they think in an unexpected way, they think more brilliant, and they think longer-term.

"Time skyline exchange" implies that if speculators figure out how to think long haul and can see past the day by day and quarterly commotion, they can increase a genuine high ground. In 1964, American Express was an extraordinary organization however the stock was getting pounded because of a protection embarrassment.

The organization needed to pay a huge number of dollars in fines because of inadvertently endorsing barrels of vegetable oil that ended up being water. That is actually when Warren Buffett started buying the stock. The best financial specialists look past transient trouble and keep their eyes on the long haul skyline.

"Just purchase something that you'd be splendidly glad to hold if the market shut down for a long time." - Warren Buffett

Great COMPANIES MAKE GOOD INVESTMENTS

Individuals need to comprehend that contributing isn't care for putting down a wager on whether the Cowboys will cover the spread against the Packers in the major event. Contributing isn't attempting to get the quarterly official statement a microsecond before the other individual. It isn't even about attempting to anticipate which stock that you think will go up the most. Basic Investing is purchasing an unmistakable bit of a business, or a portion of that business. What's more, your venture portfolio (the accumulation of all the various offers you possess) is just in the same class as aggregate of the organizations in that portfolio.

On the off chance that you purchase portions of great organizations at sensible costs, you'll end up with an excellent portfolio with less hazard. It's as basic as that.

Great organizations are ones that have an exceptional bit of leeway that others can't duplicate. Great organizations are ones that produce exceptional yields on capital.

Great organizations don't have to acquire a ton on the grounds that their business is self-financing.

"It's much better to purchase a magnificent organization at a reasonable cost than a reasonable organization at a great value" Warren Buffett

"It's much better to purchase a magnificent organization at a reasonable cost than a reasonable organization at a great cost"

RULE 3: BUY WITH A MARGIN OF SAFETY

About each expert financial specialist started his vocation perusing Benjamin Graham's, The Astute Investor. Warren Buffett called it, "by a long shot, the best book on contributing at any point composed." What makes it so uncommon? One reason is on the grounds that it presented the significant idea "Edge of Safety."

In contributing, an edge of wellbeing is shaped when one purchases a speculation at not as much as its worth, while utilizing traditionalist suspicions. The possibility of an edge of wellbeing is that you need to purchase a business at a value that is low enough that your appraisal could be totally off-base and you wouldn't lose a lot.

## Chapter Three: Investing in stocks

**DO YOU OWN HOMEWORK AND OWN WHAT YOU KNOW**

There is not a viable alternative for your very own work. Purchasing a stock in light of the fact that CNBC prescribed it, or on the grounds that your uncle suggested it, or the stock graph looks great is a certain method to lose cash.

Fruitful speculators comprehend what they possess. They purchase supplies of organizations with items they have confidence in. Effective speculators go the additional mile to break down the financials of the organization to ensure they're not missing anything. Keep in mind, a large portion of the uncommon increases made in the financial exchange come after a stock is rebuffed or after it has just risen a great deal, yet you're not going to have the conviction to stay with it except if you truly know the organization.

"You need to realize what you claim, and why you possess it." - Peter Lynch

RULE 5: DON'T FOLLOW THE HERD, STAY CALM AND RATIONAL

The ordinary purchaser's choice is normally intensely affected by people around him: purchase when others are purchasing, sell when others are selling. Shockingly, this is a formula that will undoubtedly blowback. The best financial specialists are ones that can battle this inclination and resist the urge to panic through a tempest, and stay uninvolved through an air pocket.

The world's most noteworthy financial specialist Warren Buffett said all that needed to be said, "Be dreadful when others are avaricious, and be insatiable when others are frightful!"

RULE 6:DON'T PUT ALL YOUR EGGS IN ONE BASKET,

Be that as it may, DON'T HAVE TOO MANY BASKETS, EITHER

Expansion is one of the most basic procedures for your portfolio so that on the off chance that one stock explodes, it won't sink the whole ship. As much as we might suspect we won't commit an error, we will. Indeed, even the bosses do and that is the reason we can't place all our investments tied up on one place.

There's capacity in expansion.

In any case, look into recommends that 90% of broadening advantages can be gotten in many markets with an arrangement of a little more than 20 stocks. The more you broaden past that, the less you think about every venture (See Rule #4). Your first and second best thoughts are in every case superior to your 100th best thought, so while broadening is vital, make the most of your best thoughts! Warren Buffett

"We attempt to abstain from purchasing a tad bit of either when we are just tepid about the business or its cost. At the point when we are persuaded as to appeal, we put stock in purchasing beneficial sums".

RULE 7: NEVER STOP LEARNING

Maybe the most significant standard is learn, find out additional, and afterward keep learning. Te fun thing about contributing is that the business sectors are constantly unique what's more, organizations are always showing signs of change.

Learn constantly about organizations, learn constantly from other extraordinary financial specialists, and learn constantly from your very own slip-ups. Modesty and an enthusiasm to learn are two attributes found in the entirety of the incredible financial specialists. Indeed, even Warren Buffett credits his accomplice Charlie Munger with instructing him that it's smarter to purchase an incredible organization at a reasonable cost than a reasonable organization at an extraordinary cost.

"The round of life is the round of everlasting learning. At any rate it is on the off chance that you need to win." - Charlie Munger

Eighth BONUS RULE WHEN YOU MAKE A LOT MON-EY, FIND MEANINGFUL WAYS TO GIVE IT BACK.

Bill and Melinda Gates took their fortune and lifted a great many individuals out of destitution through their establishment. Warren Buffett has done likewise with his billions. On the off chance that you make millions or even billions of dollars through the ideas instructed by YIS, we trust that you will take it and improve the world a spot. What's more, regardless of whether you don't make millions, you can discover significant approaches to offer back to your locale. Giving, should be possible with cash, yet additionally with your time, your vitality and your abilities. At YIS, we trust it's conceivable to truly make the most of our ventures. That's for what reason we're putting resources into you.

KEY TAKEAWAYS

Warren Buffett and numerous others clarified that it is truly conceivable to make excellent comes back from the financial exchange, keeping a couple of straightforward guidelines.

Contributing is straightforward, however it is difficult. The Golden Rules of Investing are generally known yet hard to follow by and by. By putting resources into a stock you are owning a segment of a business.

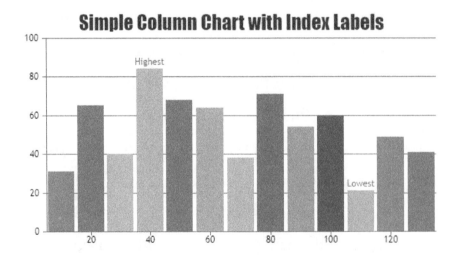

# Chapter Four: Day and Swing Trading

## THE VALUE OF A STOCK

Presentation

Envision before you is a crate of twelve doughnuts. What amount would you pay for one doughnut? In the event that every one of the doughnuts in the container are the equivalent, would one say one is worth more than the other? Consider the possibility that the world had a deficiency of sugar and this was the last box of doughnuts on the planet, with none having the option to be made for the following year. Does the shortage increment the estimation of the great? What about in the event that you just ate a case of doughnuts and can't eat additional, does the worth you would pay for a doughnut decline? The container of 12 doughnuts speaks to an organization. At the point when you separate the organization, everybody has a chance to claim a portion of the doughnuts, or part of the organization. Be that as it may, individuals may pay uncontrollably various costs for a similar doughnut. On the off chance that you need to amplify the estimation of a crate of doughnuts, what may be the best approach? One strategy is to persuade individuals that these are the most delicious doughnuts on the planet and they might be around temporarily.

More or less, this is the manner by which the market works. The financial exchange is comprised of individuals that get amped up for something or tired of something relying upon their state of mind. What is evident is that every so often the market goes crazy!

Consider watching the accompanying video to perceive how incredible financial specialist Warren Bufett reacts to the inquiry, "What do you do when the market goes down?" How is Warren Buffett utilizing sound judgment about when things are "at a bargain?" Do you concur?

Area 1

For what reason DO STOCK PRICES FLUCTUATE SO MUCH?

Open any budgetary paper like the Wall Street Journal. Go to the stock statement segment, pick any organization aimlessly, and take a gander at the high and low stock cost from the previous year. (or on the other hand go to yahoo.finance) Ok, how about we see here. We have GM. They make vehicles and trucks.

In the course of recent weeks, their stock exchanged as low as $28/share and as high as $39/share. They have 1.6 billion (bn) shares exceptional, with the goal that implies that the market estimation of GM was as low as $45bn and as high as $62bn. That is a distinction of $17 billion dollars in esteem. Presently the vehicle business doesn't generally change that much. You sell give or take 5% more vehicles every year. Chevy Silverado is a Chevy Silverado and they're not making sense of how to swap fuel for water, or how to travel to the moon. It's essentially a similar business this year as it was a year ago. So how on the planet could the worth vacillate by $17 billion dollars? What's more, more in this way, why is this occurrence with each and every organization in the financial exchange?

Was a year ago an uncommon year of value swings? Probably not Is there something the market realizes that we don't have the foggiest idea? No. Anyway, what's the clarification? Indeed, it tends to be summarized into four short words: "THE MARKET GOES NUTS!"

## MR. MARKET

Give me a chance to disclose to you a story. It's a story that incredible financial specialist Benjamin Graham told. It is about a colleague of yours, named Mr. Market. Envision you possess a business together. Presently, Mr. Market is a hero, however he experiences wild emotional episodes. One day he awakens, and the sky is blue and he is feeling extremely great. So he offers to purchase out your stake in the business for much more than it is value. Ten the following day, he awakens and it's coming down, he's inclination urgent, and he is shouting that the world is going to end. He offers to sell all of you of his stock in the organization for half of what you paid for it. You take it! Te following day, Mr. Market offers to pay a value that is neither remarkably high nor phenomenal low, so you simply sit idle. Presently the estimation of the business didn't generally change from everyday – what changed was the flighty mind-sets of Mr. Market.

To put it plainly, Mr. Market is one cranky man.

So does this imply we shouldn't put resources into the securities exchange, on account of these wild swings for the time being? Despite what might be expected! Te reality that we are offered bargains every once in a while should make us incredibly, energized. We will probably 1) distinguish what the organization is worth and 2) to hang tight for Mr. Market to have a terrible day and get it at an enormous markdown. Benjamin Graham considered this giving ourselves an "edge of security." This is what might be compared to purchasing dollars for fifty pennies.

Alright, you're thinking. This is just fine. Trust that the market will go insane and purchase underneath the reasonable worth. Be that as it may, there would one say one is issue: How would we be able to be certain that we can even verged on knowing the estimation of an organization?

How might we be certain that our figures (a.k.a. wild surmises) are even in the ballpark? Aren't there a huge amount of shrewd individuals and PC projects holding back to gather up a deal when it gets accessible? Shockingly, not the same number of as you might suspect.

QUESTION TO CONSIDER:

1. Consider something that you got a truly executioner bargain on that you purchased previously, how were you ready to get that arrangement? How is this like the securities exchange?

Segment 2

WHAT IS THE VALUE OF A BUSINESS?

We'll possibly put resources into an organization when the value we pay today is fundamentally not exactly the worth we will get tomorrow.

Model: Teacher picks an understudy indiscriminately. Instructor holds up a $10 greenback and asks the understudy, "What is the estimation of this bill?" Ten dollars. Educator holds up ten $1 notes. She poses a similar inquiry, "What is the estimation of these dollar notes?" Ten dollars. Educator offers to sell the understudy the $10 greenback for the ten $1 dollar notes. This is a wash so perhaps he'll take it, possibly he won't.

Ten Teacher offers to sell the $10 for just five $1 dollar notes. Obviously he should take it. Pose the inquiry to the remainder of the class everywhere, "What number of you would purchase this?" Do the turn around. Approach to sell the $10 note for twenty $1 notes? What number of would take this? None of them.

The best financial specialists can grab up $10 greenbacks when the market is just approaching $5 for them. Yet, how is this conceivable? It is conceivable in light of the fact that 1) the worth is dubious to figure and 2) the market is unreasonable.

Keep in mind the Market goes crazy. Is this something to be thankful for or an awful thing for you? It's a generally excellent thing. In the event that all financial specialists put together their speculation choices with respect to objective and moderate appraisals of inherent worth, it would be hard to profit in the securities exchange. Luckily, the members in the financial exchange are people dependent upon the consuming impact of feelings.

Numerous financial specialists will surrender to publicity around stocks, or individuals will bounce on a pattern, since they have hopeful perspectives that they can beat the framework. As youthful financial specialist prodigies, we will consistently abandon feelings purchase stocks dependent on what they are extremely worth.

Be that as it may, how would we know what the estimation of the organization is?

We should take Apple. What is the estimation of the world's biggest business of customer gadgets? Te estimation of any business is the present estimation of all future money the organization will make short the money it needs to contribute to get this going. Alright, that is somewhat of a significant piece, remain with me.

We should accept that today Apple sells 200 million (mn) items every year at a normal cost of $1,000 each. So they make $200 billion dollars per year in deals. Be that as it may, to make those 200mn items, they burn through $700 per gadget to plan and make them and $100 to purchase the hardware. So they're bringing home $200 per gadget, or 40bn dollars. OK pay $40 to get $40 one year from now? Actually no, not except if you think Apple is going to continue profiting the next year. Alright, how about we accept Apple sells 5% more items consistently at a similar cost of $1,000. One year from now they make $44bn, the next year they make $48.4bn, etc. Te estimation of Apple at that point becomes everything under the line. How about we accept Apple can keep this pattern for the following 40 years. Te aggregate sum of benefits going ahead, at the present worth is about $675 billion dollars. Not awful, eh? Gap that by the quantity of offers exceptional, and we have the estimation of the offers at about $111 dollars per share.

Yearly Profit

Items sold 200 million X Average Price$1,000 each = Sales $200 billion

- Product Cost $160 billion ($700 + $100 X 200 million) Benefit $40 billion (or $200 per gadget)

# Chapter Five: Investment Startegies

QUESTION TO CONSIDER:

1. How much benefit would Apple make in the event that it sold 500 million items every year at a similar cost and a similar benefit for each gadget?

So first we have the market meaning of what an organization's worth is and second, we have tips and deceives from other speculator prodigies. The estimation of what an organization is worth truly lays on only two inquiries:

1) How much are benefits going to develop and

2) How long are these benefits manageable?

Those are the two things that decide how much worth returns to you over the long haul as a proprietor of the business. 'To what extent will this last?' is likely the most significant inquiry you can pose to yourself, in attempting to figure out what an organization is value.

Presently, even the best speculators will reveal to you they have been dead off-base on the estimation of organizations on many, numerous events. They'll additionally admit to you that for half of the organizations available, they honestly have no clue what the genuine estimation of the organization is. Why? Since the eventual fate of numerous organizations is too dubious to even consider predicting.

On the off chance that you don't have the foggiest idea to what extent those benefits will last, you can't figure what the organization is value. For most organizations it is a wild think about to what extent those benefit s can last since they don't have any genuine protections. They don't have a financial canal. Fortunately there are some uncommon organizations with a significant canal around their palace that we know can't be contended away effectively. By putting resources into these great organizations we can have substantially more confirmation that they will have a decent worth today just as tomorrow.

These are the organizations we can feel certain that we are in any event in the correct ballpark when figuring their long haul esteem. So when Mr. Market comes to us in one of his awful states of mind needing to sell us portions of extremely extraordinary organizations at a rebate, we state, "Sure! Give me all you got!"

Area 3

UNDERSTANDING THE TERMINOLGY

A company's value – its all out worth – is called its market capitalization what's more, it is spoken to by the organization's stock cost. Market top (all things considered usually alluded to) is equivalent to the stock value duplicated by the quantity of shares remarkable.

For instance, a stock with a $5 stock cost and 10 million offers remarkable/ exchanging is worth $50 million ($5 x 10 million). On the off chance that we make this one stride further, we can see that an organization that has a $10 stock cost and one million offers remarkable (advertise top = $10 million) is worth not exactly an organization with a $5 stock cost and 10 million offers exceptional (advertise top = $50 million).

Thus, the stock cost is a family member and corresponding estimation of an organization's value what's more, just speaks to rate changes in market top at some random point in time. Any rate changes in a stock cost will bring about an equivalent rate change in an organization's worth. Tis is the motivation behind why speculators are so concerned with stock costs and any progressions that may happen since even a $0.10 drop in a $5 stock can bring about a $100,000 misfortune for investors with one million offers.

Inquiries TO CONSIDER:

1. What is the Market Cap of a Company with a stock cost of $20/share what's more, 10 million offers exceptional?

2. What is the present Market Cap of Apple? What number of offers do they have remarkable and what is the stock cost?

The following legitimate inquiry is: Who sets stock costs and how are they determined? In basic terms, the stock cost of an organization is determined when an organization goes at a bargain to the general population, an occasion called a first sale of stock.

This is the point at which an organization will pay a speculation bank a great deal of cash to utilize very complex recipes and valuation systems to infer an organization's an incentive by deciding what number of offers will be offered to people in general and at what cost.

For instance, an organization whose worth is assessed at $100 million may need to issue 10 million offers at $10 per offer or they might need to give 20 million at $5 an offer.

As we found in the model with Apple, an organization's worth is reliant on how much the organization can develop its profit later on. At the point when an organization sells more things or enters another market or improves edges, it can develop benefits.

## THE "GO-TO" WAY TO VALUE A BUSINESS: P/E RATIO

One approach to decide the estimation of a business is with the Price-to-Earnings

Proportion or P/E Ratio.

The value profit proportion can be determined as:

Market Value per Share (Stock Price)/Earnings per Share. For instance, assume that an organization is as of now exchanging at $43 an offer and its profit throughout the most recent a year were $1.95 per share. Te P/E proportion for the stock could then be determined as $43/$1.95, or about 22x.

Fundamentally, the value profit proportion demonstrates how long a financial specialist needs to hold up at the present income to recover all their cash. On the off chance that the P/E proportion is 22x, you are stating at this degree of income, it will take you 22 years for the organization to acquire the amount you purchased the stock for $43. When all is said in done, a high P/E recommends that financial specialists are expecting higher profit development later on contrasted with organizations with a lower P/E. A low P/E can demonstrate either an organization may at present be underestimated or the organization's benefits are relied upon to decay.

Think about a P/E as the value you pay for a stock.

When all is said in done, there are several Price/Earnings (P/E) general guidelines:

The normal P/E over the previous decade is 15x. A normal organization, ought to be worth about 15x.

Extremely extraordinary organizations (exceptional yields with predictable income development) will in general exchange around 20-25x P/E.

Awful organizations, ones whose income are erratic and make low returns, for the most part exchange at beneath 10x P/E.

An organization should exchange at about the P/E as its income are relied upon to develop later on. Organizations developing profits 30% every year might be justified to exchange at 30x P/E. Organizations becoming 15% every year may exchange at 15x P/E. Organizations not developing may exchange at 5-10x P/E.

At the point when the profession life of an individual starts, a constant salary starts with it. This pay is spent on essential needs and after some time it will increment. Along these lines, the capacity to spare and place these reserve funds in speculations will produce more incomes and keep up the buying influence of the person's cash which may fall back with the expansion in costs.

This is the place the requirement for how to put these reserve funds in speculation vehicles increments to help the person in accomplishing his life destinations.

An incredible cycle begins by finishing his training and entering the work arrange where he gets income or a pay from his work as

compensation or pay. It is typical for an individual to part his salary among utilization and sparing. Typically, an individual burns through the greater part of his pay on his utilization needs, for example, nourishment, apparel, convenience, a vehicle, instructive, wellbeing and stimulation administrations … and so forth. In the wake of addressing those necessities, the rest of aggregated and spared. Toward the start of a vocation, the pay is normally low. After some time, the pay improves and the individual steadily starts to increment his investment funds and utilize them in different territories so as to build his salary more and more. As the person's reserve funds increment, his riches begins to develop. Riches is characterized as the aggregated reserve funds.

The individual looks to put riches in ventures which incorporate substantial and monetary resources that bring him more prominent incomes and salary and assurance that his cash buying influence will be kept up and won't fall back when the costs rise. Unmistakable venture resources incorporate land, terrains, merchandise and others. Budgetary resources, then again, incorporate stores in banks, shared reserves, stocks, securities, outside money and others. These ventures produce more incomes added to the person's salary which he thus uses to help any future utilization. An individual expands his ventures and equalization them to guarantee accomplishing his targets. His momentary objective (as long as one year) can be purchasing a vehicle, a condo or beginning a little family. In medium term (one year as long as five years), objectives may change into beginning a family, bringing up kids well, teaching them and beginning a private business or a little endeavor which could expand the person's salary.

In the long haul, things could change into anticipating post retirement to guarantee a better than average life for him and his family and to leave sufficient legacy for those abandoned after his demise. An individual should utilize his riches to accomplish his objectives through suitable speculations that go in accordance with the capital he needs to verify the most noteworthy conceivable return for himself .In venture, it is realized that the higher hazard, the higher the profits and benefits. Then again, the lower the hazard, the lower the profits and benefits. Nonetheless, people handle chance in an unexpected way. Some hazard their cash in trust in making high and speedy benefits while others will in general dodge chance and favor wellbeing and alert in their ventures. Moreover, people vary in their capacity of being patient and holding back to experience lower returns, expanding dangers or misfortunes that may occur for the time being. To diminish venture chances however much as could be expected, one ought to differentiate his interests in monetary and unmistakable resources that have just been referenced beforehand. This idea can be reflected by the adage: "Don't place all your investments tied up on one place".

Individuals from the general public can be monetarily ordered into two gatherings: Individual speculators and savers.

Singular speculators are the individuals who want to make organizations and foundations, and build up various ventures, yet they might not have the adequate assets to do as such. Singular savers, then again, are the individuals who have the cash, however don't have the craving, learning or capacity to contribute it independent from anyone else. Generally, savers have a place with various classes of society, for example, laborers, workers and retirees who can spare piece of their pay. Financial specialists will in general utilize their spared assets to assist them with establishing organizations.

They partition corporate capital into stakes or bits where each bit is known as an offer. They offer these offers available to be purchased as every saver purchases some of those offers inside the cutoff points of his reserve funds. This makes him an investor and a member in the organization's capital. In this manner, he turns into a piece of its administration and choices as per his stake in the organization's capital. In different cases, financial specialists don't wish to share the administration and basic leadership of the organization with the savers. Subsequently, they will in general get the savers' cash through obtaining, at that point separating what they need of their corporate assets into divides, known as securities or sukuk.

Savers purchase these securities inside the points of confinement of what they need and how a lot of investment funds they have. Actually, they do this in expectation for comes back from holding these bonds, and afterward reclaiming their worth when their development is expected.

The Financial Market: a market where protections are exchanged (sold and purchased).

Protections include: stocks, bonds and furthermore money exchanging. As indicated by this, budgetary markets are separated into securities exchanges, security markets and cash markets. Stocks are proprietorship instruments to a piece of the guarantor's capital, while bonds are viewed as obligation instruments on the substance that gave them. At the point when you buy a stock, you become a member or an investor in the organization. Then again, in the event that you buy a bond, you become a lender to this organization. Savers buy stocks for two reasons: first, to get some portion of the benefits produced by the organization. This is known as profits.

Second, the costs of these stocks may go up because of more appeal because of the organization's development and the expansion in its income. Accordingly, the estimation of stocks possessed by the financial specialist increments. This is known as the capital increase. Stocks are purchased and sold available in a managed and lawful way so vendors don't lose their privileges. Typically, every one of these activities are made through money related business firms that are approved by a market controller, which is the Capital Market Authority (CMA) in the Kingdom of Saudi Arabia.

There are different kinds of stocks which are exchanged available. There are stocks that give their holder the privilege to go to the general gathering of the organization and express his supposition in transit the organization is overseen.

There are additionally extra stocks: they are free offers conceded to the proprietors of common stocks so as to increment what they claim in the organization and to build the organization's capital too. Concerning favored stocks, they give their proprietor the privilege and need to acquire his privileges from the organization. There are two principle sorts of financial exchanges: the essential market and the auxiliary market.

The Primary Market: a market where stocks are given, that is the point at which an organization is set up and offers its stocks to the vendors just because, or when the capital of a current organization is raised.

At the point when these stocks are recorded in the market, the primary purchaser of the stock can sell it on an exchanging market, which is known as the optional market. At the end of the day, stocks are first given and sold in the essential market, and afterward exchanged (purchased and sold) in the optional market.

# Chapter Seven: Bonds

Elements of Financial Market:

Budgetary showcases as a rule, and financial exchanges specifically, have extraordinary significance given their various capacities in serving the national economy. These administrations incorporate the accompanying:

• Saving Encouragement: by giving fields to utilize or contribute reserves, particularly for those whom their salary is higher than their costs, and need more time to focus on venture ventures they need to begin. Subsequently, putting resources into the securities exchange gives wise speculation openings that urge savers to expand their reserve funds, make the most of venture openings in the market and give sufficient money to organizations to make speculations and continue their business.

• Risk alleviation: putting resources into the financial exchange diminishes the dangers of losing reserve funds and cash if the saver himself put them in different zones where he needs more experience. What's more, one of the venture dangers, lacking liquidity, can be wiped out on the grounds that the financial specialist can sell his offers effectively and rapidly. He can likewise exchange them at whatever point cash is required.

• Increase monetary development; financing undertakings and ventures recorded in the securities exchange adds to creating more products and enterprises and supporting monetary development. This prompts an expansion in vocation open doors for work searchers.

What's more, choosing portions of stocks in explicit activities and organizations adds to controlling the cash and investment funds towards progressively achievable and productive tasks.

Qualities of Financial Markets:

By and large, money related markets have various particular qualities that recognize them from other customary markets like ware or land markets and others. The deal and buy in customary markets is accessible for products and ventures in a physical substantial manner in addition to they offer advantages to the individuals who devour them. In protections markets, in any case, there is no compelling reason to have unmistakable Sukuk or protections... and so forth in light of the fact that the tasks are helped out through PC systems. Besides, protections like securities and stocks are not devoured without anyone else's input but instead used to get returns and benefits produced from ventures. Every day exchanges in budgetary markets are tremendous contrasted with different markets . They can surpass billions in money related markets, while they can't go past millions in different markets. The law some of the time requires vendors in the protections market to purchase and sell through a money related merchant. In customary markets, nonetheless, there is no commitment to utilize the administrations of a representative.

Productivity of Financial Markets

The productivity of budgetary markets implies that the cost of a security (stock or security) is resolved by all the accessible data about the economy, divisions and organizations giving that security. Money related markets are productive if the costs

of stocks and exchanged protections are resolved effectively. The correct cost of a security, regardless of whether it was a stock or a bond, is the one that mirrors all the accessible data in an auspicious way about that security. So as to state that a monetary market is proficient, it must have a few highlights. For instance, all the significant data to pass judgment on a stock or bond and decide their correct cost ought to be accessible for all vendors. A genuine case of this, is the data about organizations and their benefit, changes in the executives or the data about contenders, the agreements they made and other data influencing the acquiring and selling choices. Also, vendors ought to be able to get legitimate investigations of the got data to help in making a decision about the correct cost for the stocks or bonds . Merchants and purchasers ought not have – because of their high money related limit - the capacity to impact the correct market costs upwards or downwards or force limitations on the opportunity of selling and buying for any broker at whenever.

Fundamental Concepts: Nominal Value, Book Value and Market Value :

A financial specialist needed to build up a plastic organization. In the wake of considering the venture's cost, he discovered that the organization's capital must be ten million Riyals. Since he doesn't have this sum, he went to the savers' cash to take an interest in helping to establish the organization. Because of the enormous measure of capital required, he isolated it into million offers. Each is worth 10 Riyals. The ten Riyals for this situation are known as the offer ostensible worth. Since the normal benefit of the task is high, a developing number of savers acknowledged to add to this venture and buy the gave stocks. The necessary capital was raised and the organization was built up. Toward the finish of the primary year, the organization have created a benefit of 2,000,000 Riyals, for example two Riyals benefit for each portion of the organization's offers. The corporate administration met to choose one of the accompanying choices:

Appropriate benefits to investors, convey some portion of the benefits and keep the remaining, or don't disperse the benefits of this current year by any means. Obviously, when the choice is to keep the benefit or part of it, the held profit are utilized in financing the organization's extensions and speculations or in making arrangements and stores to confront any crises. In the event that the appropriation isn't made, the estimation of the organization resources for this situation will be twelve million Riyals. This incorporates plots, structures, apparatus, gear, creation supplies accessible in the organization, its cash in treasury and in ledgers, and so on... . At the point when the organization's benefits increment to twelve million Riyals, the book estimation of a solitary offer becomes twelve Riyals. (12 million Riyals ÷ one million stocks = 12 Riyals).

Ostensible Value: The offer esteem when the organization is set up.

Book Value: What investors hope to get if the organization were exchanged. The book worth can be determined by isolating the organization's advantages by the quantity of offers.

Arrangements: Amounts of benefit that are held or cut off from the organization's income to be discarded in one of the particular parts of real uses, (for example, purchasing new hardware or plots to extend the organization) or for potential crisis consumptions, (for example, fire, higher generation costs, or diminished organization profit).

Income Per Share: Profits that are apportioned to each share. It isn't restrictive that income ought to be in real money. They can be extra offers circulated to investors. These benefits, or even extra offers, may likewise not be dispersed, but instead reinvested and subsequently the market estimation of the organization's offers increments.

All out Return on Stock: return on the stock in addition to capital gain. Market esteem: the estimation of the offer in the market. It is influenced by the inventory ( the quantity of stocks accessible to speculators) and the interest ( the quantity of stocks financial specialists wish to purchase). The speculator can realize the market estimation of an offer through the Saudi Stock Exchange (Tadawul) site notwithstanding different methods for broad communications.

Market Capitalization: it is determined by duplicating the quantity of an organization's stocks by the present market cost of the stock.

The organization has advanced, the work extended and the quantity of costumers has expanded. Toward the finish of the subsequent year, its stocks were glided in an IPO in the securities exchange at a cost of fifteen Riyals. Because of the great notoriety of the organization, the market cost of the stock has ascended to twenty five Riyals on the primary exchanging Day. At the end of the day, the market estimation of each offer rose by ten Riyals from the offering cost.

Universal Stock Markets

Paper and media features are loaded with news about worldwide financial exchanges. As it's been said: the world has become globalized where the news is spread between its gatherings effectively and basically. The most significant news to be distributed about these business sectors is the presentation files which we will characterize its idea at that point survey a portion of the universal and territorial records as the accompanying:

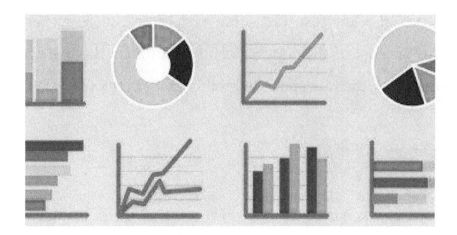

# Chapter Eight: Mutual Funds

Securities exchange Index:

A number that abridges the value development of all stocks recorded in a market and for the most part speaks to the normal of those costs. Stocks are not approach in their rate portrayal of the record. Speaking to an organization's stock relies upon its weight in the market estimated by the market estimation of the organization partitioned by the market estimation of every single recorded organization in the market. Stock costs rise and fall because of organic market. At the point when the interest for some corporate stock surpasses the stockpile, the cost of this stock ascents and hence the market record increments with the rate spoke to by this stock in the file.

The Importance of the Index:

The financial exchange record mirrors the state of the national economy by and large and the monetary presentation of recorded organizations in the market specifically. On the off chance that the interest for the organizations' creation expanded because of the financial lift, at that point the deals and income of these organizations are required to increment just as their profits to investors, which thusly pushes the costs of their stocks up and the entire market record. For this situation, the market list turns green. Be that as it may, if the exhibition in the market decreases, the pointer changes its shading to red.

**A portion of the Global Indexes:**

Worldwide money related markets have two sorts of files: General records that measure the market circumstance all in all, and segment lists that measure the market circumstance as per a specific division, for example, banking, mechanical, rural, correspondences and different areas. In the accompanying focuses we address the most significant worldwide and provincial records.

U.S. Market Indexes:

• DOW Jones: is a significant record that comprises of four sub-files and the most well known of which is the Dow Jones Industrial Average. The estimation of the list is determined dependent on the supplies of the thirty biggest modern organizations in the United States of America.

• Standard and Poor's 500 (S&P 500): It involves the loads of the main 500 organizations in a few regions, including: fabricating, transportation, utilities, cash, banking, protection, innovation and administrations. These organizations speak to roughly 80% of the market estimation of offers exchanged on the New

York Stock Exchange.

• NASDAQ: is the biggest among all U.S. lists. It contains the loads of 3,200 organizations, generally mechanical.

European Market Indexes :

• United Kingdom : Financial Times 100: (FT-100) this list incorporates the 100 most significant UK organizations' stocks in the London showcase, speaking to 70% of the all out capital of enlisted organizations.

• France

CAC 40: this file incorporates the supplies of the forty most significant French organizations in Paris showcase.

• Germany

DAX: this file contains the supplies of the 30 most critical organizations, speaking to 70% of the market estimation of the organizations enlisted in Frankfurt advertise.

Asian Market Indexes :

• - Japan

Nikkei Index : contains the loads of 225 organizations, speaking to about 70% of the market estimation of the organizations enrolled in the Tokyo Stock Exchange.

• Other Asian Indexes :

1. South Korea: KCS Index

2. Hong Kong : HANG SENG Index

3. Malaysia: KLSE Index

4. China : Shanghai Index

Middle Easterner Market Indexes:

Middle Easterner securities exchange are developing markets because of the extraordinary capability of financial development in Arab nations. The Saudi stock trade is viewed as the most huge market in all Arab nations.

It speaks to around 33% of the capital estimation of all Arab markets joined. Notwithstanding Saudi Arabia, there is various other significant Arab budgetary markets, for example, :

• The United Arab Emirates: (Dubai and Abu Dhabi markets ).

• Oman: MSM • Kuwait: KSE

• Egypt: CMA • Bahrain: BSE

• Morocco: MASI • Qatar: CBQ

The Saudi Stock Exchange - Historical Background

The Saudi stock trade is one of the recently settled developing markets. Market managing started when the primary business entity (the Arab Automobile) in the Kingdom of Saudi Arabia was set up in 1354H (1953).

Stock exchanging began in the Saudi showcase in an immediate and quick manner among venders and purchasers.

With the consistent development, an electronic framework, known as "Tadawul", was propelled in 1422H (2002)

. The framework permits enlisting, exchanging, clearing and settling shares right away. It is legitimately connected to Saudi business banks, and gets requests of selling and purchasing stocks. At that point, it executes exchanges and moves shares proprietorship in a computerized and exact way. In 1424H (2004), the Capital Market Law (CML) endorsement of the money related market has turned out and the significant highlights was to build up the Capital Market Authority to accept the elements of managing the market, create it, sort out the issuance of protections, control it, secure financial specialists, accomplish equity, productivity, straightforwardness, manage and control the revelation of data and others. The framework likewise incorporates the foundation of a business opportunity for exchanging protections under the name of "The Saudi Capital Market ".

Attributes of the Financial Market:

The Saudi financial exchange is new contrasted with the business sectors of created nations, for example, the U.S., Japan, or the EU nations. It is portrayed by the modest number of recorded organizations in the market given the enormous size of the Saudi economy. The volume of exchanges in the market is viewed as generally constrained contrasted with the quantity of gave stocks.

This can be characterized as a tight market, which prompts huge vacillations in stock costs. Various elements and factors impact the cost of exchanged stocks available. They incorporate local monetary conditions, financial development, just as the issues the economy may experience the ill effects of like expansion and joblessness. The productivity of business entities and current advancements in worldwide financial exchanges impact it just as the household monetary approaches as far as use and government use on administrations and undertakings notwithstanding the measure of cash and liquidity in the economy. The organizations recorded in the

Saudi securities exchanges are disseminated to the accompanying fifteen segments:

Every division has a file that estimates the presentation by following the costs of organizations' stocks in that segment. The general list, known as "TASI", is utilized to gauge the general execution of the whole market and it is a weighted normal of the stock costs of the organizations in working the market.

As recently expressed, the Saudi market is described by being "tight" and "restricted" contrasted with other comparative developing markets (127 organizations toward the finish of 2008, contrasted with around 350-400 organizations in comparative developing markets).

Note that the quantity of organizations has been developing since the initiation of the Capital Market Authority (CMA) in 1424H. The market has a "tight" base because of the restrictions in exchanging stocks, particularly those of significant organizations, since government possessed stocks can't be exchanged. There is another explanation that contracts the measure of exchanged stocks and fends off potential financial specialists from these organizations which is that some significant proprietors control a generous possession stake in organizations. The biggest ten Saudi organizations represent around 60 – 70% of market size estimated by any of the typical criteria: volume, exchanging, or benefits.

It is normal that the view on the Saudi financial exchange stays positive and hopeful in the nonstop improvement of the exhibition of the Saudi economy at the large scale level, and the use of all important enactment to guarantee the guideline of work in the market, increment the quantity of organizations, increment the market capital and the utilization of the ongoing government activities to look after soundness.

Money related Investment Strategies:

There are a great deal of money related and genuine speculation open doors for savers. Some lean toward the monetary venture by placing the entirety of his reserve funds in bank stores, some favor owning stocks and securities while others incline toward genuine interest in lands, land or private ventures. In the accompanying parts, we will clarify the major factors that influence savers' choices to put resources into a specific region of the abovementioned with center around monetary venture.

The most significant factor is the normal degree of profitability. In spite of the fact that the arrival on venture has numerous ideas which will be tended to at the appropriate time, it is concurred that it is the contrast between the estimation of reserve funds before speculation and their incentive after a specific time of interest in explicit territories.

Sorts of Financial Investments:

There are three angles for reserve funds venture: stocks, securities and common assets.

• Stocks: putting resources into stocks is portrayed by a high pace of return in the long haul with a high possibility of hazard, which implies that the financial specialist may continue some misfortune in his contributed capital.

• Bonds: it is realized that privately owned businesses need financing and in this manner offer securities to savers to get the necessary assets. Conceding to this apparatus in the Kingdom for now is restricted.

The administration likewise falls back on giving bonds to fund undertakings, for example, building schools, colleges, emergency clinics, developing streets, building spans, control plants and other open ventures.

Despite the fact that the administration assets originate from oil and charges, now and again it might need to issue securities so as to verify extra subsidizing.

• Mutual Funds: these assets pool investment funds through a Muniment of title with equivalent qualities like stocks. They are called venture units. Financial specialists will in general purchase supplies of these assets to utilize a portion of the points of interest that these assets have from the long involvement with overseeing speculation.

Likewise, these assets can expand their speculations, henceforth, lessening the dangers on account of the assets accessibility. Speculators depend the substance that deals with their shared assets to take choices for their sake.

As a rule, the arrival on these stocks will in general be more secure with an arrival of more than the bond's and not exactly the stock's arrival .

The most significant factor that drives speculators to putting resources into a specific sort of protections is looking for a venture that creates an exceptional yield and have a level of hazard which the financial specialist can endure.

The Financial Investment Strategy

By and large, a methodology is characterized as a long haul intend to accomplish a particular vision and goals. Any getting ready for the future starts by examining the current circumstance and deciding the vision and goals, at that point deciding the most ideal approach to accomplish that vision and targets. Money related speculation goals contrast starting with one individual then onto the next. The most extreme benefit might be the objective of a particular financial specialist, while the nonappearance of hazard may be the most significant goal for another, and satisfactory liquidity could be the target of a third financial specialist. In this manner, the financial specialist ought to have the learning and abilities that assist him with arriving at his destinations.

Components of the Financial Investment Strategy

A sound monetary speculation procedure requires deciding the accompanying components:

• Objectives.

• Financial potential accessible to the speculator.

• Time outline important to accomplish the goals.

• Expected rate of profitability.

• Alternatives: some other accessible speculation territories in which the arrival on venture can be accomplished.

Coming up next are contemplations that must be taken into account in setting up the money related venture system:

• Realism: targets must be feasible and not far away from the real world. For instance: in the event that we assume that somebody could spare (50 thousand Riyals) a year and someone else could as it were spare (10 thousand Riyals) a year, and that both of them are intending to purchase a house for up to (500 thousand Riyals) following 10 years, it is clear that the primary individual's arrangement is more reasonable than the subsequent one

• Flexibility: it implies the capacity to modify the targets what's more, choices through the transfer of current ventures and supplant them with new ones as per any advancements all together to accomplish the goals.

• Familiarity with the essentials of monetary venture: It means realizing the venture apparatuses what's more, systems so as to abstain from putting the financial specialist in danger and making him ready to take the best venture choices.

Basics of Financial Investment:

The most significant essentials of budgetary venture are:

• Identifying venture qualities: For instance, offer worth and return are influenced by the level of achievement and disappointment of giving organizations

. They are additionally influenced by monetary vacillations in the residential and worldwide economy. It is ordinary that these variances mirror the offer costs particularly for the time being. In the long haul, be that as it may, putting resources into stocks is viewed as one of the ventures that produces exceptional yields contrasted with other money related protections. Concerning the bonds, the arrival will in general be steady as the government guarantees that the investor can get the arrival expressed in the bond at the hour of development. What's more, organizations that care about their position and money related notoriety ensure the bonds gave by them. Partaking in common assets for youthful financial specialists guarantees dependability in the estimation of their reserve funds because of the experience these assets' throughs have.

• Identifying dangers related with contributing: Risks in the least complex sense implies the likelihood that a speculation can accomplish a genuine benefit after a time frame that is not exactly the normal benefit, or the speculator experiences misfortune in his capital. Venture fluctuates as per the uncertainty related with the accomplishments of anticipated benefits. There are ventures related with high dangers and others related with low chances. The financial specialist in stocks must realize that the pace of degree of profitability is related with dangers in an immediate (positive) relationship. In different words, the speculator can accomplish higher return on the off chance that he is happy to endure higher dangers.

Additionally, he should acknowledge lower paces of return if the hazard is lower. It must be noticed that the financial specialist's capacity to endure hazard differs depending on the accessible potential outcomes just as the specialist's age and nature which mirrors his own inclination to go out on a limb. A financial specialist who stays away from dangers likes to obtain portfolios which accomplish guaranteed little returns. Unexpectedly, a financial specialist who cherishes going out on a limb wants to have money related portfolios which create higher comes back with higher dangers.

Dangers that face financial specialists can be characterized into three classifications:

• Company-explicit hazard: the wellspring of hazard is from inside the organization that gave the protections.

The wellsprings of this kind of hazard are various furthermore, result from the idea of the organization's business , being caught in obligations, having deficient

liquidity to direct the business, a chapter of this book furthermore, liquidation. For this situation, the need is to pay out the organization's commitments to the banks, not the investors.

• Market chance: it is connected to the monetary conditions confronting all organizations simultaneously.

In instances of downturn, the interest for all merchandise, in the market decays which antagonistically influences organizations' profit. This makes the estimation of stocks decays. Political factors additionally impact the market's solidness.

• Concentration chance: it is the place a money related portfolio is undiversified and comprises of one stock or then again a couple of stocks. This implies any potential decrease in the presentation of the organization giving the stock may prompt extraordinary misfortunes. Regularly these dangers can be overwhelmed by expanding the territories of money related speculation.

• Investment Preference Criteria: They are the criteria by which speculations are picked; they incorporate returns, hazard, broadening and liquidity.

• Return: is the level of progress in resource esteem (subject of speculation). The financial specialist for the most part looks for budgetary speculations that accomplish the most noteworthy conceivable return.

• Risk: estimated by the vacillation of the benefit esteem. As such, the money related venture level of hazard increments with the expansion of value changes between one period and another.

Accordingly, the financial specialist must pick the kinds of ventures that have satisfactory hazard limits.

• Diversification: differentiated speculations implies that the monetary portfolio contains different and various sorts of protections (different stocks + securities + common assets) with various returns what's more, hazard levels. One of the characteristics of assorted variety is that it prompts decreasing venture dangers which is one of the ideal attributes in any portfolio.

Openings and Challenges

Money related markets give numerous open doors that increment the capability of gainfulness and development.

These business sectors likewise face a great deal of difficulties that diminish their proficiency and increments monetary speculation dangers . In the accompanying area we address the most significant chances and challenges and close with a general guidance for speculators.

# Chapter Nine: Options Trading

SOME BASIC RULES TO STOCK MARKET

Rule 1: Don't Put all of your investments tied up on one place

The main essential standard of contributing is to spread the hazard around. The greatest mix-up you will ever get is to put a lot of cash-flow into any one stock. Indeed, even Warren Buffett fails to understand the situation!

So absolutely never lose trace of what's most important. Be brilliant. Broaden your hazard!

Give me a chance to outline this with a model. Beneath you will see five stocks. You will see that the greater part of the stocks had amazing returns for 2016 yet there was one stock, Gilead, which failed to meet expectations.

Consider two diverse sort of speculators:

1. Unsafe Steve: Wants to win enormous and quick!

1. Savvy Pat: Is glad to make steady returns over a more extended timeframe.

Unsafe Steve

Steve needs to make a fortune rapidly. In 2016, he had $5,000 to contribute. He chose to put all $5,000 into Gilead. Gilead is a magnificent organization with phenomenal essentials and the valuation looked great. Be that as it may, Gilead performed seriously during the year and fell 15.9%.

Dangerous Steve lost $795. His portfolio is presently worth just $4,205. Despite the fact that Gilead is a brilliant organization, the slip-up Steve made was to put the entirety of his cash into one stock.

Indeed, even incredible organizations have a terrible year! He ought to have broadened his hazard. Presently, think about Pat.

Keen Pat

Pat has $5,000 to contribute. Pat is an increasingly reasonable financial specialist and is glad to make reliable returns after some time. A year ago he chose to put similarly into Apple, Southwest Airlines, Royal Caribbean, Stryker and Gilead. This implied Pat put $1,000 into every one of the five stocks. Toward the finish of 2016

- $1,000 put into Apple was worth $1,405

- $1,000 put into Southwest Airlines was worth $1,344

- $1,000 put into Royal Caribbean was worth $1,279

- $1,000 put into Stryker was worth $1,267

- $1,000 put into Gilead was worth $841

Pat produced an absolute benefit of 22.7% for 2016 (even with Gilead in it). This is the likeness a benefit of $1,136! His portfolio is currently worth $6,136.

The explanation Pat performed superior to Steve is on the grounds that Pat fabricated a less unsafe

speculation portfolio.

You might be of the sentiment that Risky Steve could have made a fortune on the off chance that he put everything into Apple. He would have made a 40.5% benefit. That is valid, yet the issue is that Steve needs to get fortunate all the time with this sort of technique. At the point when he fails to understand the situation and as far as I can tell even the best financial specialists on the planet miss the point, he will lose a great deal of cash.

These misfortunes may dissolve the entirety of his past increases and that's only the tip of the iceberg.

The Lesson_

Despite the fact that Gilead was and still is an awesome organization, it had a downright awful year in 2016 and fell in esteem. This can occur with any organization, it doesn't make a difference how great it is.

In the event that you conceded to putting just in Gilead, you would endure a misfortune of $795. Yet, by spreading your hazard around four different stocks, this misfortune was more than balance by the additions in the four different stocks. The outcome was a less unsafe portfolio which conveyed a decent 22.7% benefit.

Expansion works

1. Expand your hazard by contributing close to 5% or 1/twentieth of the estimation of your portfolio in any one stock. For instance, on the off chance that you have a $5,000 portfolio, put close to $250 in any one stock.

2. Put resources into stocks from various ventures. For instance, don't put resources into 20 banks. Spread the hazard through various segments and enterprises... .Airlines, Energy, Healthcare, Technology and so forth..

3. Continuously recall that you don't have a precious stone ball and neither does any other person. Things can turn out badly in the present moment for any organization.

Rule 2: Know your Investor Profile

So as to set yourself up for accomplishment in the financial exchange you have to comprehend what kind of speculator you are and what sort of hazard resilience you have.

When in doubt of thumb, the more noteworthy the reward, the more prominent the hazard you should take. A great many people would prefer not to lose cash however might want to make a ton.

Sadly, there is nothing of the sort as a free lunch in the securities exchange. All together

to benefit, you should go out on a limb.

Finding that harmony among hazard and reward is basic. Taking a rude awakening

presently will set you up for achievement later on. You have to recognize your resilience

for chance.

Take 5 minutes to finish this Investor Profiling exercise

Answer the accompanying 12 inquiries. Record the quantity of the response to each question which most precisely reflects you. There is no set in stone answer here simply answer genuinely for yourself.

Question 1: What is your significant objective for putting resources into the Stock Market?

1. Secure retirement pay

2. Security for retirement however I don't care for fluctuating returns

3. I wouldn't fret momentary instability yet need long haul development

4. Augment development of the portfolio over the long haul

Question 2: How long do you mean allowing your to venture develop?

1. Under 3 years

2. 3-7 years

3. 8-12 years

4. Over 12 years

Question 3: During the following 5 years what segment of your portfolio do you plan

to pull back?

1. 100%

2. 75%

3. half

4. Under 25%

Question 4: What is your present age?

1. More than 70

2. 55-70

3. 35-55

4. under 35

Question 5: Which of the accompanying best portrays your family salary?

1. Under €30K

2. €30K-€45K

3. €45K-€75K

4. Over €75K

Question 6: What is your family total assets in the wake of deducting all credits, contracts

and so on… ?

1. Under €30K

2. €30K-€50K

3. €50K-€125K

4. Over €125K

Question 7: How might you rate your general money related circumstance?

1. Not Good – No Savings, or almost no reserve funds and huge obligation

2. OK – Some reserve funds and reasonable obligation

3. For the most part Debt Free and sparing consistently

4. Secure – Debt Free

Question 8: Other than securities exchange pay what other salary will you have at retirement?

1. Nothing

2. Investment property

3. Different investment funds/annuities

4. Myself and accomplice reserve funds, annuities and ventures

Question 9: How might you rate your speculation information?

1. Negligible

2. Unobtrusive – Know a little however very little experience

3. Great – I've been contributing some time and made due at any rate one crash

4. Awesome – Experienced and OK with the good and bad times of the market

Question 10: Stock markets have slammed previously and recouped yet recuperation can take some time. To what extent would you be able to hang tight for a recuperation?

1. Not exactly a year

2. 1-2 years

3. 3-4 years

4. More than 4 years

Question 11: What level of momentary hazard would you say you are alright with?

1. Not exactly a 20% drop

2. A 20%-30% drop

3. 30%-40% drop

4. Over 40%

Question 12: The securities exchange is tied in with weighing up hazard and reward which best depicts you?

1. I generally think about the amount I lose first

2. I consider the misfortune more than the reward

3. I consider the reward more than the misfortune

4. I just spotlight on remuneration

Presently include the entirety of the numbers to the appropriate response of the 12 inquiries above.

Rule 3: Invest in Fundamentals not graphs!

The basics of an organization will drive the offer cost. Specialized Analysis/Charts

try not to offer you any measurable favorable position when purchasing shares. Outlines are a 'get out' for apathetic speculators who are searching for snappy and simple approaches to discover motivations to purchase or sell a stock.

Graphs can be extremely helpful to get an image of the 'past', yet that is all you will get, diagrams are not an indicator of things to come.

On the off chance that you need to check the future estimation of an organization you have to do a touch of look into - there is no alternate way. It will at last come down to the normal future development pace of the deals and benefits of an organization.

This isn't advanced science. It is a procedure of the asking yourself some fundamental questions and all the more significantly responding to the inquiries:

1. What does the organization do and how would they profit?

2. How huge is the organization?

3. To what extent has the organization been doing business?

4. How aggressive is the market?

5. Does the organization have a reputation of conveying deals and benefit development? Development is the catchphrase.

6. What are the obligation levels of the organization?

7. Does the organization pay a profit? What is the Dividend Yield? Is the profit economical.

8. What are the future deals and benefit development projections?

9. How is the organization esteemed versus their rivals of comparable size?

10. How unpredictable is the offer cost?

11. Does the organization essentials fit my financial specialist profile?

Give me a chance to give you a case of essential research we did on Apple before we put resources into 2016. We sold under 1 year later for a 39% benefit!

Rule 4: Have a Target 'Purchase' Price and a Target 'Sell' Price

The model with Apple gives you a thought of the a portion of the fundamental research you have to do before you put resources into an organization. This is the way you recognize potential 'esteem'. At the point when you do this, your prosperity rate in the business sectors will take off. Such a large number of individuals contribute on a tip from a companion or in light of the fact that an outline appears as though it is giving a purchase signal. This isn't shrewd.

We as a whole have organizations that we love … . Google, Facebook, Amazon...the rundown goes on.

● But would they say they are great worth?

● What cost would it be advisable for you to get them at?

• What is the future development potential resemble?

• What is the objective cost for the stock? This is the one inquiry most amatuer financial specialists bomb pose and answer.

• You need an exit strategy...at some point stocks can turn out to be excessively costly and it's an ideal opportunity to get them out of your portfolio. We sold Apple at $130.05. We felt at that stage the worth was not longer there in the organization with the data close by. From that point forward Apple has risen further to $160. Knowing the past is an awesome thing.. am I irritated? no ..in light of the fact that I have set principles that I pursue, the data accessible at the time recommended a stock that was completely esteemed. Keep in mind you don't have a precious stone ball... pursue your worth contributing standards and you will do fine and dandy after some time.

Rule 5: Evaluate the Stock at Earnings

Each quarter openly cited organizations make an 'income' declaration. This is the place the organization advises the market and speculators with respect to how their deals and benefits have performed for as long as 3 months.

During an income discharge the organization will likewise control their normal execution for the following quarter and at times the following year. This enables you at that point to reassess the essentials of the organization. What's more, thus re-survey your objective selling cost.

Give me a chance to give both of you instances of this:

1. Apple: After we put resources into Apple in May 2016 there were two profit discharges. Because of those profit declarations we changed our objective selling cost from $120 to $130. This was on the grounds that offers of their

I-Phone had expanded more than anticipated.

2. Gilead: After we put resources into Gilead we re-estimated our objective cost down to $75 from $92. This was on the grounds that the organization gave a benefit cautioning. The basics should direct your selling cost. Stay with reassessing the basics on a month to month premise and modify your selling cost appropriately.

Keep these five principles and you will be on the correct way to effectively contributing in the financial exchange. Considerably, better get some training in a constant, genuine world test system.

A short outline

1. Differentiate your hazard - Do not place all of your investments tied up on one place.

2. Realize your speculator profile - This will assist restricted with bringing down the stocks you ought to be search for.

3. Discover stocks that meet your financial specialist profile - we can give you how.

4. Try not to contribute dependent on a graph - there is no preferred position to you!

5. Put resources into the basics - we will tell you the best way to do this.

6. Discover quality stocks at the correct cost to purchase - we will give you how.

7. Have an objective cost for each venture - This will keep you centered and help you to remember why you are putting resources into the organization.

8. Get taught - like everything throughout everyday life, there is a correct path and there is an incorrect way. Gain proficiency with the correct way!

9. Take a free preliminary - You have nothing to lose and everything to pick up!

## Chapter Ten: Beginners' Mistakes

Some Basic phrasings

- A partnership is an organization that is a different lawful substance claimed by investors. At the end of the day, the partnership capacities like a solitary individual separate from its proprietors (investors). Hence, the investors have restricted risk, (the interest in the stock they claim).

Regular stock speaks to possession in an enterprise. At the point when you purchase basic stock, you are purchasing the partnership's plants, structures, and items. Normal stock is sold in shares. Each portion of regular stock speaks to the fundamental unit of responsibility for enterprise.

Stock resembles a Pizza, each portion of stock speaks to an equivalent bit of the pie (organization). Also, Price gratefulness happens when you sell your stock for more than you paid for the stock while profits are the bit of an organization's benefit that is paid to investors. As the organization develops, your bit of the pie develops too. On the off chance that the organization is fruitful and develops by 25%, the estimation of your offers will develop too. Profits are paid out of a partnership's benefit after duties have been paid. The partnership can, be that as it may, hold some portion of the benefit and reinvest it in the company. This part is known as held profit and it is every now and again utilized for innovative work or extension. A company doesn't need to pay profits. Profits don't need to be paid with cash. The top managerial staff can choose to issue stock profits. At the point when this is done, the present investors would get a greater number of portions of the company's stock as opposed to money.

At the point when financial specialists sell stocks for more than they paid, the benefit produced using the deal is the speculator's capital addition. At the point when a stock sells for not exactly the speculator paid for it, the financial specialist endures a capital misfortune. The cash a financial specialist uses to purchase stocks is called value capital. Since you can profit through ventures, you should decide the measure of cash that you can bear to lose without hurting your way of life. The measure of cash a financial specialist can bear to lose is called hazard capital, and that is the sum that ought to be contributed. Keep in mind, contribute just what you can bear to lose.

Organizations might be arranged from multiple points of view. On the off chance that stock is accessible for buy by the general population, it is an open organization. The enterprise is legally necessary to reveal its budgetary condition.Most huge partnerships are open companies.

A shut organization is one whose stock isn't accessible to outcasts, it doesn't issue stock to people in general and isn't required to reveal openly its money related condition. All enterprises must issue stock. The state giving the Articles of Incorporation approves the quantity of offers a company can issue. That number speaks to every one of the offers an organization can issue without returning to the state and mentioning that the state enable more offers to be given. These are the portions of stock that the organization has sold (gave). The gave offers speak to proprietorship. Approved however not gave are held for future deals to raise reserves (capital) for future development.

At the point when an organization needs to open up to the world, or to be exchanged on stock trades, it must satisfy some exacting guidelines.

- The New York Stock Exchange (you don't begin here)

- A pre-charge pay of $2.5 million for the earlier year or $2.0 million every year for two earlier years

- Net unmistakable resources of $18 million

- Two thousand investors who each have at least 100 offers

- At least 1.1 million freely held offers

- Outstanding shares with an estimation of $18 million

A yearly report is a monetary report given to investors toward the finish of each working year. A yearly report will show the money related state of the enterprise, the names of the top managerial staff, the area and date of the following investor's yearly meeting, an inspector's report confirming the genuineness of the monetary information, and the investor's letter. The accounting report records the company's advantages and liabilities. (What they possess less what they owe)

The salary proclamation records the income (pay), costs, and benefit or misfortune for the year. (How a lot of cash did they make). An investor can get a smart thought of the monetary state of a company from breaking down the asset report and the salary proclamation. A few partnerships will even incorporate a five-year money related rundown.

Security And Exchange Commission

The Securities and Exchange Commission is a guard dog office. It secures the financial specialist by upholding government laws relating to the financial exchange. The SEC screens protections, stock trades, corporate announcing, venture firms, stockbrokers, and open utility holding organizations.

Approved offers are the offers an enterprise is permitted to issue.

Given offers are the offers really given and offered to financial specialists.

Offers repurchased by a company are called treasury offers, or treasury stock.

Offers acquired by investors are called exceptional offers, shares hanging out in the hands of general society.

The market estimation of a stock is the value individuals are happy to pay for the stock at present. The market worth is dictated by the interest for the company's stock.

The book estimation of an enterprise is equivalent to its absolute resources less its complete liabilities. (Accounting report).

At the point when stock is given to people in general just because by an enterprise, it is known as an essential appropriation. (Initial public offering) The organization is acquired by a venture bank and they offer offers to financial specialists.

After the essential appropriation of stock, every single resulting closeout of the stock happen in optional markets (for instance, the New York Stock Exchange or the Over-the-Counter Market). Individuals who purchase stocks are investors. At the point when either liked or basic stocks are obtained, the investor gets a stock authentication.

A security trade, regularly called a stock trade, is a charitable association that gives offices to its individuals to purchase and sell protections.

The individuals from a stock trade are agents who purchase enrollments (called seats) with the goal that they may utilize the trade. No one but individuals can exchange on the floor of the trade. The country's biggest stock trade is the New York Stock Exchange (NYSE) situated in New York City. The American Stock Exchange (AMEX), additionally situated in New York City, is the country's second biggest trade. There are additionally littler provincial trades, for example, the Pacific, Midwest, Cincinnati, Philadelphia, and Boston trades.

Notwithstanding trades situated in the United States, there are likewise different worldwide trades, for example, those situated in Tokyo, London, Frankfurt, Zurich, Paris, Milan, Amsterdam,

Stockholm, Brussels, Sydney, Hong Kong, Singapore, and Toronto.

A stock trade is fundamentally the same as an enormous flea market or swap meet. As indicated by legend, it began in 1792 when specialists met under a buttonwood tree on Wall Street and consented to an arrangement that they would exchange stocks. An organization's name was gotten out and offers on that organization's stock were traded. In the end the trade moved inside and got known as the New York Stock Exchange (additionally alluded to as the Big Board).

A financial specialist who wishes to purchase stock will in all probability put in a request with a stockbroker. A stockbroker is an operator authorized by the SEC to purchase and sell protections for customers.

A stockbroker who works for a full-administration business firm gives investigate data, recommends venture techniques, and offers exhortation on economic situations.

A stockbroker who finishes a very exhaustive protections test known as the "Arrangement 7 Exam" is known as an enlisted agent.

A stockbroker gets a commission dependent on the complete dollar volume of each request. The commission rate shifts with every financier firm.

Rebate financier firms are an option in contrast to paying the maximum commissions that full-administration business firms charge speculators.

Rebate financier firms frequently offer no guidance or conference about contributing; they just execute a customer's requests.

Three of the basic sorts of stock requests are market orders (spot orders), limit requests, and stop misfortune orders. A market request is a request to purchase or sell a stock at the most ideal cost.

The agent will execute the financial specialist's directions at whatever value the exchange requests on that day.

Most requests are market arranges and are completed that day.
Farthest point Order

A farthest point request is a request to a dealer to purchase or sell shares at a particular value no more noteworthy than a particular sum. A cutoff request isn't executed except if the securities exchange value arrives at the point of confinement the financial specialist has set.

A stop misfortune request is a request to a dealer to sell a stock if the value drops to a foreordained level. This constrains the speculator's misfortunes or ensures a specific benefit. At the point when a request is put with a stockbroker, the financial specialist likewise should tell the stockbroker to what extent that request should stand.

A day request advises the stockbroker to dispatch the request that day. Toward the day's end, the request is dropped. A decent until dropped (GTC) request remains until it is filled or until the speculator drops it.

Stock requests are by and large set in additions called round parts. A round parcel is a numerous of (100, 200, 300, 400, and so forth.) shares. An odd parcel is various shares that isn't a numerous of 100, for example, 50 offers or 322 shares.

The Dow Jones Industrial Average (DJIA), regularly called the Dow, is a file of 30 significant corporate stocks recorded on the New York Stock Exchange. Another significant list is the Standard and Poor's 500 Stock Index. This record of 500 key stocks additionally manages partnerships recorded on different trades and is an a lot more extensive based file than the Dow Jones Industrial Average. An organization hazard is a hazard that influences the stock costs of one organization or industry. Interest for an item is an organization chance. On the off chance that an organization's item or administration is popular, the cost of its stocks will for the most part rise. In the event that an organization's item or administration isn't sought after, the cost of its stocks will for the most part fall.

Wouldn't you love to be an entrepreneur while never appearing at work? Suppose you could sit back, watch your organization develop, and gather the profit checks as the cash comes in! This circumstance may seem like a pipe dream, yet it's nearer to reality than you may might suspect. As you've most likely speculated, we're looking at owning stocks. This remarkable class of money related instruments is, no ifs, ands or buts, probably the best device at any point designed for building riches. Stocks are a section, if not the foundation, of about any speculation portfolio. At the point when you start on your street to money related opportunity, you have to have a strong comprehension of stocks and how they exchange on the financial exchange. In the course of the most recent couple of decades, the normal individual's enthusiasm for the securities exchange has developed exponentially. What was at one time a toy of the rich has now transformed into the vehicle of decision for developing riches. This interest combined with propels in exchanging innovation has opened up the business sectors so these days about anyone can claim stocks. In spite of their prevalence, be that as it may, a great many people don't completely get stocks.

Much is found out from discussions around the water cooler with other people who likewise don't have the foggiest idea what they're discussing. Odds are you've just heard individuals make statements like, "Sway's cousin raked in huge profits in XYZ organization, and now he has another hot tip..." or "Watch out with stocks- - you can lose your shirt in only days!" So quite a bit of this falsehood depends on a make easy money attitude, which was particularly common during the astounding dotcom showcase in the late '90s. Individuals felt that stocks were the enchantment answer to moment riches with no hazard. The following dotcom crash demonstrated this isn't the situation. Stocks can (and do) make huge measures of riches, yet they aren't without dangers. The main answer for this is instruction. The way to securing yourself in the financial exchange is to comprehend where you are putting your cash. It is thus that we've made this instructional exercise: to give the establishment you have to settle on venture choices yourself. We'll begin by clarifying what a stock is and the various kinds of stock, and afterward we'll discuss how they are exchanged, what makes costs change, how you purchase stocks and considerably more.

Plain and straightforward, stock is an offer in the responsibility for organization. Stock speaks to a case on the organization's benefits and profit. As you obtain progressively stock, your proprietorship stake in the organization gets more noteworthy. Regardless of whether you state offers, value, or stock, everything implies something very similar. Being an Owner Holding an organization's stock implies that you are one of the numerous proprietors (investors) of an organization and, all things considered, you have a case (but normally exceptionally little) to everything the organization possesses. Indeed, this implies actually you possess a minor bit of each household item, every trademark, and each agreement of the organization. As a proprietor, you are qualified for a lot of the organization's profit just as any democratic rights appended to the stock.

A stock is spoken to by a stock declaration. This is an extravagant bit of paper that is confirmation of your possession. In the present PC age, you won't really get the opportunity to see this report on the grounds that your business keeps these records electronically, which is otherwise called holding shares "in road name". This is done to make the offers simpler to exchange. Before, when an individual needed to sell their offers, that individual physically brought the testaments down to the financier. Presently, exchanging with a tick of the mouse or a telephone call makes life simpler for everyone.

Being an investor of an open organization doesn't mean you have a state in the everyday running of the business. Rather, one vote for each offer to choose the governing body at yearly gatherings is the degree to which you have a state in the organization. For example, being a Microsoft investor doesn't mean you can call up Bill Gates and disclose to him how you figure the organization ought to be run. In a similar line of reasoning, being an investor of Anheuser Busch doesn't mean you can stroll into the processing plant and get a free instance of Bud Light! The administration of the organization should expand the estimation of the firm for investors. On the off chance that this doesn't occur, the investors can cast a ballot to have the administration evacuated, from a certain point of view. In all actuality, singular financial specialists like you and I don't claim enough offers to impact the organization. It's extremely the enormous young men like huge institutional speculators and tycoon business people who settle on the choices. For conventional investors, not having the option to deal with the organization isn't such a major ordeal. All things considered, the thought is that you would prefer not to need to work to profit, correct? The significance of being an investor is that you are qualified for a part of the organization's benefits and have a case on resources. Benefits are at times paid out as profits. The more offers you possess, the bigger the bit of the benefits you get. Your case on resources is just important if an organization fails. If there should be an occurrence of liquidation, you'll get what's left after every one of the loan bosses have been paid. This last point merits rehashing: the significance of stock proprietorship is your case on resources and profit. Without this, the stock wouldn't merit the paper it's imprinted on. Another critical component of stock is its constrained obligation, which implies that, as a proprietor of a stock, you are not by and by at risk if the organization can't pay its obligations. Different organizations, for example, associations are set up so that if the organization fails the banks can come after the accomplices (investors) by and by and auction their home, vehicle, furniture, and so forth. Owning stock implies that, regardless, the greatest worth you can lose is the estimation of your speculation. Regardless of whether an organization of which you are an investor fails, you can never lose your own benefits. Obligation versus Value Why does an organization issue stock? For what reason would the organizers share the benefits with a huge number of individuals when they could hush up about benefits? The explanation is that sooner or later every organization needs to fund-raise. To do this, organizations can either acquire it from someone or raise it by selling some portion of the organization, which is known as giving stock. An organization can obtain by taking a credit from a bank or by giving bonds. The two techniques fit under the umbrella of obligation financing. Then again, giving stock is called value financing. Giving stock is invaluable for the organization since it doesn't require the organization to pay back the cash or make premium installments en route. All that the investors receive as a byproduct of their cash is the expectation that the offers will some time or another be worth more than what they paid for them. The primary clearance of a stock, which is given by the privately owned business itself, is known as the first sale of stock (IPO). It is significant that you comprehend the qualification between an organization financing through obligation and financing through value. At the point when you purchase an obligation speculation, for example, a security, you are ensured the arrival of your cash (the head) alongside guaranteed premium installments. This isn't the situation with a value venture. By turning into a proprietor, you accept the danger of the organization not being fruitful - similarly as an entrepreneur isn't ensured an arrival, nor is an investor. As a proprietor, your case on resources is not as much as that of loan bosses. This implies if an organization fails and sells, you, as an investor, don't get any cash until the banks and bondholders have been paid out; we call this outright need. Investors gain a ton if an organization is effective, however they additionally remain to lose their whole speculation if the organization isn't fruitful. Hazard It must be underscored that there are no ensures with regards to individual stocks. A few organizations pay out profits, yet numerous others don't. What's more, there is no commitment to pay out profits in any event, for those organizations that have customarily given them. Without profits, a speculator can profit on a stock just through its gratefulness in the open market. On the drawback, any stock may fail, in which case your venture merits nothing. In spite of the fact that hazard may sound all negative, there is additionally a brilliant side. Going out on a limb requests a more noteworthy profit for your speculation. This is the motivation behind why stocks have generally beated different speculations, for example, securities or investment accounts. Over the long haul, an interest in stocks has truly had a normal return of around 10-12%.

# Chapter Eleven: Individual Retirement Accounts

Various Types Of Stocks

There are two principle sorts of stocks: regular stock and favored stock. Regular Stock Common stock is, well, normal. At the point when individuals talk about stocks they are typically alluding to this sort. Actually, most of stock is given is in this structure. We fundamentally went over highlights of normal stock in the last segment. Normal offers speak to possession in an organization and a case (profits) on a segment of benefits. Financial specialists get one vote for each offer to choose the board individuals, who administer the significant choices made by the board. Over the long haul, basic stock, by methods for capital development, yields more significant yields than pretty much every other venture. This better yield includes some major disadvantages since regular stocks involve the most hazard. In the event that an organization fails and sells, the normal investors won't get cash until the loan bosses, bondholders and favored investors are paid. Favored Stock Preferred stock speaks somewhat of possession in an organization yet typically doesn't accompany a similar democratic rights. (This may differ contingent upon the organization.) With favored offers, financial specialists are normally ensured a fixed profit for eternity. This is not quite the same as normal stock, which has variable profits that are never ensured. Another bit of leeway is that in case of liquidation, favored investors are satisfied before the regular investor (yet at the same time after obligation holders). Favored stock may likewise be callable, implying that the organization has the choice to buy the offers from investors at whenever under any circumstances (for the most part for a premium). A few people believe favored stock to be more similar to obligation than value. A decent method to think about these sorts of offers is to consider them to be being in the middle of bonds and normal shares. Various Classes of Stock Common and favored are the two primary types of stock; in any case, it's additionally workable for organizations to alter various classes of stock in any capacity they need. The most well-known explanation behind this is the organization needing the democratic capacity to stay with a specific gathering; hence, various classes of offers are given diverse democratic rights. For instance, one class of offers would be held by a select gathering who are given ten votes for each offer while a below average would be given to most of speculators who are given one vote for every offer. When there is more than one class of stock, the classes are generally assigned as Class An and Class B. Berkshire Hathaway (ticker: BRK), has two classes of stock. The various structures are spoken to by setting the letter behind the ticker image in a structure this way: "BRKa, BRKb" or "BRK.A, BRK.B".

How Stocks Trade

Most stocks are exchanged on trades, which are places where purchasers and dealers meet and settle on a cost. A few trades are physical areas where exchanges are done on an exchanging floor. You've presumably observed photos of an exchanging floor, in which merchants are uncontrollably hurling their arms, waving, hollering, and motioning to one another. The other sort of trade is virtual, made out of a system of PCs where exchanges are made electronically.

The reason for a financial exchange is to encourage the trading of protections among purchasers and dealers, lessening the dangers of contributing. Simply envision how troublesome it is sell shares on the off chance that you needed to call around the area attempting to discover a purchaser. Extremely, a financial exchange is just a super-modern ranchers' market connecting purchasers and venders. Before we go on, we ought to recognize the essential market and the auxiliary market. The essential market is the place protections are made (by methods for an IPO) while, in the optional market, financial specialists exchange beforehand gave protections without the inclusion of the giving organizations. The auxiliary market is the thing that individuals are alluding to when they talk about the securities exchange. Understand that the exchanging of an organization's stock doesn't straightforwardly include that organization. The New York Stock Exchange The most lofty trade on the planet is the New York Stock Exchange (NYSE). The "Enormous

Board" was established more than 200 years back in 1792 with the consenting to of the Buttonwood Arrangement by 24 New York City stockbrokers and dealers. Right now the NYSE, with stocks like General Electric, McDonald's, Citigroup, Coca-Cola, Gillette and Wal-bazaar, is the market of decision for the biggest organizations in America.

The NYSE is the principal kind of trade (as we alluded to above), where a great part of the exchanging is done up close and personal on an exchanging floor. This is additionally alluded to as a recorded trade. Requests come in through business firms that are individuals from the trade and stream down to floor merchants who go to a particular spot on the floor where the stock exchanges. At this area, known as the exchanging post, there is a particular individual known as the expert whose activity is to coordinate purchasers and venders. Costs are resolved utilizing a sale technique: the present cost is the most elevated sum any purchaser is eager to pay and the least cost at which somebody is happy to sell. When an exchange has been made, the subtleties are sent back to the financier firm, who at that point tells the speculator who put in the request. In spite of the fact that there is human contact in this procedure, don't imagine that the NYSE is still in the stone age: PCs assume an immense job simultaneously. The Nasdaq The second kind of trade is the virtual sort brought an over-the-counter (OTC) showcase, of which the Nasdaq is the most mainstream. These business sectors have no focal area or floor merchants at all. Exchanging is done through a PC and broadcast communications system of vendors. It used to be that the biggest organizations were recorded distinctly on the NYSE while all other second level stocks exchanged on different trades. The tech blast of the late '90s changed this; presently the Nasdaq is home to a few major innovation organizations, for example, Microsoft, Cisco, Intel, Dell and Oracle. This has brought about the Nasdaq turning into a genuine contender to the NYSE.

On the Nasdaq businesses go about as market creators for different stocks. A market producer gives consistent offer and ask costs inside an endorsed rate spread for shares for which they are assigned to make a market. They may coordinate purchasers and venders straightforwardly however as a rule they will keep up a stock of offers to satisfy needs of financial specialists. Different Exchanges The third biggest trade in the U.S. is the American Stock Exchange (AMEX). The AMEX used to be an option in contrast to the NYSE, however that job has since been filled by the Nasdaq. Actually, the National Association of Securities Dealers (NASD), which is the parent of Nasdaq, purchased the AMEX in 1998. Practically all exchanging now on the AMEX is in little top stocks and subordinates. There are many stock trades situated in pretty much every nation around the globe. American markets are without a doubt the biggest, yet despite everything they speak to just a small amount of all out venture far and wide. The two other fundamental money related center points are

London, home of the London Stock Exchange, and Hong Kong, home of the Hong Kong Stock Exchange. The last spot worth referencing is the over-the-counter release board (OTCBB). The Nasdaq is an over-the-counter market, however the term generally alludes to little open organizations that don't meet the posting necessities of any of the directed markets, including the Nasdaq. The OTCBB is home to penny stocks in light of the fact that there is practically no guideline. This makes putting resources into an OTCBB stock dangerous.

What Causes Stock Prices To Change?

Stock costs change each day because of market powers. By this we imply that offer costs change in light of market interest. On the off chance that more individuals need to purchase a stock (request) than sell it (supply), at that point the value climbs. On the other hand, if a bigger number of individuals needed to sell a stock than get it, there would be more prominent stockpile than request, and the cost would fall. Getting market interest is simple. What is hard to fathom is the thing that makes individuals like a specific stock and aversion another stock. This comes down to making sense of what news is certain for an organization and what news is negative. There are numerous responses to this issue and pretty much any financial specialist you ask has their very own thoughts and methodologies.

That being stated, the foremost hypothesis is that the value development of a stock demonstrates what speculators feel an organization is value. Try not to compare an organization's an incentive with the stock cost. The estimation of an organization is its market capitalization, which is the stock value increased by the quantity of offers remarkable. For instance, an organization that exchanges at $100 per share and has 1 million offers remarkable has a lesser incentive than an organization that exchanges at $50 that has 5 million offers exceptional ($100 x 1 million = $100 million while $50 x 5 million = $250 million). To further confound things, the cost of a stock doesn't just mirror an organization's present worth, it additionally mirrors the development that speculators expect later on. The most significant factor that influences the estimation of an organization is its profit. Income are the benefit an organization makes, and over the long haul no organization can make due without them. It bodes well when you consider it. In the event that an organization never profits, it won't remain in business. Open organizations are required to report their income four times each year (when each quarter). Money Street watches with out of control consideration at these occasions, which are alluded to as profit seasons. The purpose for this is investigators base their future estimation of an organization on their profit projection. On the off chance that an organization's outcomes shock (are superior to expected), the value hops up. In the event that an organization's outcomes disillusion (are more awful than anticipated), at that point the cost will fall. Obviously, it's not simply profit that can change the assumption towards a stock (which, thusly, changes its cost). It would be a somewhat basic world if this were the situation! During the dotcom bubble, for instance, many web organizations rose to have showcase capitalizations in the billions of dollars while never making even the littlest benefit. As we as a whole know, these valuations didn't hold, and most web organizations saw their qualities psychologist to a small amount of their highs. In any case, the way that costs moved that much shows that there are factors other than current profit that impact stocks. Speculators have grown truly several these factors, proportions and pointers. Some you may have just known about, for example, the value/profit proportion, while others are very convoluted and cloud with names like Chaikin oscillator or moving normal assembly uniqueness. Things being what they are, the reason do stock costs change? The best answer is that no one truly knows without a doubt. Some accept that it is beyond the realm of imagination to expect to foresee how stock costs will change, while others believe that by drawing graphs and taking a gander at past value developments, you can decide when to purchase and sell. The main thing we do know is that stocks are unstable and can change in cost very quickly. The significant things to get a handle on about this subject are the accompanying:

1. At the most central level, organic market in the market decides stock cost. 2. Value times the quantity of offers extraordinary

(advertise capitalization) is the estimation of an organization. Contrasting only the offer cost of two organizations is useless. 3. Hypothetically, income are what influence financial specialists' valuation of an organization, yet there are different pointers that speculators use to anticipate stock cost. Keep in mind, it is financial specialists' conclusions, frames of mind and desires that at last influence stock costs. 4. There are numerous speculations that attempt to clarify the manner in which stock costs move the manner in which they do. Lamentably, there is nobody hypothesis that can clarify everything.

Purchasing Stocks

You've currently realized what a stock is and a smidgen about the standards behind the securities exchange, however how would you really approach purchasing stocks? Fortunately, you don't need to go down into the exchanging pit shouting and shouting your request. There are two primary approaches to buy stock: 1. Utilizing a Brokerage The most widely recognized strategy to purchase stocks is to utilize a financier. Financiers come in two distinct flavors. Full-administration businesses offer you (as far as anyone knows) master exhortation and can deal with your record; they likewise charge a great deal. Markdown businesses offer little in the method for individual consideration however are a lot less expensive. At once, just the affluent could manage the cost of a merchant since just the costly, full-administration intermediaries were accessible. With the web came the blast of online rebate intermediaries. On account of them about anyone would now be able to stand to put resources into the market. 2. Dribbles and DIPs Dividend reinvestment plans (DRIPs) and direct venture plans (DIPs) are designs by which individual organizations, for a negligible expense, enable investors to buy stock legitimately from the organization. Dribbles are an extraordinary method to contribute limited quantities of cash at standard interims.

The most effective method to Read a Stock Table/Quote

Sections 1 and 2: 52-Week Hi and Low - These are the most elevated and least costs at which a stock has exchanged over the past 52 weeks (one year). This commonly does exclude the earlier day's exchanging. Section 3: Company Name and Type of Stock - This segment records the name of the organization. On the off chance that there are no extraordinary images or letters following the name, it is regular stock. Various images suggest various classes of offers. For instance, "pf" signifies the offers are favored stock. Segment 4: Ticker Symbol - This is the special alphabetic name which distinguishes the stock. On the off chance that you watch budgetary TV, you have seen the ticker tape move over the screen, providing the most recent cost estimates close by this image. In the event that you are searching for stock statements on the web, you generally look for an organization by the ticker image. On the off chance that you don't have the foggiest idea what a specific organization's ticker is you can look for it at: http://finance.yahoo.com/l. Segment 5: Dividend Per Share - This demonstrates the yearly profit installment per share. On the off chance that this space is clear, the organization doesn't right now pay out profits. Section 6: Dividend Yield – This expresses the rate return on the profit, determined as yearly profits per offer separated by value per share. Section 7: Price/Earnings Ratio - This is determined by separating the present stock cost by profit per share from the last four quarters. For more detail on the best way to decipher this, see our P/E Ratio instructional exercise. Section 8: Trading Volume - This figure shows the absolute number of offers exchanged for the afternoon, recorded in hundreds. To get the genuine number exchanged, include "00" as far as possible of the number recorded.

Segment 9 and 10: Day High and Low - This demonstrates the value run at which the stock has exchanged at for the duration of the day. As such, these are the greatest and the base costs that individuals have paid for the stock. Segment 11: Close - The nearby is the last exchanging value recorded when the market shut on the day. On the off chance that the shutting cost is up or down over 5% than the earlier day's nearby, the whole posting for that stock is undeniable. Remember, you are not ensured to get this cost on the off chance that you purchase the stock the following day in light of the fact that the cost is continually changing (considerably after the trade is shut for the afternoon). The nearby is just a pointer of past execution and with the exception of in outrageous conditions fills in as a ballpark of what you ought to hope to pay. Segment 12: Net Change - This is the dollar worth change in the stock cost from the earlier day's end cost. At the point when you catch wind of a stock being "up for the afternoon," it implies the net change was sure. Statements on the Internet Nowadays, it's unquestionably progressively advantageous for most to get stock statements off the Internet. This strategy is predominant in light of the fact that most destinations update for the duration of the day and give you more data, news, diagramming, look into, and so forth. To get cites, essentially enter the ticker image into the statement box of any major monetary site like Yahoo Finance, CBS Marketwatch, or MSN Moneycentral. The model beneath shows a statement for Microsoft (MSFT) from Yahoo Finance. Deciphering the information is actually equivalent to with the paper.

The Bulls, The Bears And The Farm

On Wall Street, the bulls and bears are in a consistent battle. On the off chance that you haven't knew about these terms as of now, you without a doubt will as you contribute. The Bulls A positively trending business sector is when everything in the economy is extraordinary, individuals are securing positions, total national output (GDP) is developing, and stocks are rising. Things are out and out ruddy! Picking stocks during a positively trending business sector is simpler on the grounds that everything is going up. Buyer markets can't keep going forever however, and now and again they can prompt perilous circumstances if stocks become exaggerated. On the off chance that an individual is hopeful and accepts that stocks will go up, the person is known as a "bull" and is said to have a "bullish viewpoint". The Bears A bear market is the point at which the economy is awful, downturn is approaching and stock costs are falling. Bear markets make it extreme for financial specialists to pick gainful stocks. One answer for this is to profit when stocks are falling utilizing a strategy called short selling. Another methodology is to look out for the sidelines until you feel that the bear market is approaching its end, just beginning to purchase fully expecting a positively trending business sector. On the off chance that an individual is skeptical, accepting that stocks are going to drop, the person in question is known as a "bear" and said to have a "bearish viewpoint".

The Other Animals on the Farm - Chickens and Pigs Chickens are reluctant to lose anything. Their dread abrogates their need to make benefits thus they go just to currency advertise protections or escape the business sectors totally. While the facts confirm that you ought to never put resources into something over which you lose rest, you are likewise ensured never to perceive any arrival in the event that you maintain a strategic distance from the market totally and never go out on a limb, Pigs are high-hazard financial specialists searching for the one major score in a brief timeframe. Pigs purchase on hot tips and put resources into organizations without doing their due steadiness. They get restless, avaricious, and passionate about their speculations, and they are attracted to high-chance protections without placing in the best possible time or cash to find out about these venture vehicles. Proficient merchants love the pigs, as it's regularly from their misfortunes that the bulls and bears procure their benefits. What Type of Investor Will You Be? There are a lot of various speculation styles and systems out there. Despite the fact that the bulls and bears are continually at chances, the two of them can profit with the changing cycles in the market. Indeed, even the chickens see a few returns, however not a great deal. The one failure in this image is the pig. Ensure you don't get into the market before you are prepared. Be traditionalist and never put resources into anything you don't get it. Before you bounce in without the correct information, consider this old securities exchange saying:

"Bulls profit, bears profit, however pigs simply get butchered!"

Stock implies possession. As a proprietor, you have a case on the advantages and income of an organization just as casting a ballot rights with your offers.

Stock is value, bonds are obligation. Bondholders are ensured an arrival on their speculation and have a higher case than investors.

This is for the most part why stocks are viewed as more dangerous speculations and require a higher pace of return.

You can lose the entirety of your speculation with stocks. The other side of this is you can rake in some serious cash on the off chance that you put resources into the correct organization.

The two fundamental kinds of stock are normal and liked. It is additionally workable for an organization to make various classes of stock.

Stock markets are places where purchasers and dealers of stock meet to exchange. The NYSE and the Nasdaq are the most significant trades in the United States.

Stock costs change as per market interest. There are numerous elements affecting costs, the most significant of which is income.

There is no agreement about why stock costs move the manner in which they do.

To purchase stocks you can either utilize a financier or a profit reinvestment plan (DRIP).

Stock tables/cites really aren't that difficult to peruse once you comprehend a big motivator for everything!

Bulls profit, bears profit, however pigs get butchered!

All organizations need to monitor their funds. This implies the organization is monitoring the entirety of the cash coming in and cash going out, just as other exchanges that don't really include the trading of cash. Toward the finish of every month, quarter (a quarter of a year), and year, an organization will plan budget reports, which are an outline of all the money related exchanges for that period.

For an organization that is traded on an open market (which means portions of the organization stock are sold on a securities exchange) it is necessitated that the organization plan and document quarterly and yearly fiscal reports so the administration and people in general can perceive how the organization is getting along.

# Chapter Twelve: Annuities

## WHO USES FINANCIAL STATEMENTS?

Loads of various gatherings will be keen on the budget summaries of an organization.

In the first place, the organization's administration and directorate will utilize the budget summaries to follow execution. The fiscal summaries show how the organization has done before, and will assist the executives with settling on choices about what's to come.

Moneylenders (like banks who have made advances to the organization) may likewise need to see the fiscal summaries. A few advances may have certain prerequisites, for example, the organization's obligation to value proportion can't be more than 0.3 so as to get that credit. Or on the other hand, the bank may simply need to perceive how a lot of money the organization needs to assess how likely it is the organization will have the option to pay back the advance and enthusiasm for an auspicious way.

Speculators are likewise extremely keen on observing the fiscal reports. They are settling on choices about whether to purchase or sell stock in the organization, so they have to know how the organization is getting along to help illuminate their choices.

Would you be able to consider any other individual who may utilize the budget summaries of an organization, other than the board, banks and speculators?

## WHAT ARE THE THREE FINANCIAL STATEMENTS?

We should take a gander at Apple, Inc. to find out about budget summaries. There are three essential budget reports, 1) the accounting report, 2) the pay articulation, what's more, 3) the announcement of incomes. See beneath to locate Apple's 2014 monetary proclamations.

## THE BALANCE SHEET

We should begin by watching this video, made by Wall Street Survivor, an accomplice organization of YIS.

The accounting report (above) is a depiction of the business at a solitary point in time. Consider it like a photo. It is an image of what the business resembles on the day the image is taken. The accounting report shows a depiction of the organization's advantages (its assets that it hopes to make an incentive later on), liabilities (the advances and different commitments because of others), and proprietors' value (otherwise called investors' value or investors' value—the stake that the proprietors or financial specialists have in the business).

Apple, Inc. arranged an accounting report for the year finished September 27, 2014. Here are a portion of the benefits the monetary record appears: $13.8 billion Cash (in fund terms, money isn't simply dollar greenbacks, however all cash held in financial records, investment accounts, and so on in addition to genuine dollar notes close by, assuming any) $17.5 billion Accounts Receivable (this implies another person purchased something from Apple, yet as opposed to paying immediately, regardless they owe the cash, and Apple is hoping to get it later on) $2.1 billion Inventories (these are the Macs and iPhones and iPads that

Apple right now has in stockrooms and stores, planned to be offered to clients) $20.6 billion Property, plant and hardware (this is the measure of land, structures, and apparatus that the organization possesses and uses to produce and sell merchandise)

Here are a portion of the liabilities the monetary record appears:

$30.2 billion Accounts Payable (this is the other side of Accounts Receivable, so for this situation, Apple has purchased something from others and has vowed to pay them for it later on)

$18.5 billion Accrued Expenses (this could incorporate things like the commitment to pay enthusiasm to loan specialists and charges to the legislature)

$29.0 billion Long-term Debt (this implies credits from a bank)

Here are a portion of the value adjusts the monetary record appears:

$23.3 billion Common Stock (this is the stock offered to financial specialists available)

$87.2 billion Retained Earnings (this is the measure of benefits made in earlier years that has been reinvested in the business to enable it to develop, as opposed to circulated to investors as profits)

THE INCOME STATEMENT

The pay articulation shows a business' exhibition over some stretch of time, such as a year. Consider it like a video. It shows what befalls the business after some time. The pay proclamation shows how much income the organization made throughout the year, the amount it cost to sell its primary items, the amount it cost to pay its representatives over the course of the year, and the amount it owed in intrigue and expenses for the year. On an essential level, if the organization makes more income than it spends in costs, it is a beneficial business. In the event that the organization's expenses are more prominent than its incomes, at that point it's anything but a productive business.

It is in every case great to recollect not to take a gander at only one budget summary and think it recounts to the entire story of the business. A decent speculator ought to figure out how to peruse all the

fiscal summaries, and see patterns happening after some time, from monetary record to

accounting report and from pay proclamation to pay articulation.

Apple, Inc. arranged an Income Statement for the year finished September 27,

2014. The salary explanation shows that Apple has offers of $182.8 billion during that year. That is how a lot of income Apple produced using every one of its offers of PCs and telephones and applications and melodies on iTunes and everything else it sells. This is an expansion from $170.9 billion of every 2013 and $156.5 billion of every 2012.

Next, the Income Statement shows costs, beginning with Cost of Sales of $112.3 billion. This implies so as to make every one of the items it sold for that $182.8 billion income, it cost Apple $112.3 billion. Different costs incorporate $6.0 billion innovative work costs, $12.0 billion selling, general, and managerial costs, and $14.0 billion duty cost.

At last, the Income Statement shows Net Income, which is known as the base line on the grounds that – you got it! – it shows up at the base of the Income Statement.

Apple's Net Income for the year finished September 27, 2014, was $39.5 billion.

Inquiries TO CONSIDER:

1. Why the salary explanation is significant?

2. Which two lines on the salary explanation do you believe are the most significant?

THE STATEMENT OF CASH FLOWS

The third of the essential fiscal reports is the announcement of incomes. The explanation of incomes shows how a lot of money came into the business and how a lot of money left the business. It's critical to note here that when we utilize the term money in the fund world, we mean not just dollar greenbacks, similar to you may consider, yet additionally checks and electronic exchanges and the equalization in the financial balance. Indeed, most organizations will do a ton of their exchanges through electronic exchanges, yet regardless we call this money. Consider money simply meaning all types of cash.

Money produced from working exercises, is one of the most significant measurements to screen. Think about this as income or net benefit, yet the real money profit. Ordinarily if an organization has enormous non-money charges or gains in a year, the more exact benefit number is found on the Cash Generated from Operating Activities.

The other key measurement to pay special mind to in the Statement of Cash Flows is the Capital Expenditure (likewise alluded to CAPEX), or the Payments for obtaining of property, plant and gear. Aggregate for this class is the money used to put resources into the business. Warren Buffett and numerous incredible financial specialists is the Free Cash Flow.

This is determined by: Net Income + Depreciation – CAPEX = Free Cash Flow. This is how a lot of money the business created that year.

Movement: Can you figure the Free Cash Flow for Apple utilizing the announcements in this exercise?

Hint, a portion of the measurements are found on the Income Statement and some are found on the Statement of Cash Flows.

## HOW DO I FORECAST REVENUES OF A COMPANY?

In its least complex structure, future income can be determined by increasing the normal selling cost of the organization's item by the quantity of expected items sold. In any case, determining income isn't that straightforward and can include considering various variables. For example, Apple would see expanded income in the event that it sold its iPhone for more cash per unit, however just if the quantity of telephones sold didn't diminish because of the cost increment. Apple would cherish for both the cost per unit and the quantity of units offered to increment, however these two things can move in inverse ways as individuals will in general purchase less units as the cost of that unit increments. Apple can likewise build the quantity of units sold by growing geologically. If it somehow managed to start selling telephones in another nation it hadn't recently sold in, that would include income. There can be other counterbalancing factors as well, in any case. At the point when Apple previously presented the iPhone, iPods were very mainstream, however when individuals started to purchase iPhones, which included incorporated computerized music players, they started purchasing less iPods. This impact made it so that while Apple picked up heaps of income from the clearance of its iPhones, it started losing its ordinary iPod income.

Organizations can likewise increase extra income by taking piece of the pie from contenders. In the event that, for example, the quantity of cell phones sold on the planet is 1.2 billion every year and Apple sells half of those this year and 60% one year from now, it will see an income increment, all else being equivalent. This implies Apple sold 600 million telephones (half of 1.2B) this year and will sell 720 million telephones (60% of 1.2B) one year from now. This is known as "taking piece of the pie," as Apple basically took a greater bit of the pie by going from half of the market to 60% of the market. Another way an organization can develop income is by being in a market where the market itself is developing. For example, if the market (i.e., the quantity of cell phones sold) developed by 10% from 1.2 billion telephones to 1.32 billion telephones, regardless of whether Apple held a half piece of the overall industry, it would in any case sell 10% more telephones. Organizations can likewise develop incomes through opening or building new stores, obtaining different organizations, and so forth.

To figure the incomes of an organization, one must assess the business, the organization, and its rivals. Taking a gander at an organization's income development rate for a long time is a decent start. Be that as it may, you should be mindful so as not to accept that an irregular timeframe is in certainty typical. For example, Apple's income development rate was well over 10% every year since the mid 2000s, and it even arrived at paces of over half after the organization discharged the iPhone and iPad, however by 2013 Apple was an exceptionally huge organization with no new items in quite a while, bringing about a development pace of under 10% for the year.

Had the expert expected that the organization would develop income at half a year for incalculable years to come, he/she would've been in for a severe shock. Taking everything into account, determining income includes a variety of factors, however an adroit investigator who has done his/her schoolwork ought to have the option to create a decent estimate in time.

# Conclusions

Action: FORECAST REVENUES

Picked an organization that is on your rundown from Lesson 4 that you can up with from screens or from a supermarket visit, or from different sources:

- How quick has this organization been developing incomes in the course of recent years?

- How quick did this organization develop incomes a year ago?

- Has this organization been becoming quicker or more slow than its rivals?

- What do you expect they will develop at throughout the following 5 years?

Use assets, for example, Morningstar.com, Zacks.com and Yahoo.Finance to inquire about these measurements.

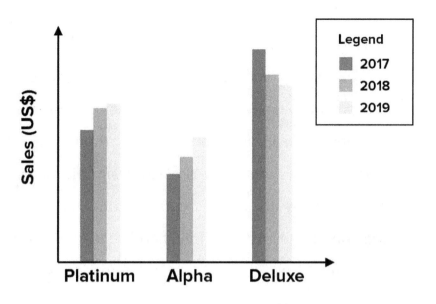

HOW DO I FORECAST MARGINS OF A COMPANY?

When investigating stocks, you will probably audit the pay proclamation, monetary record and explanation of incomes. The salary proclamation gives a money related outline of the working consequences of the firm over some undefined time frame, for example, a quarter or year. The main segment of the salary articulation shows net edges, essentially the absolute income (deals) less the expense of merchandise sold.

Budgetary organizations and administration situated organizations will in general have high net edges since they frequently have lower expenses of products sold. Though modern and assembling organizations have lower net edges as they have significant expense of merchandise sold.

Does the vehicle assembling organization Toyota have high or low gross edges? That is correct they have low gross edges! Vehicle assembling has one of the greater expense of merchandise sold out of any industry, one vehicle is comprised of thousands of parts. Including every one of those parts rises to a significant expense of products sold and lower net edges. Keep in mind the gross edge is basically subtracting the expense of merchandise sold from the all out income. Which can be useful when seeing two organizations in a similar industry, take Apple versus Samsung.

The two of them make great mobile phones, who might you supposition has higher gross edge?

A. Samsung

B. Apple

Apple has the higher gross edge and for what reason is that significant? Regardless of whether they charge a more significant expense or they have lower cost of merchandise sold can prompt upper hands as time goes on.

Going above and beyond on the pay articulation you will notice working wages or EBIT. Working Income isolated by complete incomes is Operating edge. Working edge is a proportion of gainfulness, the amount of every dollar of income is left over after both expense of merchandise sold and working costs. The working costs incorporate finance, deals commissions, advertising, transportation, travel, lease and other general costs. It's imaginable simpler to fathom on the off chance that you consider purchasing some jeans. You are in the shopping center and need to purchase some jeans that expenses $50, that is a some jeans right? They felt so pleasant you feel free to get them, did you know it just cost $20 to make those jeans. That is the expense of merchandise sold right, $20. Did you pay excessively? We should consider it. After the organization made the jeans, they needed to deliver the jeans to the store by semi-truck, somebody needed to empty the

shipment of jeans, the organization pays lease to have a store in the shopping center, the store

has workers who put the jeans in plain view and offered them to you, a business

was made to advance the jeans and these working costs signify $25 on

top of the $20 cost of merchandise sold. Leaving the organization with a benefit of $5 or gross working edge of 10%.

Gathering ACTIVITY: MARGIN MATCHING

How about we play a coordinating game! Match the organization with the working edge they make: Walmart and Facebook.

Organization A has working edge of 24%

Organization B has working edge of 5%

Insight, the mystery behind Walmart is they offer the least costs and keeping in mind that they make little benefit per great sold, they compensate for it since they sell quite a lot more socks, cleanser, and oat than any of their rivals.

Match the working edge to the accompanying three organizations, Coca-Cola, Nike and Boeing.

Organization A has working edge of 8%

Organization B has working edge of 13%

Organization C has working edge of 25% your first seven day stretch of Spanish class. A little lost with a parting migraine. Be that as it may, give it a touch of time and you're well on your approach to being capable communicate in the language of account. Regardless of whether you become a world-well known stock speculator later on, a bookkeeper, or possibly only a dental specialist attempting to keep the records of the business, figuring out how to peruse budget summaries is basic. The more familiar you are, the more effective you will be in practically any industry of business.

Extra Information

1. Fund has a language (bookkeeping) that you figure out how to talk.

2. There are three fundamental budget summaries, The Balance Sheet, The Income Statement and the Statement of Cash Flows

3. You should have the option to estimate an organization's income and edges accurately

on the off chance that you need to put resources into them.

Movement

Circumstance: MIXED UP FINANCIAL STATEMENTS Let's expect you handled a late spring entry level position working for the unbelievable speculator, Warren Buffett himself. One group will be picked to be his next protégés, and will in the end assume control over his $60 billion dollar domain, Berkshire Hathaway.

One morning, Buffett, comes to you all excited. He clarifies he was doing examination on organizations and experiencing their fiscal reports. He printed off their monetary records and pay articulations, however forgot about the names of the organizations. He says, "Would you be able to coordinate the rundown of organizations I was doing chip away at with the right budget reports? I'm sure on the off chance that I can coordinate the right organizations, I will have the option to locate the following multi-billion dollar venture thought, and I will procure you to run my organization!"

Attempt to coordinate the right the fiscal reports in APPENDIX A with every one of the accompanying organizations. The group with the most right answers is the victor. NO CHEATING BY LOOKING ONLINE!

Inquiries to Consider: (HINTS)

1. Does the organization make high edges (Gross benefit/Revenue)?

2. What do development patterns of income and overall gain let you know?

3. Is the business capital serious (do they require a ton of resources for profit)?

4. Does the organization hold a ton of inventories comparative with their general deals level?

# STOCK MARKET INVESTING
# - ADVANCED COURSE -

*David Lazarus*

# Table of Contents

# Introduction:

# Understanding the Different Ways to Buy and sell stock

The office of Investor training and Advocacy is giving this Investor Bulletin to help instruct financial specialists about the various kinds of requests they can use to purchase what's more, sell stocks through a financier firm. Coming up next are general depictions of a portion of the regular request types and exchanging guidelines that financial specialists may use to purchase and sell stocks. If it's not too much trouble note that a portion of the request types and exchanging guidelines depicted beneath may not be accessible through all financier firms. Besides, some financier firms may offer extra request types and exchanging directions not portrayed beneath. Speculators should contact their financier firms to figure out which kinds of requests and exchanging directions are accessible for purchasing and selling also the organizations' particular approaches with respect to such accessible requests and exchanging guidelines.

# Chapter One: The Importance of Investing

## Market and Limit Orders

The two most basic request types are the market request and the farthest point request.

## Market Order

A market request is a request to purchase or sell a stock at the best accessible cost. By and large, this kind of request will be executed right away. In any case, the cost at which a market request will be executed isn't ensured. It is significant for speculators to recollect that the last-exchanged cost isn't really the cost at which a market request will be executed. In quick moving markets, the cost at which a market request will execute frequently strays from the last-exchanged cost or "ongoing" quote.

Model: A financial specialist submits a market request to purchase 1000 portions of XYZ stock when the best offer cost is $3.00 per share. On the off chance that different requests are executed first, the financial specialist's market request might be executed at a more significant expense.

What's more, a quick moving business sector may cause portions of a huge market request to execute at various costs. Model: A financial specialist puts in a market request to purchase 1000 portions of XYZ stock at $3.00 per share. In a quick moving business sector, 500 portions of the request could execute at $3.00 per share and the other 500 offers execute at a more significant expense.

## Utmost Order

An utmost request is a request to purchase or sell a stock at a particular cost or better. A purchase breaking point request must be executed at the utmost cost or lower, and a sell farthest point request must be executed at the cutoff cost or higher. A farthest point request isn't ensured to execute. A breaking point request must be filled if the financial exchange's value arrives at the farthest point cost.

While cutoff requests don't ensure execution, they help guarantee that a financial specialist doesn't pay in excess of a foreordained cost for a stock.

Model: A financial specialist needs to buy portions of

ABC stock for close to $10. The financial specialist could put in a breaking point request for this sum will possibly execute if the cost of ABC stock is $10 or lower.

Uncommon Orders and Trading Instructions notwithstanding business sector and point of confinement orders, financier firms may enable speculators to utilize exceptional requests and exchanging directions to purchase and sell stocks. Coming up next are depictions of the absolute most basic exceptional requests and exchanging guidelines.

**Stop Order**

A stop request, additionally alluded to as a stop-misfortune request, is a request to purchase or sell a stock once the cost of the stock arrives at a predefined cost, known as the stop cost. When

the stop cost is come to, a stop request turns into a market request. A purchase stop request is entered at a stop cost over the present market cost. Speculators by and large utilize a purchase stop request to restrain a misfortune or to ensure a benefit on a stock that they have undercuts. A sell stop request is entered at a stop cost beneath the present market cost. Financial specialists by and large use a sell stop request to restrain a misfortune or to ensure a benefit on a stock that they possess.

Before utilizing a stop request, speculators ought to think about the accompanying:

Momentary advertise vacillations in a stock's cost can enact a stop request, so a stop cost ought to be chosen cautiously.

The stop cost isn't the ensured execution cost for a stop request. The stop cost is a trigger that causes the stop request to turn into a market request. The execution value a financial specialist gets for this market request can digress essentially from the stop cost in a quick moving business sector where costs change quickly. A financial specialist can maintain a strategic distance from the danger of a stop request executing at a surprising cost by putting in a stop-limit request, however the breaking point cost may keep the request from being executed.

For specific kinds of stocks, some business firms have various guidelines for deciding if a stop cost has been come to. For these stocks, some business firms utilize just last-deal costs to trigger a stop request, while different firms use citation costs.

Financial specialists should check with their business firms to decide the particular decides that will apply to stop orders.

Stop-limit Order

A stop-limit request is a request to purchase or sell a stock that joins the highlights of a stop request and a point of confinement request. when the stop cost is come to, a stop-limit request turns into a point of confinement request that will be executed at a predefined cost (or better). The advantage of a stop-limit request is that the financial specialist can control the cost at which the request can be executed.

Before utilizing a stop-limit request, financial specialists ought to think about the accompanying:

Similarly as with all farthest point arranges, a stop-limit request may not be executed if the stock's value moves from as far as possible value, which may happen in a quick moving business sector. Momentary advertise vacillations in a stock's cost can actuate a stop-limit request, so stop and farthest point costs ought to be chosen cautiously.

The stop cost and the cutoff cost for a stop-limit request don't need to be a similar cost. For instance, a sell stop point of confinement request with a stop cost of $3.00 may have a farthest point cost of $2.50. such a request would turn into a functioning point of confinement request if market costs reach $3.00, in spite of the fact that the request must be executed at a cost of $2.50 or better.

For specific kinds of stocks, some financier firms have various gauges for deciding if the stop cost of a stop-limit request has been come to. For these stocks, some financier firms utilize just last-deal costs to trigger a stop-limit request, while different firms use citation costs. Financial specialists should check with their financier firms to decide the particular decides that will apply as far as possible requests.

Day Orders, Good-Til-Cancelled Orders, and Immediate-Or-Cancel Orders

Day orders, Good-until Cancelled (GtC) orders, and Immediate-or-Cancel (IoC) orders speak to timing directions for a request and might be applied to either market or restrict orders. except if a financial specialist determines a time period for the termination of a request, requests to purchase and sell a stock are Day orders, which means they are great just during that exchanging day.

A GTC request is a request to purchase or sell a stock that goes on until the request is finished or dropped. Financier firms commonly limit the period of time a speculator can leave a GtC request open.

This time allotment may fluctuate from representative to dealer. Financial specialists should contact their financier firms to figure out what time farthest point would apply to GtC orders.

An IOC request is a request to purchase or sell a stock that must be executed right away. Any segment of the request that can't be filled promptly will be dropped.

Fill-Or-Kill and All-Or-None Orders two other regular extraordinary request types are Fill-Or-Kill (FOK) and All-Or-None (AON) orders. A FoK request is a request to purchase or sell a stock that must be executed promptly completely; something else, the whole request will be dropped (i.e., no incomplete execution of the request is permitted). An Aon request is a request to purchase or sell a stock that must be executed completely, or not executed by any means. In any case, not at all like the FoK orders, Aon orders that can't be executed promptly stay dynamic until they are executed or dropped.

Opening Transactions

Financial specialists ought to know that any request put outside of normal exchanging hours and assigned for exchanging just during ordinary hours will for the most part be qualified to execute at an opening cost. Speculators should contact their financier firms to discover their merchant's strategies with respect to opening exchanges.

Related Information

For extra instructive data for speculators, see the office of Investor training and Advocacy's landing page. For extra data identifying with the sorts of requests financial specialists may use to purchase or sell stock, if it's not too much trouble perused our distribution "orders."

Speculation includes creation of a penance in the present with the desire for determining future advantages. Two most significant highlights of a speculation are current penance and future advantage.

Speculation is the penance of certain present qualities for the unsure future reward. It includes various choice, for example, type, blend, sum, timing, grade and so forth, of venture the basic leadership must be proceeds just as speculation might be characterized as an action that submits assets in any monetary/physical structure in the present with a desire for getting extra return later on. The desire carries with it a likelihood that the quantum of return may shift from a base to a most extreme.

This plausibility of variety in the real return is known as speculation hazard.

Therefore every venture includes an arrival and hazard. Venture has numerous which means and features. Be that as it may, venture can be translated extensively from three edges -

- Financial,

- Layman,

- Monetary.

Financial venture incorporates the dedication of the reserve for net expansion to the capital supply of the economy. The net augmentations to the capital stock methods an expansion in building hardware or inventories over the measure of proportionate merchandise that existed, state, one year prior simultaneously.

The layman employments of the term venture as any dedication of assets for a future advantage not really as far as return. For instance a dedication of cash to purchase another vehicle is surely a venture from an individual perspective.

# Chapter Two: Stock Market Fundamentals

**How the Stock Market and Online Trades influence Forex Trade**

The financial exchange has a significant job in the assignment of assets, both legitimately as a wellspring of assets and as a determinant of firms' worth and obtaining limit.

In any case, a developing assortment of experimental proof has raised a few questions about whether value markets are proficient in the feeling of properly reflecting significant and available data.' The enormous swings in value costs in a few nations during the 1980s gave extra proof that market valuations were more factor than the income prospects of firms. These scenes empowered recommendations for changes planned for restricting volatility,* in light of the fact that abundance unpredictability or misevaluating could have unwanted genuine outcomes and lead to a misallocation of assets.

The point of this paper is to analyze the connection between value costs and business speculation, tending to the topic of whether venture is impacted by wasteful evaluating in value markets. It considers: regardless of whether offer costs impact venture once a portion of the significant macroeconomic determinants of speculation are controlled for; whether assessments of the deviation of offer costs from their evaluated harmony esteems influence speculation; and the conduct of venture and offer costs in periods when offer costs seem to have strayed generally from essentials. The outcomes recommend that, while there is a noteworthy connection between offer costs and business interest in certain nations (the United States, Japan, the United Kingdom and Canada), this to a great extent reflects stock value relationship with, and expectation of, other macroeconomic advancements. This recommends estimating wasteful aspects, to the degree they are available, don't affect business venture.

There are various significant admonitions to endure as a top priority when considering the examination endeavored in this paper. In the first place, trial of securities exchange effectiveness are joint trial of productivity and a model creating anticipated returns. Henceforth, the exact proof exhibited in Section I and somewhere else can't be utilized to dismiss the proficiency theory fundamentally. All things considered, the aggregating weight of proof proposes that financial arrangement ought not underestimate proficiency. Second, a portion of the tests introduced in the area require assessments of the deviation of genuine offer costs from those that would be found in a proficient market. Effective market costs are not perceptible and must be controlled for or proxied somehow or another. In this way, a finding that deviations from these evaluated productive costs influence speculation might be expected exclusively to a gauge of the balance value that overlooks the impacts of certain significant components. Consequently, these tests will be one-sided towards finding that wasteful valuing in value markets affects venture.

Indeed, even with this predisposition, be that as it may, the outcomes displayed later don't firmly bolster such a finding.

The examination is organized extravagantly in the segment as it looks at the proof on whether value markets cost effectively. The connection between Forex, speculation and stock costs is then viewed as additionally communicated in the book.

The proficient markets speculation expresses that security costs ought to completely mirror all accessible, applicable data. If so then deviations of real comes back from expected returns ought to be arbitrary - they should, all things considered, to be zero and uncorrelated with data accessible to the market. To test whether costs fulfill these conditions it is important to indicate a model of the conduct of anticipated returns and to contrast this and their real execution. Therefore, trial of market proficiency are joint trial of the productivity theory and the accepted model of anticipated return.

The most direct approach to test proficiency is to accept that the normal rate of return is consistent. If so, at that point changes in offer costs ought not be sequentially connected since the previous history of offer costs is the most promptly accessible snippet of data in the market and any data in this history should as of now be implanted in the present cost. Value changes should just reflect new data getting to be accessible. Over short skylines (every day and week after week returns for instance) this has all the earmarks of being the situation. In any case, value changes in certain business sectors have been seen as sequentially associated over longer skylines. A typical component of this finding is that low-request value autocorrelations are sure however turned out to be negative over longer slacks. A few specialists recognized such conduct in stock costs in the United States. This sort of conduct is additionally obvious in different nations. A few pictures contains the correlogram of quarterly changes in stock costs in the significant seven OECD nations. This example, positive relationship at short skylines and negative connection at longer skylines, appears to happen in various nations. Much of the time, the theory that the value changes are not sequentially associated can be dismissed. demonstrate that this sort of example isn't kept to financial exchanges. It shows up in a wide scope of advantage advertises over various nations.

This joint speculation likewise infers that value changes ought not be unsurprising utilizing other promptly accessible data. Ongoing proof demonstrates this may not be the situation. Basic proportions of the deviation of the current cost from a gauge of the harmony value appear to anticipate future value developments. The relationship demonstrates that the hole between a steady various of genuine profits {their intermediary for crucial impact on stock costs) and the present stock value predicts future changes in stock costs. The coefficient on this term will in general be certain, showing that when current costs are underneath the evaluations of basics, costs are bound to ascend than to fall hence. This conduct is likewise evident, however to a lesser degree, in other resource markets.

It has been recommended that these examples demonstrate that the theoretical conduct of market members may drive costs from balance in the short run (henceforth the positive sequential relationship) however that after some time costs gradually return to harmony.

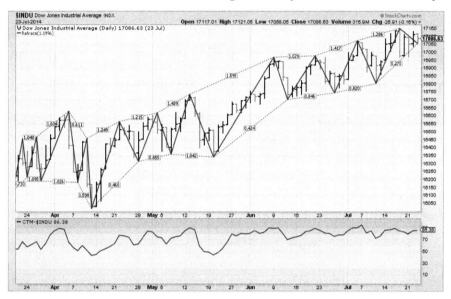

## Venture AND SHARE PRICES

Proof recommending that market-driven marvels can impact offer costs in the momentary combined with the huge vacillations in offer costs during the 1980s have driven some to contend that different principles or "circuit breakers" ought to be put on business sectors to constrain their unpredictability. Understood in these contentions is the view that wasteful aspects in value markets can prompt a misallocation of assets. The accompanying area will endeavor to reveal some insight into this issue by looking at the connection between offer costs and business speculation.

## A. Hypothetical contemplations

There are various motivations to accept that offer costs may impact venture. Hypothetically, financial exchange valuation assumes a key job in Q-type models of speculation assurance. At the point when the market estimation of an extra unit of capital surpasses its substitution cost a firm can raise its benefit by contributing. A connection between speculation and offer costs could likewise emerge if there are data asymmetries in monetary markets. An ascent in offer costs will improve the monetary record position of a firm, expanding its capacity to legitimately store ventures or to give security to outer account. In either case, the hazard that loan specialists face is decreased, in this way lessening the expense as well as expanding the accessibility of outer financing. The significance of the connection between asset report positions and the genuine economy can be found in the slow recuperation in numerous OECD nations from the downturn recently 1990/mid 1991. The corporate areas' craving to improve powerless monetary record positions has been a significant imperative on business speculation. Another ongoing limitation on speculation, which is incompletely connected to stock costs, has been the accessibility of bank loaning. Falling stock costs, especially in Japan, may have restricted the financial frameworks' ability to expand new advances (see O'Brien and Browne, 1992 for an exchange of the ongoing conduct of credit).

Exactly, share costs appear to give helpful driving data about venture and the economy all the more for the most part.

Ongoing occasions and research discoveries progressively propose that the financial exchange isn't driven exclusively by news about basics. There appear to be great hypothetical just as experimental motivations to accept that financial specialist supposition, likewise alluded to as trends and molds, influences stock costs. By speculator supposition we mean convictions held by certain financial specialists that can't be judiciously advocated. Such financial specialists are once in a while alluded to as clamor dealers. To influence costs, these not exactly judicious convictions must be connected crosswise over clamor dealers, generally exchanges dependent on mixed up decisions would counteract. At the point when financial specialist slant influences the interest of enough speculators, security costs wander from essential qualities.

The discussions over market productivity, energizing as they seem to be, would not be significant if the financial exchange didn't influence genuine monetary action. In the event that the financial exchange were a sideshow, showcase wasteful aspects would just redistribute riches between keen speculators and clamor dealers. Yet, on the off chance that the securities exchange impacts genuine financial action, at that point the speculator conclusion that influences stock costs could likewise in a roundabout way influence genuine action.

**Financial specialist Sentiment and the Stock Market**

Since Robert Shiller's showing of the overabundance unpredictability of securities exchange costs, inquire about on the productivity of budgetary markets has detonated. In resulting work, Shiller recommended that trends and designs, just as basics, impact resource costs. Eugene Fama and Kenneth French just as James Poterba and Lawrence Summers have figured out how to recognize mean inversion in U.S. stock returns. While this proof is steady with the nearness of mean-returning financial specialist assumption toward stocks, it is likewise predictable with time-differing required returns. Maybe all the more convincing proof on the job of financial specialist slant originates from the investigations of the accident of October 1987. Shiller reviewed financial specialists after the accident and discovered rare sorts of people who imagined that essentials had changed.

Nejat Seyhun found that corporate insiders forcefully purchased supplies of their own organizations during the accident, and made a great deal of cash doing as such. The insiders accurately observed no adjustment in essentials and ascribed the collide with an estimation move. The push of the proof is that stock costs react not exclusively to news, yet in addition to conclusion changes.

Follow-up concentrates to the work on mean inversion endeavor both to demonstrate the impact of financial specialist estimation on stock costs and to detach proportions of assumption. One gathering of studies concerns shut end common assets supports that issue a fixed number of offers, and afterward put the returns in other exchanged protections. On the off chance that financial specialists need to exchange their possessions in a shut end subsidize, they should offer their offers to different speculators, and can't simply reclaim them as on account of an open-end support. Shut end assets are amazingly helpful in monetary financial matters since it is conceivable to watch both their net resource esteem, which is the market estimation of their stock possessions, and their cost, and think about the two. A notable normal for shut end assets is that their stock cost is regularly not quite the same as their net resource esteem, proposing that business sectors are wasteful.

Indeed, Bradford De Long, Andrei Shleifer, Lawrence Summers, and Robert Waldmann, following crafted by Martin Zweig, have contended that the normal markdown on shut end assets can fill in as an intermediary for individual financial specialist opinion. At the point when individual speculators are bearish on stocks, they sell shut end assets just as different stocks. In doing as such, they drive up the limits on shut end reserves (that is, their value comparative with those of the stocks in their portfolio) in light of the fact that institutional financial specialists normally don't exchange these assets thus don't balance the bearishness of individual speculators. Alternately, when people are bullish on stocks, they purchase shut end reserves so limits thin or even become premiums. Charles Lee, Andrei Shleifer, and Richard Thaler present proof recommending that limits may in reality fill in as an intermediary for individual financial specialist conclusion. We won't audit the hypothesis and proof here, however will utilize shut end store limits as one proportion of financial specialist assessment, and will contemplate the connections between limits, speculation, and outer financing.

The observational proof on the potential significance of speculator assumption has been supplemented by a scope of hypothetical contentions that clarify why the impact of supposition on stock costs would not be disposed of through "exchange." Arbitrage in this setting doesn't allude to riskless exchange, as comprehended in money related financial aspects, but instead to hazardous, contrarian methodologies whereby brilliant speculators wager against the mispricing. Stephen Figlewski and Robert Shiller have both brought up that when stock returns are dangerous, exchange of this sort is likewise unsafe and consequently not totally successful. " I For instance, if an arbitrageur purchases undervalued stocks, he runs the hazard that central news will be terrible and that he will scrub down on what had at first been an appealing exchange. Since exchange is unsafe, arbitrageurs will restrict the size of their exchanges, and financial specialist notion will affect costs in balance. Others have taken this contention further. They call attention to that if financial specialist assessment is itself stochastic, it adds further hazard to exchange in light of the fact that slant can betray an arbitrageur with a short skyline. An arbitrageur purchasing undervalued stocks runs the hazard that they become significantly more undervalued sooner rather than later, when they may must be sold. This clamor dealer hazard makes exchange considerably more hazardous, permitting the impacts of opinion on costs to be much progressively articulated. The end result of these models is that the hypothetical contention that exchange keeps speculator assessment from impacting costs is just off-base.

Most models of financial specialist conclusion manage assumption that influences the entire securities exchange or possibly a major piece of it. At the point when notion influences countless protections, inclining toward the breeze means bearing precise hazard, and is along these lines expensive to chance disinclined arbitrageurs. In the event that, conversely, slant influences just a couple of protections, wagering against it means bearing just the hazard that can be differentiated, and along these lines arbitrageurs will wager all the more forcefully. Hence, speculator assessment can pronouncedly affect costs just when it influences countless protections.

This determination holds in an ideal capital market, with no exchanging limitations or expenses of getting to be educated about the mispricing of protections. All the more reasonably however, exchange is an expensive action and exchange assets will be given to specific protections just if returns legitimize bearing the expenses. Subsequently, speculator assessment toward individual protections won't be arbitraged away and will influence their costs, since arbitrageurs' assets and tolerance are restricted. On the off chance that a stock is mispriced, just a couple of arbitrageurs would think about it. The individuals who do know may have elective uses for assets, or may not hold up until the mispricing vanishes. Holding up is particularly expensive when exchange requires undercutting a security, and guidelines don't give the short merchant full utilization of the returns. Additionally, taking a huge situation in a security means bearing a lot of particular hazard, which is exorbitant to an arbitrageur who isn't completely expanded. At last, as worried by Fischer Black, arbitrageurs frequently can't be sure how mispriced a security is, further restricting their ability to exchange it. Every one of these expenses recommend that the assets inclining toward the mispricing of some random security are very constrained, and, thusly, even particular speculator slant may impact offer costs.

To finish up, late research has created an assortment of exact proof proposing that financial specialist feeling impacts resource costs. A parallel research exertion has shown that the typical models in budgetary financial matters, wherein speculators are hazard loath, suggest that speculator slant should influence costs. The contention that market-wide speculator supposition influences costs is especially solid, yet one likewise expects firm-explicit opinion to influence individual stocks. These speculations and proof bring up the conspicuous issue: does the impact of financial specialist feeling on stock costs feed through to business venture spending?

To address this inquiry, we first survey how stock costs influence interest when all is said in done.

# Chapter Three: Investing in Stock

## The Stock Market and Forex

The way that stock returns foresee venture is entrenched. In this area, we present the four perspectives that can conceivably represent this connection. In the consequent areas, we assess these perspectives exactly.

## The Passive Informant Hypothesis

As per the latent witness perspective on the securities exchange, the market doesn't assume a significant job in apportioning venture reserves.

This view fights that the supervisors of the firm know more than the general population or the econometrician about the speculation openings confronting the firm. The financial exchange, along these lines, doesn't give any data that would enable the administrator to settle on speculation choices. The market may tell the administrator what market members think about the company's ventures, yet that doesn't impact his choices. This "sideshow" perspective on the securities exchange says not just that financial specialist estimation doesn't influence venture, yet in addition that the supervisor doesn't take in anything from the stock cost.

The uninvolved witness speculation suggests that the explanation behind the watched connection between stock returns and ensuing venture development is that the econometrician's data set is littler than the manager's. In the event that the econometrician knew it all that the director does, the variety in speculation could be represented utilizing just the factors known to the supervisor when he chose the amount to contribute. The detached witness speculation has some natural intrigue. It is conceivable that untouchables know next to no about the firm that insiders do not additionally know, since outcasts gather data that is to a great extent given to understanding insiders' activities. Numerous a money related investigator's fundamental duty is conversing with organization administrators. This prevalence of insiders' learning appears to be particularly likely regarding firm-explicit basics, where data about the firm is destined to hit administrators first. One may contend, be that as it may, that the market teaches insiders something new about the future condition of the total economy thus passes on data helpful in settling on speculation choices.

Some help for the aloof witness theory originates from investigations of insider exchanging. Seyhun, for instance, demonstrates that insiders make cash on exchanging their organizations' stock. Also, insiders effectively anticipate both future quirky returns and future market returns, recommending that insiders' unique information causes them with both total and firm-explicit conjectures. Simultaneously, the proof doesn't dismiss the view that despite the fact that insiders can figure a few parts of profits that are firm-explicit, they don't figure different segments.

That is, they can make cash exchanging and still take in something from stock returns. They could possibly utilize this information in settling on speculation choices for their organizations.

## The Active Informant Hypothesis

The dynamic witness theory doles out a more noteworthy job to the financial exchange. It says that stock costs anticipate venture since they pass on to supervisors data valuable in settling on speculation choices. This data can precisely, or erroneously, foresee basics. In any event, when the securities exchange is the best accessible indicator, it can blunder because of the natural unconventionality of the basics, or in light of the fact that stock costs are sullied by supposition that chiefs can't separate from data about essentials. Regardless of whether the securities exchange sends an off base sign, the data may in any case be utilized thus the stock return will impact venture.

The market can pass on an assortment of data that bears on the inborn vulnerability confronting a firm, for example, future total or individual interest. On the other hand, the market can uncover financial specialists' evaluation of the fitness of an association's administrators and their capacity to make wise ventures. Data passed on by stock costs can likewise help settle extraneous or balance vulnerability. For instance, if an economy can be in one of a few unavoidable equilibria, the securities exchange can total convictions go about as a "sunspot' - in regards to which balance is grinding away. Obviously, this sort of job can be played by the total securities exchange just; it's anything but a thought when assessing the reliance of individual firms' choices on their eccentric returns.

Another critical element of stock is its restricted risk, which means that, as a proprietor of a stock, you are not by and by subject if the organization isn't ready to pay its obligations. Different organizations, for example, associations are set up so that if the association fails the lenders can come after the accomplices (investors) by and by and auction their home, vehicle, furniture, and so on. Owning stock implies that, regardless, the greatest worth you can lose is the worth of your venture. Regardless of whether an organization of which you are an investor fails, you can never lose your own advantages.

## Obligation versus Value

For what reason does an organization issue stock? For what reason would the originators share the benefits with a large number of individuals when they could remain quiet about benefits? The explanation is that sooner or later every organization needs to fund-raise. To do this, organizations can either acquire it from someone or raise it by selling some portion of the organization, which is known as giving stock. An organization can acquire by taking an advance from a bank or by giving bonds. The two techniques fit under the umbrella of obligation financing.

Then again, giving stock is called value financing. Giving stock is invaluable for the organization since it doesn't require the organization to pay back the cash or make premium installments en route. All that the investors receive as an end-result of their cash is the expectation that the offers will some time or another be worth more than what they paid for them. The main closeout of a stock, which is given by the privately owned business itself, is known as the first sale of stock (IPO).

It is significant that you comprehend the qualification between an organization financing through obligation and financing through value. At the point when you purchase an obligation venture such as a security, you are ensured the arrival of your cash (the head) alongside guaranteed intrigue installments. This isn't the situation with a value speculation. By turning into a proprietor, you accept the danger of the organization not being fruitful - similarly as an entrepreneur isn't ensured an arrival, nor is an investor. As a proprietor, your case on resources is not as much as that of lenders. This implies if an organization fails and exchanges, you, as an investor, don't get any cash until the banks and bondholders have been paid out; we call this outright need. Investors acquire a ton if an organization is fruitful, however they additionally remain to lose their whole speculation if the organization isn't effective.

**Danger of Stock on Forex and Online Trading**

It must be accentuated that there are no ensures with regards to person stocks. A few organizations pay out profits, yet numerous others don't. Also, there is no commitment to pay out profits in any event, for those organizations that have generally given them. Without profits, a financial specialist can profit on a stock just through its gratefulness in the open market. On the drawback, any stock may fail, in which case your venture merits nothing.

In spite of the fact that hazard may sound all negative, there is likewise a splendid side. Going out on a limb requests a more noteworthy profit for your speculation. This is the motivation behind why stocks have generally beated different speculations, for example, securities or investment accounts. Over the long haul, an interest in stocks has generally had a normal return of around 10-12%.

# Chapter Four: Day and Swing Trading.

**Various Types of Stocks**

There are two principle sorts of stocks: regular stock and favored stock.

**Regular/Common Stock**

Regular stock is, well, normal. At the point when individuals talk about stocks they are for the most part alluding to this sort. Actually, most of stock is given is in this structure. We essentially went over highlights of basic stock in the last area. Normal offers speak to proprietorship in an organization and a case (profits) on a bit of benefits. Speculators get one vote for every offer to choose the board individuals, who administer the significant choices made by the executives.

Over the long haul, regular stock, by methods for capital development, yields better yields than pretty much every other venture. This better yield includes some significant pitfalls since basic stocks involve the most hazard. On the off chance that an organization fails and exchanges, the regular investors won't get cash until the leasers, bondholders and favored investors are paid.

**Favored Stock**

Favored stock speaks somewhat of proprietorship in an organization yet ordinarily doesn't accompany a similar democratic rights. (This may differ contingent upon the organization.) With favored offers, financial specialists are typically ensured a fixed profit until the end of time. This is unique in relation to basic stock, which has variable profits that are never ensured. Another bit of leeway is that in case of liquidation, favored investors are satisfied before the normal investor (yet at the same time after obligation holders). Favored stock may likewise be callable, implying that the organization has the choice to buy the offers from investors at whenever in any way, shape or form (generally for a premium).

A few people consider favored stock to be more similar to obligation than value. A decent approach to think about these sorts of offers is to consider them to be being in the middle of bonds what's more, typical offers.

# Chapter Five: Investing Strategies

## How Stocks Trade

Most stocks are exchanged on trades, which are places where purchasers and dealers meet and settle on a cost. A few trades are physical areas where exchanges are done on an exchanging floor. You've presumably observed photos of an exchanging floor, in which dealers are fiercely hurling their arms, waving, shouting, and motioning to one another. The other sort of trade is virtual, made out of a system of PCs where exchanges are made electronically. The motivation behind a financial exchange is to encourage the trading of protections among purchasers and dealers, lessening the dangers of contributing. Simply envision how troublesome it is sell shares on the off chance that you needed to call around the area attempting to discover a purchaser. Extremely, a financial exchange is simply a super-refined ranchers' market connecting purchasers and venders.

Before we go on, we ought to recognize the essential market and the optional market. The essential market is the place protections are made (by methods of an IPO) while, in the auxiliary market, financial specialists exchange already gave protections without the contribution of the giving organizations. The optional market is the thing that individuals are alluding to when they talk about the financial exchange. Understand that the exchanging of an organization's stock doesn't legitimately include that organization.

## The New York Stock Exchange

The most lofty trade on the planet is the New York Stock Exchange (NYSE). The "Enormous Board" was established more than 200 years back in 1792 with the consenting to of the Buttonwood Arrangement by 24 New York City stockbrokers and vendors. Right now the NYSE, with stocks like General Electric, McDonald's, Citigroup, Coca-Cola, Gillette and Wal-store, is the market of decision for the biggest organizations in America.

The NYSE is the principal kind of trade (as we alluded to above), where a significant part of the exchanging is done up close and personal on an exchanging floor. This is additionally alluded to as a recorded trade. Requests come in through business firms that are individuals from the trade and stream down to floor dealers who go to a particular spot on the floor where the stock exchanges. At this area, known as the exchanging post, there is a particular individual known as the pro whose activity is to coordinate purchasers and merchants. Costs are resolved utilizing a closeout technique: the present cost is the most elevated sum any purchaser is happy to pay and the least cost at which somebody is ready to sell. When an exchange has been made, the subtleties are sent back to the financier firm, who at that point informs the speculator who submitted the request. In spite of the fact that there is human contact in this procedure, don't feel that the NYSE is still in the stone age: PCs assume a tremendous job all the while.

## The Nasdaq

The second kind of trade is the virtual sort brought an over-the-counter (OTC) showcase, of which the Nasdaq is the most well-known. These business sectors have no focal area or floor merchants at all. Exchanging is done through a PC and broadcast communications system of sellers. It used to be that the biggest organizations were recorded distinctly on the NYSE while all other second level stocks exchanged on different trades. The tech blast of the late '90s changed this; presently the Nasdaq is home to a few major innovation organizations, for example, Microsoft, Cisco, Intel, Dell and Oracle. This has brought about the Nasdaq turning into a genuine contender to the NYSE.

On the Nasdaq businesses go about as market creators for different stocks. A market producer gives nonstop offer and ask costs inside an endorsed rate spread for offers for which they are assigned to make a market. They may coordinate purchasers and merchants legitimately however for the most part they will keep up a stock of offers to fulfill needs of speculators.

## Other form of Exchanges

The third biggest trade in the U.S. is the American Stock Exchange (AMEX). The AMEX used to be an option in contrast to the NYSE, however that job has since been filled by the Nasdaq. Indeed, the National Association of Securities Dealers (NASD), which is the parent of Nasdaq, purchased the AMEX in 1998. Practically all exchanging now on the AMEX is in little top stocks and subsidiaries.

There are many stock trades situated in pretty much every nation around the world. American markets are without a doubt the biggest, however despite everything they speak to as it were a small amount of absolute speculation around the world. The two other primary budgetary center points are London, home of the London Stock Exchange, and Hong Kong, home of the

Hong Kong Stock Exchange. The last spot worth referencing is the over-the-counter announcement board (OTCBB). The Nasdaq is an over-the-counter market, yet the term regularly alludes to little open organizations that don't meet the posting prerequisites of any of the managed markets, including the Nasdaq. The OTCBB is home to penny stocks in light of the fact that there is practically zero guideline. This makes putting resources into an OTCBB stock unsafe.

The proof displayed in the paper doesn't give solid help to the view that securities exchange wastefulness, to the degree that it exists, has a monetarily critical effect on business venture. At the point when different determinants of venture are controlled for, share costs don't appear to clarify a great part of the variety in interest in any of the G7 nations. For certain nations, there is proof that a gauge of the part of offer costs not identified with accessible data is corresponded with venture to a measurably critical degree. Be that as it may, the extent of this relationship is too little to ever be important monetarily, and the plan of the tests are one-sided towards such a finding.

There are various potential clarifications of these outcomes. The first is that offer costs may basically condense data effectively accessible to supervisors. They will at that point be associated with, however not a causal effect on, speculation. Offer costs will be high and speculation development increasingly fast in those occasions when venture prospects are great just in light of the fact that this is useful for both value markets and venture. The second is that supervisors may basically disregard momentary changes in costs on the off chance that they don't harmonize with their perspective on fundamental prospects. Financial exchanges may give false flag however these sign are disregarded. At long last, the executives may react to these bogus flag essentially by rebuilding their accounting reports instead of by adjusting genuine choices. The Japanese experience priqr to 1990, when a drawn out decrease in Japanese value markets started, is by all accounts a case of this. The quick run-up of value costs in 1988 and 1989 supported huge scale value financing, both straightforwardly and by implication as value warrants connected to bond issues. This was not, in any case, utilized exclusively to expand acquisition of fixed venture. Or maybe, money related resources were obtained. It has been proposed that one purpose behind this was enterprises seen high value costs as transitory and hence didn't consider them figurings of the long haul cost of capital utilized for settling on choices about fixed speculation.

Money related venture is the responsibility of assets for a future return, in this manner speculation might be comprehended as a movement that submits assets in any monetary or physical structure within the sight of a desire for accepting extra return in future. In the present setting of portfolio the executives, the venture is viewed as money related speculation, which infer work of assets with the target of understanding extra pay or development in estimation of venture at a future date. Contributing includes very traditionalist situation just as theory the field of speculation includes the investigation of venture process. Speculation is worried about the administration of a financial specialists' riches which is the whole of current pay and the present estimation of every future salary.

In this content speculation alludes to monetary resources. Budgetary ventures are duties of assets to determine salary in type of intrigue, profit premium, annuity advantages or gratefulness in the estimation of introductory speculation. Subsequently the acquisition of offers, debentures post office reserve funds endorsements and protection strategies all are money related speculations. Such venture produces money related resources.

These exercises are embraced by anyone who wants an arrival, and is willing to acknowledge the hazard from the money related instruments.

Venture VERSES SPECULATION:

Frequently venture is comprehended as an equivalent word of hypothesis. Venture and hypothesis are somewhat extraordinary but then comparable in light of the fact that theory requires a speculation and venture are at in case some what theoretical.

Likely the most ideal approach to make a differentiation among venture and hypothesis is by thinking about the job of desire. Ventures are typically made with the desire that a specific stream of salary or a specific value that has existed won't change later on.

Where as theory are normally founded on the desire that some change will happen in future, there by coming about an arrival.

Along these lines a normal change is the reason for hypothesis however not for speculation. A venture likewise can be recognized from hypothesis when skyline of the speculator and regularly by the hazard return normal for speculation. A genuine speculator is keen on a decent and predictable pace of return for an extensive stretch of time. Conversely, the examiner looks for circumstances encouraging huge return earned inside a brief timeframe because of evolving condition. Theory includes a more elevated level of hazard and an increasingly questionable desire for returns, which isn't really the situation with speculation.

The distinguishing proof of these qualifications of these differentiations characterizes the job of the financial specialist and the examiner in the market. The financial specialist can be said to be keen on a decent pace of return of a reliable premise over a generally longer length. For this reason the speculator processes the genuine worth of the security before putting resources into it. The theorist looks for enormous comes back from the market rapidly. For an examiner, showcase desires and value developments are the fundamental variables affecting a purchase or sell choice. Theory, in this manner, is more unsafe than venture.

In any stock trade, there are two primary classifications of theorists called the bulls and bears. A bull purchases partakes in the desire for selling them at a more significant expense. When there is a bullish inclination in the market, share costs will in general go up since the interest for the offers is high. A bear sells partakes in the desire for a fall in cost with the aim of purchasing the offers at a lower cost at a future date. These bearish inclinations bring about a fall in the cost of offers.

An offer market needs both venture and theoretical exercises.

Theoretical action adds to the market liquidity. A more extensive dispersion of investors makes it fundamental for a market to exist.

Speculation PROCESS

A sorted out perspective on the speculation procedure includes dissecting the fundamental nature of venture choices and sorting out the exercises in the choice process.

Venture procedure is administered by the two significant aspects of venture they are hazard and return. In this way, we initially think about these two fundamental parameters that are of basic significance to all financial specialists and the exchange off that exists between anticipated return and hazard.

Given the establishment for settling on venture choices the exchange off between expected return and hazard we next consider the choice procedure in speculations as today is commonly rehearsed. Albeit various separate choices must be made, for authoritative purposes, this choice procedure has generally been isolated into a two stage process: security examination and portfolio the board. Security examination includes the valuation of protections, while portfolio the board includes the administration of a financial specialist's speculation determinations as a portfolio (bundle of benefits), with its very own one of a kind attributes.

Security Analysis

Conventional venture investigation, when applied to protections, underlines the projection of costs and profits. That is, the potential cost of a company's regular stock and the future profit stream are guage, at that point limited back to the present. This natural worth is then contrasted and the security's present market cost. On the off chance that the present market cost is underneath the characteristic worth, a buy is prescribed, and if the other way around is the situation deal is suggested.

Albeit current security examination is profoundly established in the crucial ideas simply sketched out, the accentuation has moved. The more present day way to deal with normal stock investigation underscores return and hazard appraises instead of minor cost and profit gauges.

Portfolio Management

Portfolios are mixes of advantages. In this content, portfolios comprise of accumulations of protections. Customary portfolio arranging underlines on the character and the hazard bearing limit of the financial specialist. For instance, a youthful, forceful, single grown-up should purchase stocks in more up to date, dynamic, quickly developing firms. A resigned widow should buy stocks and bonds in old-line, set up, stable firms, for example, utilities.

Present day portfolio hypothesis proposes that the conventional way to deal with portfolio examination, determination, and the executives may yield not exactly ideal outcomes. Thus an increasingly logical methodology is required, in light of appraisals of hazard and return of the portfolio and the frames of mind of the financial specialist toward a hazard return exchange off coming from the examination of the individual protections.

# Chapter Six: Exchange Traded Funds

Qualities of Investment

The qualities of venture can be comprehended as far as

- Return,

- Hazard,

- Wellbeing,

- Liquidity and so on.

Return: All ventures are described by the desire for an arrival. Truth be told, ventures are made with the essential goal of inferring return. The desire for an arrival might be from salary (yield) just as through capital appreciation. Capital gratefulness is the contrast between the deal cost and the price tag. The desire for come back from a venture relies on the idea of speculation, development period, showcase request, etc.

Hazard: Risk is inborn in any speculation. Hazard may identify with loss of capital, delay in reimbursement of capital, delinquency of return or changeability of profits.

The danger of a venture is dictated by the speculations, development period, reimbursement limit, nature of profit duty thus for.

Hazard and expected return of a venture are connected. Hypothetically, the higher the hazard, higher is the normal returned. The better yield is a pay expected by speculators for their eagerness to endure the higher hazard.

Security: The wellbeing of venture is related to the sureness of return of capital without loss of time or cash. Wellbeing is another component that a financial specialist wants from ventures. Each financial specialist hopes to get back the underlying capital on development immediately.

Liquidity: A venture that is effectively able to sell without loss of cash or time is said to be fluid. An all around created auxiliary market for security increment the liquidity of the speculation. A financial specialist will in general incline toward amplification of anticipated return, minimization of hazard, well-being of assets and liquidity of venture.

Speculation classifications:

Speculation by and large includes duty of assets in two sorts of advantages:

- Real resources

- Financial resources

Genuine resources: Real resources are unmistakable material things like building, autos, land, gold and so on.

Money related resources: Financial resources are bit of paper speaking to a roundabout guarantee to genuine resources held by another person. These bits of paper speak to obligation or then again value responsibility as IOUs or stock endorsements. Interests in budgetary resources comprise of –

- Scrutinized (for example security types of) speculation

- Non-protections speculation

The term 'protections' utilized in the broadest sense, comprises of those papers which are cited and are transferable. Under area 2 (h) of the Securities Contract (Regulation) Act, 1956 (SCRA) 'protections' include:

I) Shares, scrip's, stocks, securities, debentures, debenture stock or other attractive protections of a like sort in or of any joined organization or other body corporate.

ii) Government protections.

iii) Such different instruments as might be pronounced by the focal Government as protections, and,

iv) Rights of interests in protections.

In this way, in the above setting, security types of ventures incorporate Equity shares, inclination shares, debentures, government securities, Units of UTI and other Mutual Funds, and value offers and obligations of Public Sector Undertakings (PSUs). Non-security types of ventures incorporate each one of those speculations, which are not cited in any financial exchange and are not unreservedly attractive. viz., bank stores, corporate stores, post office stores, National Savings and other little investment funds declarations and plans, fortunate assets, and protection strategies. Another mainstream interest in physical resources, for example, Gold, Silver, Diamonds, Real home, Antiques and so on. Indian financial specialists have constantly believed the physical advantages for be very appealing ventures. There are an enormous number of venture roads for savers in India. Some of them are attractive and fluid, while others are non attractive, Some of them are exceptionally unsafe while some others are nearly hazard less. The speculator needs to pick appropriate roads from among them, contingent upon his particular need, hazard inclination, and return desire. Speculation roads can be comprehensively classified under the accompanying heads: -

1.Corporate protections

. Value shares .Preference shares

. Debentures/Bonds . GDRs/ADRs

. Warrants . Subsidiaries

2.Deposits in banks and non-banking organizations

3.Post office stores and endorsements

4.Life protection arrangements

5.Provident reserve plans

6.Government and semi government protections

7.Mutual store plans

8.Real resources

CORPORATE SECURITIES

Business entities in the private division issue corporate protections. These incorporate value shares, inclination offers, and debentures. Value offers have variable profit and thus have a place with the high hazard exceptional yield classification; inclination offers and debentures have fixed comes back with lower chance. The order of corporate protections that can be picked as speculation roads can be delineated as demonstrated as follows.

Value Shares-: By putting resources into shares, financial specialists fundamentally purchase the possession right to that organization. At the point when the organization makes benefits, investors get a lot of the benefits as profits. Moreover, when an organization performs well and the future desire from the organization is exceptionally high, the cost of the organization's offers goes up in the market. This enables investors to sell shares at benefit, prompting capital additions. Speculators can put resources into shares either through essential market contributions or in the optional market. Value offers can be arranged in various manners yet we will utilize the phrasing of Investors.

It ought to be noticed that the line of boundary between the classes are not clear
what's more, such characterization are not totally unrelated.

Blue Chips (likewise called Stalwarts) : These are supplies of high caliber, monetarily solid organizations which are typically the pioneers in their industry.

They are steady and developed organizations. They pay great profits consistently and the market cost of the offers doesn't vacillate generally. Models are supplies of Colgate, Pond's Hindustan Lever, TELCO, Mafatlal Industries and so forth. Development Stocks: Growth stocks are organizations whose income per offer is becomes quicker than the economy and at a rate higher than that of a normal firm in a similar industry. Regularly, the income are furrowed back so as to utilize them for financing development. They put resources into innovative work and broaden with a forceful showcasing strategy. They are confirm by high and solid EPS. Models are ITC, Dr. Reddy's Bajaj Auto, Sathyam Computers and Infosys Technologies ect.. The high development stocks are frequently called " Glamor STOCK' or HIGH FLYERS'.

Pay Stocks: An organization that pays an enormous profit comparative with the market cost is called a pay stock. They are additionally called cautious stocks. Medication, nourishment and open utility industry offers are viewed as salary stocks. Costs of pay stocks are not as unpredictable as development stocks.

Patterned Stocks: Cyclical stocks are organizations whose income vary with the business cycle. Patterned stocks by and large have a place with framework or capital merchandise businesses, for example, general designing, auto, bond, paper, development and so on. Their offer costs additionally rise and fall pair with the exchange cycles.

Markdown Stocks: Discount stocks are those that are cited or esteemed beneath their presumptive estimations. These are the portions of wiped out units.

Underestimated Stock: Under esteemed offers are those, which have all the possibility to become development stocks, have excellent essentials and great future, however by one way or another the market is yet to value the offers effectively.

Pivot Stocks: Turn around stocks are those that are not so much doing admirably as in the market cost is well beneath the natural worth for the most part in light of the fact that the organization is experiencing a terrible fix however is en route to recuperation with indications of pivoting the corner in the slick future. Models EID – Parry in 80's, Tata Tea (Tata Finlay), SPIC, Mukand Iron and steel and so on.

Inclination Shares: Preference offers allude to a type of offers that lie in the middle of unadulterated value and obligation. They have the quality of proprietorship rights while holding the benefit of a steady degree of profitability. The cases of these holders convey higher need than that of normal investors however lower than that of obligation holders. These are given to the overall population simply after an open issue of standard offers.

Debentures and Bonds: These are basically long haul obligation instruments.

Numerous sorts of debentures and bonds have been organized to suit financial specialists with distinctive time needs. Despite the fact that having a higher hazard when contrasted with bank fixed stores, bonds, and debentures do offer more significant yields. Debenture venture requires checking the market and picking explicit protections that will take into account the speculation goals of the financial specialists.

Storehouse Receipts (GDRs/ADRs): Global Depositary Receipts are instruments as a depositary receipt or declaration made by the abroad depositary bank outside India and gave to non-occupant speculators against customary offers or Foreign Currency Convertible Bonds (FCCBs) of a giving organization. A GDR gave in America is an American Depositary Receipt (ADR). Among the Indian organizations, Reliance Industries Limited was the main organization to raise assets through a GDR issue. Other than GDRs, ADRs are likewise prevalent in the capital showcase. As financial specialists look to broaden their value property, the alternative of ADRs and GDRs are exceptionally worthwhile. While putting resources into such protections, financial specialists need to distinguish the capitalization and hazard qualities of the instrument and the organization's presentation in its home nation (basic resource).

Warrants: A warrant is an endorsement giving its holder the privilege to buy protections at a stipulated cost inside a predetermined time limit or unendingly.

Now and then a warrant is offered with obligation protections as an instigation to purchase the shares at a last date. The warrant goes about as a worth expansion in light of the fact that the holder of the warrant has the privilege yet not the commitment of putting resources into the value at the demonstrated rate. It tends to be characterized as a long haul call alternative gave by an organization on its offers.

A warrant holder isn't qualified for any profits; neither does he have a democratic right. Be that as it may, the activity cost of a warrant gets balanced for the stock profits or stock parts. On the expiry date, the holder practices a choice to purchase the offers at the foreordained cost. This empowers the speculator to choose whether or not to purchase the offers or sell the obligation from the organization. In the event that the market cost is higher than the activity value, it will be beneficial for the financial specialist to practice the warrant. Then again, if the market value falls underneath the activity value, the warrant holder would like to exchange the obligation of the firm.

Subordinates: The presentation of subsidiary items has been one of the most huge advancements in the Indian capital market. Subordinates are useful hazard the board devices that a speculator needs to take a gander at for diminishing the hazard natural in as venture portfolio. The primary subsidiary item that has been offered in the Indian market is the list future. Other than record prospects, other subsidiary instruments, for example, file alternatives, investment opportunities, have been presented in the market. Stock prospects are exchanged the market consistently and as far as turnover, have surpassed that of other subsidiary instruments. The liquidity in the fates market is packed in not many offers. Hypothetically the contrast between the fates and spot cost ought to mirror the expense of conveying the situation to the eventual fate of basically the intrigue. In this manner, when prospects are exchanging including some hidden costs, it is and sign that members are bullish of the fundamental security and the other way around. Subordinate exchanging is a theoretical action. Be that as it may, speculators need to use the subsidiary market since the chance of diminishing the hazard in value developments is conceivable through interests in subordinate items.

# Chapter Seven: Bonds

Among non-corporate speculations, the most prevalent are stores with banks, for example, investment accounts and fixed stores. Reserve funds stores convey low financing costs while fixed stores convey higher loan fees, shifting with the time of development, Interest is payable quarterly or half-yearly or every year.

Fixed stores may likewise be repeating stores wherein investment funds are saved at normal interims. A few banks have reinvestment plans whereby reserve funds are redeposited at ordinary interims or reinvested as the premium gets accumulated. The head and collected premiums in such venture plans are paid on development.

Investment funds Bank Account with Commercial Banks:

A sheltered, fluid, and advantageous speculation alternative, a reserve funds financial balance is a perfect venture road for saving assets for crises or unforeseen costs. Financial specialists may want to keep a normal parity equivalent to a quarter of a year of their everyday costs. A bank fixed store is prescribed for those searching for safeguarding of capital alongside ebb and flow salary for the time being. Notwithstanding, over the long haul the profits may not keep pace with expansion.

Organization Fixed Deposits:

Numerous organizations have thought of fixed store plans to activate cash for their needs. The organization fixed store market is a dangerous market and should be taken a gander at with alert. RBI has given different guidelines to screen the organization fixed store showcase. In any case, FICO score administrations are accessible to rate the danger of organization fixed store plans.

The development time frame shifts from three to five years. Fixed stores in organizations have a high chance since they are unbound, yet they guarantee more significant yields than bank stores.

Fixed store in non-banking monetary organizations (NBFCs) is another speculation road open to savers. NBFCs incorporate renting organizations, employ buy organizations, venture organizations, chit reserves, etc. Stores in NBFCs convey more significant yields with higher hazard contrasted with bank stores.

Mail station Deposits and Certificates:

The venture roads gave by post workplaces are non-attractive. Notwithstanding, the vast majority of the investment funds conspires in post workplaces appreciate charge concessions. Post workplaces acknowledge reserve funds stores just as fixed stores from the general population.

There is additionally a common store plot that is an instrument of ordinary month to month reserve funds.

National Savings Certificates (NSC) is likewise promoted by present office on speculators. The enthusiasm on the sum contributed is aggravated half-yearly and is payable alongside the head at the hour of development, which is six years from the date of issue.

There are an assortment of mail station reserve funds endorsements that take into account explicit investment funds and speculation prerequisites of speculators and is a hazard free, high yielding venture opportunity. Enthusiasm on these instruments is absolved from personal expense. A portion of these stores are additionally excluded from riches charge.

Disaster protection Policies:

Insurance agencies offer numerous speculation plans to speculators. These plans advance investment funds and furthermore give protection spread. LIC is the biggest extra security organization in India. A portion of its plans incorporate life strategies, convertible entire life affirmation arrangements, gift confirmation approaches, Jeevan Saathi, Money Back Plan, Jeevan Dhara, and Marriage Endowment Plan. Protection strategies, while taking into account the hazard pay to be looked later on by financial specialists, likewise have the benefit of winning a sensible enthusiasm on their venture protection premiums. Life coverage approaches are additionally qualified for exception from annual duty.

Opportune Fund Scheme:

Opportune reserve plans are store plans, appropriate to representatives in people in general and private parts. There are three sorts of fortunate finances appropriate to various divisions of work, to be specific, Statutory Provident Fund, Recognized Provident Fund, and Unrecognized Provident Fund. Notwithstanding these, there is an intentional fortunate reserve conspire that is available to any financial specialist, utilized or not.

This is known as the Public Provident Fund (PPF). Any individual from the general population can join the PPF, which is worked by the State Bank of India

Value Linked Savings Schemes (ELSSs):

Putting resources into ELSSs gets financial specialists an expense refund of the sum contributed. ELSSs are fundamentally development shared assets with a lock-in time of three years. ELSSs have a hazard higher than PPF and NSCs, yet have the capability of giving better yields.

**Benefits Plan:**

Certain told retirement/annuity assets qualifies speculators for an expense refund.

UTI, LIC, and ICICI are some budgetary foundations that offer retirement plans to financial specialists. Government and Semi-Government Securities:

Government and semi-government bodies, for example, the open segment endeavors acquire cash from people in general through the issue of government protections and open division bonds. These are less unsafe roads of speculation on account of the believability of the legislature and government endeavors. The administration issues protections in the currency showcase and in the capital market. Currency market instruments are exchanged the Wholesale Debt Market (WDM) exchanges and retail fragments. Instruments exchanged the currency market are transient instruments, for example, treasury bills and repos. The administration additionally presented the pricatisation program in numerous corporate undertakings and these protections are exchanged the auxiliary market. These are the semi-government protections. PSU stocks have performed well during the years 2003-04 in the capital showcase.

Shared Fund Schemes:

The Unit Trust of India is the primary common store in the nation. Various business banks and budgetary organizations have likewise set up common reserves. Common assets have been set up in the private area too. These common supports offer different speculation plans to financial specialists. The quantity of common subsidizes that have sprung up lately is very enormous and however, on a normal, the shared reserve industry has not been indicating great returns, select assets have performed reliably, guaranteeing the financial specialist better returns and lower chance choices.

Genuine ASSETS

Interests in genuine resources are additionally made when the normal returns are exceptionally alluring. Land, gold, silver, money, and different ventures, for example, workmanship are additionally treated as speculations since the desire from holding of such resources is related with better yields.

Land: Buying property is a similarly strenuous speculation choice. Land speculation is regularly connected with the future advancement plans of the area. It is critical to check the worthwhile choosing to buy a versatile/steady property other than structures. Other than making an individual evaluation from the market, the help of government-affirmed valuers may likewise be looked for. A valuation report sign the estimation of the every one of the significant resources and furthermore the premise and way of valuation can be acquired from an affirmed valuer against the installment of a charge. In the event of a ranch, a valuation report may likewise be acquired from perceived private valuers.

# Chapter Eight: Mutual Funds

**Mutual Fund Trade Market.**

What are being traded on this market are not stocks or securities, however monetary forms (monies) from around the globe.

As it were, the Forex market is where U.S. dollars, Euros, Yen and other significant monetary standards are purchased and sold. It speaks to the biggest money related market on the planet by volume.

The roots of the remote trade market go back to 1944, when The United Nations Monetary Fund met in Bretton Woods, New Hampshire to devise an arrangement for balancing out the world economy.

The British Pound had been, up until World War II, the financial unit of decision when looking at the general estimation of remote monetary forms. Be that as it may, Hitler's system figured out how to downgrade the Pound by method for a gigantic forging plan. Something must be done rapidly so as to deflect an overall financial downturn.

Out of this gathering came the Bretton Woods Accord. This new strategy executed the Gold Standard, tying the worth the U.S. Dollar to the cost of one ounce of gold ($35.00 per ounce at the time). It was additionally concurred that the Dollar would supplant the British Pound as the benchmark "money of trade".

Every single other cash were adjusted to the Dollar, and a 'fixed conversion scale" of +/ - 1% was built up.

At the end of the day, an outside money could change up to a limit of 1% higher or lower than the Dollar. Any vacillations past this breaking point required that the 'culpable' country's national bank step in to address the unevenness.

The Bretton Woods accord stayed as a result until 1971, when it was resolved that the U.S. dollar could never again hold consistent comparative with gold. As of now, the 'fixed conversion scale' model was surrendered for the 'drifting swapping scale' despite everything we use today.

The significant thing to see right presently is that Forex exchanging among private speculators is still moderately new. The market once worked only between government (national) banks and business banks until advances in correspondence, for example, the Internet and PC banking, permitted examiners simpler access to the market.

The Forex Market today speaks to the biggest and most 'fluid' of all business sectors on the planet.

The day by day 'turnover' of exchange volume, talking in U.S. dollar terms, is on the request for trillions.

The significant players associated with these exchanges are:

- Banks

- Governments

- Speculators

- Corporations

- Other, related budgetary markets and establishments (e.g., merchants)

Presently, one of the main things you should comprehend is that these establishments are NOT all on a level playing field with each other.

As it were, not all Forex dealers have equivalent access to similar costs. The offer cost and asking cost (otherwise called the "spread") between monetary forms is to a limited extent dictated by the size and volume of the exchange.

The more cash an exchanging substance can put on hold, the better the 'spread'.

As you may gather, the focal and world financial organizations (the 'between bank' advertise) are at the highest point of the level. They are pursued next by governments and enormous monetary establishments or organizations.

The short response to this inquiry is: they don't. Not all alone. Singular dealers like you and I are known as "Retail Traders", and must experience retail business firms so as to purchase and sell monetary standards on the outside trade showcase.

You should know in advance that online retail exchanging by people (spoke to by online retail agents) is still in its early stages. Preceding the Internet, and ensuing accessibility of ongoing business sector information, it was basically outlandish for the normal individual to engage in the remote trade advertise with any level of progress enroute as you purchase and sell stocks. Everything has been mechanized and connected up electronically.

In light of a legitimate concern for total honesty, you ought to likewise realize that Forex exchanging isn't as direct as exchanging stocks on the stock trade. There are many, numerous factors to mull over with regards to deciding vacillations in cash esteems. There is a great deal of 'language' to learn, and a decent amount of complex ideas which must be aced.

Lamentably, there are deceitful organizations out there who exploit this 'expectation to absorb information', and endeavor to trick would-be retail dealers. Forex opportunity tricks are as yet common - a few evaluations place the number as high as 90%.

Thusly, it is basic that you gain proficiency with the nuts and bolts of Forex before you get included with any 'propelled' instructional classes, exchanging frameworks or online merchants!

While a full intense training on Forex is past the extent of this report, you will become familiar with the essentials here. I can't make you a specialist, however I can give you the learning you have to settle on an educated choice about whether to get included - and whether the retail intermediary you're managing is ok.

This guide will show you the outright nuts and bolts of Forex. You'll gain proficiency with the basic ideas what's more, terms associated with a normal exchange, just as...

- How cash esteems are resolved

- How and why cash esteems are relative

- Why cash is exchanged 'sets', and what that implies

- The distinction between the 'offer cost' and the 'solicit cost' of a money

The connection between 'Pips', 'Parcel Sizes' and 'Spreads', and what every one of those methods

- What your representative methods by 'influence', 'usable edge' and 'edge calls'

- Factors influencing money valuations

- Where to get more data

Envision that you're going out traveling to France. You have $1,000 U.S. dollars to spend on nourishment, transportation, gifts and visits. You're a shrewd voyager, however, so you don't need to convey the majority of that $1,000 as money in either cash.

Rather, you put $500 into explorer's checks for safety's sake, and convert the remaining $500 into Euros (the Franc was supplanted by the Euro at the development of the European Association, of which France is a part).

On the real day that you go to get your cash changed over, the remote swapping scale is

set at 1 US Dollar = 0.68679 Euro. This rate is the authority, interbank rate for severe cash to money changes.

After you crunch the numbers, you see that your $500 in U.S. Dollars transforms into a negligible $343.397 Euro. Ouch! You've quite recently endured a shot as much as $156.60 immediately in term of purchasing control, despite the fact that you haven't spent a penny. What was the deal?

What's happened is that the Euro was more grounded than the Dollar at the time you made the trade. Your Dollar wasn't worth as much as the Euro. Hence, you couldn't buy 500 Euro with 500 Dollars.

Remember, be that as it may, this wouldn't really confine your purchasing power. The amount you need to spend while in France relies upon the typical cost for basic items. For instance, if what might be compared to a $15 dinner in the U.S. is just $12 in France, you may spare enough to counterbalance the hit you took on the conversion standard.

Presently, recall that you're a savvy explorer. You stay aware of the budgetary markets, and check the conversion scale every day of your outing. On the third day, you see that the Dollar is proceeding to debilitate against the Euro.

You choose to feel free to money out your explorer's checks before things deteriorate, at a pace of 1 US Dollar = 0.67679 Euro. This gives you $338.395 extra Euro.

When your outing closes, you've burned through the greater part of the $343.39 you accompanied, yet at the same time have the $333.39 you changed over from explorer's checks. Suppose you have an even 400 Euro with you on the excursion home, just to make things simple.

You set the cash away when you return home, and continue watching the market. Half a month pass by.

Abruptly, the news reports that a significant mid-east oil arrangement has mobilized and fortified the Dollar, bringing the swapping scale to: 1 US Dollar = 0.72679 Euro. Bingo! It's an ideal opportunity to uncover those 400 Euros from underneath the sock cabinet, and go repurchase your Dollars.

After the trade is done, you have $550.36. Remember - you began with $1,000 and lost $156.60 of it immediately, leaving you with what could be compared to $843.40. You burned through $449.64 of that on your excursion, so you ought to actually just have 393.76 left.

You don't, however. You have $550.36 on the grounds that the Euros you returned home with purchased a greater number of dollars than you initially held.

This speaks to the least difficult benefit on a trade of monetary standards, just as the most natural thought behind the Forex idea: purchase low and sell high.

Presently, while this model is agent, it isn't completely exact.
Elements impact hazard: What makes monetary resources hazardous. Customarily, speculators have discussed a few components causing danger, for example, business disappointment, advertise vacillations, change in the loan fee swelling in the economy, variances in return rates changes in the political circumstance and so on. In view of the components influencing the hazard the hazard can be comprehended in following habits Interest rate chance: The changeability in a security return coming about because of changes in the degree of loan fees is alluded to as financing cost chance. Such changes for the most part influence protections contrarily, that is different things being equivalent, security value move conversely to loan cost.

Market chance: The changeability in returns coming about because of vacillations in generally showcase that is, the concur get financial exchange is alluded to as market hazard. Market hazard incorporates a wide scope of variables exogenous to protections them selves, similar to downturn, wars, basic changes in the economy, and changes in customer inclination. The danger of going down with the market development is known as market hazard.

Swelling hazard: Inflation in the economy likewise impacts the hazard innate in speculation. It might likewise bring about the arrival from speculation not coordinating the pace of increment when all is said in done value level (expansion). The adjustment in the swelling rate likewise changes the utilization design and thus speculation return conveys an extra hazard. This hazard is identified with loan cost chance, since financing cost by and large ascent as swelling increments, since banks requests extra expansion premium to make up for the loss of buying power.

Business hazard: The progressions that occur in an industry and nature causes chance for the organization in winning the operational income makes business chance. For instance the conventional phone industry faces significant changes today in the quickly changing media transmission industry and the cell phones. When an organization neglects to procure through its tasks because of changes in the business circumstances prompting disintegration of capital, there by faces the business hazard.

Budgetary chance: The utilization of obligation financing by the organization to fund a bigger extent of advantages causes bigger fluctuation in comes back to the speculators in the essences of various business circumstance. During success the speculators get better yield than the normal return the organization wins, yet during trouble speculators faces plausibility of fluctuate low return or in the most pessimistic scenario disintegration of capital which causes the budgetary hazard. The bigger the extent of advantages fund by obligation (instead of value) the bigger the inconstancy of profits hence ale the money related hazard.

Liquidity hazard: A speculation that can be purchased or sold rapidly without critical value concession is viewed as fluid. The more vulnerability about the time component and the value concession the more prominent the liquidity chance. The liquidity hazard is the hazard related with the specific optional market in which a security exchanges.

Swapping scale chance: The adjustment in the conversion standard causes an adjustment in the estimation of remote possessions, outside exchange, and the benefit of the organizations, there by comes back to the financial specialists. The swapping scale hazard is material principally to the organizations who work directs. The conversion scale hazard is only the changeability in the arrival on security brought about by monetary forms vacillation.

Political hazard: Political chance additionally alluded, as nation hazard is the hazard caused because of progress in government strategies that influences business possibilities there by return to the speculators. Approach changes in the assessment structure, concession and toll of obligation to items, unwinding or fixing of remote exchange relations and so on convey a hazard part that changes the arrival example of the business.

Sorts OF RISK

Hitherto, our dialog has concerned the all out danger of an advantage, which is one significant thought in speculation investigation. Anyway present day venture investigation arranges the conventional wellsprings of hazard recognized already as causing changeability in returns into two general sorts: those that are unavoidable in nature, for example, advertise hazard or loan cost chance, and those that are explicit to a specific security issue, for example, business or money related hazard.

In this manner, we should think about these two classifications of all out hazard. The accompanying exchange presents these terms. Partitioning absolute hazard in to its two segments, a general (advertise) part and a particular (issue ) segment, we have methodical hazard and unsystematic chance which are added substance:

All out hazard = general chance + explicit chance = market chance + guarantor chance = deliberate chance + non precise chance

Orderly chance: Variability in a protections all out return that is legitimately related with by and large minute in the general market or economy is called as methodical chance. This hazard can't be maintained a strategic distance from or wiped out by differentiating the speculation.

Typically broadening wipes out a piece of the complete hazard the left over after expansion is the non-diversifiable bit of the all out hazard or market chance.

For all intents and purposes all protections have some methodical hazard in light of the fact that precise hazard straightforwardly includes the financing cost, market and swelling hazard. The speculator can't get away from this piece of the hazard, on the grounds that regardless of how well the individual differentiates, the danger of the general market can't be stayed away from. On the off chance that the financial exchange decreases pointedly, most stock will be antagonistically influenced, in the event that it rises unequivocally, most stocks will acknowledge in esteem. Obviously imprint hazard is basic to all financial specialists.

Non-precise hazard: Variability in a security absolute return not identified with generally showcase inconstancy is called un efficient (non advertise) chance. This hazard is one of a kind to a specific security and is related with so much factors as business, and budgetary hazard, just as liquidity chance. Albeit all protections will in general have some non-deliberate hazard, it is commonly associated with regular stocks.

# Chapter Nine: Options Trading

Estimating RETURNS:

Return is the out happened to a speculation. Estimation of return possesses a vital significance in speculation investigation as the venture is attempted so as to get returns in future.

All out Return

A right returns measure must consolidate the two parts of return, yield and value changes. Returns crosswise over time or from various protections can be estimated and analyzed utilizing the complete return idea. Officially, the all out return (TR) for a given holding period is a decimal (or rate) number relating all the incomes got by a financial specialist during any ideal timespan to the price tag of the advantage. All out return is characterized as:

TR = any money installments got + Price changes over the period

Cost at which the advantage is obtained

Every one of the things are estimated in rupees. The value change over the period, characterized as the distinction between the start (or price tag) and the closure (or deal) cost, can be either positive (deals value surpasses price tag), negative (price tag surpasses deals cost), or zero. The money installments can be either positive or zero. Mesh the two things in the numerator together and partitioning by the price tag brings about a decimal return figure that can without much of a stretch be changed over into rate structure. Note that in utilizing the TR, the two parts of return, yield and value change have been estimated.

The incomes for bonds originate from the intrigue installments got, and that for a stock wants the profits got. For certain advantages, for example, warrant or a stock that pays no profits, there is just a value change. Albeit one year is regularly utilized for comfort, the TR count can be applied to times of any length.

In rundown, the absolute return idea is significant as a proportion of return since it is comprehensive estimating the complete return per rupees of unique venture. Complete return is the fundamental proportion of the real profit earned by speculators for any money related resources for a particular timeframe. It encourages the examination of advantage returns over a predetermined period whether the correlation is of various resources, for example, stocks versus bonds, or of various protections must be sold inside a similar kind, for example, a few regular socks.

Geometric mean is a superior proportion of the adjustment in riches over the past. It is a regressive looking idea, estimating the acknowledged compound pace of return at which cash developed over a particular period.

Estimating RISK:

Hazard is frequently connected with the scattering in the conceivable results. Scattering alludes to fluctuation. It is accepted to emerge out of inconstancy, which is reliable with our meaning of hazard as the opportunity that the genuine result of a speculation will vary from the normal result. In the event that a benefits' arrival has no inconstancy, basically it has no hazard. Consequently a one-year treasury bill obtained to yield 10 percent and held to development will, actually, yield (an ostensible) 10 percent.

No other result is conceivable, notwithstanding default by the administration, which isn't thought about a sensible probability.

STANDARD DEVIATION:

The hazard can be estimated with an outright proportion of scattering, or inconstancy. The most normally utilized proportion of scattering over some time of years is the standard deviation, which estimates the deviation of every perception from the number juggling mean of the perceptions and is a dependable proportion of inconstancy, since all the data in an example is utilized.

The standard deviation is a proportion of the absolute danger of a benefit or a portfolio. It catches the all-out fluctuation in the benefits or portfolio's arrival, whatever the source(s) of that inconstancy.

In synopsis, the standard deviation of return estimates the all-out danger of one security or the all-out danger of an arrangement of protections. The recorded standard deviation can be determined for singular protections or arrangement of protections utilizing TRs for some predetermined timeframe. This ex post worth is helpful in assessing the complete hazard for a specific verifiable period and in evaluating the all-out hazard that is relied upon to beat some future period.

Basic STOCK VALUATION:

The utilization of present-esteem hypothesis by bond and favored stock financial specialists is settled. The valuation assignment is moderately clear since advantages are commonly steady and sensibly certain. One manages perpetuities, or unbounded life protections with consistent profit receipts, with straight favored stock. Bonds speak to consistent pay streams with a limited, quantifiable life Common-stock valuation is diverse in light of the fact that income and profit streams are unsure with regards to the planning of receipt and the measure of the profit.

The estimation of a typical stock at any minute in time can be thought of as the limited estimation of a progression of dubious future profits that may develop or decay at different rates after some time. The more hypothetical present-esteem way to deal with regular stock valuation will be contrasted and the more conventional and down to business capitalization or multiplier approach in the following a few areas.

What befell income? We naturally feel that income ought to merit something, regardless of whether they are paid out as profits or not, and wonder why they don't show up in the valuation condition. Truth be told, they do show up in the condition yet in the right structure. Profit can be utilized for one of two purposes: they can be paid out to investors as profits or they can be reinvested the firm. In the event that they are reinvested in the firm they should bring about expanded future profit and expanded future profits. To the degree profit whenever, state time t are paid out to investors, they are estimated by the term 'Dt' and to the degree they are held in the firm and utilized beneficially they are reflected in future profits and should bring about future profits being bigger than Dt .To limit the future income stream of a portion of stock would be twofold checking since we would tally held income both when they were earned and when they, or the profit from their reinvestment, were later paid to investors.

The consistent development model is frequently guarded as the model that emerges from the supposition that the firm will keep up a steady profit strategy (keep its standard for dependability steady) and gain a steady profit for new value speculation after some time.

By what means may the single time frame model be utilized to choose stocks? One route is to foresee one year from now's profits, the association's long haul development rate, and the pace of return investors require for holding the stock. The condition could then be unraveled at the hypothetical cost of the stock that could be contrasted and its present cost. Stocks that have hypothetical costs over their real cost are possibility for procurement; those with hypothetical costs beneath their real cost are contender available to be purchased.

Another approach to utilize the methodology is to discover the pace of return understood in the cost at which the stock is currently selling. These should be possible by substituting the present value, assessed profit, and evaluated development rate into a condition and unraveling for the rebate rate that compares the present cost with the normal progression of future profits. In the event that this rate is higher than the pace of return thought about proper for the stock, given its hazard, it is a possibility for procurement.

It appears to be coherent to accept that organizations that have developed at a high rate won't keep on doing so limitlessly. Also, firms with poor development may improve later on. While a solitary development rate can be discovered that will create a similar incentive as a progressively mind boggling design, it is so difficult to assess this single number, and the resultant valuation is so delicate to this number numerous experts have been hesitant to utilize the steady development model without adjustment.

Two-Stage Growth:

The most intelligent further augmentation of the steady development model is to accept that a time of remarkable development (positive or negative) will proceed for a specific number of years, after which development will change to a level at which it is relied upon to proceed uncertainly. Firms normally experience life cycles; during part of these cycles their development is a lot quicker than that of the economy all in all. Car makers in the mid 1980s are models.

A theoretical firm is relied upon to develop at a 20 percent rate for a long time, at that point to have its development rate tumble to 4 percent, the standard for the economy. The estimation of the firm with its development example is controlled by the accompanying condition:

Present cost = PV of profits during better than average development period + Value of stock cost toward the finish of better than average development period - limited back to show

Value Stock Analysis

The essential thought process in purchasing stock is to sell it later at an improved cost. By and large, the speculator likewise anticipates a profit. Both cost and profit are the foremost fixings in a financial specialists return or yield.

In the event that the speculator had satisfactory data about and information of stock costs and profit yields he would have the option to make attractive returns.

Be that as it may, in all actuality complexities of political, monetary, social and different powers prevent the expectation of stock developments and comes back with any assurance. Lord saw that on a normal over a large portion of the variety in stock costs could be credited to a market impact that influences all financial exchange files.

Yet, stocks are likewise dependent upon industry impact far beyond the impact regular to all stocks. Ruler noticed that industry impact clarified, on the normal, 13 percent of the varieties in a stocks price.In aggregate around 66% of variety in the costs of stocks saw in the lords study was the aftereffect of market and industry. This features the need of the money related expert to look at the financial and industry impacts just as the individual organizations' exhibition so as to precisely take any speculation choices.

The huge number of components influencing a company's productivity can be extensively delegated:

· Economy-wise factors: These incorporate elements like development pace of the economy, the pace of swelling, remote trade rates and so forth which influence the benefit of the considerable number of organizations.

Industry-wise factors: These elements are explicit to the business in which the firm is working; for instance the interest supply hole in the business, the development of substitute items and changes in government arrangement identifying with the business.

· Firm explicit variables: Such as age of the plant, the nature of its administration, the brand picture of its items and its work relations.

Monetary Analysis

Return suspicions for the stock and security markets and deals, cost, and benefit projections for enterprises and almost all organizations fundamentally exemplify financial presumptions. Financial specialists are worried about those powers in the economy which influence the exhibition of association wherein they wish to take part, through acquisition of stock. By distinguishing key suspicions and factors, we can screen the economy and measure the ramifications of new data on our monetary standpoint and industry investigation. So as to beat the market on a hazard balanced premise, the financial specialist must have gauges that vary from the market agreement and must be right as a rule.

Monetary patterns can take two essential structures: recurrent changes that emerge from high points and low points of the business cycle, and auxiliary changes that happen when the economy is experiencing a significant change by they way it capacities. A portion of the wide powers which effect the economy are:

Populace

Populace gives and thought of the sort of work power in a nation. Expanding populace gives interest for more businesses like lodgings, living arrangements, administration enterprises like wellbeing, buyer request like iceboxes and autos. Expanding populace hence shows a more noteworthy requirement for monetary advancement. Despite the fact that it doesn't show the definite business that will grow.

Forex (in basic terms, cash) is additionally called the remote trade, FX or money exchanging. It is a decentralized worldwide market where all the world's monetary standards exchange with one another. It is the biggest fluid market on the planet.

The liquidity (more purchasers and venders) and aggressive evaluating (the spread is little among offered and ask cost) accessible in this checked are incredible. With the inconsistency in the exhibition in different markets, the development of forex exchanging, putting and the board is in upward direction.

0.1% under typical economic situations. With bigger vendors (where volumes are enormous), the spread could be as low as 0.05%. Influence assumes an essential job here.

**Influence**

Influence is the component by which a broker can take position a lot bigger than the underlying speculation. Influence is one more motivation behind why you should exchange forex. Hardly any cash merchants understand the upside of money related influence accessible to them. For instance, in the event that you are exchanging value advertise, the greatest influence a stock intermediary is offered is 1:2 however if there should be an occurrence of forex showcase, you will get an influence up to 1:50 and in numerous pieces of the world much higher influence is accessible. Thus, it isn't difficult to see that why forex exchanging is so well known.

High influence enables a merchant with little venture to exchange higher volumes of monetary forms and in this manner give the chance to make huge benefits from the little development in the market. Be that as it may, if the market is against your suspicion you may lose huge sum as well. Along these lines, similar to some other market, it is a two-way sword.

# Chapter Ten: Beginner's Mistakes

## High Liquidity

The size of forex market is tremendous and fluid essentially. High liquidity implies a merchant can exchange with a money. Timing isn't a requirement too; exchanging should be possible according to your benefit. The purchasers and venders over the world acknowledge various sorts of monetary forms. Also, forex market is dynamic 24 hours every day and is shut uniquely on the ends of the week.

## Openness

Beginning as a cash dealer would not cost a huge amount of cash particularly when contrasted with exchanging stocks, alternative or future market. We have online forex merchants offering "smaller than usual" or "miniaturized scale" exchanging accounts that let you open an exchanging account with a base record store of $25. This permits a normal individual with less exchanging cash-flow to open a forex exchanging account.

## Who Trades Stocks and Forex?

The forex market is gigantic in size and is the biggest market with a huge number of members. A huge number of people (like us), cash exchangers, to banks, to support investments chiefs everyone takes part in the forex showcase.

**When would you be able to exchange forex?**

Forex market is open 24 hours every day and 5 days per week. Nonetheless, it doesn't mean it is constantly dynamic. Give us a chance to check what a 24-hour day in the forex world resembles.

The forex market is partitioned into four significant exchanging sessions: the Sydney session, the Tokyo session, the London session and the New York session.

**The structure of forex: What are the best strategies in Forex trading?**

The Structure of the run of the mill financial exchange is as demonstrated as follows:

- Purchasers

- Incorporated Exchanges (NSE, BSE, NYSE)

- Vender

In any case, the structure of the forex market is somewhat special since significant volumes of exchanges are done in Over-The-Counter (OTC) advertise which is autonomous of any concentrated framework (trade) as on account of financial exchanges.

The members in this market are:

- Central Banks

- Major business banks

- Investment banks

- Corporations for worldwide business exchanges

- Hedge reserves

- Speculators

- Pension and common assets

- Insurance organizations

- Forex representatives

The Forex Market structure might be spoken to as demonstrated as follows:

- Significant Banks

- Electronic Broking Services (EBS)/Reuters Dealing 3000 spot coordinating

- Medium size and littler banks

- Retail showcase creators/Retail ECNs/Hedge assets and business organizations

- Retail Traders

- Market Participants

In the above graph, we can see that the significant banks are the conspicuous players and littler or medium estimated banks make up the interbank advertise. The members of this market exchange either straightforwardly with one another or electronically through the Electronic Brokering Services (EBS) or the Reuters Dealing 3000-Spot Matching.

The challenge between the two organizations – The EBS and the Reuters 3000-Spot Matching in forex market is like Pepsi and Coke in the customer showcase.

The absolute biggest banks like HSBC, Citigroup, RBS, Deutsche Bank, BNP Paribas, Barclays Bank among others decide the FX rates through their tasks. These enormous banks are the key players for worldwide FX exchanges. The banks have the genuine generally image of the interest and supply in the general market, and have the present situation of any current. The size of their activities viably set out the offer ask spread that streams down to the lower end of the pyramid.

The following level of members are the non-bank suppliers, for example, retail advertise creators, merchants, ECNs, speculative stock investments, benefits and shared assets, enterprises, and so forth. Speculative stock investments and innovation organizations have taken huge piece of offer in retail FX yet extremely less a dependable balance in corporate FX business. They get to the FX showcase through banks, which are otherwise called liquidity suppliers. The enterprises are significant players as they are always purchasing and selling FX for their cross-outskirt (advertise) buys or offers of crude or completed items. Mergers and acquisitions (M&A) likewise make huge interest and supply of monetary forms.

At times, governments and incorporated banks like the RBI (in India) additionally intercede in the Foreign Exchange market to stop an excess of instability in the cash advertise. For example, to help the evaluating of rupees, the legislature and unified banks purchase rupees from the market and sell in various monetary forms, for example, dollars; alternately, to diminish the estimation of Indian rupees, they sell rupees and purchase outside money (dollars).

The theorists and retail merchants that come at the base of the pyramid pay the biggest spread, on the grounds that their exchanges viably get executed through two layers. The basic role of these players are to make cash exchanging the changes the money costs. With the headway of innovation and web, even a little dealer can partake in this gigantic forex showcase.

In the event that you have voyage, you likely as of now have forex exchanging knowledge: when you purchase the money of your goal nation while paying with your own cash, that is forex exchanging. Forex brokers purchase and sell monetary standards for benefit or on the other hand to ensure speculations. An expected USD 5 trillion is exchanged day by day, the vast majority of it theoretical.

The forex market is the world's biggest monetary market, and since exchanging is between advertise members, there is no "open" or "close" of market with the exception of on ends of the week.

The forex market is the world's biggest monetary market Forex exchanging

happens from Monday morning in New Zealand until late Friday on the west shore of the USA at the end of the day, forex exchanging happens from Monday morning in New Zealand until late Friday on the west bank of the USA.

You may appreciate exchanging the significant cash matches, or know about the quality of an outlandish money, or a vibe for items; a few open doors present themselves to individuals who stay aware of news and occasions, while others require understanding investigation. Merchants carry their own qualities and inclinations to their exchanging and, after some time, make their very own exchanging style.

**Cash pair**

On the off chance that you are new to the forex advertise and have recently begun exchanging Forex on the web, you may end up overpowered and confounded both at once by the gigantic number of accessible money matches inside your terminal (like the MetaTrader4, and so on.). So what are the best money sets to exchange? The appropriate responses are not that direct as it changes with every merchant and its terminal window or with what trade (or OTC market) he is exchanging. Rather, you have to set aside the effort to break down various sets of monetary standards against your very own procedure to decide the best forex sets to exchange on your records.

The exchange Forex market happens between two monetary forms, since one cash is being purchased (purchaser/offer) and another sold (vender/ask) simultaneously. There is a universal code that determines the arrangement of money sets we can exchange. For instance, a statement of EUR/USD 1.25 implies that one Euro is worth $1.25. Here, the base cash is the Euro(EUR), and the counter money is the US dollar.

Research and mechanical improvement

The monetary powers identifying with ventures would rely upon the measure of assets spent by the administration on the specific mechanical improvement influencing what's to come. Financial specialists would like to put resources into those businesses in which the bigger portion of improvement assets are being allotted by the administration. For instance in India oil and data innovation are getting a more prominent measure of consideration and might be considered for speculation.

Macroeconomic Stability

General macroeconomic conditions are significant as far as the general atmosphere under which venture choices are made. So financial development will depend somewhat upon the solidness of the economy for example financial balance, and sensibly unsurprising degrees of expansion. Macroeconomic strength lessens the dangers of speculation and may in this manner be viewed as an important condition for development. Financial parity guarantees that there is less danger of swelling, on the grounds that there will be less danger of governments printing cash. This may likewise balance out the conversion standard and permit financing costs to be set at a sensibly low level - so further promising speculation.

Exchange Liberalization, Capital Mobility and Exchange Rate Policy

The abrogation of exchange confinements (levies and portions) is regularly observed as an important condition for development. The thought is to augment markets and in this way permit economies of scale in sending out businesses. It is regularly contended that trade rates should be balanced downwards simultaneously, to guarantee that potential exporters can contend on world markets. To support direct remote speculation confinements on universal capital streams may should be decreased.

Regular Resources and Raw Material

The regular assets are to a great extent answerable for a nation's monetary advancement and generally improvement in the state of corporate development. The revelation of oil in Middle Eastern nations and the disclosure of gas in America has essentially changed the financial and venture example of the nations.

Total national output (GDP)

Gross domestic product estimates the all-out yield of merchandise and ventures for definite use happening inside the household domain of a given nation, paying little heed to the allotment to local and remote cases. Total national output at buyer esteems (showcase costs) is the total of gross worth included by all occupant and non-inhabitant makers in the economy in addition to any charges and less any endowments excluded in the estimation of the items. Higher GDP level means that higher monetary advancement and consequently higher venture capacity.

Global Trade

Fares and Imports of products and enterprises speak to the estimation everything being equal and other market administrations gave to or got from the remainder of the world. They incorporate the estimation of product, cargo, protection, transport, travel, eminences, permit charges, and different administrations, for example, correspondence, development, money related, data, business, individual, and taxpayer driven organizations. They avoid work and property salary (some time ago called factor administrations) just as move installments.

More elevated levels of global exchange particularly higher fares are characteristic of higher income and accordingly higher financial advancement of a nation.

Expansion

Higher expansion is by and large negative for the securities exchange since it causes higher financing costs, it builds vulnerability about future costs and expenses, and it damages firms that can't pass their cost increments on to purchasers.

A few ventures may profit expansion. Common asset enterprises advantage if their generation expenses don't ascend with expansion, on the grounds that their yield will probably sell at more significant expense.

Loan fees

Banks for the most part profit by unstable loan costs since stable financing costs lead to substantial aggressive weights that crush their advantage edges. High financing costs plainly hurt the lodging and the development business.

Financial Indicators

Other than the variables talked about above there are other critical financial pointers, for example, nation's monetary arrangement, money related approach, stock costs, condition of capital advertise, work efficiency, purchaser action and so on.

Estimating methods

There are fundamentally five financial determining systems:

Studies: It is a strategy for transient estimating. It is extensively used to pass on the future course of occasions in the economy. The technique to do this is rough since it depends on convictions, thoughts and future planning of the administration.

It, in any case, comprehensively demonstrates the fate of occasions in the economy.

Monetary Indicators: It gives sign of the financial procedure through recurrent timings. These projections are a technique for getting signs of things to come identifying with business sorrows and business thriving. This technique in spite of the fact that has its preferences of giving the future signs of the economy isn't a careful strategy for discovering the monetary movement. It gives results roughly and is, best case scenario an estimation of things to come of the financial conditions.

Dispersion Indexes: The dissemination file is a technique which joins the various markers into one complete measure and it invigorates shortcomings and of a specific time arrangement of information. The dissemination record is likewise called a statistics or a composite file.

Financial Model Building: This is a numerical and measurable application to figure the future pattern of the economy. This method can be utilized via prepared professionals and it is utilized to draw out connection between at least two factors. The strategy is to make one free factor and autonomous variable and to draw out a connection between these factors. The appropriate response of drawing these connections is to get a gauge of heading just as extent.

Entrepreneurial Model Building: This strategy is the most generally utilized financial anticipating strategy. This is likewise sectoral examination of Gross National Product Model Building. This strategy utilizes the national bookkeeping information to have the option to gauge for a future transient period. It is an adaptable and solid strategy for estimating. The technique for guaging is to discover the absolute salary and the all-out interest for the conjecture time frame. To this are included the earth states of political steadiness, monetary and financial strategies of the administration, arrangements identifying with expense and loan fees. This must be added to Gross household speculation, government acquisition of merchandise in administrations, utilization costs and net fares. The figure must be separated first by a gauge of the administration area which is to be isolated again into State Government and Central Government costs. The gross private local venture is to be determined by including the operational expense for plan, development and gear changes in the degree of business. The third area which is to be taken is the utilization segment identifying with the individual utilization factor. This division is typically isolated into segments of strong merchandise, non-solid products and enterprises. At the point when information has been taken of every one of these divisions these are meant get the figure for the Gross National Product

# Chapter Eleven: Individual Retirement Accounts

When financial Analysis is made and the conjecture of economy is known, the examiner needs to take a gander at the business bunches which are promising in the coming years and afterward pick the organizations to put resources into inside those industry gatherings. There is no important co connection between monetary development and industry development a few enterprises may develop regardless of poor financial development. The business has been characterized as a homogeneous gathering of individuals doing a comparative sort of movement or comparative work. In any case, industry extensively covers all the financial action occurring in a nation to bring development. An expansive idea of industry would incorporate every one of the variables of generation, transportation, exchanging movement and open utilities. The wide grouping of industry, notwithstanding, would not be important for a financial specialist who might want to guarantee that he doesn't lose from the speculation that he makes. It is, subsequently, fundamental to qualify the business into certain attributes homogeneous gathering. As a rule, the industry is characterized in forms and in stages. It might likewise be arranged by work bunch that it distinguishes to.

## Grouping of enterprises

In India resource based industry gathering used to exist under MRTP Act and FERA Act. In any case, since monetary changes in 1991 onwards, there is no restriction to the advantage development and the characterization of MRTP and non MRTP organizations has since vanished. These days, even global firms can work in India through their backups or straightforwardly by having a greater part stake in an organization.

The size astute arrangement of enterprises is as per the following:

Little scale units: These businesses are not recorded and those which have a base paid up capital of Rs 30 lakhs can be recorded on OTCEI.

Medium Scale Industries: The units having paid up capital of Rs 5 crores or more can be recorded on provincial stock trades.

Huge scale Industries: Industrial units with paid up capital of Rs 10 crores or more can be recorded on significant stock trades like BSE.

Restrictive Based Classification

The businesses can be arranged based on proprietorship into (a) private part ventures which are available to the overall population for speculation (b) open segment (Government and semi-government possession) (c) and in joint segment.

Utilize Based Classification

(a) Basic Industries: These are in the center segment in India and comprise the foundation businesses which are for the most part in the open segment however are presently held open to the open segment. The models are manures, synthetic concoctions, coal, concrete, steel and so on.

(b) Capital Goods Industries: These are both in the private and open divisions. These are exceptionally capital concentrated ventures and are utilized to create contributions of different enterprises, for example, machine instruments, rural apparatus, wires, links and so on.

(c) Intermediate merchandise: These are products in the middle of the road phase of creation, having experienced some handling as of now however will be utilized for further generation models are tires, manufactured yarn, cotton turning, car parts and so on.

(d) Consumer products businesses: These are of two classifications, in particular, purchaser durables and shopper non-durables. These are last items for the utilization of family units. Durables are fans, bulbs, Automobiles, Cycles, Two wheelers, Telephone hardware and so on. Non-durables are nourishment items, Agro based items, tobacco, woolen and jute materials and so forth.

Info based Classification

(an) Agro based items like jute, sugar cotton, tobacco, groundnuts and so forth.

(b) Forest based items like pressed wood, paper, wood, ivory, gum nectar and so forth.

(c) Marine based items like fisheries, prawns, and so on.

(d) Metal based items like designing items, aluminum, copper, gold and so on.

(e) Chemical based items like manures, pesticides, drugs paints and so on.

Every one of the above orders is helpful for recognizing the trademark highlights of the business, its sources of info and yields or utilizes and the feasible interest for it, imperatives underway, effect of financial factors and so forth.

Industry Life Cycle

A quick investigation when anticipating industry deals and patterns in gainfulness is to see the business after some time and separation its advancement into stages like those that people progress through. The quantity of stages in the business life cycle investigation can be founded on a five phases model, which incorporates:

1. Spearheading Development

2. Fast quickening development

3. Develop development during this period is extremely little or negative net revenues and benefits.

4. Adjustment and market development

5. Deceleration of development and decrease.

Other than being valuable when evaluating deals, the investigation of an industry's life cycles additionally can give bits of knowledge into net revenues and income development.

The overall revenue arrangement commonly tops from the get-go in the all out cycle and afterward levels off and decays as rivalry is pulled in by the early achievement of the business.

1. Spearheading Development: During this beginning up arrange, the industry encounters unassuming deals development and little or negative net revenues and benefits. The market for the business' item or administration during this timeframe is little, and the organizations included bring about significant improvement costs.

2. Quick Accelerating Growth: During this stage a market creates for the item or administration and request gets significant. The set number of firms in the business faces little challenge and individual firms can encounter considerable excesses. The net revenues are exceptionally high. The business fabricates its profitable limit as deals develop at an expanding rate as the business endeavors to satisfy abundance need. High scales development and high overall revenues that expansion as firms become progressively effective purpose industry and firm benefits to detonate. During this stage benefits can develop at over 100% per year because of the low notice base and the fast development of scales and net revenues.

3. Develop Growth: The achievement in arrange two has fulfilled the vast majority of the interest for the business merchandise or administration. Accordingly, future scales development might be better than average yet it never again quickens for instance, if the over all economy is developing at 8% scale for this industry may develop at a better than average pace of 15% to 20% every year. Additionally the fast development of scales and high net revenues pull in contenders to the business which causes an expansion in supply and lower costs which implies that the benefit edges start to decay to typical levels.

4. Adjustment And Market Maturity: During this phase which is likely the longest stage the business development rate decays to the development pace of the total economy or its industry fragment. During this stage financial specialists can appraise development effectively in light of the fact that scales correspond profoundly with a monetary arrangement. Despite the fact that scales develop in accordance with the economy benefit development fluctuates by industry on the grounds that the aggressive structure shifts by enterprises and by individual firms inside the business on the grounds that the capacity to control costs varies among organizations. Rivalry delivers tight overall revenues and the paces of profit for capital inevitably become equivalent to or marginally beneath the aggressive level.

5. Affirmation of Growth and Decline: At this phase of development the business deals development decreases on account of movements popular or development of substitutes. Overall revenues keep on being pressed and a few firms experience low benefit or even misfortunes. Firms that stay gainful may show exceptionally low paces of profit for capital. At long last, financial specialists start contemplating elective uses for the capital tied up in this industry.

## Surveying the Industry Life Cycle

The business life cycle order of industry evolvement causes speculators to evaluate the development capability of various organizations in an industry. In view of the phase of industry, they can all the more likely survey the capability of various organizations inside an industry. Nonetheless, there are impediments to this sort of examination First, it is just a speculation, and financial specialists must be mindful so as not to endeavor to arrange each industry, or all organizations inside a specific industry, into slick classes that may not have any significant bearing. Second, even the general structure may not have any significant bearing to certain ventures that are not sorted by numerous little organizations battling for endurance. At long last, the reality in security examination is stock costs, an element of the normal stream of advantages and the hazard in question.

The business life cycle will in general spotlight on deals and portion of the market and interest in the business. Albeit these variables are essential to speculators, they are not the last things of interests. Given these capabilities to industry life cycle examination, what are the suggestions for financial specialists?

The spearheading stage may offer the most noteworthy potential returns, however it likewise represents the most serious hazard. A few organizations in an industry will fall flat or do ineffectively.

Such hazard might be fitting for certain speculators, yet many will wish to maintain a strategic distance from the hazard inalienable in this stage.

Financial specialists intrigued principally in capital additions ought to maintain a strategic distance from the development arrange. Organizations at this stage may have moderately high payouts in light of the fact that they have less development possibilities. These organizations will frequently offer steadiness in income and profit developments.

Unmistakably, organizations in the fourth phase of the modern life cycle, decay, are normally to be stayed away from. Financial specialists should try to spot businesses in this stage and maintain a strategic distance from them. It is the subsequent stage, extension that is presumably of most enthusiasm to speculators. Ventures that have endure the spearheading stage regularly offer great open doors for the interest for their items and administrations is developing more quickly than the economy in general. Development is fast yet precise an engaging trademark to speculators.

**Agreement Expiration and Delivery**

Any fates contract that hasn't been sold by a balancing exchange before the agreement's lapse date will be settled at that day's settlement cost. The conditions of the agreement indicate whether an agreement will be settled by physical conveyance - accepting or surrendering the real portions of stock - or with money repayment. Where physical conveyance is required, a holder of a short position must convey the basic security. On the other hand, a holder of a long position must take conveyance of the hidden offers.

Where money repayment is required, the basic security isn't conveyed. Or maybe, any security fates gets that are open are settled through a last money installment dependent on the repayment cost. When this installment is made, neither one of the parties has any further commitments on the agreement.

**Edge and Leverage**

At the point when a financier firm loans one piece of the assets expected to buy a security, for example, regular stock, the expression "edge" alludes to the measure of money, or initial installment, the client is required to store. Conversely, a security prospects agreement is a commitment not an advantage and has no an incentive as guarantee for a credit. At the point when one goes into a security prospects contract, he is required to make an installment alluded to as an "edge installment" or "execution bond" to cover potential misfortunes.

For a moderately modest quantity of cash (the edge necessity), a prospects contract worth a few fold the amount of can be purchased or sold. The littler the edge prerequisite in connection to the hidden estimations of the fates contract, the more noteworthy the influence. As a result of this influence, little changes in cost can bring about huge additions and misfortunes in a brief timeframe.

**Increases and Losses**

In contrast to stocks, additions and misfortunes in security fates records are presented on the record each day, which are dictated by the settlement value set by the trade. On the off chance that because of misfortunes one's record falls underneath support edge necessities, he will be required to put extra assets in the record to cover those misfortunes.

**Duty Implications**

The duty outcomes of a security fates exchange may rely upon the status of the citizen and the kind of position (that is, long or short, secured or revealed). For instance, for most individual financial specialists, security fates are not saddled as fates contracts. Short security prospects agreement positions are burdened at the transient capital additions rate, paying little heed to what extent the agreement is held.

Long security fates agreements might be saddled at either the long haul or transient capital increases rate, contingent upon to what extent they are held. For sellers, be that as it may, security future agreements are burdened like different fates contracts at a mix of 60% long haul and 40% momentary capital increases rates. Contingent upon the kind of exchanging technique that is utilized, there can be extra or diverse expense outcomes as well.

## Chapter Twelve: Annuities

### Assortment and Fungibility of Security Futures Contracts

Agreement determinations may differ from agreement to contract just as from trade to trade. For example, most security fates agreements require settling by making physical conveyance of the basic security, instead of making money repayment. Cautiously audit the settlement and conveyance conditions before going into a security prospects contract.

As of now, security fates exchanged on one trade are not "fungible" with security fates exchanged on another trade. This implies one may have the option to balance a situation on the trade where the first exchange occurred - despite the fact that a superior cost might be accessible for a tantamount fates contract on the equivalent fundamental security or file on another trade.

### Hedgers

Ranchers, producers, shippers and exporters would all be able to be hedgers. A hedger purchases or sells in the prospects market to verify the future cost of a product proposed to be sold sometime in the not too distant future in the money showcase. This ensures against value dangers.

The holders of the long position in prospects gets (the purchasers of the product), are attempting to verify as low a cost as could be allowed. The short holders of the agreement (the dealers of the ware) will need to verify as high a cost as could be expected under the circumstances. The fates contract, be that as it may, gives an unequivocal value conviction to the two gatherings, which diminishes the dangers related with value instability. Supporting by methods for prospects agreements can likewise be utilized as a way to secure an adequate value edge between the expense of the crude material and the retail cost of the last item sold.

## Examiners

Other showcase members, be that as it may, don't mean to limit chance yet rather to profit by the intrinsically dangerous nature of the fates advertise. These are the theorists, and they intend to benefit from the very value change that hedgers are securing themselves against. Hedgers need to limit their hazard regardless of what they're putting resources into, while examiners need to expand their hazard and accordingly amplify their benefits.

In the fates showcase, a theorist purchasing an agreement low so as to sell high later on would in all probability be purchasing that agreement from a hedger selling an agreement low fully expecting declining costs later on.

In contrast to the hedger, the theorist doesn't really try to claim the ware being referred to. Or maybe, the individual in question will enter the market looking for benefits In a quick paced market into which data is persistently being bolstered, theorists and hedgers skip off of - and advantage from - one another. The closer it gets to the hour of the agreement's lapse, the more strong the data entering the market will respect the ware being referred to. In this way, all can anticipate an increasingly precise impression of market interest and the comparing cost.

Prospects agreements are exchanged on perceived trades. In India, both the NSE and the BSE presented file prospects in the S&P CNX Nifty and the BSE Sensex. The tasks are like that of the securities exchange, the exemption being that, in file fates, the stamping to-showcase rule is pursued, that is, the portfolios are changed in accordance with the market esteems every day.

The Derivatives Trading at BSE happens through a completely mechanized screen based exchanging stage called as DTSS

(Derivatives Trading and Settlement System). The DTSS is intended to permit exchanging on an ongoing premise.

Notwithstanding producing exchanges by coordinating inverse requests, the DTSS moreover produces different reports for the part members.

Request Matching will happen after request acknowledgment wherein the framework looks for an inverse coordinating request. In the event that a match is discovered, an exchange will be created. The request against which the exchange has been created will be from the framework. In the event that the request isn't depleted further coordinating requests will be looked for and exchanges produced till the request gets depleted or no more match-capable requests are found. In the event that the request isn't completely depleted, the framework will hold the request in the pending request book. Coordinating of the requests will be in the need of cost and timestamp. A one of a kind exchange id will be produced for each exchange and the whole data of the exchange is sent to the individuals in question.

## Value Bands

There are no greatest and least value ranges for Futures and Options Contracts. In any case, to keep away from wrong request section, sham value groups have been presented in the Derivatives Segment. Further, no value groups are endorsed in the Cash Segment for stocks on which Futures and Options agreements are accessible for exchanging. Additionally, for those stocks which don't have Futures and Options Contracts accessible on them however are framing some portion of the list on which Futures and Options agreements are accessible, no value groups are pulled in gave the every day normal exchanging on such files in the F and O Segment isn't under 20 agreements and exchanged on at the very least 10 days in the first month.

## Going Short

A theorist who goes short - that is, goes into a fates contract by consenting to sell and convey the fundamental at a set value - is hoping to make a benefit from declining value levels. By selling high now, the agreement can be repurchased later on at a lower value, accordingly creating a benefit for the theorist.

## Spreads

Spreads include exploiting the value distinction between two unique agreements of a similar ware. Spreading is viewed as one of the most preservationist types of exchanging the prospects advertise in light of the fact that it is a lot more secure than the exchanging of long/short (stripped) fates contracts.

There are various kinds of spreads, including:

Schedule Spread - This includes the concurrent buy and clearance of two fates of a similar kind, having a similar cost, yet extraordinary conveyance dates. Between market Spread - Here the speculator, with agreements of that month, goes long in one market and short in another market. For instance, the financial specialist may take Short June Wheat and Long June Pork Bellies.

Between Exchange Spread - This is any kind of spread wherein each position is.

## Preferred position OF FUTURES INDEX

It is a hazard support and obliges theoretical impulse of financial specialists. It is a progressively effective technique for controlling danger on a portfolio, as it diminishes the" exchanges exchanging expenses and value pressure. Neither the purchaser nor the dealer pays the full estimation of the fundamental affirms however bargains just in contrasts, in real money without including conveyance of the advantages. The fates smoothens the advantage reallocation, gives fence support inflows or surges of money and decreases the effect of bullish and bearish ling as prospects don't include full installment on receipt both the fundamental resources is a managing in contrasts.

## Activity of Hedge of Risk

To delineate the inclusion of hazard, accept that you expect a future money inflow of Rs.50,000 per month subsequently, which you wish to put resources into values. Be that as it may, the market is bullish and costs are required to rise. At that point you purchase a list future agreement to are the normal ascent in cost. You can likewise seli short if the market is relied upon to fall in costs. Assume, you have the protections in your portfolio and anticipate that the market should fall then you can sell the prospects, rather than the protections. On the off chance that the genuine fall legend than the normal value, you will get the distinction in real money. A bullish desire makes you purchase the prospects contract and a bearish desire makes you the fates contract. On the off chance that your desires are effectively acknowledged, you can make they on the arrangements without really purchasing and selling the basic protections. s will empower you to exchange on a littler speculation as the edges you need to p for exchanging Futures is commonly 6 to 10%, and the loss of premium cash is costly then the loss of enthusiasm on a greater expense associated with purchasing and mg for conveyances of fundamental protections or offers or securities.

## Fates ON FIXED INCOME SECURITIES

Venture procedures of fixed salary protections are genuinely straightforward when contrasted with value as they put resources into government protections, corporate securities, and so on where the profits are fixed. Despite the fact that fixed pay protections have a lot of lower dangers than values, they are not totally hazard free either. Coming up next are the different dangers related with them.

## Credit hazard

Credit hazard is the plausibility of default in the reimbursement of head and enthusiasm by a borrower. Among fixed salary protections, corporate securities convey the most elevated credit chance. On the off chance that the giving organization falls into genuine monetary troubles, there is each likelihood that reimbursement will be postponed extensively and may never at any point be made. Assets diminish this hazard by putting just in bonds gave by organizations with great FICO score. Nonetheless, a great FICO assessment is no assurance that the organization would keep on performing admirably in future and respect all its budgetary duties.

Government protections convey no acknowledge chance, as the guarantor can never default, and are upheld by the sovereign assurance of the nation and are called sovereign protections. In any case, they convey lower returns than other fixed salary protections.

**Liquidity chance**

Liquidity in any market alludes to the likelihood for merchants to enter and leave positions without hardly lifting a finger in connection to volume and size of exchanges.

Profoundly fluid markets additionally diminish the effect expenses of exchanges which result from changes in costs when enormous exchanges are pushed through in a less fluid market. (The contrast between the market cost before the deal offer and the cost at which the securities are sold establishes the effect cost for the vender).

The market for government protections and transient currency markets are fluid where the effect expenses are practically immaterial, however, the profits offered by these advantages are a lot of lower than the moderately fluid corporate securities.

**Value dangers**

Corporate securities will consistently be evaluated by a presumed rating office for their financial soundness which might be changed to mirror the adjustments in the economy, industry or the organization being referred to. These rate changes can influence the market costs of the securities. This uncovered the store putting resources into such bonds to a value chance.

## Loan fee dangers

Market costs of all fixed salary protections are generally reliant on the predominant financing cost in the economy. On the off chance that loan fees are relied upon to descend in future, bonds gave in the past would turn out to be progressively appealing and bad habit refrain. Practically all ventures made by fixed pay assets are liable to loan fee dangers. Yet, the protections with longer developments are more unstable than shorter term protections.

## Different dangers

Indian common assets are permitted to put resources into abroad fixed salary protections designated in a remote cash. Such ventures are dependent upon changes in cash esteems. They are likewise presented to different political and financial dangers related with the nation in which the security was given.

## Supporting BY FIXED INCOME FUNDS

Like value reserves, fixed salary assets can likewise fence their value hazards by going into subsidiary exchanges. Be that as it may, fixed pay subordinates are not effectively comprehended and they are not exchanged an open market like stock fates.

Two basic subsidiaries utilized by fixed salary assets are:

## Financing cost swaps

Financing costs are of two kinds, fixed loan fees and gliding rates which shift as indicated by changes in a standard benchmark loan cost. A financial specialist holding a security which pays a drifting loan fee is presented to financing cost hazard. The speculator can deal with this hazard by going into a financing cost swap.

A loan cost swap is a money related understanding between two gatherings to swap or trade premium commitments of shifting nature for a concurred period.

The agreement will determine the loan costs, the benchmark rate to be pursued, the notional chief sum for the exchange, and so on.

For instance, take the instance of a shared store which has put Rs.50 crore in a gliding interest obligation of one year development. The intrigue payable by the guarantor of the security isn't fixed and will differ with the adjustments in the benchmark loan cost indicated.

The common store can go into a financing cost swap concurrence with a counter gathering who will ensure to pay enthusiasm at a fixed rate, say 10 percent, on the notional measure of Rs.50 crore for a time of one year. Consequently, the store will ensure to pay the counter party enthusiasm at the benchmark rate on Rs.50 scores for one year. As it were, the reserve will pass on the premium got on its interest in coasting rate cling to the counter party and get a fixed enthusiasm for return.

By and by, toward the finish of the agreement time frame the complete premium payable by each gathering is determined and the net sum is settled in real money. In the event that the benchmark rate, exacerbated every day for one year as it varies consistently, is lower than 10 percent the common reserve will get the distinction from the counter party. In the event that it is the other path round the reserve will pay the distinction to the counter party. In any case, the reserve is guaranteed of a loan cost of 10 percent whatever happens to the benchmark rate.

# Conclusion

## Forward rate understandings

A forward rate understanding, generally known as FRA, is another type of financing cost swap. Under a FRA, the gatherings consent to pay and get the contrast between a fixed loan fee and the benchmark financing cost winning on a future date. As on account of a swap, the financing cost, the benchmark rate and the notional sum will be referenced in the agreement. The thing that matters is that not normal for a swap wherein the benchmark loan fee for a period is considered and is determined on a day by day exacerbating premise, a FRA considers the benchmark date just on a predetermined future date.

## DISCLAIMER

The information contained within this eBook is strictly for educational purposes. If you wish to apply ideas contained in this eBook, you are taking full responsibility for your actions.

The author has made every effort to ensure the accuracy of the information within this book was correct at time of publication. The author does not assume and hereby disclaims any liability to any party for any loss, damage, or disruption caused by errors or omissions, whether such errors or omissions result from accident, negligence, or any other cause.

# Deducting | The Right Way

*David Lazarus*

## Table of Contents

# Introduction

You'll definitely have to do a lot of day-to-day daily duties, including accounting, when you first launch your small online business. Knowing how to track and forecast your business's income and expenses is a valuable skill for growth, so familiarise yourself with the basics of accounting.

And if you're willing to outsource your accounting and bookkeeping right now, learning the fundamentals can help you appreciate your finance professional's findings and correctly evaluate your company's financial wellbeing.

We've broken down all you need to understand about small online business accounting, including how to monitor and evaluate your business's main financial indicators, in the parts below.

# Chapter: 1 Online Business and its importance?

There has never been a better or easier time in history to start your own business than now. Everyone is connected now, regardless of their income status or geographic location, thanks to the development and growth of easy-to-use website creation tools and social media.

Whether you are rich and powerful or impoverished, you can now freely share your abilities and connect with people around the world. It can also be very inexpensive and simple to get started for those looking to start an online business.

Many people have started online businesses for less than 200 dollars. (the cost purchasing a domain name, hosting service and professional theme).

You can start a business if you can connect with others and fill a need. In fact, there are numerous advantages to starting and owning your own online business, ranging from increased income and freedom to assisting others in achieving their own personal goals; however, in order to keep things simple and to the point, I will only go over seven of the many advantages to starting and owning your own online business.

## 1.1 The importance of eCommerce

### 1. eCommerce Helps You Reduce Your Costs

To make your online store, it isn't essential that you have every one of your items introduced in an actual space. There're various organizations that work online where they just demonstrate all their stock through their electronic business.

This suggests not just saving by not requiring a purchase or rental of premises, yet besides all that includes electric power, the internet, and so forth or then again in the event that you need to have one, so clients have an actual space, it doesn't need to be just about as extensive as all that you offer. Regardless, you'll reduce your expenses.

## 2. eCommerce Helps Businesses Go Global

Straightforwardly identified with the previous point, this reality permits you to put your items available to be purchased anywhere on the planet. They won't have the express need to venture out to where you're to perceive what you've to bring to the table.

If you're running an actual store, it'll be restricted by the geological zone that you can support, yet possessing an eCommerce site will offer you the chance to expand your effort. It will offer your items and administrations to clients around the entire world, paying little heed to the time zone and distance.

Besides, this wipes out a wide range of topographical and etymological tango hindrances. Your online business converted into various dialects will permit them to purchase from various nations.

With eCommerce & mobile business also, the whole world is your jungle gym. Your services and products are accessible for many clients sitting on another edge of the world.

In this way, if you need to develop your online business worldwide, it is a good thought to begin making your online store & localize it in various dialects.

## 3. eCommerce Can Also Be Done through Fewer Overheads and Fewer Risk

Beginning an online store might mean essentially bring down expenses of a start-up contrasted with a physical retailer. The retailer or the online entrepreneur does not need to think about the shop rent high costs, employing a sales associate to facilitate the client, efforts, service charges, safety, and so forth. This, can empower you to sell them at good costs. Moreover, an online shop allows you to grasp expanded productivity with less danger.

## 4. eCommerce Can Broaden Your Brand & Expand the Business

Having some eCommerce store can be used to widen the scope of items or administrations available to be purchased, extending your business, bringing you a huge number of customers, and broadening your deals. It is the ideal method to take a personal brand from a conventional block & mortar store to a novice, all-around adored one.

With eCommerce, there's no compelling reason to have more than one branch, only one particular online store permitting you to completely arrive at clients without agonizing over moving areas; you can deal with your online business from home.

It's imperative to specify that eCommerce will be useful for Both B2B & B2C businesses to help personal brand mindfulness in the online market.

## 5. eCommerce Offers Better Marketing Opportunities

Your eCommerce website is the best advertising device that you could at any point have. On a web account, anybody can advertise via online apparatuses such as web-based media advertising, email promoting, web search tool advertising, pay per click advertisements, and SEO assists you in constructing valuable connections & contacts.

For instance, with great SEO, your online store will show up in the top searches of SERPs. Likewise, online media organizations will give you a stage to draw in and construct trust with your clients through audits and appraisals, just as keeping them acknowledged with normal posts about your items and offers.

## 6. Your Online Store Will Stay Open 24*7/365:

Additionally, one of the incredible significances of eCommerce that eCommerce merchants can appreciate is store timings are currently all day, every day/365 as the eCommerce stores are working 24 hours per day, 7 days per week, contrasted with the customary stores.

Along these lines, merchants can expand their deals by boosting the number of requests. Nonetheless, it's additionally useful for clients when they can buy items and administrations at whatever point they need, whether it's early morning/midnight.

## 7. eCommerce Is Easier & More Convenient

Individuals' lives are rushed; getting to an actual store implies taking a ton of time and exertion. In this way, beginning an online store implies you can find a way into your client's bustling lives, making the items they need available when they need them.

The agreeable thing about eCommerce is purchasing those choices that are fast, simple, helpful, and simple in understanding with the capability to move supports on the web.

"In web-based shopping, your product is consistently a single tick away instead of actual shopping where you might be compelled to hang tight for quite a long time or months before a product you requested is accessible," says Heritage House, who sell kid suits on the web.

On account of eCommerce's accommodation, shoppers can save heaps of time, endeavors just as cash via looking for their items effectively and making buying on the web.

## 8. Personalize Your Shopping Experience

In the event that there is one of the unmistakable favorable circumstances of having an online store, you will have the option to know what your buyer does. Genuinely, it would be entirely awkward for a likely purchaser to enter your store, and you were constantly behind him, inquiring what he needs or for what valid reason he doesn't accept your item.

Web-based business permits you, for instance, to know when in the process you left the buy midway and even recall that you left it in the center by sending an email. This, also, can assist you with improving your shopping experience for other events: shortening the means to finish the request or offering those purchaser items with comparable attributes.

## 9. Improve the Image of Your Business

Among the benefits of having some online store, there's no uncertainty that it likewise incorporates improving the picture of your organization. Offering a decent online deals stage to clients will give your organization an extraordinary corporate appearance.

Not exclusively will it end up being state-of-the-art; however, it will likewise show interest in encouraging buyer buys. For instance, it keeps you from making a trip to the actual spot of offer and permits you to analyze costs from home. Likewise, because of what we have referenced as devotion or input, you can even actualize upgrades in your items that clients will esteem emphatically

## 10. Easily Receive Feedback on Products

Have you generally needed to understand consumers' opinions about what you are selling to offer more or make it greater? Indeed, the online store will permit you to get that input to actualize enhancements in the business, through star appraisals, with the chance of leaving remarks.

Also, the client will feel heard after their buy. There could be no greater method to thank you for your trust in buying your organization's items. Besides, in the event that you offer the quality, you'll have nothing to stress over. Empowering an immediate channel where others notice what they can anticipate from the given resource is an extraordinary public illustration of trust in online business.

## 11. Maximum Security of Transactions

Today, working on the internet is practically more secure and dependable than doing this in an actual store. From home, without anybody watching on your mysterious number or Mastercard. The eCommerce site should have an SSL endorsement.

This testament not just permits safe perusing on the website. What's more, it keeps the information scrambled to be protected to add keys & passwords. This won't just be important for the client's business account yet to utilize much more touchy information, for example, Mastercard data with complete, true serenity.

It merits referencing that 33% of eCommerce specialists distinguished security, versatile installments, and portable applications as the main interests in 2019. Security will keep on being one of the best spotlights on eCommerce.

With changes in innovation, client practices, and shopping designs, dealers should give arrangements guaranteeing the trust and security of shopping measures.

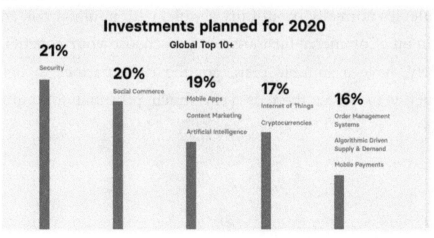

## 12 Ready for the Trade of the Future

It's another significant detail considering the long haul of the business. Search customer spending and patterns, the headway of innovation, and the most recent insights gauge that by 2040, 95 percent of buys will be executed through the web.

Along these lines, it's not just discussing a pattern of the present yet additionally about what the business relations of things to come will be. Furthermore, similarly, as though you are not on the internet, you don't exist; if your business doesn't sell on the web, it is monstrously restricting its deals.

## 13. Increase in Sales

Everything mentioned previously is centered around a certain thing: having the option to build your deals. At the end of the day, the business relies on selling more, and in this way, what it will be based on.

All the past focuses add to the way that the 10th and last bit of leeway are that there's an expansion in the acquisition of your items. Arriving at more clients, improving your items on account of remarks, or being accessible 24 hours daily will without a doubt add to the entirety of this.

As a rule, it's normally beautifully simple, with minimal risk and cost to begin an eCommerce business. As you choose your benefits/items incisively, have a suitable plan, got the right partner to help you construct your store, there is very much potential for automated revenue                    &                    high                    ROI.

# Chapter: 2 Accounting and Its Purpose

Accounting is the structured method of defining, tracking, assessing, classifying, checking, and transmitting financial records. It shows a company's profit or loss over a specified time, as well as the value and quality of its assets and liabilities, as well as its shareholders' equity.

## 2.1 Why is Accounting Important?

Accounting is very important and necessary for small business owners because it requires owners, administrators, investors, and other stakeholders to determine the company's financial results. Accounting provides key facts regarding profit & loss, costs & earnings, assets & liabilities for decision-making, scheduling, and risk management within an organization.

Accounting's main goal is to document financial transactions in books of records in order to recognize, calculate, and transmit economic results. Furthermore, tax reporting authorities mandate you to maintain simple books that track profits and expenditures.

## 2.2 What Is the Purpose of Accounting?

Accounting is regarded as the "Language of Business." It is a system of communicating financial information to multiple uses for decision-making purposes. The major objects of accounting are:

1.  **Recording transactions**

Accounting's primary purpose is to control a systematic, accurate, and full record of a company's financial activities. The accounting system's backbone is made up of these reports. When appropriate, company owners should be able to review and evaluate transactions.

## 2. Budgeting and planning

Business owners must prepare how they can distribute their limited resources, such as workers, cash, machinery and equipment to meet the company's goals.

Budgeting and planning, an integral aspect of business management, enable companies to prepare accordingly by forecasting requirements and resources. This assists in the coordination of multiple corporate segments.

## 3. Decision making

Accounting assists in a variety of decision-making processes and facilitates business owners in developing policies to improve business process efficiency. The price to be charged for products and services, the resources required to produce these products and services, as well as financing and business opportunities are all examples of decisions based on accounting information.

## 4. Business performance

Business owners may use financial records to assess how good their organization is doing. Financial reports provide a credible tool to evaluate important performance indicators, encouraging business owners to compare their output to that of their rivals as well as their past performance.

## 5. Financial position

The financial statements issued at the end of the accounting period represent a company's financial position at the time. It displays the amount of capital invested, the number of funds utilized by the company, the profit and loss, as well as the number of assets and liabilities.

## 6. Liquidity

Mismanagement of funds is a common cause of small business failure. Accounting assists in assessing a company's liquidity, which is characterized as the cash and other liquid capital available to pay off debts. Via the identification of bottlenecks, the information lowers the risk of bankruptcy.

## 7. Financing

Accounting assists business owners in the preparation of historical financial records and also financial forecasts that may be utilized while preparing for a loan or securing investment.

## 8. Control

Accounting assists in avoiding losses attributable to stealing, fraud, mistakes, injury, obsolescence, and mismanagement by enforcing different checks within the company. Internal monitoring secures the company's finances to eliminate long-term risks.

## 9. Legal requirements

Businesses must retain correct financial statements of their activities and disclose those records with shareholders, tax officials, and regulators, according to the statute. The financial statements and details are often needed for the filing of indirect and direct taxes.

# Chapter: 3 Why Is Accounting Useful for Small Business Owners?

One of the most common causes of small business failure, especially in the first year, is poor financial management. Accounting plays a critical role in providing information that assists small companies in their growth and advancement when they have a restricted budget and other resources.

Accounting is important for small business owners for the following reasons:

> Maintain a careful watch on the cash balance. You should enforce strategies for effective record-keeping and a solid financial strategy to prevent the company cash flow from running dry.

> Cost management may help small business owners grasp the principles of fixed expenses, variable costs, and how to correctly cost a project. This way, you won't waste funds on a project you felt would be profitable.

> Accounting helps you to have a clearer view of the company's health. Learn to interpret a balance sheet, financial statement, and cash flow statement to do this.

> It helps you in identifying and avoiding consumer, employee, and supplier bribery and stealing.

➢ You'll be more able to tackle investigations if you grasp corporate accounts and transactions.

➢ When working with corporate leaders who have a strong grip on the company's finances and are mindful of the financial consequences, bankers are more comfortable.

If you're a sole proprietor or have workers, the trick to expanding your small company is to monitor your financial records on a routine basis and build a comprehensive budget that helps you to recognize operating inefficiencies. Saving a little money on a few things will add up to a lot of money in the long run.

# Chapter: 4 Accounting basics How to Run a Successful Online Business

A painful task is accounting. It is the dull side of the business. But you can't ignore it if you want your business to grow. You could try to dump all your receipts into a drawer and hand them over to a stranger. Yet you are going to give them financial power. That means losing your business's future. You will hand them a sweet slice of change to do it all for you, too. I guarantee it isn't as hard as you may be afraid of, though. And, for day-to-day operations, you shouldn't require an accountant. You should still know the fundamentals yourself, even though you are paying for guidance. You may acknowledge and challenge what someone is talking to you in this context. It's your business at stake, after all.

The following accounting fundamentals help you need to know to grasp your money.

## 1. Get Accounting Software

Don't bother using excel or a calculator to piece it all together. Do yourself a favor and get software for accounting. FreshBooks are sold to clients that operate e-commerce businesses. Or there are a variety of accounting software apps you should get right in their app store if you use Shopify. Your business and interests would rely on the right choice. Make sure you choose a bookkeeping system while you're shopping in the app store. Look for software to monitor revenue, expenditures, and inventory. Keep away from programs that generate invoices only or include reports only. You want a tool that's able to do everything for you. Select one that can sync directly to your e-commerce store, whether you want apps like Shopify or go for something different. It would make things even better.

## 2. Monitor Cash Flow

Get one if you don't have a separate bank account with your business yet. You need to realize that making money is your job. And watching the cash balance is the best way to see this. When you've got more coming in than heading out, you actually do well, don't you? The timing of money going out and coming back can also be monitored. After all, what if, tomorrow, all your bills are due? When you have one million rolling's in next month, it won't mean a whole lot if you can't pay the workers by then. Bear in mind any investments on your accounts that you have. What ways of payment do you give your clients? Are some of them putting a grip on the money? From the moment a consumer spends to the time the money is in your accounts, is there a five-day delay? When you're finding out when you have resources to spare, you ought to remember this. For monitoring currency, Shopify offers a free template. With Excel, you can quickly build your own.

Per week, monitor what you plan to spend. Track the money that you plan per week to come in. You realize you're going to have a challenge if what you need to pay is more than the new bank balance and what's coming in. To improve to boost your cash flow, adopt these tips:

- Do not spend anything sooner than you have got to. If it is due within thirty days, compensate it within thirty days.

- To ensure revenue stays through, suggest selling recurring payment contracts or subscriptions to consumers.

- Hold a reserve 'just in case' in your company bank account.

- Do not overcomplicate yourself. You do not require massive statements of cash balance.

### 3. Determine how inventory should be counted

Ignore this step if you're selling a service. Inventory is the product that you sell or all the materials that you use to make that item. Do not forget to include any costs for your product being wrapped or packaged. Decide what minimum inventory volume you want to have on hand, and make sure you are tracking inventory before you pass this point so you can reorder. The last thing you want is for inventory to run out and lose sales.

Why does inventory form part of the basics of accounting?

Money equals inventory.

It is the money you spent buying that stuff. You will not make any money back until you sell your product. And while it is sitting in your warehouse, the money tied to your inventory can change (or store, or apartment).

If I purchase 50 items for 100 dollars each, and the price rises up to 150 dollars tomorrow, then immediately, my inventory is worth more.

So, if tomorrow's price falls to 50 dollars, the worth of my inventory is less.

And beware of 'shrinkage'!

That's why, unexpectedly, you have fewer inventory than you should have.

You know you've purchased 50 items. You understand that you sold and delivered 40. You should be left 10 items, right? What if you have only 8 left? This is shrinkage. Perhaps an item was misplaced, or robbed, or destroyed and had to be discarded away. There are plenty of explanations for why this happens. When you don't have a physical department location, the positive thing is the shrinkage is smaller. Currently, factory shrinkage is pretty poor. Less than 1% of the overall product is a normal shrinkage. It's also less probable that you will have shrinkage if you're running a business out of your house. After all, if you're the only person around it, you are less likely to see anyone rob the inventory. Compared with a large warehouse, it's also a lot tougher to lose stock in an apartment. Having said that, shrinkage will happen to everyone. This is why it's necessary to routinely physically count inventory. If you have missed 100 dollars worth of goods and factor it into your accounting, you ought to know.

CGS, which means cost of goods sold, is an expense directly linked to the goods sold by you. This is inventory sold, and also how much it costs to produce that inventory. Suppose say there is one widget you sell. The cost of goods sold for that widget should be whatever it costs you for the parts and also whatever it costs to build it. If the widget parts cost 60 dollars, the packaging cost is 15 dollars, and you paid someone 15 to put it together, that the total cost of the widget will 90 dollars.

| MATERIAL COST | 60$ |
|---|---|

| | |
|---|---|
| PACKAGING COST | 15$ |
| LABOUR COST | <u>15$</u> |
| **TOTAL COST OF GOODS SOLD** | 90 $ |

## 4. Calculate all Expenses

You already understand that the costs are directly tied to the volume of sales. Next, you need to know how much it costs you for anything else. Any costs that do not grow as you sell more or drop when you sell fewer are known as 'fixed costs.' Let's say If you pay a monthly rent, for instance, the price is set. If you sell one widget or a million, it won't shift. Such costs are not part of the cost of the goods sold, and the profit margin is not compensated for. However, they do control your earnings and your cash flow.

Some Common fixed expenses are

➤ Utilities

➤ Rent

➤ Interest on loan payments

➤ Property Tax

➤ Wages

These expenses are considered a fixed expense because even though you sell nothing next month, you have to reimburse them. Do not confuse this with an expense where every month is the very same amount. An expense such as electricity may be more than one month longer than the next. Or maybe there's more to it in winter than in summer. In accounting standards, it is always a fixed expense. You will use an average for budgeting if expenses change month to month.

## 5. Find out Break-Even Sales

Budgeting and planning are essential aspects of operating a business. Next, you are not only going to want to know if last month you made a profit, you are going to want to know if this month and next you want to earn more.

Your break-even sales amount is the amount of sales dollars you need to earn to cover all your costs.

Let's assume, for instance, all the fixed costs add up to 5,000 dollars a month. This ensures that you have to sell enough of the product to meet the cost of producing it (including labor cost) and also an additional 5,000 dollars only to break-even (no profit, no loss).

$$\text{Break-Even Sale} = \frac{\text{Fixed Cost}}{\text{Revenue per unit-Variable cost per unit}}$$

$$= \frac{\text{Fixed Cost}}{\text{Unit Margin}}$$

If your break-even number of units are 5,000 and you sell only 3000, then you are in problem. And if break-even 5000 and you sell 7000, then you are in a good position.

## 6. Schedule your right tax rates for customers

Here is the aspect for which most citizens groan: taxation. Taxes are necessary, and they may become very complex. At this point, you may want to contact a tax consultant specialist, if you sell a number of various goods & services to a lot of people around the world. Thankfully, systems these days are fairly smart. For you, the software can take control of much of this.

## 7. Prepare your Tax Payments

Now, if you are properly set up to collect tax, you also need to make sure you are ready to pay it. Your tax laws will rely on where you are located, actually. At a minimum, believe that as much tax as you have earned must be submitted. This suggests that it is necessary to consider that money of tax is set aside. If not, then when you submit tax return, you face some hurdles. Many online shopping platforms allow you to pay tax on your purchase price, such as Shopify.

For example, if you buy a product that price is 100 dollars and the tax rate is 20%, then you will pay the amount included tax.

| | |
|---|---|
| Product Cost | 100 $ |
| Tax Rate (15%) | 15 $ |
| **Total amount included Tax** | **115 $** |

## 8. Balance Sheet

At the end, you must understand your balance sheet. We have already addressed all as well as cash balance on the income statement. The balance sheet is the final thing to cover. This is what helps you watch the long-term performance of your business and see how your business is performing in general. An income statement is a timely overview. The broader image is a balance sheet. Assets, liabilities, and equity make up the balance sheet.

| | | | | |
|---|---|---|---|---|
| **BUSINESS CONSULTING COMPANY**<br>**BALANCE SHEET**<br>**As at December 31, 2015** | | | | |
| **Assets** | | **$** | **Liabilities & Stockholders' equity** | **$** |
| Current assets: | | | Liabilities: | |
| Cash | | 85,550 | Notes payable | 5,000 |
| Accounts receivable | | 4,700 | Accounts payable | 1,600 |
| Prepaid building rent | | 1,500 | Salaries payable | 2,000 |
| Unexpired insurance | | 3,600 | Income tax payable | 3,000 |
| Supplies | | 250 | Unearned service revenue | 4,400 |
| | | | | |
| Total current assets | | 95,600 | Total liabilities | 16,000 |
| Non-current assets: | | | Stockholders' equity: | |
| Equipment | 9,000 | | Capital stock | 50,000 |
| Acc. dep. - Equipment | 3,600 | 5,400 | Retained earnings | 35,000 | 85,000 |
| | | | | |
| Total assets | | 101,000 | Total liabilities & stockholders' equity | 101,000 |

I have finally discussed all the accounting basics you should be practicing day to day and month to month. Start with simple accounting software. It can make your life a lot easier.

Then, note that cash is king, and keep a grip on your cash flow. You should be doing this on a frequent basis unless you have a large cash reserve built.

Next, you ought to consider the revenue, expenditures, and earnings. This is your income statement, which lets you know whether you are earning money per week, month or year.

Do not neglect to schedule for taxation. Set up the e-commerce platform to receive them if you need to. Place the money together to reimburse them should you need to.

Finally, construct the balance sheet. Or let the accounting software do it for you. This will help you exactly how 'healthy' the business is long term. It's a simple way to know if you have so much debt.

There are plenty of other accounting rules and methods that will help you save money at tax time.

There will also be reporting options that can be addressed whether you're seeking to get investors or a loan for growth.

But for running your company, don't get pulled into the complicated laws. It will only distract you from your crucial day job of operating your business.

An accountant will assist you with something beyond and above the fundamentals if you require to.

# Chapter: 5 Common Accounting Mistakes and How to Avoid Them

Numerous new business visionaries handle their bookkeeping and accounting when they are beginning. Here are how to stay away from some normal DIY bookkeeping ruins.

When numerous business visionaries first begin, they attempt to deal with their bookkeeping to set aside cash. Notwithstanding, following each penny of pay, costs, charges, and seller installments are messy and tedious. Errors can happen effectively & they can charge your huge business loads of cash.

To help you forestall these monetary blunders, the absolute most regular bookkeeping ruins are below that entrepreneurs make and — all the more significantly — how to keep away from them.

## 1. Lack of organization

Accounting requires extraordinary association abilities. You'll need to record each exchange, digitize or store receipts for future reference, figure duties, and the sky is the limit from there. In case you're not appropriately following or putting away data, you'll probably miss a significant exchange or lose a receipt, which could get you into difficulty come season of tax.

## 2. Not following a regular accounting schedule

With the wide range of various duties, you have as an entrepreneur, refreshing your books may tumble to the lower part of your plan for the day. Notwithstanding, it's imperative to set a normal timetable for including late payments and costs. While every day refreshes are ideal, you ought to, in any event, enter your exchanges consistently.

## 3. Failing to reconcile accounts

While you are recording monetary information and income in your books, you need to routinely return and guarantee your ledger mirrors that equivalent equilibrium. In the event that there's a difference between the two, there's likely a mistake that requires quick thoughtfulness regarding keep the issue from deteriorating. Consistently exploring your business financial balances against your books can likewise help you get any fake exchanges that may have happened.

## 4. Ignoring small transactions

It's not difficult to disregard that little thank you blessing you sent to a customer or the ream of printer paper you got on your way back to the workplace. Regardless of how immaterial the exchange is, it's critical to record it & get some receipt. In case of an assessment review, you should have the option to give the IRS records of all your costs of doing business, even the little ones.

## 5. Not backing up your data

Envision if the gadget on which you put away your business' monetary data was lost, hacked, or taken — and you did not have it upheld up anyplace. These problems can emerge whenever, and you should be set up to reestablish your books. Luckily, there are numerous reinforcement alternatives accessible that will empower you to keep an extra, state-of-the-art duplicate of the business financials.

## 6. Not using an accounting software

In case you're monitoring your business funds in an Excel bookkeeping page or a paper record, you might need to consider moving up to programming. Putting resources into the correct bookkeeping programming can assist you with maintaining a strategic distance from botches and, at last, make it simpler to deal with your accounts.

Most bookkeeping programmings incorporate the financial balance, meaning less manual work. These projects likewise make it simple to back up your information if there should be an occurrence of a crisis. Also, if you wind up expecting to recruit a bookkeeping administration for your business, having unified programming will guarantee the bookkeeper has all the recorded information they require to deal with your books, finance, and assessments.

Regardless of whether you're taking care of your bookkeeping or moving to an expert, accounting mix-ups can cause significant issues for your business. It is ideal to forestall & face these problems.

# Chapter: 6 Business Challenges & Solutions

Small enterprises experience a number of obstacles throughout their first few years of operation. Others are more challenging to resolve than others, and according to the U.S. Bureau of Labour Statistics, about 20% of small companies collapse during their first year. Fifty percent go under by the close of their fifth year, and that figure increases to 80 percent by the tenth year.

With so poor survival rates, it's clear to see why people are worried for their first few years of the company. In fact, though, many common market issues and problems are actually fixable. You can notice several moments when you need to take a step back, make an effort to understand the pressure points that you experience and re-think your plan.

Each small business faces some problems here, including some tactical tips about how to solve them.

1. Find the Customers

2. Increasing Brand Awareness

3. Designing Email List

4. Lead Generation

5. Delighting the Customers

6. Hiring Talented People

7. Managing Workflow

8. Financial Strategy

9. Scaling

## 1. Find Customers

This first one is not just an issue for small enterprises. Marketers of well-known firms such as Toyota, Apple, KFC, and McDonald's are not yet waiting for the leads to come in: Also, the largest, most popular firms have employees working tirelessly to attract new customers every single day.

Finding consumers may be especially challenging for small companies that are not well-known. It seems, for instance, like there are too many platforms you may choose to concentrate on. How do you decide what to prioritize and where money can be allocated?

**How to solve it:**

Seeking consumers begins by deciding who the target consumer is. It does not work for everyone to spray and pray — you need to ensure you distribute the message to the correct people.

By designing buyer personas, you will get a feel of what your potential buyers are like, what they are doing, and where they spend some time online.

It will significantly boost the market outcomes by producing very particular ones. When you have developed your buyer personas, you can start developing content and reaching out to your potential buyers in areas where they invest time online and with ads that appeal to them.

## 2. Brand Awareness

Customers can not purchase from you if they don't know who you are. Often it may seem like the largest brands of today seem to have sprung up from nowhere. When did it turn into a household name? Why did they continue to spread so quickly? Is it feasible for your organization to expand in the same way?

Of note, the hard work, mistakes, and rejections of each of these businesses existed behind the scenes. But there are tactics how you can begin right away to spread the word about your company and create a strong reputation.

**How to solve it:**

There are several approaches to increase brand awareness, but concentrate on three in this book about public relations, blogging & co-marketing.

- **Public Relations**

Public relations are less about competing for a place on a news site and more about concentrating your message on the consumer and discovering your location. I suggest reading First Round Capital's excellent research about what entrepreneurs and small companies often get wrong regarding public relations, which also provides some useful guidance about how to find out who reports the industry, develop relationships, and communicate with reporters.

- **Blogging**

Running a high-quality blog on a daily basis can also help you create brand recognition. A blog not only helps push traffic to your website and turn the traffic into leads, but that also helps you to build authority and confidence among your prospects in your industry. It will also assist you in the creation of an email list, which takes us to our next step.

- **C0-marketing**

Collaborating with another brand allows you to inherit some of their name and credibility while still producing brand evangelists outside of your immediate radius. It's an ideal opportunity to complement the organic marketing activities by acquiring a wide range of potential connections. More details about how to get acquainted with co-marketing can be found in our ebook.

### 3. Designing Email List

You must create confidence by being top-of-mind and continually delivering value to drive prospects down their buyer's path to finally becoming your client.

The first move is to link prospects to your email list.

As if creating an email list is not complicated enough, the typical marketing account degraded by 22.5 percent last year. That means you'll need to expand your email list by nearly a quarter just to hold it up to date, let alone develop it. Seeking opportunities to continuously introduce fresh, different email addresses to the lists is the task of the marketing staff.

Yet what many people term "making an email list" is simply purchasing an email list, and it is never a smart idea to purchase an email list. I repeat not a good idea. It is not only a waste of resources, but it'll also damage your email deliverability and I.P. credibility. If purchasing or renting email lists is your new plan, then it's time to rebuild and find appropriate ways to position certain tools.

**How to solve it:**

Develop opt-in email lists instead of purchasing or renting lists. Subscribers who willingly give you their email address so that you can send them updates make up an opt-in email list.

The process of opting in needs the accessibility of the website that catches their email address. This can be accomplished with a shape builder or other method to transform (more on that later).

Creating a market is the other part of the puzzle. Through making excellent blog posts, you will do this and make it convenient for people to subscribe, which can help you improve your web visibility, build up search credibility, and develop evangelists from your content at the same time.

Create an informative opt-in message and email it to your old list, inviting contacts to re-opt-in and pledging to delete any contacts that don't reply.

Rising your email list does not often mean growing your sales-qualified lead list, which leads me to my next stage.

## 4. Lead Generation

Lead generation is another concern most small companies share, namely, creating sufficient leads to maintain the sales staff satisfied.

However, the most critical goal of a marketing team is to produce high-quality leads in vast amounts. A decent lead generation engine transforms website users into future buyers and maintains a constant stream of sales leads flowing in as you sleep.

**How to solve it:**

To make the lead generation method function for your business, you must first increase the conversion rate of your current website. The most critical asset you have for converting opportunities into clients is your website. Look and question yourself from your website:

Do visitors specifically direct each of the webpages to take some action, or do they leave them uncertain what to do next?

Can you use a program, like HubSpot's free lead generation tool, that instantly pulls the inputs from your forms and brings them into your communication database?

For any single campaign that you manage, can you build custom landing pages?

Do you have CTAs for any of your blog posts for lead generation? (Have you got a blog at all?)

First, prioritize the most major blogs on your website. The homepage, "About" page, "Contact Us" page, and probably one or two of the most famous blog posts are usually the sites that pull in the bulk of visitors for most companies. Learn how to decide which sites to prioritize and how to customize them in this topic.

Then, utilizing conversion applications such as:

- Hello bars, hello

- Pop-up windows

- Diaposit-ins

Finally, free lead generation tools and applications for startups can be used. It is a huge obstacle in and of itself to afford ads in general, but it can be a game-changer to identify and incorporate the most effective free marketing methods.

### 5. Delighting the Customers

A perfect target is consumer loyalty, but much greater is customer delight. After all, the ones who purchase from you again, write expert opinions and accept case studies, and recommend you to others they trust, are delighted consumers.

You have to transcend standards and offer an unmatched service in order to gain true consumer delight such that your consumers become promoters of your brand.

**How to solve it:**

For your customer, it takes effort to begin solving in a fashion that converts them into crazed fans. Here are few moves that will bring you into the proper mindset:

> ➢ Realize why you were picked by your customers and what they want and need

> ➢ At the beginning of the commitment, set clear goals

> ➢ Deliver on certain requirements (and serve the wishes of your customers)

> ➢ Dream of innovative approaches to include unique extras that go beyond and above the call of duty.

> ➢ Continue to monitor consumer loyalty and allow changes.

### 6. Hiring talented workers

Without a great team who knows your mission and encourages your actions, none of the above will happen at large.

Hiring is one of the most challenging tasks for small companies, particularly when small corporate leaders are often under-resourced to start with. Hiring new hires is a huge deal and a difficult operation, and most businesses invest about 4,000 dollars per new hire on onboarding. Employee attrition can be very costly if you do not recruit properly.

Still, as Howard Bernstein, CEO of 2020 On-site Optometry, says, it is hard to recognize anything on your own. That's why it is crucial to identify and recruit the best people and others who are genuinely passionate about what you are doing.

**How to solve it:**

For a short-term recruiting approach, it is simple to send out a work description, screen candidates, and make a decision. However, owing to the high expenses of recruiting the incorrect employee, it's essential to dedicate a considerable amount of time to the hiring phase. When you may locate excellent workers, do not settle for decent staff, even though it takes more time. Good workers are what can drive the business to the next stage.

And when you build customer personas for your employers, for your career seekers, create nominee personas. For each new job you recruit for, the personas must be different, but they may share certain basic characteristics across the culture of the business.

Next, take care in drawing applicants to the name of your company and making them involved in knowing more. This would assist you in creating a recruitment pipeline that will have the same certainty in hiring as it does in revenue. Then translate certain opportunities into applicants.

### 7.                  Managing the Workflow

When you have the staff in position to make the magic possible, handling operations as you scale is the next obstacle. You want to make sure the staff has the procedures and resources they need to perform successful work fast.

Around the same moment, as a corporate owner, you will not be everywhere at once. So, how can you remain centered on the market but still ensuring that everybody in the organization gets everything they require?

**How to solve it:**

By providing opportunities for them to get suggestions, the only approach to diagnose the barriers the team encounters and improve productivity is to build ways to identify them. It is possible to do this via:

- ➤ Surveys on employee satisfaction

- ➤ Frequent discussions of immediate reports one-on-one

- ➤ Assuring the success of your direct reports Hold one-on-one conferences for their direct reports

- ➤ Occasionally, skip-level meetings are conducted.

- ➤ Asking regarding group risks and the things that cause them the most "pain" in their positions

- ➤ Seeking the similarities & the bottlenecks in the reviews you get

## 8. Financial Strategy

More capital (whether staff, resources or time) can ideally improve productivity and output. Providing all of the support you can to the staff is the first move in maintaining smooth operations.

In principle, it seems easy, but have you realized the caveat, everything. Can you? Unfortunately, corporate owners have revenue-based and margin-based spending constraints.

It becomes a struggle then to maximise productivity when operating under such limits, investing in the company without going overboard. By making sound choices focused on strong financial planning, this is solved.

**How to solve it:**

Each business is going to be different, so by remaining in front of invoices and bookkeeping, you'll need to use business credit carefully, reduce expenses where possible, and control cash flow. You will be assisted by corporate accountants and investment planners who evaluate the financial condition and help you to make sound choices.

## 9. Scaling

According to Nick Rellas, Drizly's co-founder and CEO, "There's this balance of creating power efficiency early, versus doing just what you have to do to get it all completed."

This is a complicated one, especially because every scenario is different. This topic can be seen in any aspect of the industry, including product growth, promotion, and content design, recruiting, and so on.

Most business leaders, for instance, would drive production at all costs. However, if you develop your business too fast, you'll find yourself trying to recruit staff quickly. Since preparation requires time, this can overwhelm the more seasoned team members. And if you wouldn't adequately prepare your staff, it might backfire.

**How to solve it:**

There's no right solution here, sadly. "The scale can tip one way or the other based on where you are in your business' lifecycle," Rellas says, "although I do agree you need both at various times."

Not obsessing about every aspect, but obsessing about the correct specifics, is what it comes right down to. For example, obsessing over product excellence may be less relevant than obsessing over customer care. It is easier to set away your worries and introduce a product that is not flawless so it can be changed and enhanced at all times. After all, you will understand a lot more easily what's effective and what isn't until the goods are in possession of your consumers.

# Chapter: 7 Key Accounting Terms

The following are some standard accounting terminology that any small business owner should be acquainted with:

1. GAAP (Generally Agreed Accounting Standards)

2. Cash basis accounting

3. Accrual basis accounting

4. Accounts payable

5. Accounts receivable

## 1. Generally Agreed Accounting Standards (GAAP)

GAAP is a series of standard accounting principles that most American corporations are expected to follow. These guidelines detail how to keep track of, calculate, and report on the company's assets to third parties.

## 2. Cash basis accounting

Cash basis accounting is one of the two most popular accounting techniques, as it involves recording revenue and expenditures where they are earned and charged. Small companies like this approach because it is easy, despite the fact that it can offer a false impression of your cash flow (e.g., if you receive payment for a bill the month after you issued it).

### 3. Accrual basis accounting

Accrual basis accounting is needed for companies with a turnover of more than $25 million. You must log revenue as you charge it, rather than when it is paid, which implies you might be paying taxes on the money you haven't even received. However, opposed to cash basis accounting, it offers a more reliable long-term perspective of the finances.

### 4. Accounts payable

Accounts payable contains all unpaid payments for goods and services that you owe to suppliers. To accurately forecast cash flow, these liabilities must be considered against the company's assets and income.

### 5. Accounts receivable

Any of the money owing to the company by its consumers or clients is paid for in the accounts receivable. These accounts are normally monitored by invoices, which specify payment conditions (e.g., within a specified number of days of receipt) so you know when to expect incoming funds.

# Chapter: 8 Common Accounting Reports

As part of their financial accounting procedures, every business must learn how to prepare a few main financial reports. Outside participants, such as owners, suppliers, and creditors, can use these documents to record the business's profits and expenses.

## 8.1 Profit & Loss Statement

When it is time to file your company returns with the IRS, accountants and tax preparers would most certainly ask for a (P&L) statement, but you will still need to share it with lenders if you apply for financing. Your profit and loss statement (P&L) outlines profitability of your company by listing gross margin, profit, sales, cost of goods sold and other primary indicators over a specific time period (monthly, quarterly and annually).

*Profit and Loss Statement Template*

**[Company Name]**

[Street Address], [City, ST ZIP Code]
[Phone: 555-555-5555] [Fax: 123-123-123456]
[abc@example.com]

**Profit & Loss Statement**

**For the Period Ended** _____

| Income | $ | $ |
|---|---|---|
| Sales | 0000000 | |
| Services | 00000000 | |
| Other Income | 00000 | |
| | | |
| **Total Income** | | 0000000 |
| | | |
| | | |
| **Expenses** | | |
| Accounting | 0000000 | |
| Advertising | 000000 | |
| Assets Small | 000000 | |
| Bank Charges | 000000 | |
| Cost of Goods Sold | 00000 | |
| | | |
| | | |
| **Total Expenses** | | 00000000 |
| | | |
| **Profit/Loss** | | 00000000 |

## 8.2 Balance Sheet

Balance sheet is a "snapshot" of the company's financial condition at any specific point in time. It includes a summary of the company's capital, assets & liabilities, both of which may be used to assess the valuation of your company.

## ACCOUNT FORMAT

**BUSINESS CONSULTING COMPANY**
**BALANCE SHEET**
**As at Date_____**

| Assets | $ | Liabilities & Stockholders' equity | $ |
|---|---|---|---|
| Current assets: | | Liabilities: | |
| Cash | | Notes payable | |
| Accounts receivable | | Accounts payable | |
| Prepaid building rent | | Salaries payable | |
| Unexpired insurance | | Income tax payable | |
| Supplies | | Unearned service revenue | |
| | | | |
| Total current assets | | Total liabilities | |
| Non-current assets: | | Stockholders' quity: | |
| Equipment | | Capital stock | |
| Acc. Deal - Equipment | | Retained earnings | |
| | | | |
| Total assets | | Total Liabilities & Stockholders' equity | |

## 8.2 Cash Flow Statement

A cash flow statement is a financial statement that records and categorises each actual cost and revenue line by line, helping you to maintain track of the company's financial operation. About any line item in the cash flow statement would be identified as an operation, investment, or financing task.

You will also be liable for making a stockholders' equity statement whether the business includes shareholders or partners with equity in the company. This declaration, which is part of your balance sheet, outlines all adjustments in the valuation of the stockholders' equity rights over time, normally from the beginning of the end of the year.

| Example Corporation Statement of Cash Flows | All numbers in thousands | |
|---|---|---|
| **Operating Activities** | $ | **10,100** |
| Net Income from Operations | $ | 10,000 |
| Add: Depreciation Expense | $ | 100 |
| | | |
| **Investing Activities** | $ | **(500)** |
| Purchase of Equipment | $ | (1,000) |
| Sale of used equipment | $ | 500 |
| | | |
| **Financing Activities** | $ | **4,500** |
| Increase in Long Term Debt | $ | 2,500 |
| Issuance of Stock | $ | 5,000 |
| Dividends Paid | $ | (3,000) |
| | | |
| **Net Change in Cash Flow** | $ | **14,100** |

# Chapter: 9 Taxation

Taxation is the method of enforcing or levying a tax on individuals and corporate companies through a government or the taxing authority. Taxation applies at all levels, from corporate tax (GST) to goods and services tax.

## 9.1 What is Taxation

The federal and state governments have a major influence on how taxes are set around the country. The state and federal governments have enacted numerous policy changes in recent years to streamline the taxation mechanism and maintain accountability in the region. The Goods and Services Tax (GST) was one such reform that eased the tax system relating to the selling and distribution of goods and services in the world.

## 9.2 Purposes of Taxation

In the nineteenth century, the common assumption was that taxation could be used solely to support the nation. Governments have used taxes for more than just fiscal reasons in the past, and they do so again today. The differentiation between wealth sharing, income inequality, and economic prosperity is a valuable way to look at the function of taxes, according to American economist Richard A. Musgrave. (Sometimes global growth or progress and foreign competition are identified as distinct priorities, but they can be absorbed under the other three in general.) The first target, resource distribution, is reinforced if tax policy does not intervene with economic allocations in the absence of a legitimate justification for intervention, such as the need to minimize emissions. The second aim, wage redistribution, is intended to reduce income and wealth inequality disparities. The aim of stabilization is to sustain high jobs and market stability, which is achieved by tax reform, monetary policy, government budget policy & debt management.

## 9.2 Classes of Taxes

Taxes have been categorized in different forms in the theory of public finance, based on who pays for them, who carries the ultimate responsibility of them, the degree to which the burden may be transferred, and other considerations. Taxes are more generally categorized as either direct or indirect, such as the income tax of the former category and the sales tax of the latter. The requirements for discriminating between direct and indirect taxes are contested by economists, and it is uncertain which group such taxes, such as property tax or corporate income tax, should fall under. A direct tax is generally said to be one that cannot be transferred from the individual to anyone else, although it can be an indirect tax.

1. Direct Taxes

2. Indirect Taxes

Now we learn about direct and Indirect Taxes

**1. Direct Taxes**

Direct taxes are mainly imposed on individual citizens and are generally dependent on the taxpayer's capacity to compensate as determined by revenue, spending, or net worth. The following is a list of the most popular forms of direct taxes.

Individual income taxes are usually based on the taxpayer's gross personal net income (that might be an individual, couple, or family) that reaches a specified level. The conditions surrounding the capacity to pay, such as marital status, amount and age of the child, and financial pressures arising from sickness, are more widely tailored to take into consideration. Taxes are often charged at phased scales, which ensures that rates rise as income increases. A taxpayer's and family's personal exemptions can produce a range of income that is entitled to a zero-tax rate.

Net worth taxes are imposed on a person's overall net worth, which is proportional to value of assets less his liabilities. As in income tax, the taxpayer's specific situation should be taken into account.

Personal or direct consumption taxes (also referred to as taxes on spending or taxes on expenditure) are essentially imposed on all receipts that are not channeled into savings. In comparison to indirect spending taxes like the sales tax, a direct consumption tax may be customized to a person's financial circumstance by taking into account considerations like age, marital status, family status, and so on. This tax method has been implemented in only two nations, India & Sri Lanka, although it has long been appealing to theorists; both cases were short and ineffective. The "flat tax," which produces economic results close to those of the direct consumption tax by exempting many capital gains, came to be regarded favorably by tax analysts at the end of the 20th century. No nation has introduced a flat-rate tax base, while many have just one rate of income tax.

Inheritance taxation, in which the taxable object is the bequest earned by the individual inheriting, and estate taxes, of which the taxable object is the cumulative estate inherited by the deceased, are the two kinds of taxes imposed upon death. Inheritance taxes also take into account the taxpayer's specific conditions, such as the connection of the taxpayer to the beneficiary and his net wealth when the bequest is received. Estate payments, on the other hand, are normally phased depending on the value of the estate, although in certain nations, they include tax-free transfers to the partner and account for the number of heirs. Tax regimes which include a tax on gifts in excess of a certain threshold rendered by living individuals in order to avoid death duty from being circumvented by an exchange of property prior to death (see gift tax). Transfer taxes usually do not raise any money, if only because substantial tax collections can be prevented conveniently by estate planning.

## 2. Indirect Taxes

Indirect taxes, including imports and exports, are imposed on the output or sale of products and services or on transactions. Examples include general and limited excise taxes, VAT, taxes on some aspect of production or manufacturing, taxes on lawful purchases, and customs or import duties.

General sales taxes are levies that cover a large amount of consumer spending. The same tax rate may be extended to all taxable items, or separate rates can be applied to different products (such as food or clothing). Single-stage taxation may be levied at the retail level, like some states in the United States do, or at a pre-retail level (such as production or wholesale), as some developed countries do. At each point in the production-distribution process, multistage taxes are introduced. VAT, which grew in prominence during the second half of the 20th century, is usually collected by enabling the taxpayer to exclude from the sales debt the tax credit charged on transactions. At each point of the manufacturing and delivery process, the VAT has effectively substituted the turnover levy-a tax, with no tax relief charged at previous levels. Tax cascading, or the combined impact of the turnover tax, distorts economic decisions.

While they are usually applicable on a wide variety of items, sales taxes often exclude low-income families from the obligation to lower their tax burden. Excises, by contrast, are imposed only on individual products or facilities. Although almost all, including basics such as beef, flour, and salt, to non-essentials such as food, beer, cigarettes, coffee, and tea, to luxuries such as jewels and furs, taxes on a small category of goods, tobacco items, motor fuel, and alcoholic drinks, place excises and customs duties on most nations. Taxes on customer durables were extended on luxury items such as carriages, saddle horses, pianos, and billiard tables in earlier centuries. The car is currently a primary luxury tax item, primarily because registration regulations promote tax administration. Any nations also tax gaming & state-run jackpots have similar consequences as excises, with "take" of the government being, in essence, a gambling tax. Taxes on raw products, intermediate commodities (e.g., natural oil, alcohol), and equipment are imposed by certain nations.

Some excise duties and customs duties are particular, i.e., they are assessed on the grounds of the quantity, weight, duration, volume, or other particular features of the taxable product or service. Such excerpts, such as income taxes, are ad valorem, as determined by the price, depending on the valuation of the item. Legal transaction taxes are charged on the issue of bonds, on the selling (or transfer) of houses and land, and on sales on the stock market. They sometimes take the form of stamp duties for administrative reasons; that is, the legal or commercial paper is stamped to signify payment of the fee. Stamp taxes are regarded as an annoyance tax by many tax analysts; they are more often seen in less-developed countries & slow down the transactions on which they are applicable.

# Chapter: 10 Small Business Tax Return

Most people are dreaming of holiday shopping, celebrations, and holidays as the year draws to an end. You're already worried about your 2017 tax return as a small business owner. Filing taxes, mostly as a small company, can be perplexing, daunting, and even cause you want to rip your hair out. It won't be too terrible if you take your time to make sure you have everything you need. Here's a short guide to filing a small business tax return in five easy measures.

1.  Determine how to file

2.  Collect all the documents

3.  Find what forms you need

4.  Make sure you are getting the deductions you deserve

5.  Recheck your work with the help of a CPA

## 1. Determine how to file

The first step in planning for tax season as a small business owner is to know what sort of business you have. It would have an effect on the way you prepare your taxes. Are you a single proprietorship, an LLC, an S company, a general partnership, or a C corporation? When setting up your company, this should have already been known, but now it comes into play again. Different company forms have various criteria for tax returns, so it is necessary to consider what sort of business you are in order to understand what would be needed.

## 2. Collect all the documents

You've already learned that filing taxes needs a bunch of documentation, and this is true. Your documentation can be made up of real documents, or the documents might be digital. In any scenario, be-ensure you have them.

"The IRS says, "The company with which you are affects the kind of documents you need to maintain for federal tax purposes when it comes to what sort of documentation you can obtain. A list of your company activities should be included in your recordkeeping method. Payroll, sales slips, bank slips, bounced checks, invoices, certificates, and cash register recordings are also exampling documents. Don't forget to keep track of travel costs, any sales, and records of items you buy and are using in your company, such as furniture or machinery. Last but not least, job documents are needed. Do the utmost to maintain track of these items during the year, instead of struggling throughout the tax season, to make it easy on yourself.

## 3. Find what forms you need

It's an unfair fact that while filing the taxes, there would be some filling-out of paperwork. The kind of small company you have may influence the forms to fill out, as described earlier. Every state may have its own types and specifications, so here's a short rundown on some of the federal income tax measures:

*Form 1120 U.S. Business Income Tax Return*-Form 1120 is for tax reports submitted by C companies. C businesses are organizations where the shareholders do not incur taxes on individual reports themselves.

*Form 1120 S U.S. Income Tax Return* – For S Companies, this is the form to use. S Company owners, unlike C Companies, pay income tax on their corporate income tax reports. As a consequence, each shareholder is expected to complete a Schedule K-1 Method.

*Form 1065 U.S. Relationship Benefit Tax-* You would need to plan one of these types if your small corporation is set up as a collaboration. Since partnerships do not incur income tax, this type is just for information purposes. Every participant may also need to fill out a Schedule K-1 Form if you are part of a relationship, which goes into specifics regarding the profits, dividends, and losses of each particular partner.

*Form 1099 MISC-*This is a form that is processed and issued as part of the tax return to any independent contractors you might have employed, and it is often submitted to the IRS.

You may still need to complete separate documents for the boss, such as Form W-2 Pay and Tax Declaration.

## 4. Make sure you are getting the deductions you deserve

Deductions are the one aspect of paying the taxes that may be deemed pleasant.

Taxes are not all about the government having its due, Drew Hendricks of Forbes points out. Some tax laws are loopholes that provide for deductions – which are simply opportunities for the government to get you and your company to use money the way it wants."

You have put in a lot of time this year because operating a small company is an expensive activity. Making the best of the tax deductions, but be mindful of what is and is not an appropriate deduction. The Internal Revenue Service (IRS) offers certain basic guidance in this regard. The deductible business cost must be "usual and essential." Supplies, car costs, corporate transport, contract labor, staff compensation, pensions, employee benefits, and employee investment systems are some of the most typical ones on a small business tax return. Be vigilant not to combine personal expenditures with work expenses and be mindful of what company costs are 100% deductible versus a lower percentage.

### 5. Recheck your work with the help of a CPA

It may be confusing to submit a tax return as a private citizen, and filing as a small businessman is much, much harder. It's important to consider the measures involved in processing a small business tax return, as well as the criteria. It is advised, however, that you enlist the assistance of a licensed CPA to ensure that everything is properly and accurately filled out, particularly if this is your first filing as a small business. A CPA will help you manage all the forms, locate deductions, and advise you what reports and documentation to gather are required.

# Chapter: 11 How to Audit Your E-commerce Business

E-commerce is one of the fastest-growing business markets nowadays, so make sure you are prepared with an online business audit to help you develop the site. To boost traffic, make profits, and create a long-term consumer community, e-commerce companies need great material.

> ➢ How is the content performing?

> ➢ Is there anything that you should be doing?

> ➢ What was the last period you performed a comprehensive e-commerce audit?

It is important to take a step back and audit the material on a daily basis and ensure that it is fulfilling your company objectives. Continue reading to learn how to audit (and improve) your e-commerce material.

## 11.1 Review your current vision

Before you start your e-commerce business audit, you can do some deep thinking. This involves having a good, hard look at the new plan and finding some places that you might be falling short.
Do you really have any editorial calendar for the company's site and social network, for example? An editorial calendar is an important and basic function that many e-commerce company owners ignore.

> ➢ Take into consideration if the material is advertised. Are you making the best out of your email & social network accounts?

> ➤ Do the landing pages have well-defined objectives?

Prior to implementing some modifications or improving your approach after an e-commerce market analysis, you must first recognize existing issue areas that need to be resolved. You are already mindful of where (and why) you've been deficient in strategic guidance. Tackle certain places with passion, and bid farewell to your strategy-poor past.

## 11.2 Be critical

Now it's time to get back to work for the content auditing.

Create a list of every website on the e-commerce platform, beginning with the home & landing pages and making your way down to specific blog posts and product pages. Now go to each page and ask yourself the following questions:

> ➤ Is the website producing as it promises? Are your headings in line with your text? Do the call-to-actions execute on their promises?

> ➤ Is anything current? Since search engines don't value old material as much, it's crucial that the connections, items, and material are accurate and up-to-date.

> ➤ Is there a conceptual framework for each piece? Examine the organization on the website. It should sound normal and not haphazardly placed together.

> ➤ Is it easy to find? Internal links should be plentiful in your material, linking it all together. It's not just SEO-friendly, but it's still user-friendly.

➤ Is it efficient? Using the site analytics to see if any specific piece of material gets a tonne of traffic or converts. Don't forget these metrics if you want to expand your e-commerce business.

When undertaking an e-commerce company audit, don't be delicate with yourself: a stern eye on each material feature can sound harsh, but it will deliver the best outcomes.

## 11.3 Use tools to source the accurate data you need

Since an e-commerce company audit involves effort and time, it's a smart idea to use one of the numerous free or low-cost tools available to assist you to organize and quantify data easily. You have access to a wide variety of content resources, each of which is customized to a particular target.

➤ **Google Analytics:**

Google Analytics is helpful for finding issue areas and assessing the success of content by indicators.

➤ **Screaming Frog:**

Screaming Frog is an SEO tool that crawls your site and returns valuable (and actionable) details.

➤ **Site Analyzer:**

Site Analyzer offers a thorough review of the site, as well as an overall rating dependent on criteria such as speed, style, and copy.

➤ **Yoast:**

Yoast, a wonderful WordPress SEO plugin that offers a fast rundown of keyword targeting for blog posts and websites.

But be careful: with so many auditing tools at your hands, it's possible to get too dependent on them. To get the best out of the e-commerce quality audit, invest just in a handful and use them wisely. Don't get paralyzed by research paralysis. There are many resources that will assist you.

## 11.4 Get into auditing to maximize the value of your business

Finally, don't feel too cozy. Auditing is a constant phase that necessitates daily focus. Your content isn't a stand-alone entity; it's up against a slew of other products in a saturated sector, and standing away requires effort.

A content audit is a valuable practice that will help you keep on top of things. It's also a particularly rewarding talent to practice. Flipping websites is a popular route for aspiring entrepreneurs, and a content audit will make it simple for you to acquire an online company, transform it around, and then market it for a profit — it's a talent that can pay off again and again. It all comes down to providing outstanding web content in terms of profitability, performance, and market resale value.

# Chapter: 12 The impact of Covid-19 on eCommerce

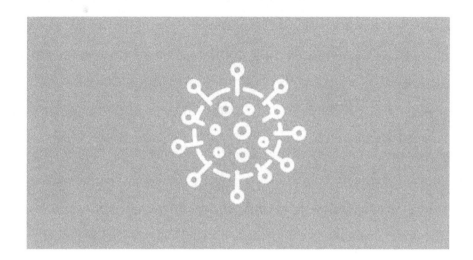

2020 was a difficult year for almost all individuals. Simultaneously, the online business developed more than ever. What would we be able to anticipate from 2021? SearchNode distributed another report on the most recent web-based business patterns and the effect of Covid-19.

A year ago, SearchNode distributed a report on online business patterns in 2020. Obviously, in those days, there was mostly secret about the Covid that would spread all over the globe. In the overview, there were loads of discussions with Magento, an improved spotlight on personalization and natural manageability.

2020 was, of course, all about Covid-19.

What has changed in a year? You should discover, as the Lithuanian tech organization distributed another report on online business patterns. In October 2020, the organization interrogated 100 internet business leaders from Europe and North America.

## 12.1 Six% eCommerce revenue decreased during the lockdown

There were inquiries concerning Covid-19. It appears to be that most web-based business organizations saw their online income increment during the worldwide lockdown in the spring of 2020. As per the study, 90% of organizations saw their online deals increment at any rate a piece, with 50% of respondents asserting it developed by more than 100%. Yet, 6% say their online business income diminished during Covid lockdown.

After the lockdown was finished, numerous purchasers began shopping at physical retailers once more. 86% of respondents say that their online incomes expanded, and just 4% say it diminished.

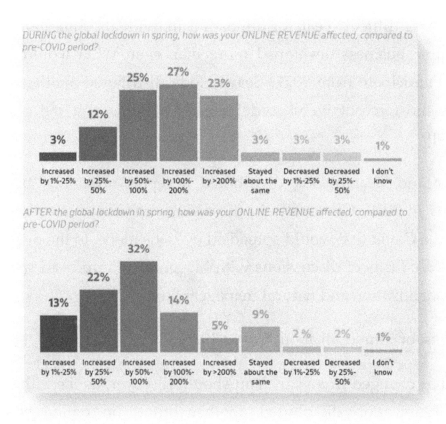

## 12.2 Online profit margin increased by 38%

Producing on the web deals is a certain something; the entire Covid-19 circumstance has additionally prompted things like disturbed inventory chains, inadequately staffed client assistance, and the sky is the limit from there. This straightforwardly influences the online net revenue. It appears to be that for 38% of internet business leaders, their online net revenue developed during the worldwide lockdown, while for a comparative rate (40%), the circumstance expressed about the equivalent. Just 15% asserted that it diminished.

## 12.3 The impact of Covid-19 on the workforce

The pandemic has, obviously, additionally prompted a few changes in organizations' labor force. Around 44% said they needed to move staff, while three out of ten recruited more individuals. The opposite side of the coin is that 26% needed to terminate a few groups, and 15 percent say they needed to lessen their workers' pay rates. Also, perhaps somewhat amazing for a few, yet 5 percent figured out how to expand compensations. What's more, much astonishing: 21% of organizations didn't change their labor force by any means.

21% of organizations didn't change their labor force.

23% of omnichannel players observed disconnected deals increment

Another intriguing finding from the investigation is that for retailers on the offline and online stores, 23% say their disconnected deals expanded, and 16 percent figured out how to keep it comparative. Lamentably, for 43%, their disconnected deals endured a shot.

## 12.4 Measurements for physical retailers

Numerous physical retailers needed to change their business on the off chance that they needed to maintain a strategic distance from to leave the business. In this way, numerous new practices were presented a year ago. Among the members, 31% presented in-store pickup, while 26% decided to present home conveyance. Sadly, around one of every five needed to close down some actual stores for great.

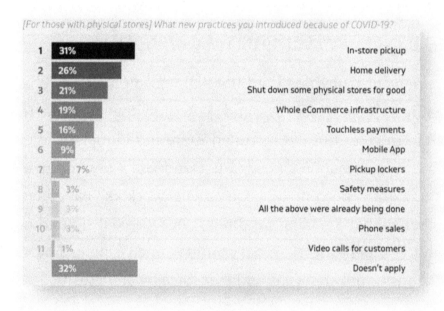

Covid has vigorously affected online retailers on various levels. Among the fundamental difficulties for internet business organizations, upset stockpile chains and satisfying interest for items were the, for the most part, referenced ones. Yet, restricted tasks because of the lockdown, overseeing stock, and the general absence of representatives were likewise vital difficulties for online retailers. What's more, 17% said it was testing since they need to shut down their actual stores.

An upset store network was the primary test for some online retailers in Europe.

## 12.5 Shifted strategies

A year ago, numerous respondents said they would generally execute, improve or change personalization, site-search and omnichannel. This year, the essential vision has moved because of Covid-19. The majority of the organizations (45%) will presently have more spotlight on the advanced piece of their business by changing the combination, putting resources into new online business programming or emphasizing additionally on internet advertising channels.

One of every five said they would increase activities, which means they need to execute their methodologies and act quicker. One out of ten says they are currently centered around actual store changes, and 8 percent went for inventory network changes, from minor ones to new store networks or coordination's.

## 12.6 Financial consequences

Notwithstanding all the terrible things occurring because of the flare-up of the Covid, monetarily 2020 wasn't so awful for some web-based business organizations. The greater part of them (63%) say the year (up to October) was effective. Furthermore, 28% case their web-based business was progressing nicely, while their actual stores didn't. What's more, an astounding 2% said the inverse!

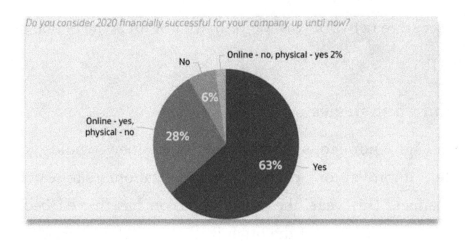

# Chapter: 13 What is the Future for Online Business?

With the online world changing apparently from one day to another and an expanding number of sites (today, there are just about 2 billion sites out there), the future for organizations working on the web consistently appears to be unsure. From the finish of unhindered internet to the limitations on YouTube adaptation to progressing computerized innovation and that's just the beginning, the inquiry is the thing that patterns will be generally noticeable for online organizations within a reasonable time-frame.

Right now, with the US economy extending, it appears to be that the not-so-distant future for online organizations is splendid gratitude to more noteworthy customer certainty and ways of managing money. What follows are new patterns in online business that have all the earmarks of growing as buyer propensities change over the following, not many years, which will significantly affect how web-based advertising is being performed.

## Expansion of Cryptocurrency

While there has been impressive information about the inconveniences related to bitcoin, digital money itself has all the earmarks of being extending quickly and turning out to be standard. With more organizations and governments going to cryptographic money as an alternative, the exchanges will turn out to be solidly advanced. This implies an adjustment in the manner purchasers purchase across all business sectors, which implies that online organizations should be set up to acknowledge this type of cash soon.

## The advent of Machine Learning

This type of innovation is ready to venture into deals and client service, implying that how organizations work with clients will be improved. AI will be through utilizing discourse examination, which better aids client assistance divisions in how to react to every one of their clients. This improves connection which means assembling a more grounded brand and enduring fewer misfortunes because of mistaken assumptions.

## Increased Security Spending

In light of ongoing hacks and break-ins that have uncovered the individual data of millions of clients, more organizations are venturing up their security conventions to keep it from happening to them. This has implied a move in accentuation from avoidance towards recognizing interruptions and reacting in like manner. Better security implies more costs, which may tremendously affect the monetary situation of little and medium-sized online organizations.

## Personalized Marketing

With such countless online organizations attempting to arrive at similar clients, it can get hard to get over the clamor. This is why individual promoting patterns have been developing and will keep on extending as more organizations spring up around the planet. Effective online organizations will zero in on brilliant showcasing that arrives at the individual, not simply the ideal buyer gathering. On account of new advanced innovation, specific Artificial Intelligence

(AI) (web-based business organizations are now confronting this test), the progressions are now occurring and will keep on developing.

## Rise of the Sharing Economy

The blend of the sharing economy, which is most broadly addressed by ride-sharing administrations like Uber. It has additionally dug into retail with monsters, for example, Google and Amazon getting into this pattern. For online organizations, the sharing economy addresses an incredible pattern ready to attack medical care and monetary administrations, which may change how numerous online organizations work.

For online entrepreneurs, the extension of the web to world business sectors implies a new wilderness of clients just as contenders. The individuals who succeed will be adaptable to the inescapable change that happens and finds a way to remain one stride ahead to guarantee their future.

# Conclusion

Accounting is described as "the processing, review, and systematic documentation of numerical business transactions, the preparation of financial reports, and the examination and evaluation of these reports for management's knowledge and guidance."

Accounting is an accounting mechanism that observes, tracks, and communicates an economic entity's monetary activities.

It is the method of defining, evaluating, and communicating economic data in order for consumers of the data to make educated choices and decisions. Human life is evolving in this ever-changing environment.

Accounting has taken on a different form as a consequence of technical advances, such as holding records mechanically.

With the widespread usage of electronic accounting tasks, a modern arena has arisen. As a consequence, it is obvious that the concept of accounting will evolve in the coming years.

# Bookkeeping and QuickBooks
# Made Easy

*David Lazarus*

# Table of Contents

# Introduction

This book is your basic guide to bookkeeping and QuickBooks. If you are a bookkeeper and want to upgrade your skillset and learn more about the QuickBooks software, this book is just for you. You will find a comprehensive detail of all the considerations, the advantages, and the ways you can become a QuickBooks bookkeeper. If you are a beginner and managing finances interests you, you can equally benefit from this book.

In the following chapters, you will find a detailed explanation of bookkeeping and why proper bookkeeping is necessary to keep businesses afloat. With people starting their businesses by the minute, the need for accurate bookkeeping is ever in demand. Small business owners invest in good financial handling software and outsourcing their account management to bookkeepers as affording an accountant is sometimes not possible for a small business owner.

You might question that bookkeeping is not as lucrative but do not pay head to that. Yes, conventional bookkeeping is becoming outdated, but still, there is demand. Most small business owners in the US use the software QuickBooks for their financial recording. Though some business owners know how to use it and keep updated, most of them will require help with crunching numbers and outsource professional bookkeepers to do the job.

QuickBooks was launched in the year 2003 by the company Intuit. After its launch, the company has launched various versions of the software to cater to different business owners' requirements. QuickBooks usage dominates the small business market by 80%. The company provides desktop-based and cloud-based versions of the software. From 2014 onwards there is a shift in trend. Before 2014, the business owners preferred the desktop model, but after the year 2014, more and more business owners are shifting to the cloud-based versions.

A whole chapter is dedicated to explaining the QuickBooks software. We discuss in detail the entire software. The services it provides and how a small business owner can benefit from it. There is a step-by-step guide to set up and install QuickBooks into your computer or other devices. After installation, guidelines are given to set up your account and add the vendor and customer accounts. A detailed explanation about how to enter employee details and how some versions can also manage automated payroll tasks. Reading about all this will make you understand the software's entire system and objective and realize how easy it is to operate. Technology has made even the most difficult and complicated tasks simpler for us. Now, it is our job to use technology for our benefit.

After you have understood the basic functioning of the software, you might want to invest in one. But this is not as easy as just purchasing one online. There are different packages of software available for different individuals. There are four basic packages available:

- QuickBooks Online

- QuickBooks Self-Employed

- QuickBooks Desktop

- QuickBooks App

Choosing the correct package that suits your requirements is also an important and difficult decision. In this book, we give you an overview of all the available packages and their specific features. All this information will hopefully make your decision easy.

In the US, the small to mid-size business market is denominated by QuickBooks users, and the owners are always on the lookout for professional QuickBooks bookkeepers for the job. You do not have to do it full time; you can manage all the accounts as a side hustle because QuickBooks software makes everything easy. You have to setup your accounting needs in the software, and most of the work is done by the software. However, it is n0t as easy as it sounds. The software is user-friendly, but you still require basic accounting knowledge and correct usage of the program. You might consider becoming a certified QuickBooks bookkeeper.

In this book, we have also discussed how in 2021, QuickBooks bookkeepers who work online make good money. There is a whole chapter in which we discuss working part-time as a QuickBooks bookkeeper is becoming a high-paying job. The average income of a QuickBooks professional in the US is discussed along with the US's best cities where you can practice QuickBooks bookkeeping. The considerations you should keep in mind while moving base to become a bookkeeper. California is the best place to be because the money QuickBooks bookkeepers are making there is approximately $10000 more than the US average per year.

There is an entire chapter dedicated to the ways you can become a certified QuickBooks bookkeeper. Sometimes a person knows what he/she wants but is unable to do anything because of the lack of guidance. This book gives you just that, proper step-by-step guidance on how to qualify yourself to become a QuickBooks bookkeeper. It does take time and effort, but you have numerous possibilities and options once you are qualified. To become a bookkeeper, you will need a certification. There are commonly three types of certifications you can choose from:

- QuickBooks Online Certification: Basic

- QuickBooks Desktop Certification: Basic

- QuickBooks Desktop Certification: Advance

The certifications are not just a one-time feat. You must keep your certifications up to date. You will require recertification each year by taking the certification exam. These tests are expensive but worth it.

Finally, we discuss the tricks and hacks you can use to use QuickBooks efficiently and effectively. These trips and hacks make your work easier and quicker. You will have to put in fewer hours. It is always wise to use trips and hacks and make the most benefit of the latest technologies. Sometimes doing online courses and certifications enable you to learn these tricks and hacks. Therefore, it is always recommended to keep your knowledge latest and keep improving your skills. The process of learning never stops. You keep learning throughout life. In present times learning has become a necessity rather than a luxury. In the ever-changing world, you will be left behind if you do not keep your skillset updated.

We hope you are going to find this book informative and helpful for your future professional endeavors. If bookkeeping is your calling, you should pursue it. It is one of the most in-demand services in the small business and mid-size business sector.

# Chapter 1. Bookkeeping

In this chapter, we will focus on the basics. We will discuss the concept of bookkeeping and how it is the one-stop solution to all your accounting needs. Before anything else, we will try to understand what bookkeeping is and its importance.

Bookkeeping is an essential part of financial management. Small business owners sometimes try to manage the bookkeeping themselves, which becomes a reason for their businesses to fail. People do not realize that bookkeeping is a full-time job. You cannot manage a business and run numbers simultaneously. For this purpose, it is always wise to hire professionals for your accounting and bookkeeping.

## 1.1.   What is Bookkeeping?

You must have heard about the term accounting. Bookkeeping is just that; it is related to managing the accounts. This term is used for business. The management of the complete finances of a business is termed bookkeeping.

To be more specific, we say that bookkeeping involves recording all the financing situations of a business. Bookkeeping is about keeping a record of all financial transactions daily, the influx and efflux of cash, the Payroll, profits, loss, investments, return on investments, and all the decisions related to the business's finance aspect. Bookkeeping helps the business owners keep track of all the information regarding the financial transactions.

After learning about what bookkeeping is, one wonders how a business owner can do all that by themselves? Not all business owners are literate about managing their finances. So, how can a business owner manage their accounts and finances? The simple answer to this question is a bookkeeper.

## 1.2. Who is A bookkeeper?

Bookkeepers are professionals who are responsible for managing all the finances of a company. They keep the owners aware of their present financial situation, record all related financial data and the total transactions made.

Correct bookkeeping is important for the business owners as well as prospected investors as well. Bookkeeping information is beneficial for the government and financial institutions as well. It will give a clear overview of the economic impacts of that certain business. Big companies and individual investors tend to research before they invest their money somewhere. The best and most reliable source of this information can be found in the company books. Looking at the books, the investor will decide whether he/she wants to invest in a certain company or project. In this way, bookkeeping is important for the owners because it is like his business introduction to the investment world. The better and more accurate the bookkeeping, the more chances of investment.

(A typical Bookkeeper)

## 1.3.  Importance of Bookkeeping

When people start a new business, they tend to neglect the importance of good bookkeeping. Finance must be taken charge from day one and cannot be neglected for a single day. Now, what does bookkeeping do? It gives the company a tangible indicator of its performance and current situation. With this information's help, it becomes easier for the owner to make proper decisions financially, revenue generated, the profits, the loss, the income goals, etc. Each transaction must be recorded; the cash influx, efflux, credits, assets, liabilities all need to be recorded.

Bookkeeping is essential to keep the business afloat. Bigger companies usually hire accountants for the financial department, but it is not always possible for small business owners. So, small business owners mostly rely on hiring a bookkeeper. There whole accounting companies from where you can outsource a bookkeeper. It is cheaper than employing a full-time accountant, and a bookkeeper can easily manage a small business account. Anyone who starts a new business should never ignore the importance of keeping a record of every dime they spent and earn. Everything should be recorded.

## 1.4. Type of Accounting Method

Each business model follows one of the two accounting methods.

- Cash Basis of Accounting

- Accrual Basis of Accounting

To implement the bookkeeping function properly, the business owner should decide which accounting method they will follow. There are two basic models for accounting which are mentioned above. Now, what is the difference between these two? We will try to explain:

Cash Basis of Accounting:

In this type of accounting, a transaction is only recorded when a payment or cash is received or spent.

For example, if you buy fifty units of a product and the payment will be done after two weeks. No transaction will be recorded. It will only be recorded after two weeks when the payment is made. This type of accounting model is now considered outdated in present times.

Accrual Basis of Accounting:

In accrual accounting, the expenses and revenue are put down when the transaction is made rather than when the payment is made.

We use the same example of buying 50 units of a product and payment must be made after two weeks. The record will be entered as soon as the receipt is received and will be recorded as payables. This is the more modern model for accounting and is widely accepted.

## 1.5. What do the bookkeepers do?

Now that you have a basic idea of who a bookkeeper is let us move to the set of responsibilities and jobs the Bookkeeper carries out. Listed are the tasks carried out by bookkeepers that make it convenient for the business owner to systematically run the business and provide a clear picture of its financial position. The responsibilities of bookkeepers include:

- Recording transactions every day.

- Sending invoices to clients.

- Keep track of payments.

- Prepare and maintain the payable ledger.

- Manage the cash flow.

- Compile and maintain all accounts.

### 1.5.1. Record the Transactions Each Day

One of the jobs of the Bookkeeper is to enter the transactions each day. These include bank transactions. Nowadays, most companies use software to manage accounts. Some software has a function to generate automated bank feeds, which makes the task easier. You must keep a check on the cash, and precious data entry time is saved.

### 1.5.2. Sending Invoices to Clients

Another responsibility of the Bookkeeper is to make receipts and invoices on purchases and send them to the clients.

### 1.5.3. Keep Track of Payments

Once the invoice is sent out, keeping a record of the payments received is also the Bookkeeper's responsibility. To keep a follow-up to receive pending payments is also the responsibility of the Bookkeeper. This is also known as being responsible for the receivable ledger.

### 1.5.4. Being Responsible for the Payable Ledger

Up to a certain amount determined by the business owner, the Bookkeeper makes the payments made on the owner's behalf. The Bookkeeper keeps records of all the payments made by the business. These include the payments to the suppliers, the extra cash available, and the other business expenses. The Bookkeeper records all this information and checks it every day.

### 1.5.5. Responsible for Managing the Cash Flow

One of the most important business rules is that a certain amount of cash is always available. The responsibility of the Bookkeeper is to always maintain the balance. This can be done by keeping a record of the day-to-day expenses and revenues. There should always be cash available for the day-to-day expenses. If the Bookkeeper suspects that the balance might be disrupted, he/she can offer advice to the owner by telling them ways to control the outflow and increase the inflow. These devices are almost always short-term fixes.

### 1.5.6. Compile All Accounts

The most important job of the Bookkeeper is to maintain the account books. The account records should all be up to date. These include all the ledgers. This is necessary for further investments and business decisions. The owner or prospect investor looks at these accounts and makes decisions according to the financial situations mentioned in the books.

## 1.6. How can a Bookkeeper be Beneficial for Business?

When you have a smaller business setup, it makes sense to manage your account yourself. But when the business expands, it is always a good idea to hire someone to take care of the bookkeeping. In this way, you can concentrate on expanding the business, and your Bookkeeper can take care of your day-to-day expenses. Many people do not hire a bookkeeper to save money but lose a lot of precious time in managing their account that they could be using to innovate and expand their business. Bookkeeping is a time-consuming job, and it should be left to the ones who are professionally trained to do so. They might as well do the job better and take less time. Following are listed a few benefits of hiring a bookkeeper:

### 1.6.1. Let you Focus on Your Business Strategy

As explained earlier, bookkeeping is a time-consuming task and demands attention to detail. Hiring a bookkeeper will save you all that time, and you will have plenty of time to focus on your business.

### 1.6.2. The Accounting Cost can be Saved.

If you have a small business, it is a better idea to hire a bookkeeper. If you hire an accountant, it will cost you more money and will become a liability. All the recording and accounts can be easily managed by a bookkeeper as well, and it will cost you a lot less money.

### 1.6.3. Double Check Your Cashflow

As a business owner, it is wise to always keep your eyes on the cashflow. But sometimes, you can get caught up, and in that situation, your Bookkeeper is there to tell you when you need to manage your cash flow. The Bookkeeper can warn your earlier, and you will still have time to manage the situation.

### 1.6.4. Be Informed of Current Financial Situation:

As the Bookkeeper is working on a day-to-day basis, he/she will be aware of all the business's financial situations. If you require any help and advice in this department, you can advise your Bookkeeper to have the complete information and explain the clear picture to you.

### 1.6.5. The Financial Data is Organized

In case you get hold of good software like QuickBooks, the Bookkeeper will work on the same software. The data is kept organized and transparent using the software because the margin for mistakes is highly reduced. The accountant can analyze the same data if you wish to get advice regarding business expansion and investment.

All in all, bookkeeping is particularly useful for business owners and investors alike. If you are not a businessperson and are interested in managing accounts for other small businesses, bookkeeping could be a good profession for you. The possibilities are limitless.

# Chapter 2. QuickBooks Explained

With a basic knowledge of bookkeeping and what it means for small businesses, we can now discuss bookkeeping solutions. 2021 is all about solutions. Bookkeeping is a difficult task. It can be made easy with the help of accounting software. In this chapter, we are going to discuss software known as QuickBooks.

## 1.7.  2.1. What is QuickBooks?

If you are a small business owner and you aim to reach the next level, you might want to start keeping track of your finances. Most people control their finances when they start with a business, but it becomes difficult once the business gains pace. If you wish to expand your business, you will have to become more proactive, take hold of your finances, plan your next financial moves, keep an eye on day-to-day transactions, and organize a cash inflow and outflow system. You should set up a payroll. All the administrative work should be organized. Reading all this must have given you a headache. You were thinking about making some money; how are you going to manage all the financial stuff?

It would be best if you were thankful for your stars that you live in the 21st Century and there is software available for everything. In this chapter, we are discussing accounting software that works like magic. The software is known as QuickBooks. QuickBooks is the perfect tool for your financial necessities.

## 2.1.1. QuickBooks

It is accounting software that has features to organize the financial aspects of small businesses. The functions of QuickBooks include:

- Recording everyday transactions

- Track and record revenue and expense.

- Report generation for planning

- Prepare bills.

- Preparation of Payroll

The software is targeted towards small to medium-sized business setups. The QuickBooks software has features that make it possible for you to manage report generation, sales, cash flow, billing, revenue, taxes, reporting and expenses. The best part about the software is that there are inbuilt templates for reports that you can easily set and customize according to your specifications. It is easy to fill in data to an already prepared template compared to create by yourself. You can take control of your finances. It is a user-friendly software, but it has a learning curve, and you must have some basic accounting knowledge to operate and use this software. To use the software effectively, you must learn and have an in-depth knowledge of the software's essential functions.

## 2.1.2. The History of QuickBooks

In 1983, two inventors Scott Cook, and Tom Proulx, created the company Intuit. QuickBooks is a product of this company and was first launched in 2003 and targeted to small businesses. Over the years, better and more functional versions of the software have been launched. It remains one of the most widely used financial software for small businesses in the US. Different versions of the software are available in the international markets as well.

## 1.8.    2.2. QuickBooks Features

QuickBooks is amazing software with multiple features and functions. Here is a list of a few features of the software.

### 2.2.1. user Friendly

This software is super user-friendly. It is easy to use and navigate. All the financial features needed for a small to medium business are present in this one program. You do not have to record your data in different locations. This single software manages all your data.

### 2.2.2. Data Migration

This is a wonderful feature. If you want to transfer any data from QuickBooks to the spreadsheet, the transition is smooth. When there is a requirement to present the data on a spreadsheet, you can easily transfer all the software from the software without manually copying it.

### 2.2.3 Smooth Navigation

To use this software is easy because the navigation is simple. Everything is displayed clearly, and working is smooth. The program interface is clear and simple. However, you will have to learn and get used to the software before you can use it. You need to learn and understand all the financial terms and data entry methods to using this software effectively.

## 2.2.4. Smooth Transactions

The bank transactions are systematically recorded. Each entry you make is recorded. You can even set up regular transactions like salary payments, commissions, and bills repeated each month or every two weeks. These transactions will be automatically recorded.

## 2.2.5. Invoices

You can set up the invoices to be generated. The software can even generate invoices from your smartphone or tablet if they are installed with the software. You are not dependent on the computer system or laptop to generate business invoices. This feature is truly per the present requirement where everything can be achieved with a click of a button anytime, anywhere.

## 2.2.6. Calculate Tax

The feature of tax calculation is included in the software. To do taxes is always a tricky business. With the QuickBooks software, you can easily calculate the taxes quickly, efficiently, and accurately.

## 2.2.7. Projections

There is an automated feature in the software that will present you with projections. The software can generate all kinds of projections, including profits, expenses, sales etc. Getting the projections makes it easy to make financial decisions.

## 1.9.    2.3. Set-up QuickBooks

To use QuickBooks, you must have basic accounting knowledge and your own business. To use this software, you must be organized and willing to manage your finances seriously and as a daily feature. Some people install QuickBooks, put in the money, and forget it for months. Some purchase it and never even learn how to use it. QuickBooks does not work in that manner. You must be willing to learn and be consistent. Consistency is the key.

Let us discuss step-by-step guidelines for using QuickBooks.

### 2.3.1. Start

The first step will be to install the software properly. For installation, you must decide how you are going to use it. When you start the program, you will have two options:

- Network

- Custom Options

You will choose the Custom settings if you use the software on only one computer and use the same computer for installations.

In case more than one computer will use the software, chose the Network setting.

After that, choose the location or folder in your PC where you wish the software to be installed. Add your details, and then set up your company file. After that, click on the QuickBooks icon on the desktop.

## 2.3.2. setup

As soon as you click on the QuickBooks program, you will see an Easy Setup Wizard to help you set up your company file. By following the simple instructions, you can set up your company file. If you are new to this kind of software, you will be favorable to take help from the wizard. It will make the setup smooth and easy.

## 2.3.3. Vendor Setup

The next step will be setting up the accounts for your vendors. You will click the Vendor Center in the toolbar placed at the top. Next, select the New Vendor option, and create a vendor account. To add a new transaction, click the New Transaction and fill in the details. You can even bring in details from MS Excel and MS Word.

Add all the vendors similarly if you have more than one.

## 2.3.4. Setup Employee Accounts

To set up the employee accounts, click the Employee Center. Then click the New Employee button and then add the related information. After the information, you click the button for New Transaction. Add the salary details and any other transaction related to that specific employee. For salary, you must add the date and time for each month. For that, you will click Enter Time and then add the specific time and frequency of salary. Some employers pay per month, and some pay by the week. Put in the information accordingly.

## 2.3.5. Set Up Customer Account

Like the vendor and employee accounts, add the customer accounts. First, you go to the customer center, then Add Customer and Job.

Here you can add it as an income source. Now add the related transaction by clicking New Transaction. Here you will add the information for payments and generation of invoices. There is a link for Excel as well as Word. You can bring the information from Excel and use Word to prepare letters for the customer.

### 2.3.6. Setup Report Generation

Next, you will go to the Report Center. All the information added by you can be viewed here. You can also customize the kind of report you want to generate. Reports for-profits, payments and expenses can be generated separately.
Add all the employees the same way if you have more than one.

## 1.10. 2.4. Using QuickBooks

After the set up let us try to understand the day-to-day working of the QuickBooks software. What should we expect from the software? How can we manage our finances? What is the essential feature of the software? All these questions will be answered in the following part of this book. Together we will try to understand how the QuickBooks software works.

### 2.4.1. Chart of Accounts

So, what can you find on the chart of accounts? It will display the company's income, liability, expense accounts, assets, and equity to assign day-to-day transactions. This is what you will find:

- All the financial information about the company. It has the balance sheets, dividend, savings, receivables, and expenses. All this can be seen in the Chart of Accounts as a list.

- All the accounts related to the business, along with the account balances and account numbers. The details of the account holder will also be shared, like the full names and contact numbers. All these accounts will appear when you click the List Menu in the QuickBooks chart of accounts.

## 2.4.2. Other Lists

These include the list of vendors you deal with. All your regular customers and customer accounts are listed. All the items you deal with and their inventory is listed.

How this is favorable for the QuickBooks user:

- You can manage everything in one place. You do not have to manage multiple lists and settings. All information is compiled in one place. Either it is the product inventory or the vendor; all can be managed in one place.

- When you have all the information in a single space, you can move back and forth with all the lists, account details and information. You can simultaneously manage all your financial situations together. Everything is easy to navigate and extremely user-friendly.

- Another feature is the easy addition ad deletion of details. It is simple to add new accounts, and it is equally simple to delete accounts. Anytime you want to change the existing settings, it is easily done.

- Apart from adding ad deleting details, you can also edit details. Correction and updating details are easy in this software.

### 2.4.3. The Reports

Report templates are already included in the software so that you can customize them according to your needs. Add the details of your vendors, customers, and items. You must add dates and times as well. Once you start adding details accordingly and you update daily transactions and activities. The reports will be forming themselves. Anytime you feel like having an overview of your business, you can pull out reports with just one click, and the reports will be generated. These reports will help you make important financial and investment decisions.

### 2.4.4. payroll

QuickBooks makes it easy to manage payrolls. With the software, you add the information, and the program will itself arrange the payroll process. The software can itself manage the accounts of the employees who have tax exemption. You can customize the settings for other incentives and deductions. If you turn on the setting, the software automatically sends emails, deposits, and receipts.

More than one person can manage the payrolls in this software, the one who has purchased the software has to allow the other users on the network by assigning permission.

### 1.11. 2.5. QuickBooks Versions

QuickBooks is available in different types and versions. Each has a different package and fee. The versions are discussed in detail in the following chapters. Here we will list down the various versions of QuickBooks software:

- QuickBooks Online

- QuickBooks Self Employed

- QuickBooks App

- QuickBooks Desktop Products

    o QuickBooks Pro

    o QuickBooks for Mac

    o QuickBooks Enterprise

    o QuickBooks Premier

o

# Chapter 3. Choosing the Best Version of QuickBooks

With the knowledge you have gained in the previous chapters, you know that QuickBooks is a financial solutions software. It was launched 25 years ago, and it has been the top choice for financial management since 2003. If you look at the company profits, they will show you an upward trend for the last 11 years straight. In addition to that, QuickBooks is used by 80% of small business owners in the US. This information enough should convince you to invest in the software.

Once you have decided to purchase the QuickBooks software, you are faced with yet another dilemma. Which version is for you? As discussed in the previous chapter, various versions of QuickBooks are available.

The QuickBooks family has a product for everyone. Here is a quick assessment of what you may want to purchase.

- If you are self-employed, run your company alone, and are looking to invest in a cloud-based accounting system, you should invest in QuickBooks for Self-Employed.

-  If you own a small business and are interested in a cloud-based accounting system, you should invest in QuickBooks Online.

- If you are a small to medium-sized business owner, you must invest in QuickBooks Desktop.

- If you are already using QuickBooks and wish to update to another version, invest in QuickBooks Apps.

One of the deciding factors in any investment is the price range and affordability. This is the approximate price of the QuickBooks Packages available, making it easy for you to decide which product is best for you and is easy on the pocket.

| Version | Usage | Price |
|---|---|---|
| QuickBooks Online | For businesspersons who want flexible financial access. This is suitable for small to mid-size business owners. | $25 up to $150/month |
| QuickBooks for Desktop | Suitable for small to medium size business owners in any sector | $399.99 with a one-time payment to $1,213 for one year |
| QuickBooks for Self-Employed | This is suitable for individual property agents, independent vendors, and Uber workers. | $15/ month |
| QuickBooks Mac | This is for small to mid-size | $399.99 paid once |

| | businesspersons who have their business set up on MAC | |
|---|---|---|

(Prices of Different Versions of QuickBooks)

## 1.12. 3.1. QuickBooks for Self-Employed

QuickBooks Self Employed is the newest addition to the QuickBooks software versions. This is cloud-based software for financial services. It is specially designed for self-employed business owners and freelance service providers. It is ideal for independent workers like Lyft and Uber drivers. Property agents can also use it.

As this is a cloud-based program, you can access it with any computer or device with the given login.

(QuickBooks Self Employed Interface)

(Display of Reports on QuickBooks Self Employed)

Using this program, you can send data to TurboTax and track personal and business expenses from a single bank account. It also calculates the Quarterly Tax and reminds you of payment.

You will find three types of packages available for QuickBooks for Self-Employed:

### 3.1.1. QuickBooks Self Employed Package

Investing in this package gives you the following features:

- Users can easily connect to their bank account through QuickBooks Self -Employed

- The users can also connect to their credit cards.

- Users can track the expenses and income from the same account but can be separated into personal and business groups.

- The software calculates taxes quarterly.

### 3.1.2. QuickBooks for Self-Employed Tax Bundle

This offers all the services provided by the simple package with an addition:

- Users can connect to Intuit Turbo Box that enables them to pay taxes online each quarter.

### 3.1.3. QuickBooks for Self-Employed Live Tax Bundle

Provides all the services as the packages mentioned above with an addition that:

- Users can consult a CPA all year round.

- The users can get the services of a CPA to review taxes.

### 3.1.4. Benefit

It can track traveling and Mileage. You can enter trips with dates, reasons, and distance traveled. The system will automatically calculate deductions.

### 3.1.5. Drawback

Does not provide a service to generate invoices and online payments.

## 1.13. 3.2. QuickBooks Online

QuickBooks Online is also a cloud-based financial solutions software. This had become exceedingly popular after 2014 when it was observed that more business owners preferred the online version over the desktop version. After that, the number of subscribers to the QuickBooks online version has been more than 1 million subscribers. This also tells us about the shift of business owners to a cloud-based system and shows their confidence in solely cloud-based software.

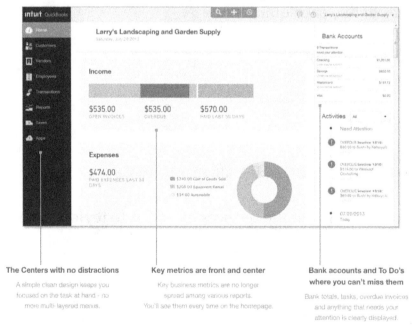

(QuickBooks Online Interface)

## 3.2.1. Common Features

The common features of QuickBooks Online are:

- Payable and Receivable Accounts:

The program can successfully manage expenses as well as income.

- Invoices and Bills:

It offers recurring or single-time invoices and can pay bills online.

- Management of Expenses:

The software can track all the business-related expenses.

- Reporting:

There are templates of prebuilt reports provided in the software, including the sales and tax reports. Simple Start gives 20 templates, Essentials gives 40 such templates, and gives 60 templates.

The QuickBooks online package does not need to be installed and comes in four packages:

## 3.2.2. QuickBooks Online Simple Start

The features provided in this package are:

- There is a single-user license.

- You can import your data from the QuickBooks Desktop version or MS Excel.

- You are entitled to consult two accounting professionals (bookkeepers and accountants)

### 3.2.3. QuickBooks Online Essentials

This version has all the abilities of the above version and, in addition to those capabilities, also has the following capabilities:

- The user is entitled to have 3 user licenses.

- The owner can set up user permissions to determine who is entitled to use the software.

### 3.2.4. QuickBooks Online Plus

All the capabilities of the Essentials version plus the following added qualities:

- Can set up 5 user licenses.

- The ability to track inventory.

- Users can create and send orders of purchase.

### 3.2.5. QuickBooks Online Advanced

This includes all the capabilities of the Plus version and the following capabilities:

- Can set up 25 user licenses.

- The ability for automated bill payment.

- The user can set up customized permissions.

### 3.2.6. Benefits

It is available for iOS, Windows, and Android devices. It can be connected to PayPal and Shopify for transactions.

### 3.2.7. Drawbacks

All the functions available in the QuickBooks Desktop are not available on QuickBooks Online. This version does not allow the addition of more than one company.

## 1.14. 3.3. QuickBooks Desktop

The QuickBooks Desktop is the most elaborated software version among all three of the versions. Most business owners prefer cloud-based financial services, but if you prefer desktop-oriented software, the QuickBooks Desktop version is for you. This version further has six more variations suitable for different types of small businesses. The six types are briefly explained as follows:

### 3.3.1. QuickBooks Desktop Pro:

This is good for most small businesses that are not involved in product manufacture.

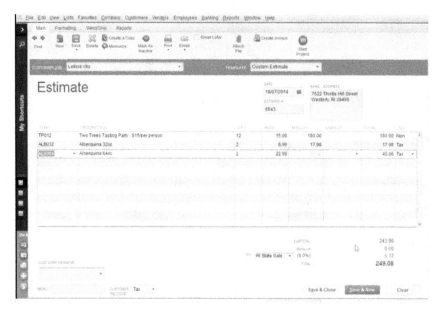

(QuickBooks Desktop Pro)

## 3.3.2. QuickBooks Desktop Premier:

This version is ideal for businesses involved in manufacturing, retail, and related to charity and non-profit organizations.

(Homepage of QuickBooks Desktop Premier)

### 3.3.3. QuickBooks Desktop Enterprise:

This is for large companies and enterprises. This version has industry reporting and a custom chart of accounts.

(QuickBooks Desktop Enterprise sales management)

### 3.3.4. QuickBooks Desktop Plus and QuickBooks Desktop Pro

The QuickBooks Desktop Plus and QuickBooks Desktop pro versions are sold as a yearly subscription rather than a one-time purchase. With these versions, your QuickBooks version is updated yearly, you are entitled to customer support, and your company data will be backed up.

### 3.3.5. QuickBooks for Mac

This is the only version compatible with Mac. It is like the QuickBooks Desktop Pro version. This is useful for most of the small businesses which are not involved in manufacturing.

## 1.15. 3.4. QuickBooks Apps

QuickBooks Apps are applications that can be used in combination with the QuickBooks software to enhance their features. These are also known as add-on applications. These add-ons can be purchased from the QuickBooks website. Some of the QuickBooks Apps are as follows:

### 3.4.1. QuickBooks Payments

This can be used as an add-on for the QuickBooks desktop to add some payment functions. This app enables the business to accept payments online as well as through credit cards. This also enables emailing of invoices.

### 3.4.2. QuickBooks Point of Sale

This is a cloud-based application. It enables the businesses to accept credit cards, track inventory and ring up sales through a point-of-sale dashboard.

### 3.4.3. QuickBooks Payroll

This app enables businesses to provide salaries to up to 50 employees by cash deposit or check. Two types of versions are available:

- Self-Service Solutions

- Full-Service Solutions

The app can calculate the state, federal, and local taxes automatically.

## 1.16. 3.5. Find the Best Version for You

QuickBooks has been a prominent player in the American market as a financial solution provider. The possibilities are numerous with this software. If you are a new business owner or plan to expand your business, QuickBooks will have a suitable version for you. But how to choose one which best suits your requirements? Here is a list of actions you can take before purchasing QuickBooks software. These activities will clear your dilemma, and the choice can be made easily:

### 3.5.1. Read Reviews

The best way to get a clear idea about a product is by reading reviews of people who have already used it. See which product is continually rated better. Read about the kind of services the software provides. Sometimes you get more knowledge about a product or service from reading someone's review. Always go through people's reviews and consider the products that most people are buying. Their performance must be the reason for their higher sales.

### 3.5.2. Take an Online Survey

When you are doing your research online, you may come across some online surveys which ask a few basic questions about your business and earnings. When you have entered your answers, the automated program will suggest the best software for you.

### 3.5.3. Talk to an Expert.

If you are still confused about which software to buy, try talking to an expert. A professional will be in a better position will suggest you according to your needs.

# Chapter 4. The Best Way to Make Money In 2021

The year is all about small businesses and freelance work. In uncertain times everyone is pushing for a side hustle. We often have a misconception that the difficult part is setting up a business; other things follow once that part is covered. We cannot be more wrong in that approach. Though getting an idea, arranging for the finances, resources, place, and the raw material is tough and difficult to obtain, keeping the business afloat once launched is the trickier part. Most businesses come to an end, not because there is a lack of work, but because they could not manage the finances. Not all are indeed good at numbers and finance, and often, help is required.

People have now understood the importance of managing finances and are eager to outsource business financing. Here enters the role of bookkeepers and financial professionals. With the small business boom, there is also a huge demand for financial management. Our focus is on QuickBooks Bookkeeping and how it is the best way to earn money in 2021. In the following chapter, we will see how much a bookkeeper earns in the US. What services you can provide as a QuickBooks Bookkeeper, and which cities are the best for practicing QuickBooks bookkeeping.

## 1.17. 4.1. Salary of Part-Time QuickBooks Bookkeepers

We hear that QuickBooks is a good way to earn money. It is a good side hustle. Be a part-time QuickBooks bookkeeper. No one tells us how much you can make and how much time should be spent to earn a certain amount.

Here we will give you a clear picture of the earnings. A breakdown by weekly, monthly, and yearly earnings.

According to the latest surveys up to 2021, in the United States of America, a QuickBooks bookkeeper's average salary is $50,618 a year. This comes to be around $4,220 per month, around $1000 a week, and about $24 an hour. This sounds very decent for a part-time job. Especially in recent times when we are surrounded by uncertainty, QuickBooks Bookkeeping is a good side hustle.

The figure of $50,618 is the average; it has been reported that you can earn as high as $95,000, and the earnings can even be as low as $29,000. If you want to look at its percentile wise it will look something like this:

- 90th Percentile earnings $93,500 yearly

- 75th Percentile earnings $ 58,500 yearly

- 25th Percentile earnings $ 36,000 yearly

As the survey is based on all kinds of bookkeepers, from entry-level ones to more professional ones, you see a huge income difference. This also suggests that the more experienced and professional abilities you acquire, the higher you will earn.

The following charts must explain the salaries of part-time QuickBooks bookkeepers in a better way.

- The Yearly Average Income of QuickBooks Bookkeepers

- The Average Monthly Income of QuickBooks Bookkeepers

- The Average Weekly Income of QuickBooks Bookkeepers

- The Hourly Average Income of QuickBooks Bookkeepers

$13.94          National Average          $45.67

$24 /hour

The following table will give you a better understanding of the earning possibilities that come with QuickBooks bookkeeping. These are the results of a recent survey. Thus, they also indicate the present trends as well.

|  | Annual Salary | Monthly Pay | Weekly Pay | Hourly Wage |
|---|---|---|---|---|
| Top Earners | $93,500 | $7,791 | $1,798 | $45 |
| 75th Percentile | $58,500 | $4,875 | $1,125 | $28 |
| Average | $50,618 | $4,218 | $973 | $24 |
| 25th Percentile | $36,000 | $3,000 | $692 | $17 |

## 1.18. 4.2. The Top 10 Highest Paying Cities for Bookkeepers in the USA

The survey also indicated that the pay varies from location to location. Here we have compiled the top ten cities in the US where QuickBooks Bookkeepers' salaries are higher than the national average.

The state that offers the highest salaries to the QuickBooks Bookkeepers is, without any doubt, California. Companies in California employ the highest paying QuickBooks bookkeepers. The top salaries are recorded from San Francisco, CA. San Francisco's salaries are around $13,636 higher than the national average. That counts for a whopping 26.9% higher average salary than the average.

The second highest is Fremont, CA. The third position is held by San Jose, CA, with a $9,337 higher average salary than the national average of $50,618. Following close behind in Oakland, CA, with an $8,668 higher average. After this is Tanana, AK, with an average yearly salary of $ 59,078, number six is Wasilla, AK, with a higher average of $8459 than the national average. Hayward, CA, has an average income of $58,044 for QuickBooks Bookkeepers. At number eight is Sunnyvale, CA, with an average income higher by $7,268 than the national average. The average salary for this part-time job in Jackson, WY, is $57,870. The last of the tip than in Norwalk, CT.

The table will give you a better understanding of the top ten cities for QuickBooks Bookkeeping.

| City | Annual Salary | Monthly Pay | Weekly Pay | Hourly Wage |
|------|---------------|-------------|------------|-------------|
| San Francisco, CA | $64,254 | $5,355 | $1,236 | $30.89 |
| Fremont, CA | $61,596 | $5,133 | $1,185 | $29.61 |
| San Jose, CA | $59,956 | $4,996 | $1,153 | $28.82 |
| Oakland, CA | $59,286 | $4,940 | $1,140 | $28.50 |
| Tanaina, AK | $59,078 | $4,923 | $1,136 | $28.40 |
| Wasilla, AK | $59,077 | $4,923 | $1,136 | $28.40 |
| Hayward, CA | $58,044 | $4,837 | $1,116 | $27.91 |
| Sunnyvale, CA | $57,886 | $4,824 | $1,113 | $27.83 |
| Jackson, WY | $57,870 | $4,823 | $1,113 | $27.82 |
| Norwalk, CT | $57,752 | $4,813 | $1,111 | $27.77 |

Having mentioned all these cities does not mean that the prospects of getting jobs are higher in these places. This is just an overview of the average income you can earn in these states. Other factors should also be considered when you decide to work in a specific location. For example, you see many six cities from the state of California. You might be tempted to search for work there. But according to research, the job market for QuickBooks Bookkeepers is not active in California. The companies might be paying higher, but the job opportunities are less. It is always smarter to work in a place where the prospects of being employed are better. However, you might be earning more if you locate in one of these locations. It all depends upon the service you provide and the requirements of the employer. It would help if you did your survey before deciding to change your location.

Another important consideration when thinking about making a location change as a QuickBooks bookkeeper is the cost of living. San Francisco may be paying the highest, but the basic cost of living is high. You might be earning more but even spending more on necessities like housing, insurance, and food. This might not prove to be a smart move. For a QuickBooks bookkeeper, an important factor in choosing a location might be the salary and a place with a lower cost of living.

## 1.19. 4.3. Best Paying QuickBooks Bookkeeping Jobs in the USA

This is true for any field of practice that your job prospects and earnings increase if you specialize in a specific field. This part will discuss the five types of specialized QuickBooks Bookkeepers who earn higher than the typical part-time QuickBooks bookkeepers. All the jobs discuss earn around $7,683 to $14,935 more than the national average. This makes the values about 14.5% to 29.5% more than a regular QuickBooks bookkeeper's salary. So, it is highly recommended that you try to specialize in a certain domain to improve your higher earnings chances. The five jobs we will be discussing are:

1. CPA Firm Bookkeeper

2. QuickBooks Remote Bookkeeper

3. Telecommute Bookkeeper

4. At home Bookkeeper

5. QuickBooks Consultant

### 4.3.1. CPA Firm Bookkeeper

The Bookkeeper associated with a CPA firm earns around $65,553 annually. This translates to a $5,463 paycheck each month, roughly $1,261 a week. In this case, you will be charging approximately $31.52 an hour. If you consider it seriously, this is quite a decent earning.

### 4.3.2. QuickBooks Remote Bookkeeper

This job fetches you a whopping $64,952 annual earning. This is more than $14,300 than the national average. You will be earning $5,413 per month, which is decent.

### 4.3.3. Telecommute Bookkeeper

According to the survey, the Telecommute Bookkeeper earns $60 795 per year. This is $10,000 higher than the national average. This brings you a decent paycheck of $5,000 per month and weekly earnings of $1,000 plus. Working as a telecommute bookkeeper, you will be charging approximately $30 by the hour.

### 4.3.4. At Home Bookkeeper

The best thing about this type of bookkeeping is that you can practice it from the comfort of your house, and you will be earning good money. You will be making savings on the commute time, fuel expenses, and outside food expenses, if you practice work from home. Continuing from home, you will still be earning $8,000 more than the national average. You will be earning around $5,000 per month from the comfort of your home.

### 4.3.5. QuickBooks Consultant

As a QuickBooks consultant, you can earn $57,986 per year. The good part about this is that you can work part-time and take home a paycheck of around $5,000 each month.

This table will give you a better understanding of the benefits of specializing and the financial prospects related to it.

| Job Title | Annual Salary | Monthly Pay | Weekly Pay | Hourly Wage |
|---|---|---|---|---|
| CPA Firm Bookkeeper | $65,553 | $5,463 | $1,261 | $31.52 |
| Quickbooks Remote | $64,952 | $5,413 | $1,249 | $31.23 |
| Telecommute Bookkeeper | $60,795 | $5,066 | $1,169 | $29.23 |
| Work From Home Bookkeeper | $58,536 | $4,878 | $1,126 | $28.14 |
| Quickbooks Consultant | $57,986 | $4,832 | $1,115 | $27.88 |

# Chapter 5. Becoming a QuickBooks Bookkeeper

Now that you have a thorough understanding of bookkeeping and QuickBooks, it must be clear that in present times the knowledge of QuickBooks is essential if you want to work in the US small business community. Sometimes learning the software is not enough. To get the job, you require to show some qualifications and expertise as well. Unfortunately, we are still living in the workplace where showing your qualifications and certificates is essential to acquire a job. But when we talk about QuickBooks, there is no harm in doing a certification. Doing a certification will open many opportunities for you. No one wants to hire an unqualified person. With this Certification, you will be considered qualified for the job. The Certification might teach you the software's basics, but the actual learning is always done practically. Nevertheless, gaining this Certification is beneficial even if it gives you a head start.

Sometimes you have this clear picture in your mind regarding what you want to do but you have no access to proper guidance. Many people want to work as bookkeepers and want to learn further to upgrade their skill set but there is no one to guide them. The information around us is so much that sometimes we are overwhelmed by the excess of information rather than its lack. Sometimes all we need is a plain simple instruction in the right direction. This chapter does just that. It will push you one step further in the right direction.

In this chapter, we will discuss how you can gain this Certification, how much it cost, how long it takes to become certified, the difficulty level of this Certification, the types of certifications available for QuickBooks; all will be discussed in this chapter. In this chapter, we will discuss:

- The type of investment required for Certification.

- Different courses available

- Information about QuickBooks Certification.

- The course fees.

- The duration of the course

## 1.20. 5.1. The Type of Investment Required for Certification

Getting a certification is a big investment. Not only are you investing your money, but you also invest your time and money in such courses as well. In present times, the world is ever-changing and keeping up with the fast-moving times has become mandatory. Otherwise, you will be left behind. Similarly, if you are a bookkeeper, you must upgrade your skillset. You might be employed right now, but what if the employer changes technology and you are no more required to work for him/her, and they hire a person with better qualifications. For such times it is important to be well prepared and keep up with times. Your aim should be to become an asset to the company rather than a liability.

## 1.21. 5.2. The Different Courses Offered

There are three types of courses offered for QuickBooks Certification. Two of them are for the QuickBooks Desktop, and one is for QuickBooks online. Nowadays, most people prefer a cloud-based financial management system, so it would be wise to take the Certification for the online version. The different types of certifications offered are:

- QuickBooks Online Edition: Basic

- QuickBooks Desktop Edition: Basic

- QuickBooks Desktop Edition: Advanced

## 1.22. 5.3. Information About QuickBooks Certification

If you are working as an employee, getting a QuickBooks certificate will reassure your employer of your abilities with the software and convince them that you are an asset to their company. Certification will enhance your credibility. This will equip you with the expertise to deal with any situation that involves QuickBooks. You will be in a better position as a QuickBooks certified employee to tackle tricky situations involving QuickBooks.

When you pass the exam, you will gain the following skills, and your certificate will be proof of your abilities:

- Easily use the main measures of QuickBooks and manage business accounts on the software.

- You can manage all the accounting functions like Payroll, transactions, invoices, and sales smoothly with QuickBooks software.

- Can solve and manage complex scenarios that come up while using QuickBooks.

One thing you should keep in mind, the certifications are not cheap, they cost high prices. But you should consider investing in this Certification as a step towards your better career. You will get profits from this investment very soon.

## 1.23. 5.4. Why Should You Invest

It is a known fact that QuickBooks Certifications do not come cheap. If you are an employer, you might feel that this is a lot of investment, and the courses are time-consuming. If you have many employees, the cost might be an issue for sure. If you are a freelance bookkeeper, the fee might be a big investment. But consider this a useful investment. This is one of the investments you should make. Some business owners consider it an initial investment, and the profits and dividends are gained when the work is done more efficiently and faster.

A lot of groups are offering QuickBooks certification courses. If you are an employer, you can look for bundle package discounts and monthly packages. If you are a freelance service provider, you should look for packages that offer monthly installments as one-time payments are sometimes difficult to pay at once.

You should always look for online courses. Nowadays, many online courses are available, and you can take them from the comfort of your home or office. This can save you the commute expenses and the time which is wasted with the commute. Always look for certifications with live tutoring. These sessions are more interactive, there are live questions and answers sessions, and you learn more this way.

You should be convinced not to take up a QuickBooks certification. If you are still not convinced, maybe this is not for you. But if you want to further your career in bookkeeping, this Certification is essential.

## 1.24. 5.5. The Certification Fee

Most bookkeepers follow the method that they do their training from a tutor and then take the certification exam. Two groups conduct the Certification:

- Intuit, through their ProAdvisor Program

- NBA (National Bookkeepers Association)

Intuit is the maker of QuickBooks, and they conduct the test for free. However, they cover their cost by making you purchase the mandatory membership, which is hundreds of dollars. You will have to become a member to get access to the test.

NBA conducts the other Certification. This is a much affordable option. If you decide to take the test through them, the fee is $150 for the ones who are taking the test for the first time. This fee includes a practice test and the actual test. At successful completion, you get a certificate. The certification must be updated every year. The fee for each subsequent year is around $75.

## 1.25. 5.6. The Length of Courses

There is no specific length for courses. The courses and workshops are carried out by professionals who specialize in QuickBooks software. The Certification is only a 2-to-4-hour program. If you are already familiar with the software, you might just book your test and pass. But for someone, the learning might take from weeks to months. All this depends upon few factors:

- Do you have basic knowledge about the software?

In this case, if you have basic knowledge and take the test straight away, the chances are that you might not be able to gain Certification. It would be best if you had more than basic knowledge to pass the Certification. You should not take these exams lightly. Since these exams are expensive, you should prepare your best before taking the exam to get greater chances of passing.

- The Certification you might wish to do.

So, there are different certifications offered. In the Desktop version certifications, there is a basic certificate and an advanced certificate. As the name indicates, the advanced certification will be harder and thus require more expertise.

- When you decide to take the test

You must be responsible when you decide the date to take the test. Do not take the test before you are fully prepared. If you decide the test date before proper preparation, the chances are that you might not be able to pass.

Mostly, the tests can be completed in one sitting. The level of the exams is according to the Certification you wish to do. It is recommended to get the basic Certification before you try to obtain an advanced certification.

# Chapter 6. Hacks and Tricks for QuickBooks

With every software, you should know about the tricks and tips to make your work more efficient and streamlined. The same is the case with QuickBooks. You can use the experience of others to better your work. You must have heard the term; time is money, and these tips and tricks save your time. And by saving time, they save your money. In present times we are blessed with technology, and we should try to benefit from t as much as possible. The lives we lead in present times are quite stressful, and the work-life balance is frankly off-balance. In such a situation, it is wise to take as much help as possible. That help can be from technology, or you can even benefit from others' experiences and mistakes. Here we will discuss some hacks and tricks the professionals from the field have agreed upon and shared with everyone to benefit from. Here is a list of a few tricks and hacks to make your work quicker and easier.

The trend of 2021 is focused more on cloud-based QuickBooks software. In this chapter, we will discuss the tips and tricks we can apply in QuickBooks Online to gain better results. We have compiled a list of six hacks that you might find helpful:

- Cash receipts should be created.

- Use attachments.

- Use keyboard shortcuts.

- Automate the emails.

- Use QuickBooks Online to track the time.

- Always use the bank rules

## 1.26. 6.1. Cash Receipts Should be Created.

It is always a good idea to organize your working space. The same is the case with finances. If you have your cash receipts created and recorded, you will easily overview all money received at any time. With QuickBooks Online, you can enter the details in the sales center and review the records anytime you want. This is a feature of QuickBooks online, which is easy to use and convenient for financial tracking.

- Usage

How you will create cash receipts is simple, go to the sales transactions and create a file med cash receipts. Next, go to the filter list and go to 'Money Received' and enter the date appropriately.

(Cash Receipt Usage)

## 1.27. 6.2. Use Attachments

This is a hack that is overlooked a lot of the time, and most people ignore using it. The hack is to attach all related forms and documents to the vendor accounts to be managed at once. For example, you can attach a W-9 to the vendor's account.

(Using Attachments)

So, when you use attachments, you can also attach the bank accounts' files and the credit card details and statements. When all the documents are attached and compiled in one place, they will be easy to review. Another pro tip will be to use naming conventions. This will make the work more streamlined and easier to track. According to experts, not using attachments wastes time you could be spending on other activities. There is no need to work so hard if you have applications in your software that make your work easier and smoother to operate. If you are using a mobile version of QuickBooks online, you can even take a screenshot of any receipt and attach it to the folder. In the same way, you can even attach the invoices and enter the yearly or monthly estimates. If you have the add-on of QuickBooks Payments, you can even receive payments.

## 1.28. 6.3. Use Keyboard Shortcuts

This is also a huge time saver. When you are working on multiple things, clicking from one program to another makes everything confusing. The same is the case with QuickBooks. When you are managing multiple entities, you need to work fast, and shortcuts are a lifesaver. Following is a summary of all the important shortcuts found within QuickBooks.

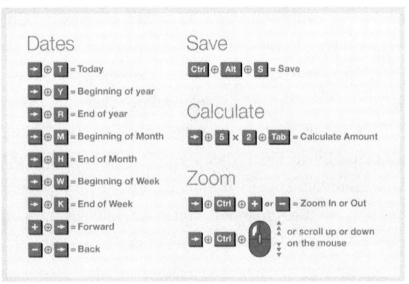

(QuickBooks shortcuts)

## 1.29. 6.4. Automate the emails.

For all the regular payments and receiving, automation is the way to go. You should automate your emails for sales, financial statements, and invoices. You must be thinking about how to go about this? It is easy; you will first set different reports scheduled to email on a specific date. For example, you can set a schedule that emails you your financial statement monthly. You can even get an email for the collection report, and the sales report every week. This will help you keep track of the open invoices.

Apart from this, you can schedule the payments that have to be sent out weekly or monthly. You can arrange for the recurring invoices to be sent automatically by email. Again, if you use the app QuickBooks payments, the received payments can be automatically recorded automatically.

## 1.30. 6.5. Use the QuickBooks Online to Track Time

If time tracking is tough for you, the newer versions of QuickBooks Online will help you. In the older versions of the program, you had to import the T reports to QuickBooks. In the newer versions, you can create the T sheets within QuickBooks online. These are the integrated T sheets. This means that any change, addition, or deletion would apply automatically to the T sheet, and it will be updated by itself. You will not have to manually update the information. This process is carried out in a seamless manner. You can create several employee T sheets and even approve several T sheets simultaneously.

## 1.31. 6.6. Always use the Bank Rules

This is a simple and logical hack. The bank rules are already made, and time tested. If you implement them and set your regular payments to the utilities, vendors, suppliers, etc., on bank rules, the task will become easier. This can save a lot of time for you as well. At the end of the month, all you will need to do is an overview of all the payments carried out in a smooth and streamlined fashion.

These hacks and tips may seem simple but implementing them can save you hours and hours' worth of labor. There will be far fewer things on your mind. It is a one-time setup, and it will be automated from then on. You will easily manage the payments, receiving, employee timesheets, Payroll, and everything else with ease, and you will become less stressed.

# Chapter 7. QuickBooks Usage in Small Businesses

Many small businesses use QuickBooks to manage their finances. The software takes care of their bill payments, monitors their cash flow, and manages invoices. QuickBooks is a good software to generated automated monthly financial reports as well as yearly financial reports. Some business owners manage their accounts themselves and are pro users of the software, but most business owners employ professionals to manage their accounts. QuickBooks certified bookkeepers are employed by small to mid-size business owners to manage their accounts.

Small business owners use QuickBooks for several functions and use. Following are the functions for which the small business owners use QuickBooks:

- Make and track invoices.

- Monitor expenses and other bills.

- Generate business and financial statements.

- Manage payroll.

- Do the inventory.

- Simplify taxes.

- Online payments.

- Record Receipts.

- Manage mileage.

## 1.32. 7.1. Make and Track Invoices

The software has the option to create invoices, and you can easily print them or directly send them to your customers. Each invoice generated by the software will be automatically recorded in the system. In this way, you can track all the amount that has already been paid, and the receivables will also be displayed.

## 1.33. 7.2. Monitor Expenses and Other Bills

You have an option to link the QuickBooks software to your accounts and credit cards. This will enable the program to record all payments and bills automatically and keep a record. It will be available for your view whenever you require.

You can enter other bills you receive in the system and take care of the payables. This will help you keep track of your expenses and payables. The software will make sure you do not miss your payments. If you attach the QuickBooks payment app, the payments can even be managed automatically.

## 1.34. 7.3. Generate Business Financial Statements

The software can generate financial statements that will give you an overview of your business performance. The kind of statements you can generate with the QuickBooks software are:

- Cashflow Statement

- Profit and Loss Statement

- Balance Sheets

## 1.35. 7.4. Manage Payroll

The software can manage the Payroll and working hours of each employee automatically. You must create a separate account for each employee, enter each employee's information, and schedule the salary, deductions, schedules, and hours. All can be managed automatically by the software. If you use the software, you can easily manage:

- Payment to the employees can be made by checks or cash.

- The taxes can be deducted automatically, and the tax-exempt employee payments are also managed.

- The software fills tax forms automatically

- The payroll taxes can be managed automatically.

## 1.36. 7.5. Do the Inventory.

The software manages the inventory. It records the quantities and keeps track of the total cost of inventory. The software will indicate when the inventory is getting low, and there is a need to replenish. This all is not done automatically, you will have to enter the amounts manually, but they will be managed and calculated automatically.

## 1.37. 7.6. Simplify Taxes

Taxes is one of the most difficult parts of the business. Most people are fearful of taxes, and in the end, their taxes are piled up. QuickBooks takes care of your taxes. The Tax becomes difficult because your financial statements are not in order. QuickBooks makes the financial statements simplified, and you can easily print them out and let a tax preparer assess the statements and use the required information.

## 1.38. 7.7. Online Payments

The QuickBooks Payments app enables you to accept payments directly from your customers. This app is integrated into the software, so all the payments are recorded in the system automatically.

## 1.39. 7.8. Record Receipts

The QuickBooks app makes it possible for the business owner to upload all the payment and expense receipts to the software, and they can be easily scanned and recorded in the system.

## 1.40. 7.9. Manage Mileage

If you use your vehicle for business purposes, a tax deduction is applied. But to receive the tax deduction, you will have to prove your traveling. You get a deduction of 57.5 cents per mile. **To record the miles, you can link QuickBooks Online to your vehicle's GPS, and it will easily record your miles, date, and time**

# Conclusion

If you have read the whole book, many of your doubts must have been cleared regarding bookkeeping and QuickBooks. This is an amazing opportunity for you to avail yourself if you want to take up bookkeeping as a profession. It is always a better idea to keep up with the current trends and technology because it ensures better job and working opportunities. Therefore, we have mentioned QuickBooks. Being a QuickBooks certified bookkeeper gives you an edge in business. This is because most small to mid-size businesses have installed the QuickBooks software for their financial management. There are different versions of QuickBooks available:

- QuickBooks Self-Employed

- QuickBooks Online

- QuickBooks Desktop

- QuickBooks Apps

QuickBooks is user-friendly and is compatible with other programs like MS Word and MS excel. Different versions are available that are compatible with iOS, android, windows, and Mac operating systems.

It will be a good idea to specialize in cloud-based QuickBooks software because, as of 2014, more and more business owners are interested in keeping their records on the cloud-based package offered by QuickBooks. If you are planning to get your Certification any time soon, the cloud-based product should be your focus. There is a basic course offered in QuickBooks Online; you should consider that.

Another consideration when thinking about QuickBooks bookkeeping seriously is what type of Bookkeeper you are going to be. According to a survey, these five types of part-time QuickBooks bookkeepers are making the highest number of average incomes:

- CPA Firm Bookkeeper

- QuickBooks Remote Bookkeeper

- Telecommute Bookkeeper

- At home Bookkeeper

- QuickBooks Consultant

The next most important point to think about is your location. At different locations in America, bookkeepers make different yearly incomes. The QuickBooks bookkeepers make the highest yearly earnings in San Francisco, California. But before quickly packing your bags towards the sunny state, keep in mind the expenses as well. Before shifting your location, always consider the basic expenses and how you will be managing them. It may be possible that you are earning less in one city, but the cost of living is cheaper, and in another city, you might be making more money, but the expenses are equally higher. In the latter case, you end up losing more money. So, always take a well-thought-out and informed decision.

In all, if you are someone good with numbers and have a consistent work ethic, you can very manage to be a QuickBooks bookkeeper. You can even work as a freelance service provider. Providing services is also generally a risk-free approach. The only investment you make is the training you do and the courses you take. After that, all is gain. In this way, you can set your schedule and take up as much work as you can manage. In present times where the future has become unpredictable, freelancing is the way to go.

# The Complete Startup Crash Course

*David Lazarus*

# Table of Contents

# Introduction

An entrepreneur is a clever fellow who wants to create an enterprise in circumstances of intense complexity. More than often, a company's priorities don't always fit the ways people need or want a service or product. New products and new projects stall at some stage or don't live up to their full potential. It is where the Lean Startup model comes in. The core philosophy behind the Lean Startup model, which is an evolution of astute businessmen's management style, promotes an atmosphere that allows new concepts to thrive while finding ways to reduce waste. Sometimes as challenging as it may be, the only way ahead might be to ditch what you have and start again from scratch. In stagnation or unfavorable economic conditions, we all are advised to do something for less. All of you must be well aware of the idea of having to do a great many things with little money along with reinventing ourselves or our systems to cater to the ever-changing needs of our consumers. Astute entrepreneurs have insight plus know means and strategies of evaluating success.

Additionally, they can determine the next steps of action, find shortcomings, and make commensurate changes to change with the changing circumstances and atmosphere to develop and further innovate. It is generally accepted that hard work and determination, combined with historical predictors, are automatic performance measures. However, the future is uncertain, and the old methods of working are just not applicable. The management of the previous century does not work with the instability of today's economy. Frustrated with conventional strategies and approaches to entrepreneurship, the creative entrepreneurs begin looking for other ideas to bring to the test. They all have come up with the Lean Startup model that focuses on innovation and getting to know customers' needs and habits to create a better product or service. It focuses on the correct process, that is, to work better and not simply harder to solve difficult circumstances. Whether it is a start-up of tech, small businesses, or a project inside a big corporation, Launching a new organization has long been a hit-or-the-miss proposition. According to the decades-old formula, you always write a marketing strategy, pitch this to the investors, build a team, launch a product, & start to sell it as much as you possibly can. & somewhere in the chain of events, you will inevitably suffer fatal failure. Most of the time, the odds aren't in your favor. A recent study by Harvard Business School reveals that 75 percent of all start-ups crash. But lately, the important countervailing factor has arisen, one which can make the task of beginning a business less dangerous. It's a technique called the "leaned start-up," & it encourages experimentation over the elaborate organizing, customer input over intuition, & iterative designs over conventional "big designs upfront" expansion. While methodology's only a few years old, and its constructs like "minimum viable product" & "pivoting"— have rapidly taken hold in the start-up community, & business schools have already started modifying the curricula to explain them. The lean start-up movement is changing traditional thinking around entrepreneurship. Newest ventures of every sort try to boost the chances of survival by pursuing the ideals of struggling quickly and learning quickly. Despite methods name, some of the greatest payoffs can be earned by the major corporations that embrace it in the long run. This book shall explore in deep as to how digital entrepreneurs utilize continuous creativity to build fundamentally profitable companies and how you can imitate them.

## CHAPTER 1: Lean Start-up

lean start-up is a strategy used on behalf of an established business to create new companies or launch a new product. Method of lean start-up advocates the development of products that customers have already shown they want so that as quick as product's launched, a market will already exist. It is in contrast to creating a brand and then hoping the demand would emerge. Developers of Product can measure consumers' interest in a product & determine how the product may need to be clarified by employing lean start-up principles. The process is referred to as validated learning & can be used to prevent unnecessary usage of the resources in the creation & development of products. If innovation is likely to be failed by lean start-ups, it'll fail cheaply and quickly instead of gradually & expensively, thence the word "fail-fast." Lean start-up's example of customers dictating the type of goods that the respective markets deliver, instead of deciding what products they would be provided.

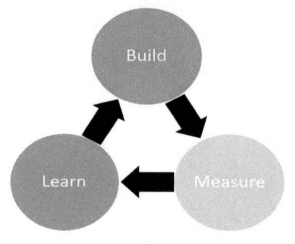

Lean Start-ups vs. the Traditional Businesses

When it comes to hiring, the lean entrepreneurship approach often differentiates itself from the conventional company model. Lean start-ups attract employees who can adapt, learn, and work efficiently, whereas conventional firms recruit employees based on knowledge and expertise. Lean start-ups employ multiple financial recording metrics also; they concentrate on the customer acquisition expenses, lifetime consumer value, client churn rate, & how viral the product maybe, instead of relying on revenue statements, balance sheets, and cash flow statements.

Requirements for the Lean Startup

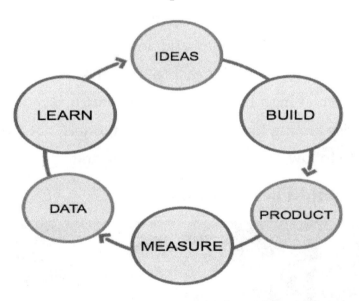

Experimentation is perceived by the lean start-up approach to be extra valuable than comprehensive planning. A waste of time is viewed as five years of business plans designed on unknowns, and consumer response is paramount. Instead of the business models, Lean start-ups use business concepts focused on assumptions that are easily checked. Before proceeding, data doesn't have to be completed; it only has to be more than enough. The start-up easily changes to limit the losses &

return to the production of goods consumers want when customers do not respond. Failure is generally regarded as the rule. Following this strategy, entrepreneurs validate their theories by engaging with prospective consumers, investors, & partners to evaluate their responses to product specifications, packaging, delivery, and customer retention. With the data, entrepreneurs make tiny changes to goods called iterations, and big adjustments known as pivots fix any major issues. To best suit the current target consumer, this testing process could result in exchanging target customers or altering the product. A problem that must be addressed is first defined by the lean start-up method. It then produces the minimum workable product or smallest product type that enables entrepreneurs to offer prospective buyers. This strategy is simpler and less risky than checking final product production, and decreasing the risk that start-ups face reduces their usual high failure rate. Lean start-ups redefine start-up as an enterprise aiming for scalable growth models, not the one that is determined to follow an established business strategy.

## 1.1 Learn to build a Lean Start-up

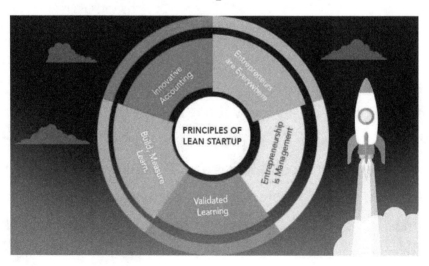

Do you know the 75 percent of all start-ups usually fail? You're likely to encounter obstacles, difficulties, and roadblocks of all sorts, no matter which type of company you're beginning to build. You could spend years on one business idea to fail if you've followed the conventional start-up formula of drafting a business plan, setting up to the investors, developing your product, & selling it. The Lean Startup Methodology is an inexpensive, fast, and less risky technique to carry your business concept to the market. Launching some form of business has always been risky. "Instead of using more traditional methods, the main distinction between building lean start-ups with Lean Start-ups Methodology is that entrepreneurs must ask themselves that "Should the products be built? "instead of "Can the products be built? It is about identifying a problem, validating the question, and creating a product that can fix the problem to create a lean start-up. When you create a lean start-up, you need to ensure that your product is consistently checked and verified, so your product's in the customer's hands as quick as possible. Subsequently, Lean Startups Methodology would help you optimize business growth. To begin creating a lean start-up, here are three moves entrepreneurs may take: Find, Execute, & Validate it.

**Find the Business Idea**

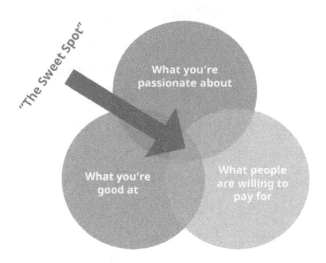

the big question is not: "could this be built?" or "Should this be built?" "It puts us in an extraordinary historical moment: the success of collective imaginations depends on our future prosperity. It's important to determine whether the product can fix is significant enough for clients to choose to buy it while selecting a company concept to pursue using the Lean Startup Approach. It can be easy to find a business idea, so it's essential to pay attention to the challenges people face daily. For the product to gain momentum, clients must be aggressively looking for solutions to a problem. It is time to execute the project after you settle on a business idea.

**Execute the Business Idea**

## STRATEGIC SWEET SPOT

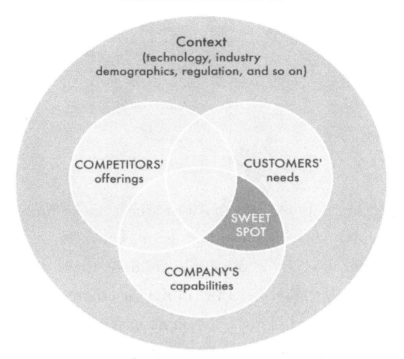

Next, you can create minimum viable products (MVP). MVP is a version of a product you plan to create, allowing the team to quickly gather as much knowledge as possible on your prospective consumers and their input on the product. Any Lean Start-up Philosophy advocates recommend that you take the "Kickstarter Approach" for your product, i.e., start selling the product before it's completed to build market value and drive demand in the product while collecting funds for the Lean Startup. It's time to validate the business plan once the business ideas are executed.

**Validate the Business idea**

## 4 STEPS FOR IDEA VALIDATION

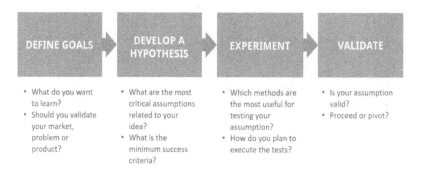

Start-ups do not only exist to make products, make profits, or even support clients. Their main target is to know how to create a profitable enterprise. By conducting multiple trials that allow the entrepreneurs to verify each aspect of the vision, this learning can be scientifically validated. Product validation's a crucial step in the development of profitable Lean Start-ups. In this phase, in the real world, it's time to play with the business idea. Early adopter or otherwise, test the MVP with actual consumers in the industry to see whether the product is feasible and to gain knowledge that you could study. Use this knowledge to determine if you can continue building your product, modifying the product, or pivoting your market plan. If the findings are mainly good from checking MVP in the marketplace, continue to develop your products using your initial approach while integrating tester input. If the outcomes of marketplace MVP research are favorable and unfavorable, tweak the product or business plan to make the product ideally suited to your consumers' desires and needs. If the findings are mainly disappointing from checking MVP in the industry, it's time for pivoting your product & business plan. To adapt vision to suit the desires and the needs of the clients would entail a radical change in your technique and work. Under certain circumstances, mainly unfavorable reviews would indicate that Lean Startup can fully quit the marketplace.

**Why should one build a Lean Start-up?**

Start-up's different way of seeing at the growth of innovative and new products, all at the same time highlighting rapid iteration & customer insights, huge vision & great ambition. Building a lean start-up is an ideal opportunity for entrepreneurs who need to start an inexpensive company and easily bring them to market. Building lean start-up essentially shortens product creation times and means that developers build products through experimentation & validated learning that satisfy consumer needs.

Example of Lean Startup

*How to start a*
**FOOD DELIVERY BUSINESS FROM HOME**

entrepreneurship in a box

For instance, a healthy meal delivery service that targets busy, single twenty-somethings in the urban areas could learn that thirty-something wealthy mothers of newborns in the suburbs have a better market. The business could then alter its delivery schedule & the types of foods it serves to provide new mothers with optimal nutrition. It could also add options for spouses or partners & other children in the household for meals. The lean start-up approach is not intended to be used solely by start-ups. In developing countries where electricity is unreliable, companies such as General Electric have used the technique to develop a new battery for cell phone companies.

# CHAPTER 2: Importance of Market Research

The method of evaluating a new product or service's feasibility through surveys carried out directly with prospective consumers is market research. Market analysis helps an organization discover the target market & collect customers' views and the other inputs on product or service participation. This form of research may be performed in-house through the organization itself or a 3rd party company specialising in market analysis. Through polls, product testing, & focus groups, it can be achieved. Usually, research subjects are compensated with the samples of goods or/and paid nominal stipends for the time. Market analysis is a vital aspect of new products or service's research and development (R&D).

The company uses market testing by engaging individuals with a prospective buyer to test its feasibility or service.

Companies will find out the target customers through market analysis and get customer reviews and input quickly.

This form of research may be performed in-house through the organization itself or an independent company specializing in the market analysis.

The study includes surveys, testing of products, & focus groups.

## 2.1 Develop an understanding of the Market Research

**Figure 2.8 Proper Definition of the Marketing Research Problem**

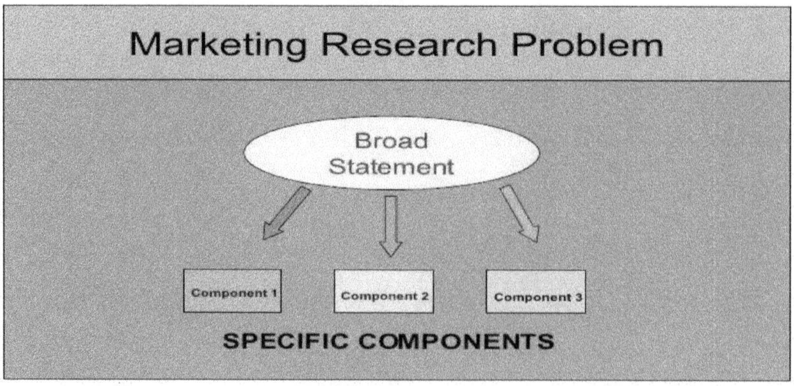

The market research aims to examine the market related to certain products or services to decide how the audience receives them. It will include the compilation of information for the market segmentation & product differentiation purposes that could be used to target promotional campaigns and assess what attributes are perceived as a concern by the customer. To complete the process of market analysis, an organization must participate in plenty of activities. Based on the business area being investigated, it needs to collect information. To assess the existence of certain trends or the related data point that it can use in decision-making, the organization needs to evaluate and understand the resulting data. Market research's a vital instrument for helping businesses identify what buyers expect, produce goods that people can use, & maintain a strategic edge over other businesses in their sector.

## 2.2 Collection of information through Market Research

The market analysis contains a mixture of the primary information, meaning what the organization or a person recruited by a company has collected, & secondary pieces of information, or what outside source has collected.

## Primary Information

The Primary data is either compiled by the organization or gathered by an individual or a business contracted to do analysis. Generally speaking, this kind of knowledge falls into two categories: exploratory &/or specific research. Exploratory analysis is a less formal choice that works by many open-ended inquiries, resulting in the presentation of questions or challenges that might need to be answered by the enterprise. The relevant study seeks the solutions to questions previously understood that are mostly called to light by exploratory researches.

## Secondary Information

Secondary data is data that has already been obtained from an external agency. It could include the demographic statistic from federal census results, research studies by trade groups, or research provided by the other organization working within the same business area.

Example of Market Research

Often firms use market analysis to evaluate potential ideas or gather customer knowledge on what types of products or the services they like and do not have at present. For instance, to test the feasibility of a product or service, a company considering going into the business might perform market research. If consumer interest is confirmed by market research, the company can proceed with the business plan confidently. If not, to make changes to the product to get it in line with consumer expectations, the organization should use market analysis findings.

Components of Market Research

The research of market involves the gathering of information about:

customers – for developing a customer profile

industry & market environment – for understanding factors that are external to the business

competitors – for developing competitor profiles.

**Learn to research the industry and market environment**

the business & market factors analysis will concentrate on knowledge regarding any legal, political, social, economic, and cultural problems or developments that may impact your organization. This external analysis will then be used to obtain knowledge about the composition of the target market, market differences, emerging market patterns, and where the new market prospects may lie. Research on the industry and business outlook could cover:

- Market size & trends
- Business regulations
- Marketing channels
- Market demographics (for example, age, gender, income)
- Sociographic (for example, beliefs & attitudes, lifestyle factors, interests).

**Sources that can be used for collecting the data**

- Pertinent <u>business & industry associations</u>
- Online trade journal
- Newspapers
- <u>Council</u> businesses support service
- Print media
- Television
- Industry expos along with trade shows

Regional councils & relevant state governmental departments (which is depending upon the industry)

consumer lists or Commercially sold marketing

search engines for Internet

**Research the customers**

To collect the relevant information about who your clients or future customers are, & what, where, when & how they shop, you can use consumer analysis.

Customer analysis will also provide you with useful insights into your consumers' perceptions towards your organization and your goods and services.

Research on customers may cover:

- Needs & expectations
- Social & lifestyle trends
- Attitude towards you
- Customer demographics (like age, income, gender)
- Attitudes towards your opponents.

**Sources for researching customers**

- Focus groups

- <u>surveys & questionnaires</u> for staff and customers
- Observations of the customer behavior
- Personal interviews
- Feedback on points-of-sale
- Sales staff
- Phone surveys
- Social media
- Development offices for local business (local council & independent)

## Research the competitors

Your study into competitors will obtain data on current and future competitors. You will use your rival's data to gain knowledge such as the existing business advantages of your competitor, shortcomings in their sales tactics, & how their consumers view their goods and services. Analysis of competitors may cover:

- Present turnover & market shares
- Pricing structures and policies
- Products & services
- Branding, marketing, advertising

## Sources for researching competitors

- Competitor marketing & advertising material, the price-lists
- Past clients
- Suppliers
- Official offices like licensing bodies
- Business directories
- Competitor stores, pages on social media, and websites

- Complaints blogs & chat sites
- Competitor print & lists of electronic mailing
- Personal & staff observations

# CHAPTER 3: Digital Entrepreneurship

It is important to academic study to consider the conditions and reasons that promote digital entrepreneurship (DE) and to direct market practice and public policies aimed at promoting this development, given its positive impacts on job development and economic growth. Digital entrepreneurship is a concept that determines how entrepreneurship can evolve as digital technology begins to disrupt industry and culture. Digital entrepreneurship illustrates trends in the practice, philosophy, and curriculum of entrepreneurs. In a modern world, digital entrepreneurship encompasses everything new and distinct about entrepreneurship, including:

- New ways of locating customers for entrepreneurial ventures
- Innovative ways of designing and offering products and services
- Unconventional ways of generating revenue and reducing cost
- Identification of fresh opportunities to collaborate with platforms and partners
- New sources of opportunity, risk, and competitive advantage

Digital entrepreneurship opens up new opportunities on a realistic basis for someone dreaming about being an entrepreneur. Some possibilities are more technical, but many others are within reach for someone who learns the fundamental skills of digital entrepreneurship. Such specific skills include looking online for potential clients, prototyping new business concepts, and improving data-based business ideas. Digital entrepreneurship is all about new ways of thinking about entrepreneurship itself and learning new technological skills, which is another way of suggesting that it introduces new entrepreneurship theories. New questions about the policy, chance, and risk are opened up by digital entrepreneurship. Digital entrepreneurship unlocks new opportunities in terms of education to train the future generation of entrepreneurs. 'Doing it' is the perfect way to practice entrepreneurship and draw on the learning. In the normal world, beginning the latest company or releasing a new product is expensive and dangerous for beginners. Not only does the modern world reduce the hurdles to beginning something new, but it provides a range of routes to growth. Educationally, it's such a different environment from case studies, simulations, and business plans. There is also controversy over the precise concept of digital entrepreneurship, partly because it is early and partly because it is changing. What is fresh in digital entrepreneurship can change over time as digital technology progresses. Maybe one day, any business projects will be born digital,' and digital entrepreneurship will cease to exist as a separate topic. However, today, there is a strong need to help educate entrepreneurs for the modern world and offer a new route to entrepreneurship to more individuals.

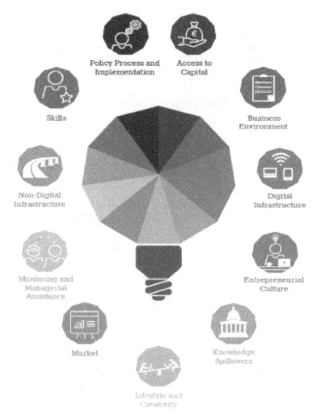

## Simple Types of Digital Business Ideas

Digital marketers don't have a good sense of what is possible at the very beginning. It is advised that they begin with one of five basic forms to help beginners conceive of new digital business ideas:

A business offering knowledge on every specialized topic

It is possible to raise revenue through advertising, referrals, sponsorship, or merchandise

A neighborhood enterprise, hosting a vibrant and helpful discussion on every specialized topic

The sales opportunities are close to the industry of information

An online marketplace that markets goods or services

The objects may be tangible or digital

A matchmaker corporation that puts together two sets of individuals. For instance, a product or service provider (for instance, prospective babysitters) and another group who will need their services are always one group (parents looking for a babysitter). Advertising income is a probability, but with good matches, a transaction fee may also be received.

A promotional organization that draws online clients to a market that already exists

A possible revenue stream here, or advertising, is fees per client referral

An ideal new business plan can be impossible to come up with right from the start, but everyone will easily develop a realistic idea among these five options. As long as they can conceive of a subject that could attract at least a few hundred other individuals, a product or service they want to market, groups of individuals that may support each other, or some small company who could use some promotional assistance, digital entrepreneurs will launch their journey from the beginning. These five basic forms often make it easy for a digital business concept to be shared. In this case, a new business concept is:

A content provider on [your subject]

A [your subject] neighborhood business

An online shop that sells [your product or service]

A matchmaking firm that connects [service providers/group A] to [service users/group B]

The promotion of an online business [a local business]

The options are nearly infinite, and they are still evolving

Digital Entrepreneurship in the face of the Pandemic

Small firms and start-ups have been struck hardest by the recent pandemic than any other area of the economy. To survive a disaster, small firms usually have few resources. Usually, small companies still have little background in the new world of becoming creative, which is now one of their best choices for weathering the storm. In this moment of recession, a variety of digital practices can be considered by small companies. The typical guidance involves applying for federal support, staying in contact with online buyers, and beginning existing products' sales using e-commerce. These are all positive moves, but studies on digital entrepreneurship suggest some additional solutions. For small companies and start-ups, here are three extra fields of digital opportunity.

**New models for doing business**

It's a smart idea to learn ways to market your current goods online but think about marketing your experience as a new online service. Many families have at least one person with increased time to develop new things or with an immediate need to discover new, more customized ways to entertain themselves. Another option is to offer digital products, such as online classes or digital how-to guides, depending on your expertise. However, digital entrepreneurship helps you pursue brand new areas of operation and offer similar new goods and services. The opportunity to pursue innovative business ideas at little or low cost is a major benefit of digital entrepreneurship. Your new digital company, for instance, may provide useful knowledge that lets customers make other buying choices. During this recession, internet traffic and investment are up and catch these emerging internet traffic sources' attention. Advertisers and marketers are involved and can pay for quality customer leads. Display advertisements, performance advertising, sponsorships, and commission fees from affiliate marketing transactions are new revenue possibilities. Another new potential for digital business is to become a matchmaker, connect individuals who need an online product or service with someone who can better provide it, and charge a purchase fee or percentage. What types of people do you meet already? During this crisis, what are their special needs? And where can you refer them to for assistance? Many of the world's major digital matchmakers, Airbnbs and Ubers, would need to be temporarily replaced by more local alternatives that fit local conditions and will be able to handle local constraints as they evolve.

**Perfect the digital business process**

An easy way to think about digital business is to see it as an ABC method with three steps: acquisition, behavior, and conversion. The acquisition adds new buyers through social media campaigns, search results, email, search, or social advertisement, among many other platforms to the digital sector. Behavior is what tourists do to fulfill their needs and help them reach their goals through their digital presence. Conversion is the task that each of your guests would like to do, whether it's finishing order, clicking on advertisements, calling for an appointment, or installing a menu. In each of these three critical regions, this problem is an incentive for the organization to develop its capability. Now is a perfect time to create digital marketing campaigns for the acquisition of consumers. When they are ready to buy again, this will make buyers and opportunities ready for it. By enhancing the digital consumer experience, behavior can be changed. To see which ones are more popular, improve interaction, try new features, new content, and new ways to organize and manage your online presence. Your friend, here is the analytics data supplied by your digital company. An integral digital business capability is to turn tourists into future or real customers. Use the time to try new calls to action. It would help if you also used this opportunity to tell clients to do something that would improve their engagement. Practice getting the guests to do easier things such as likes, comments, and shares. Then intensify the participation by signing up for updates and discounts, uploading their material, or scheduling a future appointment. Don't fail to remember how they all come together when you practice each of the digital business ABCs. With promises that can't be met or ambitions that you can't meet, it's easy to have new tourists. Acquire the right visitors who are happy and will convert.

**Start experimenting**

The freedom to innovate continuously is a key advantage of digital entrepreneurship. There are several fresh ideas to try in each part of the ABC process. Get familiar with the analytics data, which will be from Google Analytics for most digital entrepreneurs. It will provide you with reliable input on what works and what doesn't. It is still being practiced by major corporations, conducting hundreds or thousands of tests on their clients every day. If they continue to remain competitive, small firms would need to develop the skills of digital experimentation. Fortunately, the benefit of emerging start-ups is that they can hop on emerging developments that are not yet big enough to interest the big players. A crisis scenario is a hotbed of emerging developments in the quest, new hashtags, new memes, and new points for the conversation to be taken advantage of. Once digital marketers discover innovative business concepts that work with their first 100 to 1,000 visitors, it is fairly inexpensive and easy to scale up such ideas when trends take off. Be on the lookout for new 'nano trends' as these developments play out, and be ready to expand.

# CHAPTER 4: The Best Business

It doesn't need to require a big investment to start a profitable company. You can start a company without spending much capital, or even purchasing inventory, with a great business concept and the right resources. Adapting to a growing economy requires finding new, smart ways to fulfill clients' needs. To find the answer to the following important questions, you have to analyze the market:

What sorts of goods or services will fulfill the new consumer demands?

As an entrepreneur, how can your skills better fulfill those demands?

Any of the money-making, small business ideas that need very little investment are provided below.

4.1 Start your own online Dropshipper business

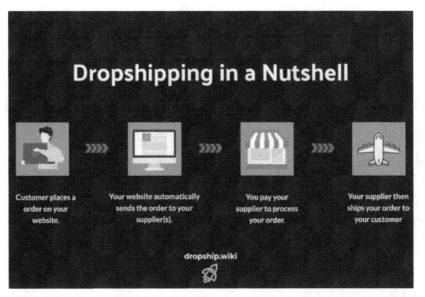

To sell online, you do not need to store inventory or spend a lot of money. You escape the expense of producing goods, handling inventory, and exporting with the dropshipping business by working with third-party vendors that do it all for you.

**How it works**

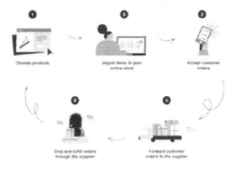

Dropshipping is a retail fulfillment technique where a retailer does not hold the items in storage that it offers. Instead, when a store sells a product using the dropshipping model, it orders the product from a third party and directly sends it to the consumer. As a consequence, the seller doesn't have to handle the items personally. The main contrast between dropshipping and the traditional retail model is that no product is held or controlled by the selling trader. Instead, to execute orders, the seller purchases inventory if appropriate from a third party, typically a wholesaler or retailer. You should start advertising your company using digital marketing tools to drive customers to your site once you're finished setting up your online store, and your site goes live. You'll get an order notice each time they make a transaction. They will complete it after the order is delivered to the supplier. You've just become the manager of your own e-commerce company. To get started with your dropshipping business, link your Wix account with Modalyst or Spocket. You can sell all kinds of great goods at your set prices after procuring products from millions of reliable suppliers. Just try to strike a balance with each sale between competitive prices and how much you earn.

**Choose products to sell**

You may need to select dropshipping items to sell before you launch your online business. Take the time for clarification of your brand and vision. To figure out what individuals are buying, do some market research. Before selling them in your store, determine the future demand, price, and profit margin of items. For an online shop, you will thrive by finding a way to stand out. Explore specialty items to source and market, and by offering a range, aim to stop placing all the eggs in one bowl. That said, to make your online store easier to browse, aim to organize your items into collections. Keep out of markets that are still saturated with stores. Take the time to set up marketing and advertising efforts to save you time and improve your revenue eventually.

**Example: Trending work from home products**

Think of what customers do at home to select the right business to establish with little investment. With equipment for living room workouts, open your online fitness shop. Open an adorable store selling puppy items for professionals working from home, such as quiet pet toys. It's all about feeling at ease in your home setting during COVID-19. It is why items such as sweatshirts, leggings, hoodies, slippers, and socks selling out everywhere. The athleisure trend has a moment. While people do not dress up at home as much, with cute pajama sets or multi-use makeup for a simple beauty routine, they may also look for ways to feel and look healthy. Your customers can also opt for at-the-home beauty items, such as grooming accessories or nail kits, with salons now less available.

As remote employees and students set up shop at home, home office products are also common. You have to dream of tech devices such as lap desks, laptop stands, desk organizers, keyboards, or home storage. The market has also spiked for ergonomic desk chairs that help posture and back alignment or convenient seat cushions. But not all of this is work and no play. As consumers search for new recreation ideas, gaming items have also become popular. As people look for things to do, at-home leisure products, such as game boards, trivia, or knitting equipment, sell well. Shoppers must spend more time cooking at home with restaurants closed. It suggests a spike in sales of kitchenware as well as online food and beverage items. Parents also need childcare and work-life to be tackled. So, consider adding quiet toys and play spaces to your dropshipping company, like the car park mats. Shoppers also like to video chat or watch Netflix with friends without holding their laptops all the time. In the dropshipping shop, try offering bedside mounts and table mounts.

**Promote your online store**

When you introduce items, it's time for your shop to be advertised. It Is where a strong approach for e-commerce marketing comes into play. Allow the best of the business software for the e-commerce website. Automate your email marketing promotions and client outreach to save time. Advertise your dropshipping business on Facebook and Instagram with paid campaigns. Work with influencers to support your brands and advertise them to their followers if it's important to your company. In promoting your online dropshipping business, your SEO strategy will also play a crucial role. It suggests the development of high-quality advertising and low-budget ads to improve the search engine results' exposure. Increase the visibility of your website with keyword optimization, for example. Let's presume you're selling home clothing for comfortable work. If you include the phrases "luxury comfort wear," "work from home," or "athleisure clothing" in your web copy, when people search for those keywords, you will have a better chance of ranking on Google.

**Get creative with branded products designed by you**

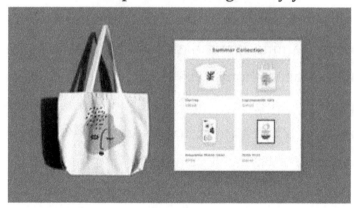

Now, let's take one step further with dropshipping. By linking Printful or Printify to your online shop, you add a personal touch with print on demand. You partner with print-on-demand businesses supplying the inventory, just like with dropshipping. Choose any customizable merchandise and introduce your creative touch, from t-shirts to phone cases, bags, and more. Go ahead and design graphics, quotations, or images to be printed on the chosen items. Start by choosing from thousands of different products to customize your online store and sell your designs. Start a business with funny quotes on a t-shirt. Add photos of your cat to Novelty Socks. Your logo or designs that match your brand create stickers — another cool option: selling goods made by you with original artwork. Yet, to market exclusive designs, you should not have to be a graphic artist. Hire and collaborate with freelance artists to create unique art for your products that are printed on-demand. You will distribute to over 90 places internationally when you receive an order. Forward your orders while managing everything from your Wix dashboard to your chosen supplier. Only think about it; shoppers would rock all over the world your exclusive creations.

**Create digital video content**

Now that individuals spend more time at home, by taking on new hobbies or returning to old ones, they're looking for ways to keep themselves occupied. Do you work in an industry, such as fitness, restaurants, or education, traditionally requires face-to-face interaction? Use this opportunity to create digital instruction videos, such as cooking demonstrations, workout routines, and more streamed online by people. The shutdown of schools and daycare services in 2021 means that parents have to spend a lot more time with their little ones at home. Moms and dads are searching for ways to keep their children busy, engaged, and learning. So if you are at home and temporarily out of a job, how can you apply your experience to satisfy this market demand? Especially now, family-friendly activities are always trendy. Get ahead of the competition by selling children-friendly video content. Create exercise videos for children if you're a fitness trainer. Promote the use of child-friendly content, such as workouts or classes for baby yoga. To help parents home-school their children, post daily lessons online. With your children, you can even create an entertaining cooking show. With digital video content, there are distinct pricing models to earn money. To give customers full access to exclusive content, you may charge a monthly channel subscription. You can monetize your content based on the number of viewers if you work with video hosting platforms like YouTube. Selling or renting your videos is another option. Over a 24-48-hour cycle, viewers may download the video or watch it on your site. To give clients an idea of your product and nudge them to make a purchase, consider offering some of your content for free. Zoom, Vimeo, and YouTube can also host live streaming or webinars. Comprehend the Supply Chain of Dropshipping

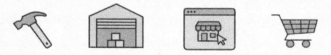

Supply chain's some fancy word that defines the journey a commodity takes to move from creation through manufacture and eventually into a customer's hands. If we are talking about suppliers of hard core chains gurus, they would insist that the supply chain stretches all towards mining products to make an object (like oil & rubber). But it's a bit intense. We do not need to be quite so specific.

The three most important participants in the dropshipping supply chain must simply be understood: wholesalers, manufacturers, & retailers.

## Manufacturers

Manufacturers produce the commodity, & most don't sell directly to the public. They sell bulks to wholesalers & dealers instead. The easiest way to buy goods for resale is to buy straight from the manufacturer, but most of them have minimum purchasing standards you'll desire to follow. When shipping them to consumers, you'll still need to store & re-ship goods. It's also cheaper to buy from the wholesaler for these purposes directly.

## Wholesalers

Wholesalers purchase products from manufacturers in bulk, mark them up marginally and then market them to the retailers to sell them to the public. They're normally much smaller than those needed by a vendor if they have buying minimums. Wholesalers normally store goods from thousands of producers, if not a hundred, and prefer to work in a single field or drop shipping niche. Many operators are exclusively wholesalers. It means that they only sell to retailers & not direct to the general public.

## Retailers

the retailer is anyone who sells the products directly to the public after adding his margin. If you are running a business that fulfills your orders through dropshipping suppliers, you are a retailer.

## Dropshipping is a service, not a role

You will find that "drop shipper" is not one of the supply chain players. Each of the three will operate as drop shippers - manufacturer, wholesaler, and retailer. If the manufacturer is prepared to supply its supplies directly to your consumer, it's "dropshipping" for your sake. Similarly, a supermarket retailer will offer drop ship, but its price would not be as favorable as a wholesaler because the manufacturer does not buy it directly. It doesn't mean you're having bulk rates simply because someone declares to be a "drop shipper." It means that, for your sake, the company would ship goods. You desire to ensure that you deal exclusively with a reputable manufacturer or wholesaler to get the best prices.

**The order process**

Let us observe how the drop shipped order is processed so that you have understood the players involved. We would follow the order put with a theoretical shop, an online seller Phone Outlet, specializing in smartphone accessories, to demonstrate. Phone Outlet dropships all its items directly from the wholesaler that we will call Wholesale Accessories. Here's a sample of what the whole ordering process could look like:

**Customer Places Order With Phone Outlet**

Allen requires a case for the new smartphone and places an order through the Phone Outlet online store. A few things happen once an order has been approved:

Phone Outlet & Mr. Allen would receive an email of confirmation (likely alike) of new orders which store software automatically generates.

During the checkout process, the payment of Mr. Allen is captured and automatically placed into the bank account of Phone Outlet.

**Phone Accessory Outlet Places the Order With Its Supplier**

The step is generally as artless as sending the confirmation of an email order to a sales representative at Wholesale Accessories by Phone Outlet. Wholesale Accessories has a credit card from Phone Outlet on file & will charge it for wholesale goods, including handling fees or shipping. Some sophisticated drop shippers will support XML Automatic (a normal format for stock files) orders uploading or the ability to place orders manually online. Still, email is the most common method to place orders with dropshipping vendors because it is universal & easier to use.

## Wholesale accessories ships the order

If items in the stock and wholesaler have positively charged the Phone Outlet card, the order will be boxed up and shipped directly to the customer by Wholesale Accessories. Although shipments come from the Wholesale Accessories, the name & address of the Phone Outlet would appear on the label of the return address, and the logo would appear on the invoice & packing slip. Wholesale Accessories would then email invoice & tracking numbers to the Phone Outlet once the shipment has been finalized.

Turnaround time is often quicker than you would think on dropshipped orders. In a few hours, most feature suppliers would be capable of getting the order outdoor, allowing merchants to publicize shipping on the same day when they use drop shipping suppliers.

## Phone outlet alerts the customer of shipment

When this tracking number's collected, Phone Outlet gives the customer tracking information, potentially using an email interface built into the online store interface. The order and delivery process is complete with the order delivered, the invoice received, and a customer told. The benefit (or loss) of Phone Outlet is the contrast between what this costs Mr. Allen & what this paid for wholesale accessories.

## Dropshippers are invisible

The drop shipper is invisible to the end buyer, despite its vital position in the ordering & fulfillment process. Just the Phone Outlet return address & signature would be on the shipment when the package is received. If Mr. Allen obtains the wrong case, he will call Phone Outlet, who would work with Wholesale Accessories behind scenes and get the right item shipped out. To the ultimate buyer, the wholesaler does not exist. Stocking and shipping dropshipping products is the sole responsibility. The merchant is responsible for all else — website creation, marketing, customer support.

## 4.2 How to Find and Work with Reliable Dropshipping Suppliers

One of the most popular questions ambitious entrepreneurs pose is: What is my e-commerce store's best dropshipping supplier? Supplier directory for dropshipping is a distributor database grouped by niche, market, or commodity. Many of the directories employ a few scanning mechanisms to ensure that legitimate wholesalers are suppliers listed. Many are managed by for-the profit corporations who charge a fee to use their directories. While membership folders, particularly for brainstorming the ideas, may be useful, they're by no means essential. If you already know the commodity or drop shipping niche that you need to sell, you must locate the big suppliers in the market with a little bit of searching & the techniques mentioned above. Plus, you once start dropshipping company, unless you want to locate suppliers for the other things, you would probably not need to revisit the directory. That said, the supplier directory is an easy way to scan for or/and browse a vast range of suppliers in 1 location easily and is useful for brainstorming ideas for marketing goods or entering niches. If you are short of time and ready to spend cash, a helpful tool may be supplier directories. There is a range of different suppliers and businesses for dropshipping.

**Best dropshipping suppliers**

CJdropshipping

Oberlo

CROV

DropnShop

Supplymedirect

Modalyst

To make this easier to select best drop shipping companies for specific needs, we will focus on the following factor:

**Location and shipping options**

So, Where do the supplier's locations exist? How much time is consumed in producing the item after the customer has put orders?

**Product types**

**Which kinds of products they dropship?**

**Recommended for**

And Is the particular suppliers suited for experienced or beginner dropshippers?

**Oberlo**

Shopify. The Oberlo is dropshipping the platform, making it easier to find AliExpress items to sell in the Shopify store. It is the best online drop shipping supplier directory for Shopify. The platform provides over 30 thirty of the latest dropshipping goods from vendors across the globe in 60 plus niche categories. Oberlo has free registration, beginning at 29.9 dollars a month for paid plans.

**Location & shipping options**

In different places around the world, Oberlo links you with suppliers. Usually, each includes many delivery solutions for the clients to send products. On each commodity page in the Oberlo app, you will find what delivery methods the supplier uses. the Popular shipping method includes:

**China Post.** Affordable / Free shipping expenses. Delivery could take 20 to 50 days.

**AliExpress Shipping.** Affordable costs of shipping. Delivery can take up to 15 days.

**ePacket.** Affordable / Free shipping expenses. Delivery could take 15 to 30 days.

**DHL/UPS/FedEx.** Express the shipping expenses. Delivery could take between five to fifteen days.

**Product types**

So You may find anything that includes bracelets, antiques, car parts, wedding supplies, sunglasses, furniture, and much more.

**Recommended for**

It's recommended for the beginner & veteran drop shipper.

**CJDropshipping**

With fast delivery, it is the best dropshipping service. CJDropshipping is a marketplace that allows retailers to scale up the drop shipping business affordably. You can conveniently import goods directly from 1688 and Taobao marketplaces into the Shopify store, usually at a price lesser than on AliExpress. Along with other dropshipping applications like Oberlo, it's also a free Shopify application that you could add to the store.

## Location & shipping options

To perform processing on the same-day for the store, CJDropshipping uses US-based warehouses. UPS, USPS, DHL, & FedEx work with it. The shipping line known as CJPacket will bring goods to the US in 7 to twelve days if you are shipping from China.

## Product types

Independent designers & owners of small businesses in China are home to the 1668 and Taobao marketplaces. Via CJDropshipping, there are 100s of millions of listings you may browse, & products vary from mainstream goods to difficult-to-find items & even the virtual product. If the CJDropshipping app does not have a product, you can upload a request & CJDropshipping would list this once the best source is identified.

## Recommended for

The retailer who needs a 1-stop location for all the things drop shipping, including inventory procurement, order preparation, distribution, and fast shipping to United States, is highly recommended.

## SupplyMeDirect

It is the strongest dropshipping provider for the UK, US, & European markets for private labels. SupplyMeDirect is a wholesale provider that supports the size of dropshipping business. The app provides private labeling & secure sourcing. It's a free Shopify application that you could contact twenty-four 7, supported by dedicated support staff.

## Location & shipping options

The SupplyMeDirect is different. The reason is that nearly 60 percent of the stock resides in the warehouses established in the United States, the UK, Canada, & Europe. It makes shipping reliable and fast. The shipping has an average time of delivery of 4 to 7 days.

**Product types**

Any product from apparel to kitchenware, the toys to the accessories, & more

**Recommended for**

It is best for the drop shippers who intend to sell in the whole world & want fast shipping.

**CROV**

For the multi-channel vendors, it is the strongest dropshipping provider. CROV links retailers from vetted lists of US vendors to a wide variety of items. It is yet another free-of-cost Shopify app to populate the store with products and automate orders.

**Location & shipping options**

In the 42 countries, shipping is available. Costs rely on vendors & their shipping processes, which can be found in a directory on every product detail page. To ship the domestic orders quicker, CROV has a US warehouse.

**Product types**

It offers extra than 35 thousand products in more than 20 other trending categories from the selected suppliers.

**Recommended for**

It is the best for eCommerce sellers. Especially for those who need to sell different products on Amazon, Shopify, & eBay.

**Modalyst**

It is the greatest supplier of dropshipping high-tickets for US apparel. For online retailers, Modalyst is an automatic dropshipping program.

It is known for delivering items that customers would enjoy from the brand names such as DSquare, Calvin Klein, Dolce, and Gabbana, & other famous brands. For any target demographic, Modalyst often features a curated collection of independent & trendy brands. The website has an official API collaboration with AliExpress Dropshipping, allowing you to access the millions of items with a Google Chrome plugin to connect to your shop with one click.

## Location & shipping options

The Modalyst has the own marketplace of US manufacturers and products that can offer domestic orders free of charge between six to eight days. Also available are UK dropshipping vendors & Australian drop shippers. Businesses, except countries in South America and Africa, will ship to more than 80 countries in the world

## Product types

It generally emphasizes premium and fashionable products. Modalyst is part of the Booster Program of AliExpress also, offering an infinite catalog of items for drop shippers to browse.

## Recommended for

It is recommended for users of Shopify who want their shops to add exclusive items. You will also market goods using Modalysts Private Label Software with your branding. You will take advantage of any of the luxury brands and vendors that Modalysts has to sell if you chose the Pro plan.

## dropship

It is the best source of dropships for French goods. DropnShop is a dropshipping program for Shopify that provides online sales of French goods. It offers inventory from the top factories of French. It takes the requests from e-commerce partners to diversify product catalog and expand your business due to partnerships with thousands of producers. There's an availability-free plan.

## Location & shipping information

To have worldwide delivery at a decent rate, DropnShop partners with numerous suppliers. Every product has different shipping information, but you may find anything you require to know on the product detail page of the app.

## Product types

Would you like to sell France's best cosmetics products in your shop? With DropnShop, you may. The supplier also sells 1000s of SKUs, all 100 percent manufactured in France, across several categories, from children's toys to the hair & products of skincare.

## Recommended for

It is the best for eCommerce stores. It is best, especially for those who desire to add the French product to the catalog.

Let us learn to find dropshipping suppliers

Suppliers are not always made equal, like most things in life. It is also more important to ensure that you are dealing with top-notch players in the dropshipping community. The supplier is a vital part of the dropshipping fulfillment operation.

## Before you contact suppliers

Okay, so you've discovered a range of good suppliers & are prepared to go forward—great! Yet you would want to get all ducks in a row before you start approaching businesses.

## It would help if you were legal

we discussed earlier, before authorizing you to register for some account, most amazing wholesalers would need confirmation that you are a legal entity. Most wholesalers report their prices to licensed consumers, but you will need to be legally authorized before seeing the type of pricing you will receive. Before contacting vendors, make sure you're lawfully integrated.

## Don't be afraid of the phone

One of the strongest worries people have is picking up phone & making the call when it comes to vendors. It is a paralyzing prospect for many. For such problems, you may be capable of sending texts, but you'll have to pick the phone up more frequently than not to get the answers you need. The good news's that this isn't as terrifying as you would imagine. Suppliers, including novice entrepreneurs, are used to having the people calling them. You're going to get someone to answer questions who's polite and happier. Here's a trick to motivate you: just type your questions down in advance. When you have a list of already written questions for asking, it is surprising how easy it's to make the call. Great vendors for dropshipping tends to have most of the following six characteristics:

## Expert staff and industry focus

There are knowledgeable distribution agents from top-notch manufacturers who truly know the market and the product lines. It's invaluable to contact a representative with concerns, especially if you're starting a store in a niche you're not too familiar with anything.

## Dedicated support representatives

individual sales agent responsible for taking good care of yourself & any concerns you have should assign you to quality drop shippers.

Problems take even longer to fix because we generally must nag the people to take care of a crisis. Getting a single interaction with a supplier allows you to locate the entity responsible for fixing your problems which is very valuable.

## Invest in technology

When there are many great suppliers with obsolete websites, suppliers that know the advantages of technology and spend extensively in it are typically a joy to deal with them. For online retailers, features like an inventory of real-time, a detailed online catalog, personalized data feeds & online searchable history of orders are pure pleasure & may help streamline the activities.

**Can take orders via email**

it may seem like a small challenge, but have to call in each order or put it manually on a website makes handling orders even more time-consuming.

**Centrally located**

It's helpful to use a centrally placed drop shipper in a big country like the United States since shipments can cover more than 90percent of the country within 2-3 business days. It may take an additional week for shipments to be delivered around the country where a retailer is based on one coast. Centrally placed vendors allow guaranteeing quicker turnaround times reliably, theoretically saving you cash on shipping costs.

**Organized and efficient**

few vendors have qualified personnel and outstanding processes that contribute to effective and often error-less fulfillment. Every 4th order will be botched by others & make you need to rip the hair out. But without ever using it, it's impossible to tell how a professional supplier is.

While it cannot give you the full picture, it will give you a better sense of how suppliers perform by placing a few small test orders. You can see:

How to order process is done

How rapidly things ship out

And How fast this follows with monitoring details and invoice quality of package when the product arrives

It is important to learn how to distinguish between genuine suppliers of wholesale & retail stores acting as wholesale suppliers when looking for suppliers. A real wholesaler buys straight from the producer & will usually offer you even better prices.

How to spot fake dropshipping companies

You will come across a significant number of " fake" wholesalers based on where you're looking. Unfortunately, historically, legal wholesalers are bad at selling and appear to be more difficult to find. It results in non-genuine wholesalers showing more often in searches, usually only intermediaries, so you'll need to be careful. Following dropshipping tips would help you decide whether it is a legal wholesale supplier.

**They want ongoing fees**

Real wholesalers don't charge their clients monthly fees for the luxury of doing a business & buying from them. It's usually not legitimate if a retailer asks for a monthly subscription or a service fee. It's necessary to distinguish between the suppliers and directories of suppliers here. Supplier directories are bulk supplier directories grouped by commodity categories or sector & screened to ensure suppliers' authenticity. Many directories, either 1-time or continuous, can charge a fee, but you do not take it as an indication that the directory itself's unlawful.

**They sell to the public**

You would need to register for a wholesale account to get real wholesale rates, demonstrate you are a legal entity, and be accepted before making your first order. So Any wholesale seller selling goods at "wholesale" to the general public is the only retailer offering the items at inflated rates. However, here are a few legal dropshipping charges that you would possibly encounter:

**Per-order fees**

Depending on the size and complexity of the goods being dispatched, certain drop shippers would charge a dropshipping fee per shipment that can vary from 2-5 dollars or more. As the prices of packaging and delivering individual order is much greater than shipping bulk order, this is common in the industry.

**Minimum order sizes**

There would be a minimum beginning order size for certain wholesalers, which is the lowest sum you may have to buy for your 1st order. They perform this to weed out window shopping vendors with questions & minor orders that will not translate into real sales and will waste their resources. If you're dropshipping, some problems may be caused. For starters, what would you might do if you have a minimum order of $500 from a supplier, but your mean order size takes about $100? Only for the privilege of making a dropshipping account do you not want to pre-order $500 of the stuff. It's best to make an offer to pay the seller $500 in advance, in this case, to create a loan with them to apply for the drop shipping orders. It helps you fulfill the retailer's minimum purchase obligation (as you are committed to buying a product at least 500 dollars in product) without having to position a single big order without accompanying any customer requests.

Tips for working with dropshipping wholesalers

It's time to start looking for vendors now you can detect a scam from the actual deal! There are a variety of different techniques that you may use, some more successful than others. In order of usefulness and choice, the ways below are enlisted, with the preferred methods enlisted first.

## Contact the manufacturer

It may be the ideal way for legal bulk vendors to be conveniently identified. Contact the manufacturer to inquire about their wholesale dealers' list if you know the product(s) you intend to dropship. To observe if they dropship and ask about setting an account up, you may then email these wholesalers. Because most wholesalers carry goods from several manufacturers within the niche, you are pursuing, and this strategy would permit you to source a range of items easily. You'll easily be able to find the leading wholesalers in that market after making few calls to leading producers in some niche.

## Use Oberlo

Oberlo helps you quickly import goods straight into the Shopify store from vendors and directly send them to your consumers, all in some clicks.

## Features

Products can be imported from suppliers

Product customization

Orders are fulfilled automatically

Inventory & price automatic updates

Pricing automation

## Search using Google

You may use Google to fetch high-quality suppliers. It is quite obvious, yet there are some factors to keep in mind:

## You have to search extensively

Wholesales are not good at marketing & promotion. Furthermore, they aren't going to cover the top search results related to "wholesale suppliers for some product X." You will have to do all the research yourself.

## Don't judge by their website

Wholesales are now infamous for making '90s-style websites. Although a quality site can suggest a successful supplier in some instances, many legal wholesalers have cringe-worthy website homepages. Don't let you get turned off by the bad design.

## Attend a trade show

trade show helps you to engage in a niche with all key manufacturers & wholesalers. It's a perfect method to make friends, all in one place, and research the commodities and suppliers. It only applies if the niche &/or product has already been chosen, and it is not possible for everybody. But it's a perfect method to know vendors and the suppliers in the region if you have the time and resources to participate.

Ways to pay dropshipping suppliers and companies

A large number of suppliers shall accept payments in 1 of 2 ways:

## Credit card

Many suppliers will ask you to make the payment by credit card as you're starting. Paying with credit cards is always the better choice after you've developed a flourishing business. Not only are they easy (no requirement to constantly write checks), but lots of loyalty frequent flier/ points miles can be racked up. You will rack up a high number of sales with your credit card without requiring to pay any real out-of-the-pocket costs when you are purchasing a product for a client who has already paid for it on your website.

## Net terms

"Net terms" on invoices are the most typical method to pay the suppliers. It assumes that you have certain days for paying the retailer with the items you have ordered. So if you're on the "net 30" term, you have exactly 30 days to pay the supplier for the items from the purchase date you ordered by bank draw or check. Usually, before providing net payment terms, a supplier would make you have credit references, so it's lending you money. It is a normal procedure, but if you have to provide any documentation while paying on net terms, do not be alarmed.

Usually, before providing net payment terms, a supplier would make you have credit references, so it's lending you the money. It's a normal procedure, but if you need to provide any documentation while paying on the net terms, do not be alarmed.Bottom of Form

Top of Form

Bottom of Form

FAQs about dropshipping suppliers

Given below are some of the frequently asked questions, along with answers about the dropshipping suppliers.

**How do I find dropshipping suppliers?**

On directory vetted such as Oberlo, you can find dropshipping suppliers, colleagues' suggestions, or look the suppliers for the products for brands you like. You may also find several excellent alternatives with some research work.

**What are the best dropshipping suppliers in 2021?**

Some top suppliers for dropshipping are Worldwide Labels, Doba, SaleHoo, AliExpress, Alibaba, Wholesale Central, & CDS.

**Is dropshipping still profitable in 2021?**

In 2021, dropshipping also represents a viable market opportunity. Since you don't need to spend on the inventory or incur holding expenses, it's a sustainable business model.

**Which platform is best for dropshipping?**

Combined with the Oberlo, Shopify allows for a streamlined setup for dropshipping. On Oberlo, you can check for vendors and make items available on the branded Shopify website for sale. You make the sales, & your drop shipping supplier will do the rest.

Common questions about dropshipping

We have compiled a list of questions that could be posed by anyone planning to start a new drop shipper business.

**How much do I need to invest in starting dropshipping?**

While it is difficult to predict exact prices for any individual company, to get started, there are few things on which each drop shipping company would need to be spending money. Here's a short rundown of the critical expenditures.

**Online store**

Estimated price: ~29 dollars per month

To establish & host an online shop, you'll need to find an e-commerce site. We suggest launching a shop at Shopify. You will be capable of syncing source items with Oberlo marketplace conveniently, and you will get access to a full range of themes & free branding software so that you can quickly get your company up & running.

**Domain name**

Estimated price: $5 to 20 per year

Without the domain name, it's difficult to develop trust with clients. Although there is a range of top-leveled domains available (example, example. co example. shop), if one is available, we recommend searching for the .com which suits the brand.

**Test orders**

**Estimated price:** Varies

While dropshipping helps you to have limited interference in managing your total product catalog, that you can set aside, also little of the time, cash to test the items you want to sell. You threaten listing products with too many flaws or faults if you don't, which will lead to disappointed consumers and a lot of the time wasted coping with refunds.

## Online advertising

Estimated price: the Scales with the business; It is recommended to start budgeting with a minimum of $500

Each e-commerce organization must look for ways of reducing the average cost of acquiring a client across organic networks such as SEO, content marketing, & word of mouth. But advertising is typically an important medium for many product-based firms to start every company. Search engine marketing (the SEM), displays advertising, social media advertising, and smartphone ads are among the most common channels.

## How do drop shippers make money?

Dropshipping businesses act like product curators, choosing the <u>best dropshipping products</u> for market to the customers; remember that marketing costs you incur, into both time & money, help the potential customers find, explain, & buy the right products. You will also have to include the cost of supporting customers whenever there is a product or a shipping problem. Last but not least is the original price for which the supplier sells a product. With all these prices to be accountable for, the dropshipping business mark up the individual products in exchange for the distribution. It's why the suppliers are okay with having drop shippers markets the products for those people – dropshipping stores also drive extra sales, which supplier would've missed out otherwise. it is good to find out how much this costs to "acquire" customer, & price the products with it in mind.

## Is dropshipping a legitimate business?

Dropshipping is essentially a fulfillment model, one used with many global distributors, and is completely legitimate. Satisfying consumer needs and creating brands that resonate with the right demographic is also vital for long-term growth, as with any company. Owing to a misconception of how dropshipping works, this question generally occurs. The bulk of discount shops at which you shop are most likely not to sell items they directly make. Dropshipping takes the curated approach & converts it into an online company-fit distribution model. of course, you must do more simple things to operate your business lawfully. To guarantee that you are doing business lawfully in your country, find a lawyer who has specialized in these matters.

Benefits of dropshipping

For emerging entrepreneurs, dropshipping is a perfect business model to start with because it's accessible. You can easily test multiple business concepts with a small drawback with dropshipping, which helps you learn a lot about picking and selling in-demand goods. In 2021, dropshipping is still a viable market opportunity. Since you don't need to spend in inventory or incur holding expenses, it's a sustainable business model. Combined with Oberlo, Shopify allows for a streamlined setup for dropshipping. On Oberlo, you can check for vendors and make items available on your branded Shopify site for sale. You make purchases, and your drop shipping provider will do the rest.

**Less capital is required**

Stocking a warehouse takes a lot of money. By using dropshipping, you can eliminate the possibility of falling into debt to start your company. You can launch a dropshipping company with zero inventory instead of buying an extensive inventory and hoping it sells and start making money immediately. Perhaps the greatest bonus of dropshipping is that an e-commerce website can be opened without having to spend thousands of dollars in stock upfront. Traditionally, manufacturers have had to bind up large quantities of inventory with capital investments. For the dropshipping model, unless you have already made the sale and have been paid by the consumer, you do not have to buy a product. It is possible to start sourcing goods without substantial up-front inventory investments and begin a profitable dropshipping company with very little capital. And because you're not dedicated to selling, as in a typical retail company, there's less danger involved in launching a dropshipping shop without any inventory bought upfront.

**Easy to get started**

Managing an e-commerce business is much easier as you don't have to deal with physical products. With drop shipping, you won't have to worry about:

Warehouse cost and management

Handling returns and inbound shipments

Packing and shipping of your orders

Keeping track of inventory for accounting purposes

Perpetually ordering products

Continuously managing stock level

**Low cost of inventory**

If you own and warehouse stock, inventory is one of the biggest costs you would have. You can end up with old inventory, causing you to find ways to reduce your inventory, or you may end up with very little inventory, resulting in stockouts and missed sales. Dropshipping lets you escape these challenges and concentrate on increasing your client base and developing your brand.

**Low Order Fulfillment Costs**

Usually, order fulfillment requires you to store, organize, label, select and carry and ship your inventory. Dropshipping lets all of it be taken care of by a third party. In this arrangement, the sole job is to ensure that they receive customer requests. They will do all the rest.

## Low overhead

Your operating rates are minimal because you don't have to do with buying inventory or maintaining a warehouse. In reality, many popular dropshipping stores are managed as home-based enterprises, needing nothing more to run than a laptop and a few recurring costs. These costs are likely to escalate as you expand, but they will still be low relative to those of conventional brick-and-mortar companies.

## Flexible location

From just about anywhere with an internet connection, a drop shipping company can be managed. You can run and handle your company as long as you can effectively connect with vendors and clients.

## A wide selection of products to sell

Without the limitations of a physical inventory and the associated costs, dropshipping allows you to rapidly, comfortably, and cheaply upgrade your inventory. You will instantly deliver it to your customers without waiting for it to arrive in your factory if you know that a product is doing well for another store or reseller. Without the risk of bringing old products, dropshipping helps you to try new products. You're paying just for what you offer. Since you don't have to pre-purchase the items you sell, you can show your future buyers various trending products. If suppliers store an item, you can list it for sale at no added cost at your online store.

## Easier to test

Dropshipping is a valuable form of fulfillment for both the opening of a new store and for company owners looking to measure consumers' demand for additional types of items, such as shoes or whole new product ranges. Again, the primary advantage of dropshipping is the opportunity to list and likely sell goods before committing to purchasing a significant quantity of stock.

**Easier to scale**

For a typical retail organization, you would typically need to do three times as much work if you get three times the orders. By leveraging dropshipping vendors, suppliers will be responsible for most of the work to handle extra orders, helping you to improve with fewer growing pains and less gradual work. Sales growth can often bring extra labor, especially customer service, but companies that use dropshipping scale particularly well compared to conventional e-commerce companies

# Conclusion

Digital entrepreneurship may be clearly described as entrepreneurial businesses which are carried through a digital medium. Most studies proved that entrepreneurship a crucial driver for economic development & also for the reduction of unemployment. I's really important to grasp all the principles relevant to entrepreneurship. For meeting market competition & achieve the business target, every entrepreneur must be up to date with changes that arise in the customer's tastes & desires and even in the market. It is often important to use certain new digital technology & softwares to connect with the consumers and increase quality demand. As today's environment is largely dependent on national & global technology, it is important to have the sector's technologies. In this way, digital entrepreneurship plays a critical role in enabling the entrepreneur to conduct all the tasks accurately and efficiently. Using software apps allows any entrepreneur to increase the market demand for his or her product & grow the business both technologically and traditionally. As the Information & communication technologies (ICT) skills are crucial elements of digital enterprise success, it's significant to learn how it allows people to improve their business so that you can use the same for creating your own successful business. It will allow any person who engages in the business to learn about digital entrepreneurship in the Present world, changing dramatically in all fields, particularly in information & communication technology (ICT). In this case, the exponential growth of emerging technology with new creative functionalities is changing competitive environment, modifying the general market strategies, systems, and the procedure. For example, on networked economy motorized by new technologies, many businesses or company is becoming tinier with just one person where the partnerships are evolving. Digital Innovative technologies, including big data, social media, and mobile & cloud platforms, are giving rise to new ways of collaborating, exploiting capital, service/product design, creation, and deployments over the open standards & collaborative technologies. They're, in turn, impacting the market activities through generating job opportunities. Like, Alibaba.com is digital technology that allowed millions of Chinese people to be entrepreneurs. It is also responsible for the creation of employment.

Even digital technologies generate vast job opportunities. They're creating several challenges also. Emerging technologies are modernizing the labor market. Several countries are facing several obstacles, such as Australia, to face economic competition. To face the obstacles and eliminate the barriers, countries are recommended for taking over digital entrepreneurship & achieve an acceptable role. Digital entrepreneurship increases jobs across ICTs like Facebook, social computing, mobile technology, and digital channels. Many firms began digital businesses by selling the products online to meet competition in the industry. As this becomes necessary, focusing on how a business venture must be started is rising with utmost significance. People who need to start a digital company should know the differences between digital versus conventional opportunities, downfalls, entrepreneurship, and digital entrepreneurship challenges. The people need a format or digital entrepreneurship system that consists all information about the new digital enterprise, including its features and objectives.

# PRIVATE LABEL CRASH COURSE

*David Lazarus*

# Table of Contents

# Introduction

A private label is where a person or corporation paying another business to make a commodity without its name, emblem, etc. The person or business then applies to the packaging their name and design. So, what sorts of items should be labeled privately? From skincare and dietary treatments and infant essentials, pet products, and kitchen utensils, pretty much all under the sun. The benefit of private labeling is that nothing innovative needs to be produced or developed by you. You can add your mark on it as long as it's not a proprietary commodity and label it yours. For the last ten years, private labels have risen by at least double the number of popular household products. In reality, there is a lot of conversation about the rise of private labels or retail brands around the world these days. Or we need to claim private brands, maybe since they are indeed labels by the end of each day. Opportunities to have ever-better-value offerings for both of us as consumers. Possibilities for everyone to push the main factors transforming the world of today and tomorrow. Yes, it's not the Private Label curse. It could well, in truth, be a present. A blessing that pushes us all to question the status quo again. A gift that pushes one to step positively with some of the main big forces that form the world of today to collaborate together more successfully and collaboratively. A blessing that is increasingly important to all of us, whether in the United Kingdom, the United States, China, or Scandinavia. If we like it or not, Private Label will soon have a single category of quick products in the country. In the last ten years, private labels have risen at least double the amount of popular consumer packaged goods brands. How did the Private Label expand at the above remarkable pace, and what lessons does it give players in the more narrowly established markets of fast-moving consumer goods? We like to think of it as a food event, but it's increasingly a complete experience of consumption. Flavors' globalization, marketers, and individuals have made Private Label a global fact. More and more, Private Label is the face of today's retailer. Comprehend it. This isn't going to go away. Act about it. Perhaps we should name them PRIVATE Companies from now on. Perhaps we might create very different tactics to survive if we began naming them brands instead of labels. Brands are concerned about combating their closest competing brand. Will they behave as though their closest advertised rival is the Private Label? Maybe they could, because maybe if they did, they might behave very differently in reality. The commodity has gone on. In turn, as Private Label has become a brand power in its own right, it has become privatized. It cannot be ignored as a single mark anymore. It's something a ton more. While taken out of context, Private Label is turning controversial for this cause, maybe more than any other, placing owners on the backhand side and retail section on the offensive. Neither group appears especially keen to publicly address it or cooperate on something outside development. Products have brought copycatting stores to court, and dealers have de-listed popular brands from their racks. There's a tiny concession space. It increasingly distorts agreed shopping habits and usage trends in order to exacerbate problems more. It is a brand that can often account for two out of three physical transactions made by your consumer. A brand that is gradually seen as an alternate product and value of parity. A company that will out-weigh and out-image any typical brand by exploiting the retailer's corporate strength and spending. A brand that can drive producers into a vicious cycle of loss in the market. A trillion-dollar market that, as you realize its sheer scale and future effects, must be the least evaluated and poorly understood industry around. An industry that in the years to come is going to get a lot larger. There would theoretically be billions of dollars of sales redirected by brand owners to this power. Are you confident your plans are ready? The remedies? But, as the solution, what do people recommend? Lower costs, increase efficiency, and be more imaginative. This is not just a remedy that you can pursue as a standard component of your business growth. It is simply not sufficient. This is an opportunity that requires the unusual and the unconventional. Or else rise to the challenge. The Private Label is a wake-up call from a brand creator. Wake up to the truth in the company. Wake up in search of a shopper. Wake up to what you might theoretically do for your company. Wake up to proactivity for real. Wake up to a chance to get the rest of the planet back into communication with your company. Private label has arisen from the conventionally held assumption that firms will benefit and conquer the competition by providing either higher value at a higher cost for their consumers (or shoppers) or fair value at a cheaper cost (retailer brands). In other terms, it's a preference between distinction (or innovation) and low cost, and it's safe to assume that only then have retailers fallen into the former to offer the latter to the shopper reliably in spades. As Coke (and Tesco) can also inform you, it pays dividends to see the brand on any street corner. However, as some of our research highlights would demonstrate, there is still a significant perception difference between Private Label and existing manufacturer labels in terms of quality/value. As long as the shopper is concerned, at least, without the other, one will not thrive, and broadly speaking, maker labels are better positioned to offer sound 'innovation' and 'value' to retailers. Just 16% of shoppers in all regions sincerely agree that a supermarket of retailer-owned goods can only be expected in the future. So, we think there is a potential for brands to constantly reinvent themselves through shopper intuition, deeper brand commitment, and creativity. The potential for retailers to continuously add value is there. The potential exists for producers to maximize their manufacturing ability and for interactions to be reinvented by agencies. But most critically, the potential is there to constantly impress and entertain the shopper, far beyond all their hopes. The other alternative frequently provided is to get yourself into making a private label. However, you may be compelled by Private Label to analyze the very simple essence of the company in which you are and to doubt whether it is strong enough to move you further. Ask for your goods. Ask how and to whom you are offering. Ask if you still are tuning into the agents of transition. Your corporate purpose issues. Ask if you have the best staff and processes to meet this crucial problem. Finally, Private Label is a concern for manufacturers alike. Knowing how to profitably manage it without undermining the very essence of the organization you are with. And the manufacturers that you work with. Yes, you may assume that you can survive without them. Yet we're advising, be very, very patient. If you want to be a genuinely successful marketing tool in terms of bringing to the shopper, you need one another. In comparison, we exist in an age in which the newspapers are building up major global supermarket chains as the latest businesses to despise. Why are you stopping this? As the messenger, you use Private Label, a messenger that not only reveals that you deliver excellent value and costs but also indicates that you think for your consumer and their long-term social needs. And you are really doing what you can to support them. Now, even more on this. The private label is, to a great degree, a hidden force. The conservative nature of the subject-matter literature tends to downplay its actual place in the world, a function far from conservative in fact, and a role in which Private Label is undeniably the single greatest influence on our businesses and goods today. Brands, engagement professionals, and scholars have consistently ignored or underestimated this. That's got to change.

## Chapter 1: Getting Started-Private Label

A private label is where a person or corporation paying another business to make a commodity without its name, emblem, etc. The person or business then applies to the packaging their name and design. So, what sorts of items should be labeled privately? From skincare and dietary treatments and infant essentials, pet products, and kitchen utensils, pretty much all under the sun. The benefit of private labeling is that nothing innovative needs to be produced or developed by you. You can add your mark on it as long as it's not a proprietary commodity and label it yours. A private label product is made and marketed under a retailer's brand name through a contract or third-party maker. You specify all about the commodity as the distributor-what goes into it, how everything is packaged, what the logo looks like-you pay to get it manufactured and shipped to your shop. This is in relation to purchasing goods with their corporate logos on them from other businesses. A successful brand identity can be the crucial base for building loyal customers, customer growth, and a competitive edge. Care of your corporate name as your company's face is how you are viewed by the audience. Without a detailed, excellently defined brand identity, the consumer might not realize who you are. In the end, you need to create a personal link. The potential exists for producers to maximize their manufacturing ability and for interactions to be reinvented by agencies. But most critically, the potential is there to constantly impress and entertain the shopper, far beyond all their hopes. The other alternative frequently provided is to get yourself into making a private label. However, you may be compelled by Private Label to analyze the very simple essence of the company in which you are and to doubt whether it is strong enough to move you further.

## 1.1 What is Private Label?

A private label product is made and marketed under a retailer's brand name through a contract or third-party maker. You specify all about the commodity as the distributor-what goes into it, how everything is packaged, what the logo looks like-you pay to get it manufactured and shipped to your shop. This is in relation to purchasing goods with their corporate logos on them from other businesses.

## 1.2 Private Label Categories

Almost every consumer product category has both branded and private label offerings, including:

- Condiments and salad dressings

- Cosmetics

- Personal care

- Frozen foods

- Dairy items

- Beverages

- Household cleaners

- Paper products

## 1.3 Different types of Private Label as profitable strategies

### Generic Private Label

Generic private-label goods are one of the conventional private label tactics used to provide the price-conscious consumer with a low-price alternative. The brand doesn't matter to these consumers. With limited advertising and no marketing, the goods are inexpensive, undifferentiated, poor inconsistency. In commoditized and low-involvement goods, these private labels are primarily present. For both discount stores in Western nations, this technique is widespread.

### Copycat Brands

In order to draw buyers, manufacturers play on the price point, retaining the packaging identical to a national brand that offers a sense of the product's similar consistency. These goods are reverse engineered, utilizing factories of identical technologies from national brand products. In wide categories that have a clear market champion, certain private labels are mostly present. In the detergent group, Massive Corporation blindly embraces the copycat brand approach. Detergents against rival products with identical packaging have been launched, albeit at a cheaper price.

### Premium store brands

Retailers now have started utilizing private labels, rather than just as a pricing strategy, as a store point of difference. Premium store brands are valued higher and are also high in performance than the national brands. Here, the customer proposal is to be the greatest brand that money will purchase. In the retailer's shop, these products get influential eye-catching locations. In the advertising, the manufacturer insists on the excellent consistency of the goods.

### Value innovators

Retailers manufacture goods that have all the value-adding characteristics and eliminate the non-value-adding characteristics in order to reduce costs, one point ahead of the copycat approach, and thus provide the customer with the best value deal. The danger of being imitated also rests in these labels. As it produces furniture under a modern market paradigm that involves self-service, assembling, and transporting yourself, Ikea is renowned for its better goods.

## 1.4 White Label vs. Private Label Dropshipping?

You can select between white label and private label dropshipping if you want to launch an online store. Both words define goods that have been branded by a reseller, but the two definitions very distinctly. Particularly to beginners, they may seem quite complicated, so let's go through each one and explain their relative benefits.

**Private Labeling**

Private marking is where a company selectively makes a commodity for a store that offers it under its own name. Costco utilizes private marking, for instance, by marketing its own "Kirkland" brand that no other store can offer. As a consequence, goods with private labels are typically less pricey than national brands. Plus, they can be very lucrative if they're promoted properly. Dropshipping is a convenient method for private-label goods to be distributed. You will find a dropshipping provider if you are an online shop owner who can offer items directly to you and incorporate your branding. Dropshipping is an e-commerce market concept in which no inventory is held by the manufacturer. The retailer, instead, manages the packaging, packing, and delivery of goods to the end customer. In other terms, for dropshipping, the goods are delivered directly to consumers, and they are never used by stores.

## White Labeling

A white-label product is a manufactured product that a company makes but is rebranded by marketers to make it look as though it had been produced. Each dealer is authorized to resell the item under its own title and labeling. Unlike private labels, several retailers may market a white-label commodity. For e.g., you can have your own branding and labels on the goods that are delivered if you wish to market a product under your brand name utilizing the dropshipping business strategy. It is often safer to search at something that already has a market when it comes to items with a white mark. It's dangerous to produce goods with white marks that consumers are not comfortable with. It's safer to go for existing brands that people regularly use. As with private labels, dropshipping makes it simple to market online white-label goods. Again, the items are delivered directly from the producers to customers, and the commodities are seldom seen by dealers.

## Advantages & Disadvantages of White Labeling

You won't have to go through the complicated logistics of making a commodity in one of these two e-commerce market models. You can save a lot of time and money without significant expenditure of time and energy in product design and production. In essence, you will concentrate on selling the commodity to the target group and branding it. In order to expand your company, you won't spread yourself thin and can concentrate on other areas of expertise. So, let's go through the common advantages and disadvantages of each business model:

**Advantages of White Labeling**

There are some real benefits of the white labeling market model, including:

- **It saves time and money.**

It's just cheaper to white mark an established commodity instead of wasting resources on developing a product from scratch.

- **Gain a large profit**

In general, white label goods are exclusively marketed by suppliers and may be bought at cheap market rates.

**Disadvantages of White Labeling**

There are, on the other side, some risks of white marking, including:

- **Limited options for branding**

Because it will be the producer or retailer who makes the white label product's bottle, label, and packaging, depending on the concept, you can just decide what it will deliver for you.

- **Limited choices of products**

Just the goods that the maker produces will be preferred, and you will not be allowed to produce anything special to the market.

- **Competition is tough**

It is challenging to stand out from the other online vendors that, white-label or not, sell the same items.

## 1.5 Dropshipping Private Label

We have addressed that different dropshipping products are among the simplest methods for private or white label items to be distributed. So, let's go about how private or white label items can be dropshipped.

**Finding a supplier**

In order to achieve the sustainability of online shops, having a successful dropshipping supplier is utterly crucial. In quest of finding a directory of dropshipping vendors who sell private label facilities, you should look at business websites or just do a search on Google. Seeking a niche will allow you and your business to stand out from other retail vendors. Make sure that you conduct consumer analysis to figure out what sort of thing you would prefer to rebrand or distribute.

**Establishing the identity with the brand**

A successful brand identity can be the crucial base for building loyal customers, customer growth, and a competitive edge. Care of your corporate name as your company's face is how you are viewed by the audience. Without a detailed, excellently defined brand identity, the consumer might not realize who you are. In the end, you need to create a personal link. Brand awareness must be expressed in the products, slogan, website, and packaging. It can offer a' derived from human attributes' to your brand. Brands with a very well-established personality make the brand intimately relatable, connecting consumers at a relational level and having to have the commodity in their lives. This is relevant for dropshipping products, including the private and white labels.

**Increase awareness about your label and brand**

Growing your brand recognition is another important move towards building a profitable brand. If the product is fresh, then identifying your target customers and discovering ways to draw consumers to your shop is the very first thing you'll want to achieve. This is so if it's the private label dropshipping goods. Here are some forms that brand recognition can be improved without any expense:

- Build content on your website with the addition of a blog

- Developing your social network online identity

- To engage and network with more clients and get product feedback.

- To maximize your keyword scores, perform SEO.

## 1.6 Deciding What to Private Label

You might be wondering about what's a competitive commodity to private label. The secret to this phase and probably the most crucial step in beginning a private label company is researching and putting efforts into finding a good product. You ought to figure out which products/services are in the market to ensure if your product would sell. To see what people, look for on the internet and get ideas about what you can offer from there, you can use programs available online.

If you intend to launch your private label company on online marketplaces, you'll want to use a testing method that actually monitors what individuals are searching for on that platform. For this, popular programs include Helium 10 and Jungle Scout. They both provide several resources to help you continue your market path with your private label.

## What Makes A Good Private Label Product?

The biggest point to hold in mind when applying for a private label for a commodity is to find one that:

**It is in strong market demand and has limited competition from sellers.**

This can help you stop being trapped with things that you will not offer.

## Has a strong margin for benefit

Taking into consideration how much the item would cost you vs. how much you will market it for. If the item is held in a warehouse, plus the expenses involved with sale online, don't neglect to take into account the delivery costs from your source to you and from you to your client, packing and storage fees.

## If you can manage the expenses

If you have a $1,000 or $10,000 startup investment budget, you need to take into consideration how many units you will need/want to buy and how much of the budget you will spend.

## How to Find Suppliers

It's time to search for a producer or trade firm that provides private label service once you have a commodity in mind that you would like to private label. You can select anywhere in the world to make your goods. And several times, the type of service/product you select would rely on where you choose to get your product made. For e.g.,

China might be worth considering if you are trying to sell toys or gadgets because they seem to produce a ton of these types of items at very low prices. Consider looking for Alibaba or AliExpress if you want to go on this path. Both of these platforms are bulk markets where the goods are identified by suppliers and trade houses, where you can find almost everything. Because with all our federal rules, it's a great choice to source in the U.S. whether you want to offer food, dietary foods, cosmetic goods, or something else you bring in or on your body. Check on Google for items sourced domestically. Say you're searching for vegan deodorant source, just type in Google "vegan perfume private label U.K." to get a list of companies that can use vegan deodorants for private label.

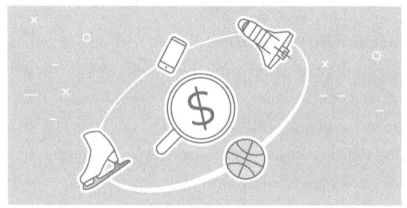

## What to Ask Private Label Suppliers

Once you've drawn up a list of possible vendors, calling each one and posing some questions is a smart idea.

## Pricing Per Unit

The price would usually already be accessible for you to see on the website for each item. However, depending on how many units you order, most manufacturers give a discount. Knowing this data would also assist you in estimating the gross margin.

## MOQ

In the private label/wholesale environment, this is a generic word used because it stands for "minimum order" or the minimum number of units you will order at a time. On their website/product listing, most vendors will mention their MOQ, although you will only have to inquire for some. The MOQ of a producer can be as few as five units, although it can be 1,000 and beyond for some. Although this may be negotiable often, asking this upfront is a smart move so that you can prepare and budget appropriately.

**Customization**

It is nice to know what the factory is and will not do in advance so that you can stop trying to swap vendors later unless you are seeking to apply your branding to the package, customize packages, or make modifications to the product.

**Production Time**

It is helpful to know how long it would take your provider to meet orders when your private label company continues to expand, and you continue to prepare for potential orders. Typically, the norm is around 15 days (depending on the commodity and order size), so it can go up from there.

**Response Time**

Take notice of how long it takes for the supplier to get back to you, bearing in mind that you are initiating a long-term future trading partnership. You would want to make sure that your communication individual is trustworthy, prompt, and specifically addresses your questions. If your provider is based in another country, take into consideration that they are in a separate time zone and that you will not automatically obtain a reply. During their business hours, being present will allow the operation easier.

**Samples**

Ask for prototypes such that the consistency and particular requirements can be measured. Many vendors can submit a sample free of charge, while others may start charging a small fee. Anyway, it's certainly not something you'd skimp on, especially if you're trying to give the highest service to your customers.

## Customizing Your Product

In how your product can market, customizing your product will play a huge role. Question yourself, "What's going to set my version apart from the competition?" The response to this is key in having a prospective customer select your product over the product of a more known, well-reviewed business. Perhaps it's as quick as providing color combinations or getting fancy packaging, or it might be easier to enhance a function that you want more in-depth. Such customizations, such as packaging upgrades, are likely to be achieved by your supplier, and some can be accomplished through yourself or by your suppliers, such as custom marking with product specifics and a logo. Customizing the goods in any form is the main message here. Stand out by having it different (and better) than the rivals '. By basically slapping the mark on it, you don't want to sell the same exact thing as another brand.

## You are selling your Private Label product.

You may pick anywhere to market your private-label line of items. Here's an extensive list of online sales places or suggestions on how to get into shops.

## A Personal Online Store

Such customizations, such as packaging upgrades, are likely to be achieved by your supplier, and some can be accomplished through yourself or by your suppliers, such as custom marking with product specifics and a logo. Customizing the goods in any form is the main message here. Stand out by having it different (and better) than the rivals '. By simply yanking your tag on it, you wouldn't want to give the same product as yet another brand.

## Brick-And-Mortar

Sitting the goods on the shelf of a physical shop offers consumers the ability to see your product that they would never have dreamed of it otherwise. In other words, customers have to practically "search" for services or products they want to buy online. But if they don't think about it, they're not going to search and probably won't find it unless you pay serious bucks promoting it. If shoppers are still in a shop and happen to see it, it builds brand/product recognition at least. Fees and requirements for getting shelf-space vary by store, but it can be a decent place to start from local, family-owned stores. Read more regarding boutique collaborations or having your own storefront.

## Markets

Markers and art fairs for producers are on the increase. Consumers love to shop locally and want to help their community's artisans. They're a perfect way to get instant input from customers, too. Find out how to start trading and find craft markets at farmer's markets.

## Don't limit yourself.

Start with a variety of channels, in-person shops, and websites. You would be able to see over a span of time how many sales you create from each one, how much money each produces, etc. You should just stick doing what's profitable, then. It is certainly a road to launch your private label company, and it will be months until you can bring the goods on the market. But the trip can be well worth it if you do your product testing, pick the best source, separate the product from the market, and price it right.

# Chapter 2: Profitable Strategies in Building Six-Figure Business

For private-label products, manufacturers may raise gross margins by managing the whole supply chain from manufacture to distribution. Clothing traders have been pushing different private-label options for years. Costco has the Kirkland private-label name. Nordstrom's got Caslon. And Kohl's has Sonoma as its in-house, billion-dollar brand. Although online stores have supplied other industries with private label labels, basic products for tangible products focused on low-cost hardware and office equipment, the move to clothes implies a brazen policy expansion. Any volume seller is looking at the advantages of growing private-label brand's goods in order to drive sustainability and connect with a more aware and conscious millennial generation who are known for not being very brand loyal.

## 2.1 Private Label for Profitability

Profits are powered by private labels. A private-labeled commodity or product with parity in operation and consistency with major labels will cost manufacturers 40 to 50 percent less to develop and sell to consumers. In order to negotiate with online marketplace empires and other online suppliers who offer low-cost products without caring about reducing margins, merchants will then switch around to provide greater discounts. Online, where customers have 100 percent pricing transparency, this is especially essential. This functions on both luxury and commodity items. Building and maintaining a private label often enables manufacturers to develop exclusive goods for higher prices or to manufacture commodity products below brands at a sustainable price. To boost their inventory rotation, manufacturers are now using private-label tactics. Retail stores with services from private labels could also have more than four seasons a year. An innovative team in private label, such as the JCPenney team of 250 designers working in-house or the internal production and procurement departments of Nordstrom, will contend on an equal footing with fast-trending fashion stores like H&M.

## Factors to be Considered

It may be dangerous to hop into this business without carefully thinking it over. Before investing and dedicating time to a privately-label approach, here are some factors to be considered:

- **Identifying low cost and high-quality manufacturer**

A colossal advantage is strong production suppliers, while poor manufacturers or suppliers are a horrific liability. Spend the effort to do it correctly. There are hundreds or thousands of suppliers capable of producing stuff that you would need. Find the producer that fits all the requirements for price and consistency; often, identifying the markets that are relevant. You may also want to learn from Portugal or Vietnam for clothing. Vietnam, South Korea, and China have manufacturing expertise in electronics. Take note that costs for suppliers differ greatly depending on the order's size.

- **Strengthen the Skills in Design and Procurement**

The private label includes relationships with producers of agricultural and consumer goods, component retailers, multinational warehouses, and distribution suppliers. Will you broaden the current partnerships between suppliers? If not, determine whether to consult the staff or purchase the expertise that will render the retail company a key competency of the strategy regarding the private label. Consider a completely dedicated bet on vertical trading, too.

- **Using brand pricing and external signs as guiding principles for pricing policy**

Research your rival brands closely while designing your own products under the banner of a private label. Retailers ought to make up their mind whether to generate the product as a luxury product and expend marketing expenses or to position it as an alternate brand by selling below national labels. If product attributes can be readily contrasted and placed as a substitute brand, it is important to consider the price point of comparable goods to position them correctly against competitors' national brand/products label brands. In other situations, were comparing features is not something very straightforward. Retailers can use a number of internal market pointers for pricing, such as site traffic, ratings, consumer feedback, and retailers can recognize the popularity of the product. Today, if a commodity is popular/interest-generating, but the converging performance is low, this can cause a price reduction/promotion intervention.

- **Acknowledge the differences in categories and manage them smartly**

Consumers can browse for functionality within a particular perceived cost sub-set for white and hard goods. Buyers searching for features are opting for a dryer or washing machine. Potential customers are looking for other qualities, such as cloth, shape, trendiness, for soft items like clothing. Those features deter similarities.

- **Decide Efficient Customized Label Blend**

The best combination of private label and branded items has to be determined by retailers. Are buyers looking for a feature in a certain product category or range on the website? Collecting web search data can help marketers make a choice. They have to remember the client base as well. If the consumer pool is predominantly 28- to 51-year-old buyers, private label goods can be more value aware and prefer small-scale proliferation.

- **Implement Algorithmic, Data-Driving Pricing Methods**

With constantly evolving customer preferences, at every given level in time, you should be able to recognize demand levels and continually seek the optimum price value. Factor in leveraging algorithms based on technology systems to easily evaluate price levels and strategies; when priced carefully with supporting data, private-label brands also deliver unexpected revenues. For e.g., the commodity was priced well below the national brand by a generic manufacturer of merchandise with a very well private label refrigerator brand, just to experience a drop in revenue. The store began checking multiple price ranges, steadily pushing up the segment. Sales started to fall with the first $200 onwards. And, magically, revenue and traffic boomed until the price reached a hidden barrier. This sounds counterintuitive, but the private-label company has already been put in a competitive area with national labels in the view of the consumer. Instead of seeing it as a lower quality commodity, clients began to see it as domestic brands. They were prepared to move since the price levels were always cheaper than domestic brands. In a considerably more profitable buyer zone, it was repositioned by moving the idea up the continuum. If consumers interpret things the same way with analytic pricing, the same SKU will gain double the profits. These are some of the most important elements in successfully initiating your private label initiative at any major retailer. Going over these basics will strip the efforts of the bulk of danger.

## 2.2 9+1 Pricing Strategies

**Want to maximize profit on your product sales?**
Aside from other publicity and business tactics, a strong pricing policy is indeed something you need to concentrate on. When setting the price for your goods or services, what considerations do you consider? When determining the prices for your goods or services, there are a number of considerations, including:

- Production cost

- positioning strategies

- competitor's products

- Distribution cost

- Target consumer base

When buying a commodity, price is a very important consideration for a buyer. A productive pricing system can also have a profound influence on the company's performance. And often, it decides whether or not the organization can succeed. So, what are those tactics you should suggest in order to improve the revenue and be more profitable?

## Premium Pricing

Marketers put rates higher than their competitors or rivals for this promotional policy. However, it is used where there is a major competitive edge, and a relatively cheaper price is safe for the marketer or the organization to charge. For small businesses that offer exclusive services or products, high pricing is perfect. A corporation, however, can check that the packaging of the goods, its promotional campaigns, and the décor or luxury facilities of the store all fit to maintain the fixed price.

- **Example of Premium Pricing**

Let's take the example of luxury specialty retail stores that charge you a little extra but sell you exclusive styles and tailored clothing.

## Penetration Pricing

To try to draw buyers? Ok, this technique is going to help you with the purpose. Lower rates are given on utilities or goods under this strategy. Although this technique is used by many emerging firms, it does appear to lead to an initial reduction of profits for the business. Over time, though, the growth of product or service recognition will drive revenues and allow small businesses to stand out. In the long run, as a business succeeds in entering the sector, its costs always end up growing to represent the condition of its role in the sector.

## Economy Pricing

The advertisement expense of a service or commodity is held at a low in this strategy. The technique is used during a certain period where the organization does not invest much in promoting the service or product.

## Example of Economy Pricing

The first few budget airlines, for instance, are offered at low rates in discount airlines to fill in the jet. A broad variety of businesses, from discount stores and generic grocery manufacturers, use Economy Pricing. The technique, though, maybe dangerous for small firms when they lack the market scale of larger corporations. Small companies can fail to make a sufficient profit with low rates, but strategically tailoring price-cuts to your most loyal customers or consumers may be a successful way to guarantee their loyalty for years to come.

## Price Skimming

This technique is meant to assist enterprises in focusing on the sale of innovative services or goods. During the preliminary process, this strategy means setting high prices. The rates are then reduced steadily when the competitor's goods or services arrive on the market. When the product is first released in the marketplace, this price approach produces an image of exclusivity and good quality.

## Psychology Pricing

This method of pricing deals with a client's psychology. For e.g., setting the price of a ring at $99 is likely to draw more clients than setting prices at $100. But the concern is, in terms of a very limited gap, why are consumers more drawn to a product's former price? Psychology suggests that on a price tag, customers prefer to give greater attention to the first digits. When stores apply $0.99 on product tags of $1.99 or $2.99, you can find identical promotional strategies. The purpose of this approach, therefore, is to build an image of greater value for the consumer.

## Bundle Pricing

How often have you been persuaded to purchase a multipack of 6 packets for $2.99 instead of purchasing one packet for $0.65? Or an SMS kit instead of texting on the individual rates? Without sacrificing efficiency, we all enjoy commodities that cost us less. This is why package selling is a success for both the vendor and the consumer and is profitable. The vendor gets to sell more of their inventory, and for less cost, the consumer gets to purchase the product in bulk. For instance, if bundle package of chips is for $1.30 and 3 multipacks for2.50$. The probability of purchasing three packs is more than purchasing only one. Bundle pricing enhances the worth sense when you are actually offering your consumers anything for free.

## Value Pricing

This technique is used when external forces such as increased rivalry or unemployment cause corporations to offer valuable promotional offerings or goods, e.g., combo offers or value meals at KFC and other restaurants, to sustain sales. Quality pricing lets a buyer know like for the same price, they are receiving a ton of product. In several respects, profit pricing is analogous to economic pricing. So, let's make this very clear that there is added benefit with regard to service or product in value pricing. Generally speaking, price cuts should not rise in value.

## Promotional Pricing

Promotional pricing is a really common method for sales and can be used in different department stores and restaurants, etc. Part of this promotional policy are methods such as money off coupons, Buy One Get One Free, and promotions.

## Cost-based Pricing

This method entails determining cost-based rates for the commodity to be made, shipped, and sold. In addition, a fair rate of profit is usually added by the corporation or sector to compensate for the risks as well as initiatives. Businesses such as Walmart and Ryanair are seeking to become low-cost suppliers. These businesses may set lower rates by constantly lowering costs whenever feasible. This undoubtedly contributes to lower profits but better profits and revenues. Companies with higher costs can, therefore, often rely on this approach to pricing. Yet, in general, in order to demand greater profits and rates, these businesses purposely generate higher costs. The aforementioned techniques are the most widely adopted strategies used by corporations to increase profit from sales of their product or service. In its own unique way, any pricing strategy is effective. Therefore, consider your marketplace and other conditions before selecting a pricing plan for your good or service to bring the most out of the strategy used. Therefore, becoming mindful of the competitive place when setting a price is important. What the clients or buyers anticipate in terms of the price should be considered in the marketing mix.

## 2.3 Best Practices in Private Label Branding

Can you recall when generic or non-national branded items with large black lettering and bad product consistency indicated simple white or yellow packing materials? After the unmemorable early days of supermarket labels, stores have clearly come a long way. In fact, many private label labels today are practically indistinguishable from their producer-branded equivalents on the shelves.

**Align with and support the master (retail) brand**

It is certainly no accident that some of the best private label company portfolios are those that tend to be in tune with the supermarket master brand's positioning and strategic purpose. Preferably, their positioning is strongly complementary to the supermarket master brand, enhancing the latter's equity and beneficial relationships.

**Bring differentiation to the category; fulfill unmet customer needs.**

When their products are additive to the supermarket, or better still, the overall competition, private label labels are maybe at their strongest. One way to achieve this is to bring the category to something completely differentiated. Another similar approach is to resolve consumer expectations that are not fulfilled by the big national labels. Importantly, this difference can be more than just a cheaper price than the brands of the manufacturer. In the good or service offering itself, private label labels can often be exclusive. Safeway is a perfect illustration of introducing distinction to the market and thereby addressing an increasingly unmet desire of the customer. Finally, creativity is another form in which private label labels may offer category and consumer distinction.

### Establish clear boundaries for private label brands

There is also a temptation to expand it everywhere and anywhere in the shop once retailers effectively establish a good private label brand. This extends horizontally across types of goods and vertically across ranges of price/value. However, the tendency to over-extend or dilute the private label brand properties is resisted by better practice retailers.

### Define brands based on emotional attributes

Since they feel an intrinsic bond to them, customers prefer to gravitate towards (and stay faithful to) products. There is no more for products with private labels than for brands with national suppliers. For private label labels, it is important that they stand for something more than just price/value and much more than a commodity attribute. They need to have an emotional advantage to which customers may connect. This essential nuance is understood by marketers that have become popular with exclusive labels and find ways to distill emotional equity through their private label brands.

### Distinguish brands with a distinct identity and appropriate brand linkages

Finally, a distinctive and highly identifiable visual identity is established by leading label labels and embraces a clear messaging approach. They still maintain clear rules specifying the degree to which the private label mark may and should be identifiably affiliated with the supermarket master brand. An attractive visual presence and strategically advantageous brand design are undeniably part of what makes private label companies popular or leads to their downfall if overlooked.

## 2.4 Positives and Negatives of Private Label

### Advantages

There is a legitimate explanation for retailers that are involved in flooding their stores with items with their brand name. Many of the main benefits of goods with private labeling include:

- **Handling Production**

Third-party suppliers operate at the behest of the supplier, providing full influence over the ingredients and consistency of the goods.

- **Control overpricing**

Retailers may also assess sales cost and efficient selling due to leverage over the product.

- **Adaptability**

In reaction to growing consumer demand for a new feature, smaller stores have the opportunity to move rapidly to bring a private label product into development, whereas larger firms might not be involved in a product or niche category.

- **Managing branding Decisions**

The company name and package concept produced by the manufacturer carry private label items.

- **Managing profitability**

Retailers monitor the amount of profitability their goods offer due to control over manufacturing expenses and pricing.

- **Increased margins**

Private labels enable manufacturers to sell and raise the profit margin more competitively on their goods. Compared to producing brands, several manufacturers gain 25-30 percent higher profit profits on private labels.

- **Customer loyalty**

Nowadays, consumers want goods manufactured locally, and they would like more if they enjoy the private label products. You would be the only outlet who would be willing to supply them with such goods. It is challenging to win the trust of individuals in the retail sector.

**Disadvantages**

As much as you have the financial capital to spend in creating such a commodity, the risks of introducing a private label brand are few. Primary drawbacks include:

- **Manufacturer dependency**

Since the manufacturing of your product range is in possession of a third-party vendor, working with accomplished businesses is critical. Otherwise, if the manufacturer gets into challenges, you might lose out on opportunities.

- **Difficulty building loyalty**

In a number of retail stores, existing household brands have the upper hand and can always be found. Only in your shops can your goods be sold, restricting consumer access to it. Restricted supply, of note, may also be an asset, providing clients an incentive to come back and purchase from you. Although private label goods are usually offered at a lower price point than their brothers of the corporate name, certain private label brands are also branded as luxury products, with a higher price tag to show it.

## 2.5 Keys to Private Label Greatness

As of late, we are doing a lot of innovative work in the Private Label sector, and here is a good refresher of The Core Values that we believe in for developing our own labels that are strategically convincing. We also see that there are particular fundamental stories in their creation throughout all great store brand cases, but there are seven values that they must abide by to be genuinely strategically convincing.

**Principles of Equity and Environment**

From a branding and design point of view, there has never been more interest in the grocery store and how we connect, affect purchasing decisions, and even construct theatre inside it. This is real in every part of the world. Of course, there is a reverence we all have to have for the cultural uniqueness of the grocery store, from country to country, since some customers are in the store just once a week, to other food and market experience where customers connect every day. Even with these diverse regional variations in frequency, familiarity, and satisfaction inside the retail shop, there is a common emphasis on making the store brand function more credibly and more convincingly with consumers in general.

## The equity connection

Immersing oneself in the retailer's overarching goal, its perception and equity distinction as it is now, and what is achievable in the future is important. To achieve this, the right branding collaborators coordinate with the senior brass of the distributors with which they operate, as well as the organization's top merchants and store name specialists. They take into account all the main targets for which a merchant is fishing and then see how to enhance store brands as being one of the key tools to accomplish their task. Store products strengthen the retailer's total equity and vice-versa, and they struggle because they do not.

## Environmental support

A kit can only do too many. Your store brand will get overloaded if it does not have the off-shelf environmental help in the vast stream of 40,000+ items that many of the largest supermarkets carry today. Beyond the box, give it existence and speech. To help your brand, use the theatre in the shop.

## Be preferential

For supermarket brands, own products, exclusive brands, and the like, there are loads of common nomenclatures. "But whatever the language, don't treat your store brands to the larger national brands as weaker "stepchildren. Don't be afraid to handle your supermarket labels preferentially in the store, beyond the incisive box template for your company. In their importance, in their distribution of space, in their positioning of shelves, and in their show and cross-merchandising all throughout the shop. No need to apologize to the CPGs or succumb to the study of planograms.

**Don't blindly follow.**

For years, there has been a "follow the herd" attitude of store labels, and today it still persists. Because of what Walmart has achieved with Such Prices, many retailers we talk to now are terrified of "white" packaging. So often, individuals are hyper-attentive to the competition and norms and what's going around the market of store labels. The bottom line is that you can build your own vision in a very creative and special way. Do not blindly obey the naming conventions, color conventions, or typically mundane price-centered store brands set by broad categories and how they have traditionally behaved in order to reconsider anything intelligently.

**Three layers have to work together.**

Make sure you are not concerned with visual language alone with the positioning of the store labels and how they are to be fully distinguished for the future. This is the responsibility of a number of production agencies, who feel they are only employed to rewrite the store brand's aesthetic vocabulary. If we want to encourage these products to be produced differently, we need to understand how the graphic language is created, indeed, but also how it is structurally packaged and the language we use to orally convey the item. Graphic, systemic, and verbal languages all cohesively operate together.

**Steve Jobs never asked the consumer.**

Apple is one of the world's most creative and well-thought-out, profitable enterprises. When questioned what Steve Jobs felt about research in a New York Times report and how Apple uses it to direct new product creation, he replied, "None... it's not the job of consumers to know what they want." There are so many retailers that use research to store products in their innovative development phase, and this is a mistake. Customers will still turn to the protection and what is comfortable with them, but if they are the only sounding board, you will not have the most creative performance.

**On the brand's positioning**

In using the name of the shop on the individual store brand packaging, there are no universal guidelines, just as there are no generalizations to create about how large the store brand should stretch. Both of these brands had a very definitive strategic positioning when producing Greenway, Hartford Reserve, and Via Roma for A&P, and this relationship that established the role of the company was a very significant part of the process. Clearly describe it, know that you want to distinguish the brand rather than sheer costs, own it thoroughly in the consumer's head, and correctly reiterate it. In the development of an ambitious store brand platform, these ideals would suit you well because they are standards that the best supermarket brands live by with true conviction. The name brand industry continues to be guided by continuing innovative creativity, a true steel hand in spreading out from the single "price" veil, and to be persuasive in their own right. And store brands need to be promoted with vigor, motivation, and media support.

# Chapter 3: Finding the Products & Starting Your Personal Brand

You should concentrate on creating a reputation before you start your company, one that is recognizable and valued, and a private label benefits both you and the retailer or supplier you select. The first move with your organization is importing the goods you choose to market, products that do not crack easily, which have satisfaction for the customer. The second and most significant move is to make your brand known to current and future clients. The more customers remember your brand, the higher it is possible that your revenue rate will be. Through selecting producers or suppliers who will submit your goods via Private Label, you will help this along. This operates by encouraging the consumer to position their orders with you, then deliver them to the retailer and directly dispatching the product. The return home address would be that of the company in most situations, but for Private Label, this will be yours. This ensures that whether they have any concerns or queries, the consumer would assume that the service/product has come from you, and they will only contact you. This helps you build up a brand reputation, but using trustworthy vendors, depends on you, and you deliver top-quality customer support. In general, manufacturers are willing to use private labels since it suggests that they do not have to be interested in any consumer problems. To sum up, while you are looking to get your brand out and develop a company without leeching on mainstream online market place/websites' popularity, a private label makes perfect sense. It will require a bit extra time to select a supplier since you must do the job yourself and guarantee that you work for the right supplier. Still, you will also gain a better profit when you take responsibility for the client support and are willing to negotiate the supplier's rates. A private label is where a person or corporation paying another business to make a commodity without its name, emblem, etc. The person or business then applies to the packaging their name and design. So, what sorts of items should be labeled privately? From skincare and dietary treatments and infant essentials, pet products, and kitchen utensils, pretty much all under the sun. The benefit of private labeling is that nothing innovative needs to be produced or developed by you. You can add your mark on it as long as it's not a proprietary commodity and label it yours.

## 3.1 How to Start Your Private Label Brand from Scratch?

Because of its profitability and consumer benefits, private labeling has boomed in prominence in recent years. To distinguish between larger vendors, more and more sellers create their products on and off e-commerce marketplaces. With 50 percent of one of the online markets, private labeling vendors, the rivalry is fierce. You need to realize what you're doing if you want to excel. To start a strong private label, you need the know-how, expertise, and money. When you place your logo and name on a standardized commodity, private labeling is. This separates the brand from related rivals and retailers. You have full power over your brand, with a private label. You establish a distinctive identity that is essential for successful promotion and the acquisition of consumers. Customers, not goods, are faithful to labels. Customer satisfaction and repeat business may be created through the private label. In the market, you still have the power of your price and place. A private label on the online marketplace enables you to build a different collection of items only for your product. This gives real estate devoted to your brand and assures that you are not vying against other retailers for the Buy Box. Since they get higher value, clients love private labels. Private-label goods are usually cheaper, but major stores' efficiency is the same, if not higher. In reality, at least one form of private label product is purchased by approximately 98 percent of customers. Depending on their lifestyle, customers may even buy goods. One study showed that clients prefer private labels for the price and choose them based on expertise. They buy from private labels that they most associate with. Ultimately, in a sea of rivals, a private label separates the name, allows you greater leverage over your revenues, and appeals to a niche client target. So, you have agreed to launch a private label of your own. The measures to take to help you start a profitable private label from design to launch are below.

## 3.2 Understand the costs of private labeling

Before digging deeper into a private label, it's important to consider the initial start-up costs. In comparison to reselling, private tagging is more costly. However, this capital input usually results in a better return on your expenditure in the long term.

**Manufacturing**

Typical development expenses, such as supplies, processing, manpower, and transportation, would have to be accounted for. You may need to consider the customization charge, too. For customizing a product with your mark, packaging, or specs, most manufacturers will charge a fee.

**Brand**

Even to design the brand itself, you would require money. To create the logo and package template, you'll definitely want to employ a graphic artist. To stress the voice of your company, you will also want to develop a content strategy.

**Marketing**

Marketing is a significant part of private labeling. Customers don't know about your company, so to become more noticeable, you need to spread knowledge. A large cost may be generated through ads such as promoted and boosted blogs. A website creator and domain name would presumably both need to be charged for. For any other unforeseen fees or modifications that pop about at the beginning of the start of a new company, you can also add a sizable buffer.

- **Choose the products you want to sell**

The majority of corporations and labels start with a commodity. The brand is how you create your cash and profits. The item is the guiding force of your business. Starting a commodity with your name helps determine your margins, demand, and availability. The brand is the consumer service, but you will need to offer your consumers a valuable product in the end. You would typically choose a branded commodity that you place your own logo on while you market a private label. This suggests that a single generic product begins with your "brand." How do you further build and broaden your branding using that product? You want high-rank and high-margin units when buying a commodity. To lower warehousing and shipping costs, you will want thin, lightweight goods. If the first product you offer doesn't work out or you choose to shift paths, you can still move goods. The aim is to stick less to one commodity than to use product testing as a prism in your overall business and niche instead. You should also accept complimentary commodities with this in mind. If you market key items, you want to think of a range of similar goods that would still blend with your brand when choosing key products. For starters, you can grow inside the travel domain or beverage industry if you sell travel mugs. You will market some eco-friendly home products as well if you sell environmentally efficient cleaning products.

- **Define your target market**

Who is the perfect consumer for you? Who would be more willing to buy your unique product? This can assist you in deciding the sorts of goods you are trying to produce and how you are going to promote such products. The consumer is your market and your brand's secret. Getting a well-defined target demographic is more relevant than ever, considering the current condition of the economy. No one is willing to afford to target everyone. By approaching a niche segment, small enterprises may successfully compete with big firms. Many firms say they are targeting "anyone interested in my services." Others say they are targeting buyers, renters, or stay-at-home moms in small businesses. These priorities are all too common. Targeting a certain market does not mean that you exclude entities that may not follow the standards. Instead, focus marketing helps you to concentrate your advertising money and brand message on a single demographic that is more inclined than other markets to purchase from you. This is a means of meeting prospective consumers and creating a business that is far more accessible, accessible, and effective. For instance, an interior design business might opt to sell to households between the ages of 34 and 63 with incomes of $160,000-plus. The business could opt to approach only those involved in kitchen design remodeling and conventional designs in order to define the segment any better. This business may be broken into two niche markets: parents on the move and baby boomers leaving. It is much simpler to decide where and how to advertise your brand with a well-specified target audience. To help you identify your target market, here are some ideas.

**Look at your current customer base.**

Who are your new clients, and why are they buying from you? Look for features and desires that are popular. What ones do other businesses carry in? It is also possible that your product/service will also help other individuals like them.

**Check out your competition.**

What are your adversaries targeting? Who are the clients at present? Don't try the same business. You might discover a niche market they are missing.

**Analyze your product/service**

Write up a description of each of the product or service specifications. List the advantages it offers next to each function. A graphic artist, for instance, provides high-quality design services. The advantage is the picture of a professional organization. More clients would be drawn to a professional image when they perceive the business as professional and trustworthy. So, basically, attracting more clients and earning more profits is the advantage of high-quality design. When you have your advantages identified, make a list of persons that have a need that suits your benefit. A graphic designer may, for instance, opt to approach organizations involved in increasing their consumer base. Although this is already too common, you now have a foundation on which to proceed.

**Choose specific demographics to target.**

Find out not only who wants the products or service and also who is most willing to order it. Consider the reasons that follow:

- Location

- Education level

- Occupation

- Gender

- Ethnic background

- Marital or family status

- Age

- Income level

- Ethnic background

## Consider the psychographics of your target.

Psychographics is a person's more intimate traits, including:

- Personality

- Values

- Interests/hobbies

- Attitudes

- Lifestyles

- Behavior

Assess how your service or product would blend with the lifestyle of your destination. How and where is the item going to be used by your goal? What characteristics are most enticing to your goal? What media for details does your goal switch to? Can the newspaper read the destination, check online, or attend unique events?

## Evaluate your decision

Make sure to consider these issues after you have settled on a target market:

- Are there enough individuals that meet my criteria?

- Is my goal actually going to benefit from my product/service?

- Are they going to have the use for it?

- Do I know what guides my aim to make choices?

- Can they afford my service/product?

- With my post, may I meet them? Are they readily accessible?

Don't smash the goal so far down there. Know, there is more than one niche opportunity you may have. Consider how, for each niche, the marketing message can be different. If you can successfully hit all niches with the same post, then maybe you have broken down the market so much. Also, if you notice that there are only 50 individuals that match all of your requirements, you may need to reevaluate your objective. Finding the right combination is the trick. You might be wondering, "How do I gather all this data?" Attempt to look online for analysis that others have done on your aim. Look for posts and blogs in publications that speak to or around the target group. Check for blogs and sites where thoughts are shared by people in the target market. Check for sample findings, or try doing your own survey. Ask for input from the new clients. The hard part is identifying your target demographic. It is much simpler to find out which platforms you should use to attract them, and what advertisement campaigns can connect with them if you know who you are approaching. You should give it only to people that suit your requirements instead of delivering direct mail to anyone in your ZIP code. In identifying the target demographic, save money and have a greater return on investment.

- **Consider your differentiating factor.**

You've settled on demand and a commodity. Now, what is going to make you distinctive in your business from your competitors? Look at the rivalry. What is their emphasis? And where are they missing? A perfect spot for you to put the brand is the field that they struggle the most. You could find, for example, that all of your rivals have a formal language; with your brand, you might take a goofy and enjoyable tone. In order for it to become a good differentiator, it doesn't have to be a big improvement. The core of your identity becomes your differentiator. Keep in mind that price may also be a defining factor. You would get a different demographic and competition than a cheap or discounted commodity, whether you are quality or luxury product.

- **Create your brand look**

Your "brand" consists of the goods, the demand, and the distinguishers. Yet, it is your material and aesthetic as well. You need a clear emblem that represents the name while private labeling is used. How you are and where the stuff comes from, the logo tells. This emblem can be included in all communications, packaging, and marking. Be sure it's accessible as a corporation and website prior to picking the brand name. This would mean that you do not infringe on any patents or fight with companies with identical names. To build the logo and package template, you'll definitely want to employ a graphic artist. This is the perfect approach to make things look respectable and trustworthy to the private label.

- **Create an experience**

A brand is, ultimately, more than a slogan, though. Your "brand" is how your business is experienced by the client. It's a consistent way for your audience to communicate. You need to work out how consumers can uniquely perceive your brand based on brand differentiation. What is your content going to look like? What could you provide that is unique to the experience of your brand? You may produce visually enticing social media photographs, for instance, that contribute to the lifestyle around your dog collars. Or you should make sure that you react to and respond to any social network statement or post. To keep your label on the edge, you can use special and exclusive packaging. Build an atmosphere, and you can turn your one-time consumers into long-term customers.

- **Find a supplier**

Acting with a good provider is an important aspect of private marking. The manufacturer must have private labeling expertise so they can help you make a return from your products. For a variety of consumers, several overseas factories will produce a standardized commodity and modify such items with private packaging for marking. You collaborate with a retailer, for instance, that produces bottles of water and T-shirts. They have ten buyers, each with their own special emblem written on the bottles, that offer water bottles. A customization and packing fee will normally be paid by the factory.

- **Build the brand**

You have put yourself in a role, built a differentiator, and found a supplier. It's time to start developing your organization now. You have to:

- Name and image copyright.

- Website configuration

- Creating a voice on social media

- Shape an LLC

Just like you would like any other legal corporation, recognize your e-commerce firm. You need yourself, your goods, and your income to be covered. You would also like to start naming the lists with online items. A private label means you don't have to fight for a Buy Package. "With a different page for your branded goods, you hold your own "real estate." In line with the brand background, this is a good chance to customize the listing.

## 3.3 Choosing the Right Products

Choosing the best market and the right goods to spend your efforts on is the greatest challenge you would have to conquer. This decision is vital to the success or failure of your company. The only biggest mistake you're going to make is selecting a product based on your own interests or personal preferences, particularly if you want to create a genuinely profitable company. You have to provide what other customers want, not what you want. Especially if you are not the type of individual to embrace patterns or the type of individual that is always perceived to be "outside of the box." We can't tell you what products to offer, but we can definitely give you some ideas about how to pick the right ones.

**How to choose the right product**

Your organization would have an uphill struggle to become profitable without a strong product portfolio. It may seem impossible to try to find out what you are trying to market, with potentially millions of items out there. The item you chose will also pose other concerns that you may need to work on. For starters, shipping may become an issue if you are planning to sell freezers. Depending on where the clients work, whether you are selling alcohol, there could be regulatory limits. Market analysis can sound daunting, but knowing the product can cater to the people you are going to attract through your site is important. You should monitor the industry dynamics if you already have an understanding of what you intend to do to see how the commodity is actually performing on the market. If you are really not sure what you'd like to offer, trends can still be helpful to you. Business dynamics will offer you an indication about what items consumers are purchasing or are interested in buying at the moment. Look for items that address a dilemma the target group is experiencing. If your consumer is fed up with the current product range, open a unique and better product to deliver them. Choosing a commodity that is not reasonably available nearby or a national brand that is coveted by a region outside of where it is actually accessible may also be a brilliant choice. Another recommendation is to find a service/ product based on your target audience's interests. This may be in the shape of a new TV show that is beginning or a fashion trend.

It often applies to aiming for a difference in chances. If you choose a product that many different competitors are already selling, find something that you can do differently or better than everybody else. This can be an enhanced product characteristic, a market that your competitors totally miss, and maybe something in your marketing plan. If you are trying to market a commodity-based on something that is trending at the moment, ensure that you capitalize early on the pattern. There tend to be more individuals who buy the product at the beginning of a trend. Everybody else is now also moving along to the next thing if you get on the hype train at the end of the trend. Do not wait too long to profit on a trend in the market unless you think that you're going to revive a dead trend. When you make your choices, it is important to take into account product turnover. It would take a lot of time and resources on a product range that varies year after year to guarantee that the product selection is held up-to-date and does not include last year's choices, which could no longer be eligible. A reduced churn product would enable you to engage in a more informative website that will be applicable for a longer time span. Don't be frightened of looking at smaller segments and niches of products. Although there may be fewer prospective customers, there will also be less competition, making it easier to get it to the top of the search engines and much more cost-effective in terms of marketing. The right product is an essential part of your success. Take your time and also don't rush into the first good-looking product.

## Looking for Product Ideas

There is no need to start a shop without a commodity to sell. Begin with something you already have, or how you can fix your own issues or the challenges of people you meet before you start looking for fresh ideas on what you can sell. There are some ways to consider:

- Which items or niches are you involved in?

- What items are your mates excited about?

- Which challenges do you have with your own life?

- Whose goods can address this?

- What kind of firms are based in your community?

- Can they be translated into a definition online?

- What will organizations in your culture cater to individuals outside of your community?

- In other areas of the planet, what items are trending?

- Is there a need inside your society for them?

- Will you build in your society a market for them?

- Is there a certain sector you like to be interested in if you are confused regarding products? In that industry, what products are popular?

- What items can you find useful from that industry?

- In other online retailers, what items are popular?

- Will this commodity have a niche that you should specialize in in sales?

- What's the social curation website trend?

- Is there an undiscovered thing out there that individuals would want to see open to them?

## 3.4 Building a Team and Starting your Personal Brand

### Choosing the Right Supplier

It can be tricky to pick a supplier for your private label company, but it can help you to realize that there are a variety of suppliers who have been doing this for several years. Some lead the industry in broad industries, and this may be the perfect place to get started in your new company since the goods you offer are already established and have gained appreciation from the market. You can have to trade-off or work in restricted strategies with your profitability, and you need to be careful in reviewing the terms and conditions of each corporation, but each of these can create a backdoor into which you can start a profitable long-term business. Not all private labels are made equally, and to guarantee that your organization is effective, you want to make sure you chose the best provider. There are certain items that your provider wants to provide and some things that are less essential but can have greater convenience. Any of the items you'll be searching for in a provider include:

- Will the retailer have members who are knowledgeable?

- Will the supplier devote them to a particular entity committed to your account?

- Are they invested in being advanced technologically?

- How can you send orders?

- Where are they situated?

- Are they a coordinated business?

- How fast are their orders shipped?

- How are they keeping you throughout the loop on product returns and items out of stock?

- How fast can they send you the tracking details and purchase order?

- What payment types do they approve?

- What kind of fees are they charging?

It may seem impossible to locate the legal firms and distinguish them from the fraudulent as you are searching for a provider. There are some tricks to choosing a decent provider for private labels. One crucial point to bear in mind when you start approaching suppliers is that they could very well be the secret to selecting the best supplier, even though they are not the right match for you. Make sure you always ask every supplier you meet if they can guide you in the appropriate path to reach a supplier that suits your company. As they're in the business, they are sure to have connections that will help you and are typically prepared to share the details. Looking at social media is another way one can improve the chances of having a reliable supplier to deal with. Often, through a family member, neighbor, or acquaintance who might be in the industry or meet someone in the industry, you may find a lead. Any lead is a successful lead, even though it leads to a dead end. In order to strengthen the partnership, you have with your supplier, there are a few items you should do:

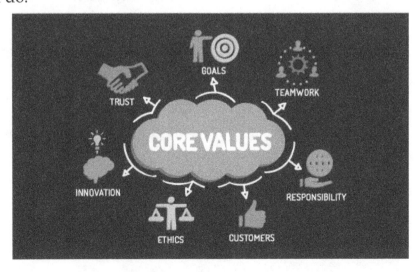

- Pay on time to develop trust and then become a reliable client.

- Set simple and realistic targets if an estimation of the goods you plan to sell in a specified period is requested

- Remember that they have other clients and do not belong to you alone.

- Learn what you need when you put orders to speed up the operation.

- If there is a malfunction, do not accuse the representative, but collaborate with them to find a remedy.

- Knowing somebody on a personal level seems to make them more likely to help you out. Build relationships with your delegate

- Train them to identify what you need, such as fresh product photos and product update updates, items out of stock, and products were withdrawn.

**Finding the Right Suppliers and Working with Them**

The one crucial part you have to do before you continue the quest for the right suppliers is learned how to say the difference between a true wholesale supplier and a department store that works like one. The manufacturer orders their stock from a genuine wholesaler and delivers far higher deals than a supermarket would. To create a good organization, you need to be able to do all of the following:

**Have Access to Exclusive Distribution or Pricing**

Being able to negotiate unique product agreements or exclusive prices would offer you the advantage without the need to import or produce your own product to sell online. These are not quick items to arrange, and you can notice that you are still out-priced, and at wholesale rates, some private label brands would still offer the same or equivalent. You need to find a way to persuade the buyers that the commodity you sell is of greater quality than the competitor, whether you can have exclusive distribution, particularly if the competition sells a knock-off product at a cheaper price. This is where the website's "about us" page becomes much more useful as it is a good way to share the fact that you are unique to the product.

**Sell at the Lowest Possible Price**

You will rob clients from such a chunk of your niche market if you are willing to sell your goods at the lowest costs. The main thing is that since you actually won't be able to appreciate the gain, you are destined to struggle. The low price is not often the primary motivating factor behind the choice of a consumer to shop. Customers seem to choose to invest their cash on the best benefit and lowest cost of a commodity. This suggests that you ought to persuade them that the best decision is to invest a little extra cash in your goods, so there is less downside and more appeal to them.

**Add Your Value Outside of the Price**

Think in terms of having data that complement the items selected. A real capitalist can fix challenges, and at the same time offering goods at high rates. In your unique niche, make sure you give suggestions and insightful recommendations. Your customer support is one extremely efficient way to bring value to the goods outside of the costs. If you are willing to address all the queries of your consumer without needing to call you and are willing to respond to any emails easily, your store website will stick out from the rest.

# Conclusion

A private label is where a person or corporation paying another business to make a commodity without its name, emblem, etc. The person or business then applies to the packaging their name and design. So, what sorts of items should be labeled privately? From skincare and dietary treatments and infant essentials, pet products, and kitchen utensils, pretty much all under the sun. The benefit of private labeling is that nothing innovative needs to be produced or developed by you. You can add your mark on it as long as it's not a proprietary commodity and label it yours. Dropshipping is a convenient method for private-label goods to be distributed. You will find a dropshipping provider if you are an online shop owner who can offer items directly to you and incorporate your branding. Dropshipping is an e-commerce market concept in which no inventory is held by the manufacturer. The retailer, instead, manages the packaging, packing, and delivery of goods to the end customer. In other terms, for dropshipping, the goods are delivered directly to consumers, and they are never used by stores. There is a legitimate explanation for retailers that are involved in flooding their stores with items with their brand name. Third-party suppliers operate at the behest of the supplier, providing full influence over the ingredients and consistency of the goods. In reaction to growing consumer demand for a new feature, smaller stores have the opportunity to move rapidly to bring a private label product into development, whereas larger firms might not be involved in a product or niche category. You should concentrate on creating a reputation before you start your company, one that is recognizable and valued, and a private label benefits both you and the retailer or supplier you select. The first move with your organization is importing the goods you choose to market, products that do not crack easily, which have satisfaction for the customer. The second and most significant move is to make your brand known to current and future clients. The more customers remember your brand, the higher it is possible that your revenue rate will be. Through selecting producers or suppliers who will submit your goods via Private Label, you will help this along. This operates by encouraging the consumer to position their orders with you, then deliver them to the retailer and directly dispatching the product. To sum up, while you are looking to get your brand out and develop a company without leeching on mainstream online marketplace/websites' popularity, a private label makes perfect sense. It will require a bit extra time to select a supplier since you must do the job yourself and guarantee that you work for the right supplier. Still, you will also gain a better profit when you take responsibility for the customer support and are willing to negotiate.

CPSIA information can be obtained
at www.ICGtesting.com
Printed in the USA
BVHW081950070421
604338BV00011B/1129

9 781802 249118